THE OLD FOREST RANGER;

OR,

Wild sports of India

THE OLD FOREST RANGER;

OR,

Wild sports of India

ON THE NEILGHERRY HILLS, IN THE JUNGLES, AND ON THE PLAINS.

BY

MAJOR WALTER CAMPBELL

GYAN

Published by

GYAN

Gyan Publishing House
5, Ansari Road
Daryaganj, New Delhi-110002
Phone: 011-47034999, 9811692060
E-mail: books@gyanbooks.com

Distribution Network
gyanbooks.com
India, USA, Canada, UK, Australia

ISBN: 978-93-6280-494-5 (HB)
First Published, 1869

2nd Impression 2024

Printed at: Gyan Press, Delhi.

THE OLD FOREST RANGER; OR, WILD SPORTS OF INDIA
Author: MAJOR WALTER CAMPBELL

LONDON, HOW & PARSONS, 1st JANY 1842.

THE

OLD FOREST RANGER;

OR,

Wild Sports of India

ON THE NEILGHERRY HILLS, IN THE JUNGLES, AND ON THE PLAINS.

BY

MAJOR WALTER CAMPBELL,

OF SKIPNESS,

Late of the Seventh Royal Fusileers.

FOURTH EDITION.

LONDON:
GEORGE ROUTLEDGE AND SONS,
THE BROADWAY, LUDGATE.
NEW YORK: 416, BROOME STREET.
1869.

TO THE

RIGHT HONOURABLE LORD ELCHO.

&c. &c. &c.

My dear Elcho,

I beg leave to dedicate this volume to you, not only as my Kinsman, but as a Brother Sportsman, and one whose unrivalled celebrity as a Horseman, and a Deer-stalker, renders him so well calculated to reflect honour on a work of this nature.

Knowing you, as I do, to be a proficient in the noble art of woodcraft, and one fully alive to the beauties of the grooved barrel, I trust that the Indian adventures of "The

Old Forest Ranger," may serve, like the silly ballads of a wandering Minstrel, to wile away an idle hour; and, if so, the "*grim auld Carle*" will have fully accomplished the object I had in view in sending him to your door.

Believe me ever,

My dear Elcho,

Your affectionate Cousin,

WALTER CAMPBELL.

Skipness House, November, 1841.

PREFACE.

There is an old Scotch saying, more remarkable for truth than elegance, to this effect—"Gie the Loon an inch, and he 'll tak' an ell," and this, I fear, may, with some propriety, be applied to me in the present instance.

The kind reception I met with, under the disguise of "The Old Forest Ranger," has encouraged me to reprint, in a connected form, my papers on Indian Field Sports, which have appeared, from time to time, in the pages of the "New Monthly Magazine," and once more to sue for favour at the hands of the public.

I have introduced two new Chapters, and made some other slight additions to the original matter, which with the aid of a few illustrations, derived from sketches made in India, and tolerably copious notes, containing descriptions and authentic anecdotes of the various animals mentioned in the work, may, I hope, induce my former kind Readers, once more to smile upon the "Old Forest Ranger," in his new jerkin.

Whether I have acted a prudent part, or not, in so doing, still remains to be proved. But, stand or fall, the deed is done. I have thrown aside the spectacles and red nightcap of *Koondah*, and now, in my own name, venture to crave, from an hitherto indulgent public, a lenient criticism of the Old Forest Ranger's many imperfections.

That there are defects of style, I am fully aware, and am prepared to submit, with resignation, to any chastisement which the Gentle Critics may see fit to inflict upon me, for my sins, in this respect. But I feel myself entitled to claim for my descriptions—*Indian stories*, though they be—the merit of authenticity.

My object in writing the following pages was to present my Readers with a faithful sketch of some of the more exciting Field Sports of India; and, to insure my doing so, I confined myself almost exclusively to the description of such scenes and adventures as either my Brother, or I, or both of us—for we hunted in couples occasionally—have witnessed. The few exceptions which occur to this general rule, are anecdotes which I have had from men, on whose word I could place implicit reliance, and for which

I have given my authority in the notes. To my Brother, Mr. George Campbell of the Bombay Civil Service, I am indebted for many valuable extracts from his Indian Journal.

My Characters are purely fictitious, and are merely introduced, like the subordinate performers in Van Amburg's exhibitions, to serve as foils to the wild beasts, and to avoid the repetition of that eternal egotistical I, which is so disagreeable in a personal narrative.

Should these pages ever meet the eye of any of my Brother Officers of the 62nd Regiment—the Regiment in which I began my military career, and in whose ranks I visited "the Land of the Sun"—I beg to assure them that "Watty Campbell" the "*Jungle Wallah*,"* in spite of time and distance, has still a warm corner in his heart for the old "Wiltshire Springers," in whose society he has spent so many happy days, by Sea and by Land, in Quarters and in Camp, at the Mess-table, and in the Hunting-field.

To my late Brother Officers of the Royal Fusiliers, I would also beg to offer a word of kind remembrance,

---

* *Jungle Wallah*—A Jungle Man, or Wild Man of the Woods—my Regimental nick-name.

with the assurance that, although circumstances rendered my stay among them more brief than I could have wished, I shall ever look back, with pride and pleasure, to the short time I had the honour of serving in that distinguished Corps.

And to all those who are kind enough to devote an idle hour to the Old Man's idle tales, I beg to offer my most grateful thanks.

W. C.

CONTENTS.

CHAPTER VII.

CHAPTER VIII.

CHAPTER IX.

CHAPTER X.

CHAPTER XI.

CHAPTER XII.

CHAPTER XIII.

CHAPTER XIV.

CHAPTER XV.

CHAPTER XVI.

CHAPTER XVII.

CHAPTER XVIII.

CHAPTER XIX.

ILLUSTRATIONS.

THE OLD FOREST RANGER.

CHAPTER I.

A WORD FROM THE OLD FOREST RANGER.

READER, couldst thou see us, as we are now, reposing in our easy chair; our once muscular limbs swathed in flannel bandages; a red woollen nightcap covering our scanty locks; and our stubborn back bending, at length, under the weight of fourscore years; thou wouldst find it hard to credit that this trembling hand, which now can scarcely guide the pen, was wont, of yore, to poise, with deadly aim, yon long-barrelled rifle; or that the grim trophies of the chase, which grace the walls of our favourite study, and on which we still gaze with all the pride of an American savage sitting amidst the smoke-dried scalps of his enemies, were fairly ta'en, in sylvan warfare, by the white-headed Old Man who now ventures to address thee.

Yet so it is Gentle Reader—The Old Forest Ranger, once the terror of Wild beasts, is now reduced to this.

—Think not, however, that we repine at our lot.—The old Dog hath had his day,—a right merry day it was too—and although in our declining years, we look back, with pleasure, to the exploits of our youth, we do so, also, with feelings of gratitude to our Maker, who hath protected us through many dangers, and brought us back in safety, from a far distant land, to lay our aged bones in the same romantic Glen of our beloved Highlands, where first we drew the breath of life.

We have been gazing, for the last hour, upon the trophies which surround us, till our head swims, and our heart burns, with glowing recollections of how each grinning savage bled and died.—The soul-stirring scenes come so vividly before us, that we feel an irresistible temptation to commit our thoughts to paper. And write we will, if it be only for the sake of furnishing one other instance of feline ferocity, besides the tragical fate of poor Monro—an anecdote which, in spite of its being half a century old, and worn to tatters by constant use, still continues to be quoted, with undiminished satisfaction, by every writer who wishes to impress his Readers with a wholesome dread of the Tiger's cannibal propensities; as if it were the only well authenticated instance on record, of such a catastrophe.

We feel it also to be due to the character of our Brother Hunters, who pursue the

"Crafty dysporte of venery"

in a gentlemanlike manner, to disabuse the minds of such of our Readers as may have been led away by the accounts of travelled Cockneys, and seduced into the belief that Indian Sportsmen indulge in the vile practices of *shooting* Hog on the plains, hunting bagged Jackals, redolent of Asafœtida, and slaying Pea-fowl in jungles frequented by Deer.

Such things are done no doubt; and done, perhaps, by men who rejoice in the name of *Sporting characters*, but not by *Sportsmen*. The man who *shoots* a Hog in a hunting country in India, is held up to greater execration than a convicted *Vulpecide* would be in Leicestershire. No man who can ride well up to an old Gray Boar, will ever demean himself or his good Horse, by following a poor, dripping, broken-hearted vermin, till he is trotted to death by a parcel of mangy curs.

And we have invariably remarked that those who habitually indulge in the innocent pastime of Peacock and Jungle-fowl shooting, are young gentlemen who having devoted their early youth to the rearing of tame Rabbits, have never learnt to appreciate the beauties of a *grooved barrel*, and have, therefore, signally failed in their attempts upon nobler game; or as a quaint friend of ours used to express himself,

"They have found the wild Bucks so extremely *bashful* that no Hunter could approach them."

We have yet another reason for writing, Gentle Reader, but this we must whisper in thine ear.

We have, long ago, wearied out our good Old Lady, the Minister, and the Doctor; indeed all the inhabitants of the Glen, who have been simple enough to let us decoy them into our Den.—Our preliminary clearing of the throat, which they recognize too well, as the prelude to an Indian story, invariably drives them from our presence; and being no longer able to command a Hearer, we have resolved upon the desperate experiment of making an attack upon the Public.

Hurra! We have renewed our youth, like the royal bird from whose wing our pen was plucked. (It is our fancy, Gentle Reader, ever to write with an Eagle's quill.) The fire of other days is in our blood.—Our eye is, once more, bright.—We cast off our spectacles as an useless encumbrance, and grasp our long neglected rifle, which for years, hath slumbered peacefully above the fire-place, reposing upon the brow-antlers of a noble Stag.—The dark Spirit of the woods is upon us. The angry roar of the wounded Tiger is in our ears. And we snort like an aged War-horse, who hath been roused by the trumpet's sound, as we look back, through the long vista of bygone years, on the sylvan warfare of our youth.

We see thee now, thou green spot in the wilderness where first we pitched our solitary hunter's tent. Oft have the gloomy arches of the eternal Forest, in which thou art embossed, echoed to the crack of our trusty rifle. Oft has thy green herbage been stained with the life-blood of the stately Bison.

Hurra! for the wild woods!

Hurra! for the headlong charge of the mighty Bull! And thrice Hurra! for the deadly grooved barrel before which he bows his proud forehead to the dust!!

But hush! We are getting beside ourselves. Our unusual fit of excitement hath got the better of our discretion. And our much respected Consort, who was approaching to administer our morning potation of

Athol-brose, hath fled in dismay, wringing her hands, and proclaiming aloud that,

"The Laird hath gaen *horn-wud!*"

We must compose ourselves, else we shall lose our character as well as our *Athol-brose.*

So! We have pacified our Better-half, quaffed our morning cup, and replaced our spectacles with becoming gravity.—The Spirit of the woods hath passed away.—We have laid aside our rifle, resumed our Eagle quill, and the Old Forest Ranger hath once more subsided into a douce and cannie Carle.

Reader, if thou art, like us, a thorough-paced old Sportsman, one who hath advanced through all the progressive stages of practical gunnery, from the firing of twopenny cannon, on the King's birth-day, to the scientific use of the grooved barrel—If thou hast a soul capable of appreciating the manifold beauties of that most perfect weapon the double barrelled rifle,—armed with which the solitary Hunter wanders fearless among the savage beasts of the wilderness.

If, in short, thou art as great an enthusiast in the noble art of wood-craft, as we were in our younger days, we trust that even our imperfect sketches of Indian field-sports, may afford thee an hour's amusement. Thou wilt be ready to make every allowance for the defects of a Brother Sportsman's style; and to thee, therefore, we think it unnecessary to make any apology, for asking thee to accompany us into the woods.—It may, perhaps, remind thee of old times.

Reader, if thou art no Sportsman, then we do feel some delicacy in asking thee to join us, lest thou shouldst be disappointed. If thou art inclined to shoulder a rifle and follow us in our wanderings, we say come, and welcome! We shall be right proud of thy company; and shall do our best to inspire thee with that wild spirit of adventure which gives the principal charm to an Indian Hunter's life. But we forewarn thee that thou wilt be introduced to savage men, and savage beasts; and if such society liketh thee not, we pray thee to remember that the blame lies not at our door.

Reader, if thou art a Critic, dogging our path for the unworthy purpose of noting every false step, and picking holes in a poor Old man's coat, we say,—Aroint thee! We go armed; and aged though we be, have not yet forgotten how to handle a rifle.

We hardly dare to hope that the Gentler Sex will so far honour us, as to illuminate our blood-stained pages, with the sunshine of their eyes. But, in the event of our being so highly favoured, we feel that, to them, some apology is due for introducing them to such uncouth scenes.

Vailing our bonnet, then, and bowing full low, we would thus crave permission to address our Fair Reader.

We are but a poor old Forester, Gentle Lady; one unfit to tell a tale in Lady's Bower. But, as Hunters of old were wont to offer up grim trophies of the chase at the shrine of beauty, so do we venture to lay this unworthy volume at thy feet. Spurn it not, Gentle Lady. It is all an Old Forester has to offer, and, for thy sake he heartily wishes it more worthy of acceptance.

CHAPTER II.

A DAY'S HUNTING ON THE NEILGHERRY HILLS

It was on one of those heavenly mornings peculiar to the climate of the Neilgherry Hills, where the brilliancy of a tropical sky is combined with the freshness of an European sunrise, that three handsome Arab horses, accoutred for the field and each led by a native Horse-keeper, might be seen slowly passing to and fro in front of one of the pretty little thatched cottages which, scattered irregularly over the sides of the hills, form the Cantonment of Ootacamund. Presently a group of three Sportsmen, in hunting dresses, issued from the doorway, and the impatient steeds snorted and pawed the ground, as if to welcome the approach of their riders.

" A fine scenting day this, lads," exclaimed the elder of the party, looking up towards the sky, and carefully buttoning a warm spencer over his green hunting-coat.

The speaker was a man apparently about fifty years of age: his hair, which had originally been dark brown, was slightly sprinkled with gray, and the corpulence of his figure would, at first sight, have led one to suppose that his sporting-days were over. But the healthy though dark colour of his cheek, showed that he had spent much of his time in the open air, whilst his firm step and steady piercing eye convinced one that he could still breast a hill, or squint along a clouded barrel with some hopes of success.

The second person in the group was a tall wiry figure, whose large bones and well-knit joints gave promise of great strength and unusual activity. He was accoutred in a short round jacket of fustian, the colour of which approached as nearly as possible to the faded tints of dead fern or dried bamboo. His legs were cased in long leggings of deer-skin, which reached half-way up the thigh, and were fastened by a strap to his girdle; his head was covered by a small cap of Astracan fur, and an ammunition-pouch of dressed bearskin was tightly buckled round his waist by a broad leathern belt, into which was also thrust a hunting-knife of unusual size, with a buckhorn handle handsomely mounted in silver. His accoutrements altogether were those of a half-reclaimed savage; but the aristocratic cast of his features, the proud glance of his eye, and his erect military carriage, declared at once the gentleman, the soldier, and the daring sportsman. His complexion had been tanned to the colour of mahogany by long exposure to a tropical sun, his short upper lip was shaded by black mustaches, and the expression of his countenance gave one the idea of a silent and reserved person, who, from long habit and perhaps from having spent much of his time in solitary rambles through the trackless forest, had acquired much of the stoical philosophy of an American Indian, and, like him, was very cautious of betraying his feelings. A keen observer of human nature, however, might have detected, in the occasional flash of his dark eye, evident tokens of a fiery and restless spirit, well disciplined, indeed, but ready to burst forth if occasion required, like the sudden eruption of a volcano.

The third person, who stood by his side, formed a striking contrast, both in appearance and dress, to the weather-beaten sportsmen. He was a slender fair-haired lad, apparently about eighteen, whose rosy complexion and boyish manner showed that he had but lately emerged from the thraldom of school-discipline, and had not as yet braved the fiery climate of India for more than a few months. In short, he had all the appearance of a gentlemanlike young man, who had but lately arrived from England, and was still in all the happy ignorance of early *griffinage.* His glossy new hat, fashionably-cut green hunting-coat, breeches of virgin-white, and well-polished top-boots, were sufficient to convince the most casual observer that he belonged to that unhappy race of mortals who, for twelvemonths after their arrival in the Honourable Company's dominions, are considered fair game both by Europeans and Natives, and get unmercifully plucked—for the very good, and to them, no doubt, satisfactory, reason, that they are only *griffins.*

The party had just descended the steps of the veranda, and were about to mount their horses, when the sylph-like figure of a lovely girl appeared in the doorway, and rushing towards the elder of the party, with her fair hair streaming in the morning breeze, playfully imprinted a kiss on his weather-beaten cheek.

"Ah! you little rogue!" exclaimed he; "what has roused you from your bed at this early hour?"

"The desire to say good morning to you, Papa,

and to wish you success. You know you never have good sport unless I see you off and give you a sprig of my charmed heather-bush to stick in your cap. The last time I did so you killed that large tiger which now stands stuffed in the veranda. But as you are so ungrateful as to forget the potency of your little Fairy's spell, you shall have no heather to-day. My gentle Cousin shall bear the palm," cried she, as she turned towards the younger of the party. "Come hither, Charles; you have declared yourself my true Knight, and as such are bound by all the laws of chivalry to wear my colours in your cap. Kneel, Sir, and receive the favour with becoming humility."

Charles knelt at the feet of his fair kinswoman, whilst she, with a roguish look of mock gravity, fixed in his cap a small bunch of heath—a plant which even in the cool climate of the Neilgherry hills is reared as an exotic—saying, as she did so,

"Arise, Sir Knight; be daring and bold, do credit to my badge, and presume not to return into this presence without some trophy worthy to be laid at my feet."

The elder Lorimer was by this time in the saddle, and shouting impatiently to his nephew.

Charles hastily kissed the hand of the pretty tyrant, while she, doing her best to look affronted at his presumption, turned from him with a dignified toss of her little head, courtesied demurely to Captain Mansfield, and bounded into the house like a young antelope. The two young men mounted in haste, and following the elder Lorimer, dashed down the hill at a smart gallop.

Charles was, or was not, in love with his pretty cousin

Kate, just as my Fair Readers (if I am so far honoured as to have any) may think probable: I am no judge of such matters. But as he rattled his fiery little Arab down the steepest part of the hill, with a careless seat and slackened rein, he certainly appeared absent, to say nothing of his humming to himself, but loud enough to be overheard by his companions, a love-lorn ditty, about music, love, and flowers. In this amusement, however, he was soon interrupted, by a long whistle of astonishment from his uncle, accompanied by a thundering injunction, to mind his bridle-hand, and not break the horse's knees, although he was perfectly welcome to take what liberties he liked with his own neck.

"Why, Charles," continued old Lorimer, "you look like a moon-struck poet, and are more fit to wield a gray goose-quill, than a rifle. Music, love, and flowers, indeed! Hang it, the boy must either be in love, or a born simpleton. Stay till you hear my pups giving tongue together, like a chime of bells, with the crack of a two-ounce rifle, and the whistle of a rugged bullet by way of accompaniment; that is the sort of concert for a man to listen to in the woods, whatever little weakness he may choose to give way to amongst the Woman-kind."

"Well, well," interrupted Charles, "never mind, Uncle; you know I have not yet had much experience in field-sports, and you can hardly expect me to be an enthusiast in the art; but I trust that, under your good tuition, I shall soon improve. I have been told that pea-fowl and jungle-fowl are very numerous in these hills, and I have brought with me a double-barrelled gun, by

Purdie, which, I flatter myself, will do some execution amongst them."

"Pea-fowl, jungle-fowl, and a double-barrelled gun!" exclaimed the old Gentleman, checking his horse, and turning towards his Nephew, with a look of the most sovereign contempt; "why, you misbegotten whelp, do you take me for one of those thistle-whipping vermin who prowl about the woods with a smooth-bored pop-gun, murdering partridges and quail? who flog their unhappy curs if they show blood enough to give tongue on the slot of a deer, and get drunk for very joy, if, by any lucky chance, one of the imps succeeds in circumventing a pea-fowl? Do you suppose, Sir, that those noble hounds, which were sent on this morning to the hunting-ground, attended by twenty well-armed beaters, are kept to scour the woods for quail, or that my favourite rifle, 'kill-devil,' which, this very season, has cut a ragged hole in the dun hides of thirty deer, not to mention a few bears and tigers, is a weapon to be soiled with the blood of jackals? I tell thee, Boy, I have not had a smooth barrel in my hands these twenty years: the thing does very well for schoolboys to shoot hedge-sparrows withal; but a rifle, Sir, a rifle, is the only weapon fit for a man to handle, and no one shall hunt with my hounds that uses any other."

"I crave your pardon, my worthy Uncle," said the good-natured Lad, with a smile; "but, as I told you before, I am no sportsman, and I was not aware that using a smooth-bored gun was considered such a heinous offence in this country."

"Well, well, boy, never mind, I was perhaps over-hasty. You shall shoot with one of my rifles to-day, and I have no doubt that, when you have learnt to handle it a little, you will fully appreciate the beauties of the weapon, and become a convert to my system. But here is the cover in sight, so a truce to talking, and let us to business."

They were now descending a rugged bridle path, which led into a sequestered valley, clothed with the richest herbage, and flanked by stupendous mountains, the sides of which were intersected with numerous and well-wooded ravines. It was a glorious sight, and one to inspire a poet or a painter, independently of the feelings which warmed the blood of the sportsmen, and made it course through their veins with a freer motion, as if purged from all the grosser particles of humanity. The higher hills were still shrouded in mist, whilst the bosom of the valley was flooded by a deluge of light, such as none but a tropical sun can impart. Thin wreaths of vapour, like the dim ghosts of Ossian, curled slow and majestic up the mountain's side, gradually revealing to the eye of the spectator the rich foliage of the woods, sparkling with dew-drops, and glowing with the deep scarlet flowers of the rhododendron. The fresh morning air came loaded with the perfume of wild orange flower and jessamine, and the harsh scream of the wary pea fowl, blended with the cheerful cry of the jungle-cock, might be heard at intervals, rising in wild discord from the inmost recesses of the woods. On a sunny bank, at the foot of the descent, the armed beaters (who had been sent on at an early hour in the morning) were scattered about in picturesque groups, leaning in careless attitudes on their broad-bladed hunting spears, or, with the natural indolence of Hindoos, availing themselves of the opportunity to enjoy a hasty nap in the grateful sunshine. A short distance apart from the rest might be seen the chief huntsman, "Ishmail Khan," sitting cross-legged on a grassy hillock, smoking his *kallioon* with true oriental gravity, and complacently stroking his long, silky beard, as, from time to time, he cast a look of paternal tenderness on the pack of noble looking hounds, which lay around him. These dogs, to a casual observer, had all the appearance of common English fox-hounds; but to the eye of a sportsman, it was evident that the original breed had been crossed with the bull-dog, or the large poligar dog of India, a cross, which, although it diminishes the beauty and speed of the animal, is found to answer better than any other on the Neilgherry Hills, where such formidable antagonists as the bear, the wild boar, the panther, and even the tiger, are to be encountered.

As the riders entered the valley the natives arose and saluted them with a respectful salaam. The horse-keepers seized the bridles of the smoking steeds, and carefully spreading a horsecloth over their loins, proceeded to bend and crack each joint of their limbs, as is done in the operation of shampooing, previously to rubbing them down, and dressing them.

"Well," exclaimed Lorimer, as he proceeded with the greatest exactness to charge a heavy double-barrelled rifle, which was handed to him by one of his attendants—"Well, Ishmail, what news of game this morning? Has that Hill-man, who promised to be upon the look out for us, made his appearance yet?"

"No, Sahib," replied Ishmail, in Hindostanee; "the slave of your highness has not yet arrived. May dogs defile his father's grave! he is slower than a tortoise."

"Here, however, comes our jackall," shouted Mansfield; "and with good tidings, too, if one may judge by the delighted grin on the visage of the ill-favoured Pagan."

At this moment the figure of a half-naked savage, with his head uncovered, and his long matted locks flowing in wild confusion over his shoulders, emerged from the neighbouring wood, and descending the hill at a few bounds, prostrated himself at the feet of Lorimer.

"Here, Ishmail," said the old gentleman, "you understand the language of the creature; desire him to rise, and ask him what information he brings."

Ishmail having questioned the messenger, turned towards his master with a look of great satisfaction. "Your slave has been successful, Sahib; he reports thirty head of deer, marked down in different woods, and a sounder of ten wild hog, headed by an immense boar, whose tusks he compares to those of an elephant, which he has just seen entering this ravine on the north side of the valley. If your highness would permit me to offer an opinion, I should say we had better attack the hogs first, else the noise of our beaters will cause them to shift their ground."

"Right, Ishmail, right; your old boar is a cunning fellow, and steals away at the first whimper of the hounds, but there is no fear of a stag moving when he once gets into good cover."

By this time six other sportsmen had arrived, making in all nine guns.

"We muster a pretty good field to-day, and shall, I think, be able to give a tolerable account of this same sounder of hog; so, Gentlemen, the sooner we take our places the better. You, Ishmail, must lead the dogs and beaters round the shoulder of this hill, so as to gain the top of the ravine without disturbing the game: and mind you wait for a signal from my bugle to throw them into cover. You, Mansfield, who know the ground, had better take Charles under your guidance, and go to your favourite stand on the other side of the glen, whilst I post these gentlemen in the most commanding positions I can find."

Ishmail had already mounted his shaggy hill pony, and was leading his myrmidons by a circuitous route to their appointed station, when Mansfield, bringing his rifle to a long trail, beckoned to Charles to follow him, and began to ascend the hill with long strides. Close at his heels followed a well-dressed *peon*, "bearded like the pard," and bearing his second rifle; and Charles was followed by a low caste native dressed in the white calico robe usually worn by household servants in India, and shouldering, with a look of great importance, an immense hunting-spear, which he had borrowed from one of the beaters. Mansfield, having crossed the ravine and ascended for some distance on the other side, halted near a large gray stone, which commanded a full view of the surrounding country.

"This is our post," said he; "and now let us dispose of ourselves scientifically. You, Sir, (addressing the *Peon*,) leave my rifle here, get on the top of that rock, keep a good look out, and make the usual signal to me if you see anything move." Then casting his eyes on the long, stooping, effeminate figure of Charles's attendant, who stood leaning on his spear with a look of vacant wonder, "Who the devil have we here, Charles? To what species does this animal belong? Are we to class him among the *Quadrumana?* or does he aspire to the more noble order of *Bimanà?*"

"I am not naturalist enough to decide the knotty point," answered Charles, laughing; "but at present he serves me in the honourable capacity of *Mussaulchee.*"

"Yes," chimed in the grinning varlet, "I master's *Maty Boy*,—very proper, very handsome *Maty Boy*,—*maty* business, *shikar* business, too much kind of business, I can do very proper. Sahib sometimes make fun, call me Heels, because Sahib say my hind leg stepped a-midship."

"Very well, Master Heels," replied Mansfield, striving to repress a laugh, "I have no doubt whatever that your talents are exceedingly diversified, but at present I do not suppose we shall have any opportunity of calling them into action; so just be good enough to coil away that misshapen figure of yours behind yonder stone, and do not allow your baboon's head to appear over it, unless you wish it to become better acquainted with the butt-end of my rifle."

The indignant Heels looked daggers, but, like a prudent person, slunk away quietly to his lair, muttering to himself some unintelligible jargon about *maty* business, *shikar* business, and *galee.* Mansfield and Charles now proceeded to conceal themselves behind a rock which overhung the ravine, allowing nothing but their heads to appear over it, and in this situation awaited the signal for putting the hounds into cover.

"Is not this considered rather an unfair style of sport?" inquired Charles. "I was told at Madras that no one ever thought of killing a wild boar in India, except on horseback, and with a spear."

"True; such is the general rule, and a very proper one. In the plains it is considered unmanly to kill a hog in any other way than by riding him down; and the shooting of one is considered as great a crime as it would be to shoot a fox in Leicestershire. But on these mountains, where the steepness of the hills and the swampy nature of the valleys renders it impossible to ride to hog, the practice of shooting them is permitted, and the rifle takes the place of the spear.—But hark! there goes the signal."

The distant notes of a bugle were now heard; and ere the echo died away amongst the surrounding mountains, the hounds came rushing over the crest of the hill, like driving mist before the blasts of autumn, and dashed gallantly into cover. Behind them advanced a line of well-armed beaters, like skirmishers, in extended order, sounding horns and beating *tom-toms* to rouse the game. For some minutes these were the only sounds heard; but presently the voice of a single hound arose upon the blast, and echoed down the rocky sides of the ravine.

"Now then, my Lad," whispered Mansfield, rising on one knee, and cocking his rifle, "look out, and screw your nerves to the sticking-place: the old Boar will soon be afoot; and if once these dogs get fairly on his trail, they will not allow him to dodge long in cover. Hush! hark!—there he goes again: 't is old Speaker; I know his voice well, and he is no babbler, take my word for it. There, now Racer chimes in—now Rodney takes it up. Steady, my Lad, steady! 'T is all right now, depend upon it."

Hound after hound now opened on the scent as it gradually became warmer, till at length, the whole pack, in full chorus, came sweeping down the glen like a hurricane, rousing the startled echoes of the woods, and making the welkin ring with their joyous music.

At this moment Mansfield's attention was roused by a low whistle overhead; and looking up towards the summit of the rock which overhung them, he beheld his *Peon* poking his head cautiously forward, and pointing with animated gestures towards the opposite side of the ravine.

"The game is afoot!" cried Mansfield, eagerly grasping his heavy rifle, and raising his body a little, so as to command a better view. "And now I have him. See there, Charles, on the opposite side of the glen, just passing that gray rock which skirts the jungle. 'T is the old Boar, and as big a one as I have seen this season. By the hump of the Holy Camel, he looms as large as a donkey!"

As he said this, his rifle was slowly raised, and the sight brought to bear upon the Boar, who was sulkily trotting up a rocky path, occasionally stopping to listen to the hounds, and churning the white foam betwixt his enormous jaws. Charles watched the deliberate movements of Mansfield with breathless impatience; but, at the very moment he expected to see him press the trigger, the weapon was again lowered.

"It is a wild shot," said Mansfield, shaking his head. "I have killed at as great a distance; but three hundred yards is too long a range, even for Clincher to throw a ball with any degree of accuracy. Besides, from the direction the beast is now taking, he must pass within fifty yards of your Uncle's station; and if he fails to kill him, (which, by the way, is not likely, for 'Kill-devil' seldom opens his mouth for nothing,) he is sure to cross to our side, and give us a good shot." Then starting to his feet, and waving his cap on high, he shouted across the ravine, with the voice of a Stentor, "Mark! Sir, mark! below you, and to the right!"

The Boar, startled by the sound of his voice, sprang forward, and began to bound up the rocky path with the agility of a goat; and at the same moment the elder Lorimer was seen slowly raising his head from amongst a thick clump of fern, in which he had concealed himself.

"See, see!" whispered Mansfield, smiling; "how cautiously the Old Gentleman raises his head above the fern, like a cunning old grouse-cock. Ah! now he catches a view of the Boar, and 'Kill-devil' is about to speak. Silence, and watch."

The sharp crack of a rifle echoed amongst the rocks; but the Boar only bounded forward with increased speed; whilst the cloud of dust which was knocked up under his belly, and the shrill whistle of the bullet, as it glanced from a stone, announced that it had fallen a trifle short of its intended mark.

"Missed him, by heavens!" cried Mansfield, dashing his cap to the ground, and stamping impatiently. "At him again, Sir—at him again. Give him the other barrel."

A projecting rock had for a moment concealed the Boar from the view of Lorimer; but the instant he again appeared, the Old Gentleman pitched his rifle forward, and fired rapidly. The report of his piece was answered by a short, savage grunt from the Boar, who staggered slightly; but immediately recovering himself, he turned sharp round, and scrambled with wonderful rapidity down the rugged side of the ravine.

"Good!" exclaimed Mansfield; "that shot told, although not exactly in the right spot. There is nothing like pitching your gun at them, and pulling quick, with swift-going animals.—And now, Charles," said he, turning to his companion, "look out, and let us see how you can handle a rifle. He is certain to cross to our side, and break within an easy shot of us, and, with an ounce of lead through his body, will not be quite so quick in his movements as he was at first. Down again behind the stone, and keep quiet."

A rustling in the bushes, directly below them, soon announced that the Boar was at hand. The next instant the brushwood was thrust aside, and the enormous brute burst forth within twenty paces of them. His small twinkling eyes flashed with malignant fire, and the foam which besmeared his jaws was slightly tinged with blood. As he gained the top of the bank, he stopped for an instant, and turned his head on one side, as if listening to the hounds which followed hotly on the scent.

"Now is the time," whispered Mansfield; "be cool,

and mind you hit him well forward, through the shoulder if possible."

Charles, trembling with excitement, thrust forward his rifle and fired, making the white splinters fly from a tree beyond the Boar, and at least three feet above him. At the same instant the unfortunate Heels, startled by the shot, sprang up with a look of wild astonishment from behind the stone where he had lain all this time enjoying a comfortable nap. The enraged Boar no sooner got a glimpse of his white dress, than, uttering a savage grunt, he made at him *au pas de charge*, tossed him over his head, and sent him rolling and shrieking down the precipitous bank. Ere Mansfield had time to raise his rifle, the hounds had come up, and dashing without hesitation at the enraged brute, seized him by the ears.

"Whoop to him, my gallant dogs! hold him and shake him!" shouted Mansfield, whilst the Boar struggled in vain to disengage himself from the jaws of the powerful hounds. "Just look at that savage devil Rodney, that large brindled dog between a hound and a bulldog; see how gallantly he stands up to him. But we must put a stop to this, or he 'll rip the dogs to pieces. Here, Charles, my boy, pick up that spear which poor Heels has dropped in his agony. You shall have the honour of giving him the *coup de grace*."

Charles, delighted at having an opportunity of making amends for his bad shot, eagerly grasped the spear and walked steadily up to the Boar. The brute, seeing him approach, redoubled his efforts, and, freeing himself by one tremendous struggle from the hounds, plunged madly forward. But Charles, whose blood was now effectually

LEARNING TO STAND A CHARGE.

roused, coolly lowered the point of his unwieldy weapon, and awaited the charge. The enraged Boar rushed with blind fury on his antagonist. The broad bladed spear buried itself deep in his brawny chest, and, with one savage grunt of defiance, he sank to the earth, wallowing in blood and foam.

"Gallantly done, my boy!" shouted Mansfield; "we shall make a Sportsman of you yet, in spite of the new tops and white inexpressibles. I see you have plenty of nerve to handle a spear, and only want a little practice to make you a dangerous fellow with the rifle."

During this exclamation, Charles, who had withdrawn his blood-stained spear, stood leaning against it, and gazing in silent wonder at the gigantic proportions of the brute which lay gasping at his feet.

"Ay, he is a big one," said Mansfield, "and his head will be a fine trophy to lay at the feet of your Fair Cousin. But he is dead enough now, and we may leave him to the beaters, who will do the needful with him, as soon as their work is over. Let us go now and examine the plight of your unfortunate page Heels, who, if I mistake not, will stand in some need of the leech's aid. Your old Boar seldom makes a charge without leaving his marks behind; and I can tell you, from experience, that they are no love-pinches. I cannot help feeling for the poor devil, although I can hardly divest myself of the idea that the creature ought to be classed amongst the order *Quadrumana*."

Having returned to the edge of the glen, they beheld a prickly bush about half way down the hill in violent agitation, although no living creature could be distinguished through its tangled branches; and from the midst of it issued lamentations like those of a condemned spirit in Limbo, mingled with fearful maledictions against the old Boar and all his ancestors, male and female, even to the tenth generation.

"How the Pagan blasphemes!" exclaimed Mansfield, laughing heartily; for he was now convinced, from the energetic manner in which Master Heels expressed himself, that he was not so seriously hurt as he had at first feared. "He is gifted with the true Malabar style of eloquence, and must have studied the noble art of abuse under the directions of his Grandmother. There is no one who understands real piquant slang like your ancient Malabar dame; I would back one of them at any time to silence the whole battery of Billingsgate market. But we must go to the relief of the poor wretch, for he is evidently unable to extricate himself from the durance vile in which he is held by that prickly bush."

Having scrambled down the hill, they succeeded, after some difficulty, in relieving poor Heels from his awkward situation. He had, almost by a miracle, escaped the deadly rip of the Boar's tusk. But in other respects he was in a very sorry plight. He was sorely battered by the fall—his white robe was torn to shreds and besmeared with blood—and his face was so dreadfully scratched and disfigured by the brambles into which he had fallen, that scarcely a feature could be distinguished. Having replaced his turban, which had been knocked off in the scramble, and wiped his face as well as he could with his sleeve, he thus addressed Charles in blubbering accents, whilst he busied himself in extracting the numerous thorns which still remained buried in his flesh.

"Suppose, Master, please I take leave. This *shikar*

business very trouble business—jungle pig not good, he too much *bobbery* make—all same like tiger. Small *shikar* I can do very proper, but this *jungle shikar* too much bad. Suppose, Master, cut off my head, I never can do that business."

The two Sportsmen, after enjoying a hearty laugh at the expense of poor Heels, relieved his mind by assuring him that his services would no longer be required to assist in the much dreaded *jungle shikar*, and that he might take leave as soon as he pleased. The poor trembling wretch made a salaam of profound gratitude, and turning his face towards the cantonment, limped away towards home with a degree of speed which nothing but mortal terror could have inspired.

CHAPTER III.

A DAY'S HUNTING ON THE NEILGHERRY HILLS.

(CONTINUED.)

THE unlucky "Heels" had disappeared in the distance, and the recall of the huntsman's bugle had brought together the scattered hounds, as old Lorimer scrambled up the steep hill-side, mounted on his shaggy little pony, "Marble."

"Come, Gentlemen," cried he, as he pulled off his green hunting-cap, and wiped the perspiration from his forehead, "don't let us lose time; the hounds are all assembled, and we have still plenty of work before us. Our next beat is to be the large wood, at the back of this hill, where we have twelve deer marked down. You all know your stations there, I believe. And after that, we shall try the rocky glen, below the '*Todah Mund*,' in hopes of finding that large bear which gave us the slip last Saturday. You must exert yourselves this time, Lads, and not let him escape again. I hear that the old blackguard has taken a fancy to human flesh of late, and has carried off a Todah Woman and a Child within the last three days. So die he must; if we hunt him for a week. As to the hogs, we have given a tolerably good account of them. This boar and three fat sows have been sent to the shades. So let's mount and be off. Ha! Charles, my boy, give me your hand; you stood up to that old boar like a man; and the way in which you handled your spear made me forget the disgrace you brought upon my rifle by that first shot of yours. Oh, you young dog, it was a devil of a miss that! a most palpable miss—worthy of my friends the 'thistle whippers!' You shut both your eyes when you fired that shot, eh?—did you not, you young dog, eh? Well, well—never look ashamed, boy—I have seen older hands than you make as bad a miss before now, and trust to their heels rather than a spear afterwards. Eh! Doctor—do you recollect that wounded sow that gave you such a devil of a *gruelling*, up the hill at 'Ralliah,' last week? Faith, you may thank your long legs and the ounce of lead I lodged in her shoulder for being now in a whole skin."

The person whom Lorimer thus addressed was a tall, bony, loose-jointed figure apparently about fifty years of age, who looked as if his limbs were attached to his body by wires. His large hands, covered with red hair and freckles, projected several inches beyond the wristbands of his scanty jacket; and his gaunt misshapen legs terminated in a sort of *palmated* foot—we can find no other word expressive of its peculiar formation—which gave to the whole limb the appearance of an ingeniously contrived machine for crushing cock-roaches or stopping a mouse in a corner. His scalp was thatched, rather than clothed, with coarse red hair. And his face,—But how can we ever do justice to that inimitably expressive countenance?—It was a face which, at first sight, gave one a lively idea of the Knight of the Rueful Countenance. There was the sallow complexion, the high cheek-bones, the capacious mouth, the interminable nose, and the solemn look of a Don Quixote. Yet, with all this, there were lines of mirth lurking round the corners of the mouth, a *pawky* expression in the eye, and an extraordinary power of motion in the extremity of the long proboscis, which, when called into action, rendered the worthy Doctor's face one of the most perfectly mirth-inspiring we have ever had the good fortune to meet with. Of his character we shall only say, that under this rough exterior our friend the Doctor carried a heart true as steel, and overflowing, not only with mirth, but with the unadulterated milk of human kindness.

He was one of our oldest and most intimate friends; and we can safely say that, either as a boon-companion, or a trusty friend in the hour of need, we have never met the fellow to *Long Jock Macphee.*

"Indeed then, Sir," replied the Doctor, glancing downwards towards his uncouth limbs, "thae same lang legs o' mine are no ill things at a pinch; and in my opeenion are mair to be lippened till than the best spear amang tham a'. But, at the same time, I was muckle indebted to you, Sir, for that bit lead ye put into the beast. It was just in the nick o' time, for I was sair taigled wi' thae lang leather spats—thae leggins, as ye ca' them;—mair fit for an Indian savage than a Christian man. And the muckle beast was just at the grippin o' me when ye cowpet her. Gude preserve us frae a' lang-nebbit things!—it gars me grue to think o't? The wild 'grumph!' 'grumph!' 'grumph!' o' the rampawgin deevil just ahint me—and me expectin' every moment to feel her muckle white teeth play chack through my hurdies. Ay, ye may laugh, Lads; but, faith, it was nae laughin' sport to me—and that ye'll ken, the first time ony o' you tries a race wi' ane o' thae wild swine. They 're just perfect deevils incarnate! My certie! ye're waur aff wi' ane o' them than Tam O'Shanter wi' Cutty Sark at his heels—for she only pou't aff the grey meere's tail; but faith, lads, it's your ain tail that's in danger when ye come to grips wi' a wild soo!"

This speech of the Doctor's elicited a roar of laughter from his companions, in which he good-humouredly joined; and the whole party, mounting their ponies, cantered over the hill to take up their positions for the next beat.

The scene is now changed to one of those wild solitary valleys through which the superfluous water of the hills makes its escape, and rushes on its headlong course down the almost perpendicular side of the mountain. From hence the glowing plains of the Carnatic are seen extended like a living map 8000 feet below the spectator. The valley itself presents a scene of wild and savage grandeur, contrasting beautifully with the luxuriant palm groves and voluptuous sunshine of the low country, over which the eye wanders, for many leagues, till it is lost in the dreamy indistinctness of the distance, where earth and sky become blended in a red fiery haze. Light fleecy clouds are hurried swiftly across the heavens, and shivered, as it were, against the craggy peaks of that granite mountain, which towers high amidst the region of storms, whilst all around is hushed, silent, and motionless, as the sleep of infancy. The only sound which breaks the death-like stillness is the wild, unearthly cry of the great black monkey—a deep, loud "wooh!" "wooh!" which rising suddenly, and at long intervals, from the gloomy recesses of the wood, has a strange, startling effect, and suggests to one's mind the idea of a stray satyr calling to his mates.

Mansfield and Charles have just taken up their position behind the shelter of a palmira bush.

The former, accustomed to such scenes, is sitting with his ponderous rifle across his knee, his thumb resting on the cock, and his head turned a little on one side, watching, with the unwearied patience of an Indian hunter, to catch the faintest sound: whilst the more romantic Charles, allowing his weapon to lie idly by his side, gazes with rapture on the glorious view, and, if I am any judge of physiognomy, is thinking more of his pretty Cousin than of the deer.

The hounds have opened on the scent.

"Down! down!—crouch like a panther!" whispered Mansfield, seizing Charles by the arm, and pulling him more behind the shelter of the bush. "Do you remark that crackling amongst the dry branches just below us? It is a deer, and he will break at that opening where you see a beaten path like a sheep-track. It is their regular run; keep your eye upon the spot, and watch."

"I see him," whispered Charles, cocking his rifle, and making a motion to rise. "I see his antlers moving above that bush of wild jessamine."

"Stay, stay, my boy—not so fast," replied Mansfield, smiling at the eagerness of his young companion. "It requires a little more experience than you have had, to judge whereabouts a stag's shoulder should lie, when nothing but the points of his horns are visible. Don't fire till you can see his body. He is listening intently to the hounds, and does not observe us, so there is no hurry. Now then he moves—now!"

A sharp crack—a dull plashing sound—the noble stag plunges madly forward—and over, over, over he rolls, staining the green herbage with his life-blood, which gushes fast from a rugged hole in his side.

Mansfield's *Peon* springs forward with the bound of a tiger, and, muttering a short prayer, like a good Mussulman as he is, buries the long glittering blade of a hunting knife in the throat of his victim. The "stricken deer" gasps painfully for breath—his wide nostril is distended—his bloodshot eye rolls wildly for a moment—his limbs quiver in the last agony—he heaves a long shuddering sigh, and dies.

This was the first deer that Charles had ever seen fall, and his heart smote him as he witnessed its dying struggles.

Is not this rather a cruel amusement? whispered conscience. Does not your savage nature relent as you see that graceful creature weltering in his blood, and, in the last agonies, bending his dark languid eye upon your face, as if asking, What have I done to deserve this? Do you not almost wish that the fatal ball had sped less truly to its mark?

Mansfield, who had watched the working of his companion's features, as he gazed pensively on the dying stag, here interrupted him with a gentle tap on the shoulder.

"I can read your thoughts, boy; and they do credit to your heart. Even I, old sportsman as I am, can sympathize with you in a feeling which many men affect to call weakness, but which I consider merely as a proof of a good heart, and one which no man need be ashamed of. I can look unmoved on the dying struggles of the foaming boar. I even experience a sort of savage satisfaction, as the last faint growl rattles in the throat of the surly bear; and the expiring roar of the vanquished tiger is music in my ears. But I never yet slew a deer that a feeling of pity, such as you now experience, did not immediately succeed the burst of exultation which invariably accompanies a well-directed shot; and yet, the very next moment, I was exerting my utmost skill to accomplish the death of some other animal, and felt all the disappointment of a baffled tiger if my ball did not take effect. We are strange unaccountable animals in this respect. But I am satisfied it is not cruelty—it is not a thirst for blood which inspires us with a love for the chase. No! it is a far nobler feeling;—a species of ambition—a love of enterprise; the pleasure arising from which depends entirely on the difficulties to be surmounted in the attainment of our object. What satisfaction, for instance, would it give a sportsman to be turned loose in a park, full of fallow deer, where, if shedding blood were his object, he might gratify that propensity to his heart's content? None whatever. There are no difficulties to be surmounted, and he would look upon himself in the light of a butcher. But after a long day's stalking through a Highland glen—after making a round of many weary miles to get down the wind of the ever-watchful red deer—after creeping through the heather like a snake, and wearing his knees to the bone amongst the coarse gravel of a dry watercourse,—how breathless that moment of intense anxiety to the sportsman when he first ventures to raise his head above the sheltering bank, and finds the object of all his labour, a noble stag of ten tines, still feeding in the very spot where he first observed him! And, Oh! the electric thrill of exultation, when the crack of his rifle is answered by that dull soft *thud*, grateful to the sportsman's ear as the voice of her he loves; and the proud stag, bounding high into air, falls gasping on the bloody heath!—Bah! the sensations of a young lady on receiving her first proposal are nothing to this. But, hark! the merry music of the hounds comes sweeping by us on the blast, and scatters all my romantic and moralizing ideas to the four winds of heaven. Hurra!"

But 't were long to tell of all the deer that fell in the course of this beat. Suffice it to say that many proud antlered heads bowed before the unerring rifle of Mansfield; and that the worthy Doctor expended more than his usual allowance of ammunition, with even less than his usual success.

The party had assembled at luncheon by the time Mansfield and Charles joined them; and, as they approached, their ears were saluted by the loud tones of old Lorimer's voice, swearing as usual by "the beard of the Prophet," and "the bones of his ancestors," while he vented his wrath, in no very measured terms, against the unfortunate Doctor.

"Well, you d—d long slip of anatomy, you expect to get something to line your ungodly maw, do you, after the good service you have done us to-day? Bones of my ancestors, man! it might grumble long enough before you filled it with venison of your own killing, although, to do you justice, you are as good a shot at a venison-pasty as any one I know. Why, you vender of ratsbane! what the devil were you thinking of, to let all those deer pass you? Fifteen shots have I seen you fire this blessed day

—fifteen shots, by the beard of the Prophet! and not a hoof to show for them. Hang it, man, that last hind passed so close, you might have thrown salt on her tail, and yet, after four shots, away she went, bounding over the hills like a kangaroo, with half the pack at her heels; and when we shall get them back again, the devil only knows. Speak, you misbegotten son of Esculapius! Why don't you speak, and let us hear what you have to say for yourself?"

The Doctor, who was well accustomed to the Old Gentleman's eccentric ways, and knew him to be one of those privileged characters who say and do whatever they like, without giving offence to any one, sat very coolly exploring the inmost recesses of a venison-pasty, whilst he listened with imperturbable gravity to this harangue. At length, bolting an enormous mouthful, and washing it down with a long pull at the *brandy-panee*, he thus replied, still keeping his knife ready to resume his attack on the pasty.

"Ca' cannie, Sir!—ca' cannie! For ony sake, dinna be puttin yersell throughither that gaet. It 's no good for the digestion. It 's an unco bad thing for a person o' your plethoric habit to be giving way to sic violent emotions sae soon after meals. Do you no ken, Sir, it 's very apt to bring on a fit o' apoplexy? Gude preserve us! but he 's gettin awfu' red in the face! It 's amaist black! I 'm thinkin, Sir, I 'll need to tak some blude frae you. Just bide a wee till I get my lance," continued the Doctor, coolly turning up his sleeves, "I 'll no be a crack."

"You and your *lance* be hanged!" roared the Old Gentleman, trying to look fierce, but quite unable to suppress a laugh. "Sit down, you vampire, and say your say without farther circumlocution."

"Weel, then, Sir," replied the Doctor, eyeing a savoury morsel which he had just impaled on his fork; "Weel, then, I 'll just tell you, in three words, that it was your ain fault, and nae fault o' mine that sae mony o' the deer jinkit past me this same day."

"My fault, Sir! how the devil do you make out that it was my fault?"

"'Deed, then, Mr. Lorimer, it was just your fault, and naebody else's. Ye *will* persist in garrin me aye shoot wi' a single bullet, and ane o' thae bits o' rifles, that lets nae mair crack than a pen-gun; although I 've threippet on you, till I 'm weariet, that I hae nae skill o' sic like new-fangled weapons, and am no fit to hit a peat-stack wi' ane o' them. But just gie me a good honest fusee, wi' plenty o' pouther, to gar it tell against a body's cheek, and a nievefu' o' grit shot on the top o' that, and I 'll cation mysell to ding as mony Staigs as ony o' you,—no exceptin yoursell, Sir; or that chiel Mansfield, wha makes sic a phraze aboot his rifle gun, and his lang ranges. As to the lang ranges, I 'll maybe no kill a beast on the ither side o' ane o' thae glens, whare ye need the prospec-glass to see whether it 's a dun deer or a grey soo that ye'r firin at. But, faith, there 's no mony o' them 'ill gi' me the jink if ance they come within a christianlike distance."

What answer old Lorimer would have given to the Doctor's heretical plan of employing "plenty o' pouther, and a nievefu' o' grit shot," is unknown, although, I suspect, he was just on the point of consigning the Doctor and his fusee to the bottomless pit. But, luckily for them, Ishmail at this moment stepped forward, with his usual profound salaam, to report that the stray hounds had been collected.

The fragments of the luncheon were quickly disposed of, the cigars lighted, and the whole party moved off in the wake of Ishmail and his hounds, to beat that famous glen, below the *Todah-Mund*, which every Neilgherry sportsman must recollect, as being the favourite resort both of bears and tigers.

It is rather a ravine than a glen. A deep rent in the side of the mountain, so narrow that the light of day can hardly penetrate. The rocky sides rise abruptly to the height of 500 feet, rugged and splintered, as if torn asunder—and no doubt they have been—by some grand convulsion of nature.

The bottom is clothed with an almost impenetrable underwood of tangled bamboo; whilst along the sides a few gnarled, misshapen trees, chiefly rhododendrons, shoot out from amongst the crevices of the rocks, stretching their fantastic branches, all glowing with scarlet flowers, across the ravine, and weaving their snake-like roots into every fissure which affords the slightest prospect of moisture; their moss-grown bark, and distorted limbs, proving how hard a struggle they must have, to extract sufficient nourishment from the niggardly soil.

The information which old Lorimer had received of his friend the Bear's man-eating propensities, made him more than ever anxious to ensure his destruction.

All the known outlets were strongly guarded, and on every high peak of rock, which commanded a good view, might be seen the motionless figure of a Native, perched like some huge bird of prey, and watching, with eagle glance, to prevent the possibility of any animal stealing away unobserved.

All being stationed at their respective posts, the gallant Ishmail contemplated the distribution of the forces with a grim smile of satisfaction, and fiercely twirling his long mustache, which curled upwards to his eyes, shouted, in a loud clear tone, to the dog-keepers, "*Chor do!*" At the signal twenty impatient hounds bounded from the leash, and dashed into cover.

"Have at him, my little tigers! Whose dogs are we that he should laugh at our beards? By the hump of the Holy Camel, he shall this day be made to eat dirt. Show your ugly snout,—meet me if you dare,—you old grey-headed *bantchoot.* I defile your mother's grave, and spit on your father's beard!" So saying, Ishmail drew his heavy *tulwar*, or native sword,—and wrapping his *cumberbund* tightly round his left arm, to act as a shield in case of necessity, stalked, with an air of determined resolution, into the gloomy jungle.

"There goes old Ishmail, with his whiskers bristling like an enraged tiger-cat," exclaimed Mansfield, laughing, as he watched these proceedings from his place of concealment amongst the rocks. "His blood is fairly up now, and he is determined to make the Bear show his grey muzzle, even if he drives him out at the point of the sword. Hark! they have found already."

Deep and angry now arose the baying of the eager hounds, from out the gloomy depths of the ravine, and wildly did the prolonged echoes reverberate the sound. But it was no longer the musical chime with which they swept along on the hot scent of the flying deer.

The sound was now stationary, and the short angry barking of the dogs was mingled with an occasional yell of pain, announcing that some unfortunate hound had suffered for his temerity, in attempting to close with his formidable antagonist.

"What an obstinate brute!" exclaimed Mansfield, as he stretched forward over a projecting rock, in hopes of getting a glimpse of what was going on in the thick jungle below. "I never in my life met with a Bear that stood so much bullying; they generally start at once, and make a running fight of it."

A tremendous roar, followed by a despairing death-shriek, now arose with fearful distinctness above the confused baying and howling of the dogs. For a moment there was a death-like silence, as if every living thing had been paralyzed by that voice of thunder. Then a strong rustling amongst the tangled bamboos,—a deep, surly growl, mingled with a stifled throttling cry,—a faint groan, and again the baying of the hounds was resumed, but less eagerly than before, and in a whining, undecided tone, betwixt anger and fear.

The shouting of the terrified beaters was now heard in all directions, and next moment many of them were seen rushing from the jungle, and scrambling up the face of the rocks; whilst, with frantic gestures, they waved to their companions below to fall back.

"By heavens, I thought so," shouted Mansfield, starting to his feet, and instinctively grasping his rifle, as the well-known roar of a Tiger reached his ear.

"Thought what?" asked Charles, astonished at the unusual excitement of his stoical companion.

"Why, that we have caught a Tartar, that 's all;—slipped the poor dogs at a Tiger, instead of a lubberly old Bear. Thank God, the beaters are all out of danger now, except the poor fellow whose death-shriek we heard, and he is, no doubt, beyond the leech's aid. But we must bestir ourselves, else the brute will not leave a hound alive."

In the enthusiasm of the moment Mansfield had slung his rifle across his shoulder, and, in spite of the remonstrances of Charles, was about to attempt the desperate experiment of scrambling down the face of the rock, and shooting the Tiger in his lair; when his motions were arrested by the voice of Ishmail.

"Stop, Sahib! In the name of the holy Prophet, stop! What madness has seized you?" shouted the poor fellow in Hindostanee, as panting and smeared with blood he scrambled painfully to the top of the rock.

"Ishmail, my boy, you are wounded!" exclaimed Mansfield, running towards him. "It was not you whom the Tiger struck down just now?"

"No, Sahib. Men do not climb rocks after being knocked down by a Tiger. It was poor Asmodine, my helper, whose cry you heard. I was standing close by him; he received the weight of the blow, and is now amongst the Houries, praise be to Allah; whilst I have escaped with a slight scratch on the shoulder."

Here Ishmail pulled aside his tattered garments, and exhibited a wound, which looked as if inflicted by a gardener's rake, and from which the blood flowed in long purple streaks over his oily skin.

"Faith, Master Ishmail, that same slight scratch will

require some square yards of Dr. Mc.Phee's plaster before you are in marching order again. But, Ishmail, what is to be done? Is there no chance of driving the brute from his stronghold?"

"Sahib, the Tiger is no fool, he will not come out to eat your Highness's bullets."

"But he is tearing the dogs to pieces, man; and unless we assist them, he will not leave one alive. I think I could manage to get down to that ledge of rock above him, and shoot him as he lies."

"No, Sahib; had that been possible he were dead ere now. But I have examined the place well: he lies in a sort of cave directly under that ledge of rock, so that it is impossible to get a view of him, except from the level ground directly in his front. May dogs defile his father's beard! he has chosen his ground well. Nothing but rockets can force him to leave it; and, please Allah, it shall not be for want of rockets, if he lives to see the sun set to-morrow. But at present we must leave him, Sahib. It would be the act of a madman to attack him in his den."

"But the dogs, Ishmail?"

"He will kill no more dogs, Sahib. Our three best hounds, the only ones who had courage to close with him, have already been destroyed, and the others are only baying him at a prudent distance. They will be glad enough to leave him when they hear the recall sounded."

"Alas! poor Asmodine, yours has been a cruel death. But it shall not go unrevenged."

So said old Lorimer, as he turned from regarding the mangled corse of his faithful follower, and wiped a tear from his bronzed cheek.

His companions had dragged the body from the jungle at the risk of their lives. And the Doctor, after examining the wounds, had just reported him dead. The remains of the poor fellow presented a ghastly spectacle, and a fearful example of the destructive powers of a Tiger. The fore part of the skull was crushed in like an egg-shell, and evidently by the mere weight of the paw, for there was no mark on the head either of teeth or claws. The glazed, bloodshot eyes were forced from their sockets: and a thin stream of black blood flowed from each nostril, and trickled slowly down the sunken, lead-coloured cheeks. Besides this, it appeared that the Tiger had seized him with his teeth; the whole of the throat and the skin of the breast being torn away; leaving the root of the tongue exposed, and the bare muscles of the chest still quivering with convulsive twitches, although it was evident, from the nature of his wounds, that the poor fellow's death must have been almost instantaneous.

"Rodney, Racer, and Speaker killed, Sahib, and others badly wounded," said Ishmail, as, with the important air of an Officer on duty, he advanced to make his report, after having mustered the hounds.

"The devil fly away with these cursed Tigers," replied Lorimer. "This makes seventeen hounds that I have lost by them since last May. Couple up the dogs, Ishmail; I have not the heart to put them into cover again to-day. See that those which are wounded be carefully carried home in *cumbleys*, and have this poor fellow's body removed into camp. And now, gentlemen, we had better mount and jog homewards. We can do no more to-day; but to-morrow——"

Here he raised his voice, shook his clenched fist, and stamping on the ground—

"By the bones of my ancestors, if we live to see to-morrow, the infernal Tiger shall pay dearly for this day's work.—Ishmail, you will see that there are plenty of fire-works provided."

"*Jo Hookum, Sahib*," replied Ishmail, sternly, casting a sidelong glance at his mangled shoulder, and grinding his teeth.

"But the Bear," asked Mansfield; "must we let him slip through our fingers, Sir?"

"I am sorry to say, Mansfield, he has done so already. The scouts report that the brute stole away whilst we were tackling the Tiger, and he is, no doubt, far beyond our reach.—Burmah, my horse."

Burmah, a little dark, square-built, bushy-whiskered Mahratta, approached, leading the powerful gray Arab horse which his master had ridden in the morning, now fresh and well groomed. And, as he patted the glossy arched neck of the noble animal, he addressed him in the most extravagant terms of endearment, such as a nurse lavishes on her child; whilst the sagacious creature, as if grateful for his caresses, pricked his small ears, and rubbed his velvet muzzle against the naked shoulder of his groom.

Most of the party had mounted, and the beaters were beginning to move off, bearing the mangled body of their companion slung on a bamboo, together with the wounded dogs, and as much of the game as they could conveniently carry; when Mansfield, who had for some minutes been gazing intently at a distant hill, shouted to his *Peon*, in a voice which made him start—

"Abdallah! my spy-glass—quick, man—quick!"

"What see you?" asked Lorimer.

"Can't say exactly, Sir; but it looks devilish like our friend the Bear."

"Impossible, man! He could never be such a fool as to take across that open line of country."

"By Heavens! it is though," cried Mansfield, with exultation, handing the glass to Lorimer; "and on ground where we can ride him, too. He is making for the large wood above Nidiwuttum. But he has two long miles of open country before him, and the devil is in it if little Bundoolah does not lay me alongside of him before he reaches it. Here 's at him, at all events—who 'll follow?"

So saying, he sprang to the saddle, snatched a spear from one of the beaters, drove in his spurs, and sitting well back, with a strong pull at Bundoolah's head, dashed down the rocky hill-side at the top of his speed.

Old Lorimer rode too heavy to attempt a racing pace over such break-neck ground. And the rest of the party, with the exception of Charles, being mounted on little short-legged hill-ponies, had no chance.

Charles, however, was well mounted, and his young blood boiled to rival the daring feats of Mansfield, the pride of the Mysore country. Glancing around him in search of some weapon, his eye rested on the ornamented hilt of Ishmail's sword.

"This will do famously," cried he, as Ishmail handed him his *tulwar* with an ironical smile, which seemed to say, "It will do all *your* work as well as anything else—a broomstick might serve your turn, for that matter."

But this was lost upon Charles, who eagerly clutched the sword, and waving it triumphantly around his head, rattled down the hill in hot pursuit of his companion.

"You 'll find that a queer tool to tackle a Bear with, my hearty," shouted old Lorimer, laughing, as he and the rest of the party followed at a steady canter. Charles only answered by another wave of his sword and an extra dig of the spurs.

But we must follow Mansfield. The tremendous pace at which he rattled over the ground soon brought him up with the chase. He was now within fifty yards of the Bear, who, finding that matters began to look serious, was shambling along at his best pace, his foaming jaws distended, and his tongue lolling far out of his mouth. Three strides more would have brought him within spear's length. But Bundoolah began to show symptoms of distress. And there being no rival at hand to dispute with him the honour of the first spear, Mansfield pulled up for a moment, to let his panting horse gather fresh wind before going into action with an enemy who, in all probability, would try the mettle both of horse and rider.

The spear which Mansfield had snatched up in his hurry was not exactly such a one as a sportsman would have selected from choice. It was a heavy unmanageable weapon, headed with about half a ton of iron, well covered with rust, and not much sharper than the fluke of an anchor.

"A small touch of the file would do no harm here,"

thought Mansfield, as he felt the point with his finger, and thought of the razor-like edge of his favourite hog-spear; "but never mind, I must only give it *the more powder*. Now then, Bundoolah, we 'll try it."

So saying, he gathered up the reins, fixed himself well in the saddle, and closing his heels, the trusty Bundoolah bounded forward like an antelope. A true son of the desert, he feared neither beast nor devil, and dashed up to the bear without hesitation, in spite of the growl of defiance with which he was saluted. Taking a steady pull at his horse's head, and closing his left heel, ready to wheel off as the blow was struck, Mansfield poised his harpoon-like spear, and drove it with his whole strength into the broad back of his surly antagonist.

"That 's through your d——d black hide, tough though it be, else there 's no virtue in iron——No, by the Lord—no blood!" and Mansfield ground his teeth with vexation, as the blunted spear glanced off the Bear's shaggy hide, only inflicting a slight scratch. The enraged brute turned on his pursuer with a tremendous roar. Quick as thought Mansfield wheeled off to avoid the charge; but in doing so his horse stumbled; and ere Bundoolah could recover himself, the gigantic fore paws of the Bear were clasped round his neck, his teeth firmly fixed in his throat, and horse and rider rolled together on the ground.

At this critical moment Charles appeared in sight, thundering over the stones at headlong speed—his horse in a lather of foam,—his bloody spurs driven to the head at every stride,—and his sword-blade flashing in the sun, as he waved it over his head.

Half mad with excitement, the impetuous boy never dreamt of gathering his horse together as he neared the Bear, but dashed at him at speed, and with a slackened rein. The consequence was, that the animal—terrified by the smell of blood, and the piteous groaning of poor Bundoolah, as he lay gasping in the deadly embrace of the Bear—bounded suddenly to one side, reared up on end, and spun round. Charles, although a good horseman, was taken by surprise, lost his balance, and fell. Nothing daunted, however, he instantly scrambled to his feet, rushed towards the Bear, who still continued to hold down the struggling horse, and buried his sword up to the hilt in his body.

The wounded monster quitted the horse, and rushed, open-mouthed, at his new assailant. Charles sprang back to avoid the first rush, and watching his opportunity, when the Bear reared on his hind legs, plunged the sword deep into his chest. Fortunately for Charles it pierced his heart. The enormous brute fell heavily forward; a stream of black blood gushed from his mouth; and the much-dreaded Bear, the man-eater, the monarch of the rocky glen, lay at the feet of his conqueror, a harmless mass of black fur and bear's grease.

"Hurra!" shouted Mansfield, who was just beginning to recover from the stunning effects of his fall, and had raised himself on his elbow, "killed him, by the Lord, and killed him well, too—Charles, you are a lucky dog; I would have given a month's pay to have struck that blow. But you may thank your good stars that you happened to touch his heart, for these infernal Bears have as many lives as a cat, and had you stabbed him in any other part, he would have had your head half way down his throat before I could have come to your assistance. However, all's well that ends well—so lend me a hand to rise, Charles—Ha! confound it, how stiff I am. I verily believe Bundoolah must have rolled over me, for I feel as if my back were broken."

Mansfield, although stunned and severely bruised, had escaped all serious injury, and was quite fresh by the time the rest of the party came up.

"Ishmail's old *tulwar* has proved a better weapon for '*tackling*' the Bear than you expected, my venerable Uncle," cried Charles, pointing with an air of triumph to the dead brute.

"Ishmail's *tulwar!*—Why, you little bantam-cock, you don't pretend to say that you killed the Bear!"

"And why not?" replied Charles, coolly wiping the bloody sword, and returning it to Ishmail.

"The devil you did! but how did you manage it?—and what was Mansfield about with his spear? It was wont to be a deadly one."

"It played me false this time, however." And Mansfield proceeded to relate the particulars of the adventure. In the mean time the Doctor was stooping over the dead Bear, and examining the tremendous muscular development of his limbs with great interest.

"Od, but it 's an awfu'-like beast," muttered he, half soliloquizing. "Did any leevin ever see the like o' thae fore-paws—they 're as grit as my waist, and fit to squeeze the life out o' a bull, let alone a Christian—and to think o' that bit slip o' a Laddy fechtin him wi' a sword! Od, it 's just past belief—It minds me o' the story o' Dauvid and Goly-o'-Gath."

The rest of the party having duly admired the size of the Bear, the length of his claws, and the richness of his fur, there was nothing further to be said on the subject; so "boot and saddle" was the word. A spare pony was provided for Mansfield,—poor Bundoolah being too severely wounded to be fit for work—and in five minutes they were all cantering homewards.

Night had closed in, before they reached the Cantonment; and the chill mountain-breeze whistled bleak and cheerless through the woods. But a good dinner and a bright fire awaited them—and one there was who fondly hoped that the smile of beauty would greet his return; so with light hearts they pushed merrily forward, smoking their cigars, and talking over the adventures of the day.

We remarked, that evening, that Master Charles succeeded in getting up a very comfortable flirtation with the blooming Kate; and from the sunny smile which danced in her deep blue eye, and played around her pretty mouth, as she listened to his half-whispered conversation, we felt satisfied that the flaming account of his exploits, given by Mansfield at dinner, had not been lost upon her.

Charles retired to rest with his head and heart brimful of love; and that night his pillow was beset by fleeting visions of blue eyes and Bear-skins, Tigers, turtle-doves, and true-love-knots.

CHAPTER IV.

A TIGER HUNT ON THE NEILGHERRY HILLS.

"What the devil brings you here?" exclaimed old Lorimer, as Ishmail, armed to the teeth, advanced to hold the stirrup whilst he mounted his horse; "I thought Dr. Mc.Phee had ordered you to keep your bed."

"He did so, *Sahib;* but I could not rest. There is blood between that Tiger and me, and my wounds will not heal till I have been revenged on him. With the permission of Your Highness, I must have a hand in his death."

"Well, well, so be it, you blood-thirsty old savage, and much good may it do you. But is all prepared?—have plenty of fireworks been sent to the ground?—and has the ravine been watched during the night?"

"The slaves of Your Highness never sleep, *Sahib.* Our best scouts have been on the watch ever since sunset yesterday; a mouse could not pass them unobserved; and I myself have seen that there are plenty of fireworks prepared. By the Holy Prophet! it shall not be for want of fire if he beats us this time."

"Good!—Then mount and follow us."

The sun was just peeping over the hill-tops as our party came in sight of the ravine, where they had left the Tiger the evening before. Under the shelter of a large tree, a group of natives, who had been relieved from their cheerless watch, sat enveloped in their dark *cumbleys*, couching round the embers of a wood fire, and shivering with cold, as they handed from one to another the sociable *kallioon*, the never-failing comfort, and almost only luxury of the temperate Hindoo.

"These poor fellows have had a cold night's work," remarked old Lorimer, as the natives arose to salute him; "but never mind, we shall soon find employment for them, that will warm their blood, else I 'm mistaken. Here, Ayapah, what news of the Tiger? Have you marked him in?"

"*Ho, Sahib*," replied Ayapah, bringing the palms of his hands together, and raising them to his forehead, as in the attitude of prayer. "The Tiger awaits Your Highness's pleasure."

"Where is he? In this ravine?"

"No, *Sahib*. He killed a bullock last night, and is now lying in a small ravine close to the *Todah Mund*."

"All the better; we shall have less trouble in driving him out. Ayapah, show us the way."

Ayapah shook the dew from his *cumbley*, drew his *cumberbund* more tightly round his loins, thrust a long hunting-knife into his belt, and, grasping his matchlock, led the way down a rocky path which crossed the large ravine, in the direction of the *Todah Mund*.

"Are not these a fine race of men?" remarked Mansfield, as they approached the village, pointing to a group of *Todahs* who were lounging about with the bold careless air of independent mountaineers.

"How different is their manner from that of the effeminate Hindoos. You see they are perfectly respectful, and salute us with a gentle inclination of the head; but there is nothing cringing or timid in their mode of doing so. They are too dignified even to evince curiosity, which they consider womanish, and appear to be almost unconscious of our presence. Look at that fine venerable old patriarch leaning against his hut, which appears hardly large enough to contain him; his high and strongly marked features bear the native stamp of dignity, whilst his finely formed head, covered with a profusion of short curling hair, and the lower part of his face almost concealed by his enormous whiskers and long flowing beard, might serve as models for a bust of Hercules."

"They are indeed a noble race of people," replied Charles, "and not only their appearance, but their dress is perfectly classical. That single web of coarse cloth, thrown around them in graceful folds, is exactly the Roman toga."

"And here comes a Roman matron," added Mansfield, pointing to a very handsome *Todah* woman, who approached them, followed by a laughing group of naked children. She was dressed in a web of cloth, similar to that worn by the men, but arranged so as to conceal more of the person. Her complexion was not much darker than that of an Italian, and her skin so transparent that the blue veins could be distinctly traced under it. Her long silky hair, the arrangement of which had evidently cost her some little trouble, hung in flowing ringlets over her shoulders, and her only ornaments were some heavy bracelets formed of brass. Her easy, natural, yet graceful carriage was that of a true child of nature;

ignorant of crime, and happy in her ignorance; whilst her clear hazel eye, beaming with confidence and innocent simplicity, formed a striking contrast to the dark rolling voluptuous orbs of the more coy beauties of the plain. She displayed none of the haughty reserve so remarkable in the men; but coming up to the party, with a smiling air, began, like a true daughter of Eve, to talk with great energy, laughing and gesticulating all the time, and appearing perfectly satisfied with herself; although it was evident, from the manner of her hearers, that they did not understand a single word she said.

"Who would have supposed that this pretty young creature is the wife of ten or a dozen husbands?" remarked Mansfield.

"The wife of a dozen husbands!" exclaimed Charles in astonishment. "Why, Mansfield, you are laughing at me. A plurality of wives is bad enough, but who ever heard of a plurality of husbands? The thing is impossible."

"Both possible and true," replied Mansfield, "all these men, whom you see lounging about, are her husbands. The law of the *Todahs* allows but one wife to the inhabitants of each village, and, till within the last few years, a still more barbarous custom existed amongst them, that of destroying all the female children, except one, which was reared to supply the place of the mother. I am happy to say, however, that Government have succeeded in putting a stop to this horrible system of infanticide. You may remark that there are now as many female as male children, and as these grow up, the plurality of husbands will no doubt gradually fall into disuse."

"Now, then, lads," exclaimed old Lorimer, bustling up with his heavy rifle across his shoulder, "let 's to work, and see who'll win the Tiger-skin. Bones of my ancestors! boys, I never saw so pretty a place to kill a Tiger, in all my life: but come and see—I think I have arranged it so that he can hardly slip through our fingers."

The place, into which the Tiger had been marked, was a small ravine at the back of the village; the tangled brushwood, which grew out of the sides, meeting over it, in the form of an arch, so as to exclude the rays of the sun even at mid-day. A few large trees grew along the banks, perched upon which the sportsmen might defy the rage of their formidable enemy; and the ground, for several hundred yards on each side, was open, and free from brushwood, so that the Tiger could not possibly break cover without exposing himself to a murderous fire.

"Now, then, gentlemen, we have no time to lose," cried Lorimer, "you must each climb into one of these trees: Ishmail and his gang will scour the ravine with rockets, and the moment the Tiger is afoot you will be good enough to give the alarm, that the beaters may fall back to the shelter of the village. As to you, Father Long-legs," addressing the Doctor, "I beg that you will keep your eyes open, and try for once to shoot like a gentleman. By the beard of the Prophet! if you allow the Tiger to pass you, as you did the deer yesterday, I shall be tempted to send you a messenger from old 'Kill-devil,' that will make you jump off your perch like an electrified frog."

"Hoot toot! Maister Lorimer, but you 're awfu' raised

like this mornin'," replied the Doctor, grinning like an ogre! "I'm thinkin ye'r turnin daft on our hands a' thegether. To speak o' knockin a dacent man aff the top o' a tree like a hoody-craw!—Shootin an M. D. wi' as little ceremony as if he were a muckle black ape!—O'd Sir, you'r no canny—you'r waur than the Tigre himsell—I'll just speel up, and be out o' your reach, afore the deevle gets the upper hand o' you."

So saying, the Doctor sprang to the nearest tree, into which he climbed with wonderful agility; and having perched himself, astride, on a comfortable branch, sat dangling his long legs, and grinning defiance like an overgrown baboon. The rest of the party followed his example, and were soon perched on the various trees which skirted the ravine. Old Lorimer alone remained on foot, being too unwieldy to attempt such feats of agility.

"What do you intend to do, Sir?" inquired Mansfield, hailing him from a tree; "you are not going to remain on foot, are you?"

"Not exactly on foot," replied Lorimer, "I intend to sit on that bush;" pointing to one, on a little rising ground about two hundred yards from the ravine. "I shall look on, and if you all miss the Tiger, I shall be ready to *wipe your eye*—so mind your hits."

"You don't mean to say you will trust yourself on that bush!" exclaimed Mansfield in astonishment. "Why, it is not three feet from the ground—and if the Tiger charges, you are perfectly at his mercy."

"It is not exactly the most desirable seat in the world," replied the Old Gentleman, laughing; "but it is better than nothing. The Tiger is less likely to charge me there, than if I were on foot. And supposing he does come at me, I must just trust to Providence and old 'Kill-devil,' as I have often done before. Here, Ishmail, throw a *cumbley* over it, to keep out the thorns, and help me to get up. So, so!—that 's very comfortable—now then, my rifle, and then to work. Don't spare the rockets—singe his whiskers for him, the blackguard."

Ishmail grinned a fiendish smile as he moved off to obey his orders.

The bush which Lorimer had selected for his seat was one of those thorny shrubs which, growing in round isolated masses, become so densely matted and interwoven together as to afford an excellent seat, and, when covered by a thick blanket, to defend one from the thorns, is almost as comfortable as an air cushion. On the top of this sat old Lorimer, much to the amusement of his young companions, with his legs crossed under him, and his rifle resting on his knees, looking perfectly happy, and very much like the figure of a Chinese Mandarin on a mantel-piece.

Whizz!—crack!—away goes a rocket darting through the tangled brushwood in a zigzag course, like a fiery serpent.

It is answered by a tremendous roar which makes the earth tremble.

Hurra! a whole volley of rockets sweep the ravine, like a storm of fire. Now then he must show himself—nothing but a salamander can stand this. Every rifle is cocked, and every eye strained to catch a glimpse of the skulking savage.

" Look out! he is afoot!" shouted Mansfield, as a low growl and a rustling in the bottom of the ravine announced that the Tiger was at hand. " Be ready for a start, Ishmail, and see that all the beaters make a dash for the village the moment he shows himself."

Again all was hushed in breathless silence, but no Tiger appeared.

" Confound the skulking brute!" roared old Lorimer, *hotching* about on the top of his bush in an agony of impatience. " Blaze away, Ishmail, give him more fire, man; blow the cowardly beast to the devil!"

Again a shower of rockets swept the ravine from end to end. Again the beaters rent the air with their shouts, but still no Tiger. Ishmail actually foamed with rage, and Mansfield, unable longer to curb his impatience, sprang from the tree.

" I see how it is," cried he, snorting like a war-horse. " He has got into a cave again, as these rascally hill Tigers always do, when they can. But though it be deep as Hell and dark as Erebus, I'll have him out. Here, my hearties, lend a hand to cut away some of these bushes, that we may see what we are about."

The bushes having been partly cleared away, so as to admit sufficient daylight, Mansfield cautiously descended into the ravine, closely followed by the trusty Ishmail. After a short search they discovered a small rocky cave in the bank of the ravine, the entrance to which was about four feet from the ground.

" He must have taken shelter here," remarked Mansfield; " and if so, it strikes me I shall be able to manage him. The entrance to the cave being so high above the ground, I can peep in without showing anything but my head; and if I can only catch the glare of his eyes, I think I can plant a ball between them before he has time to make up his mind for a charge."

"It is a dangerous experiment," replied Ishmail, shaking his head, "but your fortune is great, *Sahib;* the Tigers tremble at your presence; we shall try it."

"Not both of us, Ishmail, you can be of no service to me here; I must attempt it alone. But do you go and withdraw the beaters to a safe distance, and tell the gentlemen to be ready to pour in a volley in case he should charge."

Ishmael felt much inclined to grumble at this arrangement, which prevented his sharing in the adventure. But he well knew that Mansfield's orders were not to be disputed, and accordingly withdrew, muttering prayers, and invoking the aid of the Prophet in his behalf.

Mansfield having removed the caps from his rifle, to ascertain that the powder was well up in the tubes, replaced them with fresh ones, so as to prevent the possibility of his weapon missing fire. He then crept quietly along till he was right under the cave, and raising his head, peeped cautiously into the gloomy recess. At first all was impenetrable darkness; but as his eye became gradually accustomed to the subdued light, he perceived two bright green orbs glaring upon him, from the inmost recess of the cavern.

"Now then for a steady hand," thought Mansfield, as he slowly raised himself so as to bring his rifle to bear. A low surly growl announced that the Tiger was on the alert, and a certain impatient switching of the tail, which invariably precedes a charge, did not escape the practised ear of Mansfield.

Full well he knew there was no time to be lost. Quickly but steadily the heavy rifle was raised to his shoulder, his finger was on the trigger—another instant would have sent a two-ounce ball crashing through the Tiger's skull, when a terrific roar burst from the cave—a huge mass of yellow fur shot over his head, as if projected from some powerful engine—the rifle exploded in the air, and our hero found himself sprawling on his back in the bottom of the ravine, and, strange to say, unhurt.

With one bound, the Tiger gained the top of the opposite bank, and bursting through the tangled brushwood, started across the open ground at racing speed. A shower of balls saluted him as he made his appearance, but not a single shot took effect.

The only chance now remained with old Lorimer, and every eye was fixed upon him as "*Kill-devil*" was slowly raised, and the sight brought to bear upon the Tiger.

"Noo then," exclaimed the Doctor, twisting his features into the most extraordinary contortions, and wriggling about on his perch in a perfect ecstasy of excitement. "Noo then, Maister Lorimer, noo, Sir, for the love o' goodness haud straight. Od's my life, if you miss him noo, we'll never see mair of him. O! man, tak a good vizzy; O! Sir.—Hurra!—he's deed—he's deed,"—shouted the doctor, almost screaming with delight, as "*Kill-devil*" poured forth its deadly contents, and the wounded Tiger, uttering a shrill roar, bounded high into the air. But this triumphant shout was changed to a groan of horror, as the enraged brute turned from his course, and dashed with terrific bounds towards the bush on which Lorimer was seated.

Again his rifle was raised with the coolness of despair —again the report was answered by a short angry roar, announcing that the ball had taken effect, but the Tiger only dashed forward with increased speed. Nothing now can save him—every rifle has been discharged—three bounds more, and poor old Lorimer is a mangled corse. The Tiger has gathered himself together for the last spring—Charles can bear it no longer, but burying his face in his hands, groans aloud. Ha! he 's down—it 's all over—No!—hark to that shot—'t is Mansfield's rifle —the ragged bullet whistles through the air, and the Tiger, rearing up to his full height, falls back gasping in the last agonies.

A simultaneous shout of triumph burst from the assembled multitude as Mansfield stepped from the ravine, and dropping the butt-end of his rifle to the ground, drew a long breath like one who has just had a heavy load of anxiety removed from his mind.

"My blessing on you, for a trusty companion," murmured he, regarding his favourite weapon with a look of affection, as if it had been a living creature—"You have stood my friend in many a hard pinch, but never before did you put forth your beauties in so good a cause. There was life and death on that shot—I had but one barrel left, and had I failed—it makes me shudder to think what that poor old man would now have been."

The moment it was ascertained that the Tiger was

fairly unable to rise, the beaters and villagers rushed down in a body to glut their eyes with the dying struggles of their vanquished foe, and many were the curses and maledictions showered upon the expiring tyrant, as he lay, terrible even in death, still glaring fiercely on his tormentors, and making feeble attempts to growl, whilst the frothy blood bubbled in his throat, and choked his dying sobs.

"God bless you, my boy!" exclaimed old Lorimer, grasping Mansfield's hand in both of his, and squeezing it hard; whilst the tear of gratitude dimmed his eyes. "I have not words to thank you as I could wish, but I feel it—I feel it in the bottom of my heart, and my poor dear motherless child will bless you, and pray for you, whilst she lives, for having saved her old father from a cruel death."

Mansfield blushed like a bashful maiden at hearing the praises which were lavished upon him on all sides, and turned away to hide his confusion, whilst he busied himself, with more than usual care, in reloading his rifle.

"Poo! poo! nonsense," cried he at last; "what a fuss you all make about knocking over a Tiger. Why it was not much of a shot, after all, although it happened to be put in at a lucky moment; any one of you might have done the same had your rifles been loaded."

"I 'm no' just so sure o' that," remarked the Doctor, with a *pawky* leer; "there are some of us no' just that good at the lang ranges, and yon was a deevle of a lang range. But be the shot good, or be it bad, it saved the life o' the best friend I hae on earth, although he did threaten, no' half an hour ago, to ding me aff the tree like a pyat; and for that same I shall hae a respect for you, and your rifle gun, and your lang ranges, till my deein day—so gie 's your hand, my trusty friend, and my blessing go wi' you."

In the mean time Ishmail, who had dispatched the Tiger by firing a matchlock into his head, was busily employed, with a lighted match, in singeing off his whiskers.

"How do you like that, you sulky-looking old *bant-choat?*" muttered Ishmail, as he squatted in front of the dead Tiger, singeing away with great industry. "You little thought, half an hour ago, that you should have me for a barber; but I 've got you by the beard now, and the devil a bristle shall I leave on your ugly snout. No, no, I had trouble enough with you when alive, and have no fancy to be haunted by your ghost now that you are dead."

Ishmail having finished the singeing operation to his entire satisfaction, the dead Tiger was placed upon a cart drawn by four bullocks, and driven off towards the Cantonment, followed by a crowd of natives, blowing horns, beating drums, and shouting forth the praises of the victor.

CHAPTER V.

DEER-STALKING, AND IBEX SHOOTING, ON THE NEILGHERRY HILLS.

How much of romance, and old tradition, is associated with the very word, "Deer!"

Does it not, Gentle Reader, conjure up before thee many a legend of the olden time—many a scene of ancient Chivalry?—The Douglas and the Percy?—The bloody field of Chevy Chase?—The ancient Forests of our Kings?—Robin Hood and his merry-men?—Shakspeare, and the mad pranks of his youth?

We can hardly fancy the most phlegmatic Alderman, gazing on a fat haunch, without thinking of honest Jack Falstaff, and Windsor Forest; and remembering that, in all ages, the Deer has been the theme of Poets' song—the game of Kings.

As such, we have a regard for "the bonny dun Deer" above all other animals of the chase. We look upon him as a noble animal of ancient family. And we never behold him wandering over his wild Domains, with the lofty bearing of a Feudal Baron, that a certain feeling of respect does not creep over us.

There are many Indian field sports, in which we have played our part, of a grander and more exciting nature than that of Deer-stalking; but there are none to which we look back with greater pleasure. We have certain romantic ideas connected with this sport, which we do not associate with any other, and which we can only trace to the sublime nature of the scenery amidst which it has been enjoyed, coupled with the silent, solitary, character of the sport itself;—for we have ever agreed in thinking, with the quaint old Author of "*The Treatyse of Fyshynge wyth an Angle*," that, in Deer-stalking, as in the "*Gentle craft*,"

"*Whanne ye purpoos to go on your dysportes, ye shall not desyre gretly many persons wyth you.*"

Dearly did we love those solitary rambles among the wild Hills; nor did we ever miss, or seek for any society but our own thoughts. And dearly do we now love to look back to the happy days we have spent in "hunting of the Deer." To remember how we have watched him, with his Herd, feeding in some lone Glen;—or looming through the mist like a gray spectre;—or cutting the sky-line, like a sculptured image, on the pinnacle of a mountain, where he keeps his watch, at break of day, scanning the surrounding hills with jealous eye. We love to remember how the Royal Hart hath led us many a weary mile, in the exciting contest of Man's reason against the unerring instinct of the Brute;—our manœuvres, foiled by the keen vision, and exquisite sense of smell, which Nature has bestowed upon the Stag for his protection, and which he uses with the skill of a consummate General;—the wild scenes through which we have followed the chase; far away from the haunts of man; where no sound is heard but the plash of the distant waterfall, and the sighing of the wind through the long rank grass;—the pure air of the mountains bracing the nerves, and setting fatigue at defiance.

Mile after mile have we thus passed over in the heart-stirring pursuit,—hour after hour has thus flown by, equally unheeded,—till the shades of night have closed around us, and the wailing cry of the Jackall has warned us to retrace our weary steps over the moonlit hills.

So great an enthusiast are we in the art of Deer-stalking, that we look upon it as the poetry of hunting. It is a pursuit which calls forth all the energies of the Hunter's mind as well as of his body. It is a campaign in miniature. It is a study for a General. And it is a sport which, if followed in a proper spirit, with due moderation, and by a person of tolerably cultivated tastes, ought to make the solitary Deer-stalker, not only a wiser but a better man.

We have never gazed upon the glorious works of Nature with such profound feelings of reverence, and gratitude towards the Beneficent Creator of all things, as, when sitting alone on a wild hill side, in the warm twilight of a tropical evening, surrounded by all that is grand and beautiful in mountain scenery, we have watched the wary Deer feeding securely in the green valley below; and, by means of that wonderful instinct which their merciful Creator has bestowed upon them, defying the utmost skill of Man to approach them. We have never sat down to a sumptuously covered table, with half the feeling of gratitude towards Him who gives us our daily bread, that we have, in our solitary tent, to a frugal supper of broiled venison, earned with the sweat of our brow. And never have we retired to rest in a happier frame of mind, or enjoyed more balmy slumber, than after the successful termination of a hard day's Deer-stalking.

It has often proved a subject of wonder to us, that this sport of Deer-stalking, in spite of the many charms which it possesses in our eyes, finds so few followers amongst the Sportsmen of India.

We have known hundreds of men who rode well to Hog, who were undeniable rifle shots, who were good Sportsmen in every respect, and who used to prove the life and soul of our merry parties in the Jungle; but, amongst those, we could point out but few who had poetry enough—or perhaps foolish romance enough—in their composition, to appreciate the delights of the solitary Deer-stalker's life.

Indeed amongst all our Sporting Friends—if we except our Brother, who was, and still is, a perfect enthusiast—Mansfield was the only one who could fully sympathize with us, in our ardent love for this sport. He was an enthusiastic admirer of Nature. He understood the poetry of the thing. And much as he had distinguished himself in the various manly field-sports of India,—much as he enjoyed the society of his Brother Sportsmen,—much as his society was courted by them,—he never appeared so much in his element, as when following a shy old Stag, through the solitary wilds of the Neilgherry Hills—and no man knew better than he, how to do so with success.

It was therefore with no small feeling of satisfaction, that he availed himself of a quiet day, after the encounter with the Tiger, to initiate his young Friend Charles into the mysteries of his favourite pursuit.

The ground selected for this day's sport, was Chenykonoor; a spot amongst the *Ghats*, on the edge of the Hills, which, on account of the extreme difficulty of the ground, and its remoteness from the Cantonment of Ootacamund, was little known, and less frequented, by any one except the staunch Deer-stalker Mansfield himself.

It still wanted more than an hour of daylight, when Charles, who, partly owing to the cold—for this was the first night he had passed under canvass on the Hills—and partly from over-anxiety, had enjoyed but broken slumbers, started from his hard camp bed, and roused Mansfield out of a sound sleep.

The full moon had, for the last hour, been shining on the young Sportsman's face, and the bellowing voice of the old Stags, calling from hill to hill, was a temptation he could no longer resist.

Mansfield, delighted at the ardour of his Young Companion, quickly obeyed the summons;—and having ascertained that Charles was properly clothed in the sober habiliments of a Deer-stalker—the two Sportsmen, followed by Mansfield's favourite *Peon* Ayapah, proceeded, over the moonlit hills, towards the edge of the *Ghats*.

Here, by rights, the Sportsmen ought to have separated, each taking his own beat. But Charles being a novice in the art, it was necessary, on this occasion, that he and Mansfield should keep together.

Daylight was beginning to appear, as they reached the ground, where Mansfield expected to find deer; and the occasional bellow of a Stag afforded welcome evidence that his expectations would not be disappointed. But the hills were enveloped in so dense a mist, that no object could be distinguished; and the Sportsmen sat down, in silence, to await its clearing off.

By slow degrees, the white curtain arose, gradually unclothing a conical hill, in front, till all was bare, except the rocky summit, on which the vapour hung like a silver veil. And now, through the gray mist, on the very pinnacle of the highest peak, loomed forth a shadowy outline, like the dim ghost of a gigantic Deer.

Mansfield laid his hand gently upon the arm of his Companion, and both crouched low upon the ground.

As the sun rose, behind the sleeping mountains, its rays shot through the fog, dispersing it like magic, and a flood of crimson light struck full upon a noble Stag. From a mere shadow, he now stood forth in bold relief, his stately form and wide spreading antlers showing so vividly distinct against the sky-line, that distance was forgotten, and Charles could have sworn that the wild jealous glance of his eye met his, as they watched each other.

After making a rapid survey of the surrounding ground, Mansfield shook his head.

"I fear, Charley my boy, he is too old a Soldier for us.—He has taken up so commanding a position that there is little chance of our getting near him; but we may try."

So saying Mansfield arose, for there was no means of effectually concealing themselves, and began to saunter off carelessly, in an opposite direction to where the Deer stood, in hopes that, by so doing, they might be enabled to make a wide detour, and approach him under cover of the hill.

The Stag did not attempt to leave his post; but stood watching their motions, turning as if on a pivot, so as to keep his head always towards them, till a mass of rock concealed them from his view, when he took the alarm; and, on again coming in sight of the conical hill, the Sportsmen found its rocky summit untenanted.

"I thought so"—remarked Mansfield, looking somewhat disappointed, for the Stag had exhibited a pair of antlers, such as even he had seldom had the good fortune to meet with—"But never mind; there are plenty more good heads where that one came from. We shall have blood on the knife yet before night."

The fog had, by this time, rolled away from the Hills, leaving a clear blue sky over head. But, some hundred feet below the Spectators, as they stood upon the edge of the *Ghat,* a level mass of white vapour extended to the very horizon, from which the rays of the sun were reflected with intense brilliancy, as if the Hills had been surrounded by an interminable desert of frozen snow. Slowly, and imperceptibly, the dense mass of vapour yielded to the increasing heat, till the features of the plain below could be faintly traced, as if through a curtain of thick gauze. Another moment, and the veil was rent asunder;—the thin sheet of cloud was broken into detached masses, which condensed with the rapidity of steam;—and the glowing scenery of the Low-country, its varied features dwindled into Lilliputian proportions, and bathed in glowing sunshine, burst upon the sight, like a bright vision of Fairy Land.

The effect was magical.—And so wrapped in admiration was Charles, that Mansfield was obliged, more than once, to repeat his warning whistle, before he became aware that the keen Deer-stalker was already on the top of a rising ground, at some distance, carefully sweeping the horizon with his telescope.

"There"—said Mansfield, placing the glass in the hands of his Companion, and pointing to a range of hills about a mile off—"Take a look, and tell me what you see."

Charles looked in the direction indicated, threw down the glass, jumped to his feet, and began capering about, in an ecstasy of delight.

"A whole herd of deer, by all that is beautiful!—Come Mansfield—come—let 's be at them at once!"

So saying, the eager young Sportsman snatched up his rifle, and set off, at a trot, in the direction of the Deer.

"Hark back!—Hark back!"—exclaimed Mansfield, laughing—"Not so fast, Youngster. There are two or three things to be considered before we proceed any farther. Pray can you tell me from what point the wind blows, this fine fresh morning?"

"The wind!" replied Charles, looking a good deal astonished, and glancing around, as if to make out the points of the compass. "Why, I can hardly tell. I should think it was somewhere about South-East. But what has the wind got to do with it?"

"The points of the compass, indeed, have not much to do with it"—replied Mansfield, smiling. "But had you followed the line you were taking, you would have found, to your cost, that the direction of the wind, with reference to the position of the Game, is a trifling circumstance worth attending to, in Deer-stalking. Do you not perceive that the wind blows directly from where we stand, towards the Deer?"

"To be sure I do. But what of that?"

"Simply this; that were we to attempt to approach them from this side, with every advantage of ground in our favour, we should see the whole herd toss up their noses, and gallop off, before we were within a quarter of a mile of them. The wonderfully acute sense of smell possessed by the Deer, is the thing of all others to be guarded against in stalking. We must get round them, and approach them, *up the wind*, even if it costs us a day's march to accomplish our object."

The nature of the ground was favourable for stalking, and Mansfield soon gained a position from whence the Deer might be approached without alarming their keen sense of smell. There still remained much difficulty in approaching them unseen. But long experience had given to Mansfield a correctness of eye, an almost instinctive faculty of availing himself of the slightest inequality of ground, which few Deer-stalkers ever attain, and, after surmounting innumerable difficulties, the Sportsmen at length found themselves under cover of a little hillock behind which the Deer were feeding.

Here the Sportsmen halted; and Mansfield motioned to Charles to remove the caps from his rifle, and replace them by fresh ones, in case they might have become damp in creeping through the long grass.

All being ready, Mansfield crawled, on hands and knees, to the top of the hillock, and, lying flat upon the ground, peeped cautiously into the little valley beyond.

There were the Herd, still at feed, and well within range. Mansfield could have picked off any one of them. But nothing met his eye save long-eared, timid looking Hinds, who might thank their stars they were not overlooked by a *Pot-hunter*.

Mansfield was too good a Sportsman to shoot game, merely for the sake of boasting, afterwards, that he had killed a certain number in a certain time—as we regret to say is too often the case among men who aspire to that character—and made it a rule never to kill a Hind except when Deer were scarce, and his People in want of food.

Charles being a promising Pupil, and one in whose sporting education he took a pride, Mansfield thought this a good opportunity to impress upon the mind of the young Sportsman, a useful lesson of coolness, forbearance and mercy; and, although Charles, more than once, attempted to raise his rifle—keeping his eyes all the time riveted upon the Hinds, with a longing, loving, look, such as a young Pointer casts upon a dead bird, which, although close under his nose, he does not dare to touch,— Mansfield was inexorable, and held him down with a grasp, against which it was in vain to contend.

The wily Deer-stalker knew well that where so many Hinds were congregated, there must be a Stag at no great distance, and therefore remained perfectly still, allowing them to feed on quietly, whilst he watched their graceful motions, and stored his mind with characteristic attitudes to be introduced at some future period in his drawings.

Presently the Hinds began to look about, and one of them called.

Now he knew their Lord was coming—and a slight motion of the hand made Charles aware of the fact.

The rifle was silently cocked, and next moment the young Sportsman had brought his sight to bear upon the bristling shoulder of a Royal Stag, as he slowly emerged from a thicket of gigantic fern.

It was the identical Stag they had first seen, and attempted, in vain, to stalk. Mansfield recognized his noble head at a glance.

The ragged bullet sped hissing through the air, and the Hinds startled by the report of the rifle scampered off in wild confusion. The Stag made one sickly reel, but immediately recovered himself, and followed them with blood bubbling from a wound in the shoulder.—Mansfield fired, right and left, and planted two balls in his side before he was out of range, but without any apparent effect upon the enormous brute, who rattled down the *Ghat*, without a stagger, clattering over the rocks like a cart-horse.

The difficulty now was how to proceed. A young hand would naturally have followed the wounded Deer, who, with three large balls through his body, could not be expected to go far. But Mansfield was well aware of the extraordinary tenacity of life possessed by this species of Deer, and also knew that, if followed, he would pursue his downward course, as long as life remained, and probably be lost in the heavy forest jungle which encircles the base of the Hills. And yet, if allowed to get out of sight, he would as probably be lost amongst the high fern and lemon-grass, or in one of the deep wooded ravines with which the country abounded. Fortunately, however, the elevated position occupied by the Hunters, gave them an advantage, of which no man knew better than Mansfield, how to avail himself; and by skilful manœuvring he managed to creep from point to point, keeping the wounded Deer in sight, without frightening him, or driving him into the Low-country.

The Stag, finding he was not pursued, and never having seen the Hunters from the first, soon stopped.

But he was in a very ticklish position, and Mansfield felt that his utmost Generalship must now be called into play—for if frightened, or missed, that noble Stag was lost to him for ever. The animal was, by this time more than half way down the *Ghat* with a clear run below him into the heavy forest jungle—and a few hundred yards beyond him was a dark and dangerous ravine, for which he was evidently making, and from which, if he once gained its sanctuary, there was little chance of ever recovering him.

Desiring Charles and the *Peon* to remain perfectly quiet, Mansfield, with a rifle in each hand, began to creep down the steep descent, with the stealthy pace of a Panther.

About a hundred and fifty yards from the spot where the wounded Deer stood gazing stupidly around him, there grew a small clump of stunted date trees, which did not escape the practised eye of the Deer-stalker;—this was the point at which he aimed, and, by dint of creeping on hands and knees, he at last succeeded in getting behind it.

Stopping for a moment to draw breath, Mansfield brought his heavy two-ounce rifle to bear upon the shaggy neck of the Stag, and fired. Down dropped his noble head, and a stream of blood gushed from his throat, but still he stood firm.

Now for the double rifle. One ball crashed through his ribs, another plunged into his shoulder,—He only winced, and before Mansfield could reload he was off, making for the deep ravine before alluded to. But his gallant heart was sinking.—His strength failed him before he reached the stronghold.—He halted, and stood tottering beneath the shade of a tree.

The Stag was now so close to the ravine that Mansfield did not dare to venture on a long shot, at three hundred yards, for fear of missing him, and the nature of the ground would not admit of his approaching any nearer.

For a full hour, by his watch, Mansfield kept sentry over his quarry, expecting every moment to see him drop. His heart smote him as he marked the laborious breathing of the poor animal.—He felt disgusted with himself—as every one must have felt who has been forced to have recourse to such a scene of butchery in securing his game—and almost wished that the first shot had never been fired.—But it was now too late to retract. The death of the poor animal was inevitable, and the sooner he was put out of pain the better.

Once the Stag lay down, and then Mansfield fancied all was over—but he rose again, and having ascertained, by the aid of his glass, that the animal was gaining strength, rather than getting weaker, he determined upon risking a long shot.

The first ball fell short,—the second hit, bringing the animal on his knees. But the Stag immediately re-gained his footing—made a rush, rather than a run—and disappeared in the dark ravine, for which he had been making from the first.

And this with seven balls through his body ! !

Now we are aware that what we have just narrated, must appear to the Reader very like an *Indian* story, and if he doubts our veracity we can hardly blame him. We have only to say that every particular was noted down on the spot, and that we have related them word for word as they occurred.

Tired and dispirited, Mansfield abandoned the pursuit, and retraced his weary steps towards the place where he had left his Companions.

Ayapah, one of the most indefatigable *Shikarees* we ever knew, now volunteered to undertake the forlorn hope of retrieving the wounded Deer. A council of war having been held on the subject, it was settled that he should descend the *Ghat* by a rather dangerous path, which would enable him to reach the bottom of the ravine, taking a rifle with him to dispatch the Stag, if he found him; whilst the two Sportsmen watched above in case he should move.

Another anxious hour passed. At length the trusty Ayapah was seen to reach the foot of the *Ghat* in safety—he descended into the ravine,—and, next moment, a faint report announced that the death shot had been administered.

As previously arranged, the two Sportsmen set off to the nearest Burgher Village to procure people to carry home the Deer; and by two o'clock the noblest pair of antlers, which now grace the walls of our *Sanctum*, were hanging from the pole of Mansfield's tent—and a dozen happy Villagers were trudging home, under a welcome load of venison.

Ayapah reported that he had found the Stag dying, under a rock, but that he got upon his legs, and made a feeble attempt to *charge*, before he fell.

Verily, there is no more gallant brute in nature than a Neilgherry Stag.

After partaking of some luncheon, the Sportsmen again sallied forth.

As it was still too early in the day for Deer to be again at feed—the only time there is much chance of finding them, without hounds, in a country abounding with such strong cover,—Mansfield took a new line, proceeding to a wild precipitous part of the *Ghats* which he knew to be frequented by a herd of that rare animal the Ibex of the Neilgherries.—If the Reader be a Naturalist he may perhaps find it worth while to glance at the description of this animal given in our notes.

The heat had, by this time, become oppressive. The wild animals had all retired, for shelter, to the dark woods, and deep ravines. And, even with the aid of the telescope, not a living thing could be seen, over the wide extent of country, which the elevated position of the Hunters enabled them to command.

They had already scrambled along the precipitous face of the *Ghats* for several weary miles; now following a narrow deer-track; now descending to avoid a bluff headland of rock, or an impenetrable ravine; and now cl'mbing painfully up the dry bed of a mountain torrent, filled with loose round stones, which rolled from under the feet at every step, and went thundering down the side of the mountain, rendering the ascent both difficult and dangerous.

Charles, unaccustomed to such severe exercise, was beginning to exhibit evident symptoms of fatigue, and to moralize on the folly of risking one's precious neck for the sake of an Ibex, when Mansfield suddenly stopped; and, laying his hand upon the arm of his Companion, pointed, silently, towards a lofty crag, some thousand feet above them, upon the pinnacle of which, between them and the sky, stood a noble male Ibex, the watchful sentinel of his herd.

The distance was so great, and the animal so perfectly motionless, that Charles fancied they had not been observed, and instinctively crouched behind the nearest rock.

"It is too late to attempt concealment,"—remarked Mansfield. "There is no more vigilant sentry than an old buck Ibex, and I'll engage that fellow had his keen eye upon us, long before we observed him. But, sharp as he is, I think I can show you how to circumvent him, provided you are a tolerable cragsman, and can stand another hour's climbing."

Charles, whose spirits had rallied at the sight of game, declared himself ready for anything.

"Follow me then,"—said Mansfield—"and look well to your footing, for we have some dangerous ground to pass over."

The great point, in approaching Ibex, is to get above

them. From below, it is impossible for the most skilful Stalker to elude their vigilance; but they rarely, or never look above, to guard against danger. Mansfield was well aware of this peculiarity, and knew that if he could once get out of sight, without alarming the watchful Sentinel, his knowledge of the ground would enable him to reach a point above the game, from whence, with a little care, and attention to the direction of the wind, he could easily approach within shot.

Without attempting to conceal themselves, the two Sportsmen moved off, directly away from the Ibex, taking a course which enabled the watchful animal to keep them in sight for nearly a mile; when—having ascertained, by means of his telescope, that the suspicious Sentinel was lulled into fatal security—Mansfield suddenly dived into the bed of a dry watercourse, and began to ascend the steep face of the *Ghat* with all diligence. It was a weary climb to the top, and, in many parts, exceedingly dangerous. But excitement enabled the Sportsmen to overcome difficulties, which, in cold blood, would have been considered insurmountable, and, after an hour of severe toil, they found themselves safely landed on the top of the cliffs.

"Now!"—exclaimed Mansfield, throwing himself upon the grass, and indulging in a low chuckle of satisfaction, as he wiped away the big drops of perspiration which fell from his forehead like rain—"I think we have circumvented that old rogue, at last; and, if he has not left his post, I can bring you near enough to distinguish his whiskers."

Mansfield's correct eye enabled him, at a glance, to

recognize that portion of the cliff, which he had marked, from below, as overhanging the position of the Ibex; and, the direction of the wind being favourable, it was reached without difficulty.

Lying flat upon the ground, the two Sportsmen now crawled to the edge of the precipice, and, peeping cautiously over, beheld a sight which amply repaid them for all their toil.—Directly under them fifteen Ibex were feeding amongst the ledges of rock, and, on the same peak where they had first observed him, the shaggy old Buck still kept his post, watchful as ever, but quite unconscious of the danger which threatened him from above.

"Take him in the head"—whispered Mansfield—"He is not above fifty yards off."

Charles, resting his rifle on the edge of the cliff, took a steady aim and fired.—The sentinel Buck, in the last agony, sprung, with a convulsive bound, from his giddy post, and down, down, down, he shot, cleaving the air like a bird, in his headlong descent, till he fell, a shattered mass, among the pointed rocks, two thousand feet below.

The remainder of the herd, startled by the shot, and missing their leader, skipped about from ledge to ledge, and from point to point, trying in vain to discover from whence the danger proceeded. One sprung upon the very rock from whence the unfortunate Sentinel had so suddenly been dislodged, and actually stared Mansfield in the face. He had hardly secured his footing, before a two-ounce ball crashed through his head. But he too, reeling from his lofty pedestal, took the awful leap, and, after bounding from crag to crag, was lost, for ever, in one of those wild chasms where the foot neither of man nor beast has ever dared to tread. Quick as lightning, the second barrel was discharged amongst the startled herd, and a fine Buck fell dead without a struggle, at the same moment that the nearest female dropped from a narrow ledge, shot through the heart by Charles.

This fresh disaster appeared to open the eyes of the bewildered animals. The Leader, looking upwards, uttered his shrill note of alarm, and away rattled the wild herd, taking their own narrow path—it looked a mere line—along the dark face of the scarped precipice, where it appeared hardly possible even for a bird to find footing. Along this fearful road, the Ibex pursued their course, at headlong speed, skipping, like winged creatures, from crag to crag, till they had reached a place of safety ; when forming in line, with an old hoary Patriarch at their head, they cast one wild glance at their baffled pursuers, and moved off, at a more sober pace, to some far distant haunt.

Ropes having been procured from the neighbouring village, a Burgher was induced, by the promise of some venison, to venture down the precipice, and the two Ibex last shot were slung up, after some difficulty. The others—as is too often the case in Ibex shooting—had fallen far beyond the reach of man, and were reluctantly abandoned to the Vultures.

Mansfield having congratulated Charles, on the good success of his first attempt in the difficult and dangerous sport of Ibex shooting, and having refreshed him, after his labours, with a mouthful of brandy and water, of which he stood in much need, the game was left in charge of the Villagers, who agreed to carry it to the tent, and the Sportsmen strolled towards home, by a circuitous route, keeping a good look out for Deer as they went along.

The sun was now getting low, and the wild cry of the pea-fowl arose from the wooded valleys; but no Deer were yet visible. Soon, however, the distant bellowing of a Stag was heard, echoing amongst the silent hills. This was a sure sign that the Deer were moving out to feed, and Mansfield now proceeded with great circumspection, scanning the hills with his glass, and peeping cautiously over every rising ground, before venturing to show himself. Once or twice a Hind started from amongst the long fern, almost at the feet of the Sportsmen. But, Charles having been previously cautioned by Mansfield not to fire at anything but Stags, they were allowed to go off unharmed. At length, on turning the abrupt shoulder of a hill, a crash was heard, proceeding from a thicket below, and, next moment the head of a fine Stag appeared, forcing his way through the tangled brushwood, and tossing the branches aside with his sweeping antlers. He was far out of range, so the two Sportsmen crouched behind a rock, and watched his proceedings in silence.

Having cast his jealous eye around, and apparently satisfied himself that all was right, the majestic animal began to graze, feeding up slowly towards the Hunters, and lazily brushing off the flies with his horns. Half an hour had thus passed, and the Stag had approached within about a hundred and eighty yards of Mansfield's place of concealment, when he suddenly appeared to scent danger on the wind, and threw up his head with a wild snort. It was answered by the sharp report of Mansfield's rifle, and the Stag drawing himself together with a convulsive shudder, dropped apparently quite dead. He was about to press the trigger of the second barrel, when his *Peon* gave an alarm that Deer were passing behind, and Mansfield ran round the hill to intercept them; but he was too late, and when he returned the Stag was still lying in the same spot where he had fallen.

Ten minutes having now elapsed since the first shot had been fired, during which the Stag had never shown any symptoms of life, Mansfield thought it needless to make a target of his body; but drawing his hunting knife walked towards him.

Having to cross two deep ravines, before he reached the Stag, Mansfield took the precaution, of leaving Charles and the *Peon*, to watch in case, by any chance, he should come to life again—and it was well he did so,—for he had not got more than half way, when a shout from the *Peon*, and the sharp report of a rifle, announced that the Stag was once more upon his legs. Mansfield rushed forward and was just in time for a snap shot, as the animal was disappearing, at a smart gallop, over the ridge of a hill. Down he came again, but rose in an instant and trotted off.

Leaving his discharged rifle, Mansfield gave chase, armed with his long hunting knife, and soon came up with the quarry, for he was sick and faint from the effects of the last shot.

Killing the Stag at Bay

The wounded Stag, finding himself unable to escape, turned, in despair, and stood at bay. His mouth was besmeared with foam, and his bloodshot eye rolled savagely as he lowered his head for a charge. On he came with mane erect. Mansfield, who watched his motions with the eye of a hawk, stepped nimbly aside to avoid the deadly stroke of his horn, and drove the hunting knife, up to the hilt, in his chest. One vigorous struggle separated them; and away went the Stag, actually splashing the bushes with his blood, yet facing a steep hill, at a pace which left Mansfield, dead beat, far behind. But he could not go far. He reeled—staggered—made one desperate effort, to reach a dark ravine—and dropped dead upon the brink.

By the time this Deer was broken up, the sun had already set, and the Sportsmen—after having tied a handkerchief to his horns to prevent the wild dogs from attacking the carcass during the night—made the best of their way towards the tent.

Darkness succeeded sunset, with that rapidity peculiar to a tropical climate, and the wailing notes of the Jackall came sweeping by them on the night wind, before they had proceeded half a mile over the hills.

It was already so dark that objects could no longer be distinguished at the distance of a hundred yards, and Charles had just called the attention of Mansfield to the beautiful effect of the full moon which was rising behind a rocky hill before them, when suddenly, as if by magic, the figure of a noble Stag which had hitherto been shrouded in darkness, rose between them and the light, and remained perfectly motionless, his graceful form thrown out strongly against the red disk of the moon, like a figure reflected by a magic lantern.

Mansfield slowly raised his rifle, the fine sight of which, being opposed to the light, showed as clear as if it had been noonday.

The sharp report was answered by a fiendish yell from the startled Jackalls—and the form of the Stag disappeared as suddenly, as if it had, indeed, been only a phantom. The ball had passed through his heart,—and he died without a struggle.

The moon was now shining cold and bright, over the wild *Ghats.* By her pale light the Hunters performed the last offices to the departed, and, strapping his glorious head upon Ayapah's back, they struck out over the hills, and soon reached the welcome shelter of their tent.

After enjoying a hearty supper of broiled venison, and discussing the events of the day over a cup of hot coffee, and a sociable cigar, the wearied Hunters retired to rest with light hearts, and the pleasing reflection that the produce of their day's sport had supplied a whole Burgher Village with a week's supply of animal food, which to these poor People is the greatest of all luxuries.

Gentle Reader, if you wish to enjoy Deer-stalking in perfection, and without restraint, go to the Neilgherry Hills !

CHAPTER VI.

A RIDE IN THE GREAT WALIAR JUNGLE.

Old Lorimer being laid up with an attack of gout, and Ishmail not yet sufficiently recovered from his wounds, to enable him to resume his duties as Huntsman, Mansfield had made arrangements with Charles, and the Doctor, for a few days' hunting in the Great Jungle, which extends from the base of the Hills, towards the Western Ghauts, and in which Bison, Deer, and wild Elephants are found in abundance.—The tents, and camp equipage had been sent on, two days in advance, in charge of Mansfield's *Peon* Ayapah; and, on a fine bright morning, our three Friends started, on horseback, for their hunting ground.

As they rode slowly down the romantic pass which leads from the Hills to the heavy forest jungle below, their conversation naturally turned upon Mansfield's late adventure with the Tiger.

"Od, man, but yon was a narrow escape ye had frae the Tigre," remarked the Doctor; "I canna' think hoo he gae'd o'er you without gie'n you a skilp wi' ane o' thae muckle paws o' his, for they 'r gae an' ready wi' them by ordinar!"

"Faith, Doctor, that 's more than I can tell you myself," replied Mansfield; "all I recollect is hearing a roar, seeing some large object fly over my head, and finding myself sprawling at the bottom of the ravine, with one barrel of my rifle discharged. I must confess it was a fool-hardy attempt on my part, and I have got out of the scrape much better than I deserved. I received a lesson in my early days, which ought to have taught me prudence, and made me cautious of attacking anything in the shape of a Tiger for the rest of my life."

"May I ask what that was?" inquired Charles, who now began to take a deep interest in Mansfield's anecdotes of jungle warfare.

"It is a melancholy story, and one which, even now, I cannot think of without a feeling of remorse for my folly. But I shall tell it you, as it may prove a good lesson, and prevent your being guilty of any such rash act, in the commencement of your jungle campaign. It happened soon after my arrival in this country, when I was yet a boy, and, like all *Griffins*, addicted to the vice of *pot-hunting*, or, as your worthy uncle emphatically terms it, *thistle-whipping*.

"One fine morning, I was following my usual avocation, attended only by a Moorish Boy, who had charge of my dogs, a fine game little fellow, about twelve years of age, and a few cockers. The boy and his dogs beat the bushes vigorously; quail and partridge were plentiful; and in spite of my missing every second shot, my bag was beginning to fill rapidly. I fancied myself a very Nimrod, and continued to load and fire with unwearied industry and great delectation. In the midst of our sport, a large Panther sprang from the bushes; and, strange to say, took to flight, followed by my pack of yelping curs, till they drove him into a cave, on the side of a rocky hill, at no great distance. I had never before seen anything in the shape of a Tiger, and was struck dumb with astonishment. Not so my little Moor Boy. He was the son of a famous *Shikaree*, and although I believe he had never seen a Tiger any more than myself, he had often heard his Father talk of his exploits amongst the wild beasts of the forest; he knew me to be a *Griffin*, and his little heart swelled with the proud consciousness of superior knowledge in woodcraft.

"'Suppose Master please,' said he, drawing himself up, and assuming an air of immense importance, 'I show *Sahib* how to kill that Tiger. I know very well *burrah shikar* business.'

"In my simplicity I looked upon the daring little imp, who talked thus confidently of killing a Panther, with a degree of respect almost amounting to awe; and, without hesitation, put myself under his guidance.

"According to his directions, I extracted the shot from my gun, and reloaded it with some bullets, which I happened to have in my pocket.

"'Now then,' exclaimed my young *Shikaree*, as he placed me behind the shelter of a large stone, directly in front of the cave! 'now then, I show *Sahib* how to make Tiger come. *Sahib* make Tiger eat plenty balls; that proper *shikar* business.' So saying, he marched directly up to the entrance of the cave, and began to pelt the Tiger with stones, abusing him, at the same time, in choice Hindoostanee slang.

"Sure enough this did make 'Tiger come' with a vengeance. The enraged brute, uttering a shrill roar, darted from the cave, seized the poor boy by the back of the neck, threw him over his shoulder, and dashed down the hill like a thunderbolt. My blood curdled at the sight; but I instinctively fired, and, I suppose, hit the beast, for he instantly dropped the boy, who rolled into a dark ravine at the foot of the hill. The Panther having disappeared in the neighbouring jungle, I descended into the ravine, to look after poor little 'Kheder.' There he lay, weltering in blood, dreadfully mangled, and evidently in a dying state, but still quite sensible. The gallant little fellow never uttered a complaint, but fixing his large black eyes steadily on my countenance, as if he could there read his fate, asked in a faint tone of voice for some water. I was stooping down to collect some in my hat, when I was startled by a surly growl and the noise of some animal snuffing amongst the brushwood, which closed over my head and almost excluded the light of day. It was the Panther, who had returned. My first impulse was to fly, and leave the boy to his fate. But poor 'Kheder,' seeing my intention, fixed his glassy eyes upon me with an imploring look which cut me to the heart, and made me blush for very shame. Kneeling by his side, I raised his head, wiped the bloody froth from his parched lips, and poured a few drops of water down his throat. This appeared to revive him.

"'You have not killed the Tiger, *Sahib*,' said he, speaking in Hindoostanee: 'I am sorry for that. I should like to have sent his skin to my father. But you will tell him, *Sahib*, that I died like a *Shikaree*. I was not afraid of the Tiger: I never cried out when I felt his teeth crunching through my bones. No! I stuck my knife in him twice. See! that is Tiger's blood!' and his glazing eye flashed wildly for a moment, as he held up a bloody knife, which he clutched firmly in his right hand. 'My Father will be proud to hear this. But my poor Mother will cry much, and her heart will turn to water, when she hears that I am dead.'

"And here, for the first time, the hot tears began to trickle down his cheeks. For a few minutes he remained motionless, with his eyes closed, and the big drops stealing, slowly and silently, through the long silken eyelashes. But, suddenly starting up, with his eyes bursting from their sockets, and gasping painfully for breath, he screamed, as if in a fit of delirium,

"'The Tiger has seized me again!—save me, *Sahib*, save me!' cried he, in a hoarse voice; I feel his teeth in my throat! my breath is stopped!—ah!—ah!' he gasped like a person drowning, his eyes turned in his head till nothing but the white was visible—his jaws became firmly locked—a cold shudder ran through his limbs—and the gallant little 'Kheder' fell back in my arms, a stiffened corpse.

"I was young then, and unused to witness death; and that scene has made an impression on my mind which will never be obliterated.

All this time the Panther continued to pace up and down the edge of the ravine, nearly on a level with my head, growling fearfully, and, ever and anon, poking his snout into the bushes, and snuffing at me, as if debating with himself whether or not he should jump down. The bushes were so thick that he could not distinguish me through them, and it is to this circumstance that I attribute my escape. For a full hour, I remained in this dreadful state of suspense; and, during that fearful hour, many were the good resolves I made against Tiger-hunting. But, like many other good resolves, they were only made to be broken on the first tempting opportunity. The Panther, at last, as if tired of keeping watch, walked quietly off; and I escaped to tell the tale, which I trust will prove a warning to you, Master Charles, and to all other *Griffins* who may chance to hear it."

"Eh! Captain Mansfield, but that 's an awfu' affectin' story," exclaimed the Doctor, inhaling an enormous pinch of snuff; "the death o' that puir bit Laddy gar't the tears come into my een, and amaist set me greetin'. I wonder, Sir, it hasna' had some effect in makin' you a wee thing mair wiselike. But I 'm thinkin' you 're waur than ever. Od, man, it 's just frightsome to see the way your een glance, when onything comes across you, to set your birse up. By your leave, Sir, you 're just a perfect maniac for the time being. As true as death it gar't me grue to see the wild demented look ye had, yon day, when ye gaed into the glen after the Tigre. What will you do, Sir, when ye gang hame, whare ye 'll hae nae Tigres nor Wild Soos to hunt? Think o' that, Sir! Od, ye 'll no be chancy! I expect to hear o' your ridin' aboot the country wi' a pot-lid on your head, like Don Quixote, spearin' the puir folks' swine, wi' the cook's spit; or maybe creepin' up ahint a dike, and takin' a shot at a brindled stirk, amang the bushes, in mistake for a Tigre.

And, noo that I think o't, I 'm no just sure that you 'll be able to remain in the Airmy. Na, Sir, you canna do 't. You 'll need to sell oot—and you 'd better do 't afore ye get amang your freens and expose yoursel'. Ye ken, Sir, when ye gang hame, the grenadiers 'll get back the bearskin caps; and the smell o' the bear's fur, on a hot day, 'll raise your corruption, and set you demented. Ye 'll begin first to snuff and snort, the way you did the day, when the Tigre wadna come out. And then you 'll cry out to the Commandin Offisher, 'Look out, Sir! look out!—the bear 's afoot—I smell him!' And then—and then—hoot, fie, Sir, it 'll never do; you maunna gang hame, on nae account; you maun get an exchange, without loss of time. If ance ye gang to England, they 'll hae you in a straight jacket, wi' your head shaved, and spinnin' about in a big creel, hung frae the tap o' the room, for a' the world like a rattan in a wire cage, afore you 're twenty-four hours on shore."

"You be hanged!" cried Mansfield, unable longer to keep his gravity, and bursting into a loud laugh.

The Doctor grinned mightily at his own conceit, exhibiting a set of yellow teeth, which, barring the colour, might have been envied by a wolf; and, following the example of Mansfield and Charles, spurred his horse into a canter.

Our friends have, by this time, accomplished more than half the descent; and a remarkable change is already perceptible, not only in the temperature of the air, but in the scenery and in the natural productions. The cloth dress, which had been found necessary in the bracing climate of the Hills, now begins to feel oppressive to the wearer. The Rhododendron trees, wild jessamine, and high-waving fern, which have hitherto clothed the sides of the hills, now give place to stunted bamboo and dwarf Palmyra bushes; whilst turtle doves, tookans, paroquets, and other tropical birds, unknown on the summit of the hills, begin to make their appearance.

As they continued to descend, the heat, and the tropical character of the scenery, gradually increased, till, at the foot of the pass, the road suddenly plunged into the great forest jungle which encircles the hills; that wilderness of trees, where the stupendous Elephant and the prowling Tiger have, for ages, held undisputed sway.

Here, the tall feathery bamboo, the stately teak, and other large trees peculiar to an Eastern climate, flourish in all their glory. The glare of an Indian sun is suddenly quenched in the deep gloom of the forest. The deathlike silence of the wilderness reigns around; and the confined air of the woods becomes close and suffocating.

Under the shade of a large Banian tree, at the entrance of the forest, our party found a relay of fresh horses, which had been sent on during the night.

The saddles were quickly transferred to their backs, and, leaving their smoking steeds in charge of the Horse-keepers, the three Sportsmen pushed along the rugged path, which led into the forest, at a round pace.

"Come, Æsculapius," cried Mansfield, addressing the Doctor, who was beginning to lag behind, and exhibited strong symptoms of being somewhat saddle-sick, "that old jade of yours will fall asleep under you, unless you make better use of your heels.—Give him the spur, man."

"Oich? Hoich!" grunted the Doctor, as he drove the spurs into his long-legged, raw-boned *Cutch* horse, and came shambling up to the rest of the party, at a pace which very much resembled the action of a Dromedary, and must have been about equally pleasant to the unfortunate rider—"Od, Captain, this is a deevle o' a pace ye 'r gaun at—man nor beast is no fit to stand this, at least, no' withouten leather breeks and tap-boots."

"O, ho!" cried Mansfield, laughing, "is that your complaint, Doctor?—sorry for you, my worthy Galen—very sorry, indeed—nothing so unpleasant as feeling the want of a pair of leathers in a long ride; but I much fear there is no help for it. We have still twenty long miles before us, and unless we make play now, we shall get benighted and lose our way, which in this forest would be no joke. Give him his head, man, and let him go."

"Weel, weel," sighed the Doctor; "but just bide a wee till I dight my face, and get a pinch out o' my mull." Here the Doctor pulled off his hat, and began to mop his face with a snuffy pocket handkerchief. "By your leave, Gentlemen, I 'm just sweetin' like a bull, and my poor beast is no muckle better."

"Hark forward!" cried Mansfield, giving the reins to his horse, after he had allowed the Doctor sufficient time to enjoy a hearty pinch of snuff. "Good night to you, Doctor; I suppose we shall hear of you in the course of to-morrow, provided the Tigers or wild Elephants do not make free with you during the night."

The Doctor, finding there was no help for it, took heart of grace, and by dint of plying the spurs vigorously, managed to make the old Dromedary keep up wonderfully well, although not without many a grin, and many an uneasy shifting of his seat.

As they penetrated deeper into the woods, the gloom became more intense, and the deep silence of solitude more imposing. It almost inspired them with a feeling of awe. Not a bird, not even an insect, was heard. It appeared as if no living thing had ever disturbed the solitude of the primeval forest. And yet there were occasional traces of life. The tall rank grass which grew up amongst the trees, to the height of ten or twelve feet, was in many places trampled down by the wandering herds of wild Elephants—several recent footmarks of Tigers might be traced along the sandy path—and once or twice a jungle-dog was seen to glide across the road, with the drooping tail and stealthy pace which indicate the prowling savage.

Here and there an occasional opening in the tree-tops varied the monotony of the scene, exhibiting a gorgeous view of the Mountains. Their stupendous crags, hanging woods, and sparkling waterfalls, backed by a sky of deeper blue than even Italy can boast, formed a striking contrast to the sombre gloom of the forest, and made the panting travellers sigh for the fresh mountain breezes which they had so lately left.

Mansfield and Charles had just pulled up for a moment to admire one of these beautiful glimpses, and to allow the Doctor, who had again fallen behind, to come up, when the former, casting his eyes upon the ground, discovered a huge snake, a Boa-constrictor about twenty feet long, basking amongst the dry leaves by the side of the path.

"Hurra, Doctor! Hurra! Screw him along. Here's a shot for you; a piece of *shikar* quite in your line"—and Mansfield hastily unslung his rifle, which he always carried at his back ready loaded.

"What is 't, man?—what is 't?" cried the Doctor, coming up, quite out of breath.

"See there," replied Mansfield, pointing to the snake; "what do you think of that fellow, Doctor? Would he not be a fine addition to your museum?"

"Od's my life, man, but that's a grand beast," exclaimed the Doctor, jumping from his horse. "An indubitable Boa, and longer by six feet than ony specimin I ever met wi'. Gi' us the rifle, Captain, gi' us the rifle, till I shoot him—I wouldna' lose that specimin for a pund-note."

"Steady now, Doctor," said Mansfield, handing him the rifle; "let's see you take him in the head."

"Na, na! we maunna injure the heed on no account; it would spoil him for a specimin," replied the Doctor, firing right and left into the snake.

The balls passed through the body of the enormous reptile without apparently doing him much injury; he merely gave a convulsive start, and glided rapidly into the jungle.

"Hark to him, Doctor! Go it, my sporting Æsculapius! Never mind the thorns!" shouted Mansfield, laughing till he nearly fell from his horse, as the worthy Doctor, in the excitement of the moment, dashed through brake and briar in hot pursuit of the wounded snake.

Charles, who had never before seen a Boa, was quite as anxious as the Doctor to secure the prize. Throwing the reins of his horse to Mansfield, he sprang to the ground, and joined in the chase, shouting aloud, and brandishing a hog-spear which he happened to carry in his hand.

In this manner they followed the snake for some distance, the Doctor pounding away with the butt-end of the rifle, and Charles striving in vain to transfix him with his spear. At length the snake reached the brink of a dry watercourse filled with dense tangled brushwood, into which he glided. He was just about to disappear, when the Doctor, inspired with a desperate fit of courage, dashed forward, seized him by the tail, took a turn of it round his arm, and throwing himself on his back, with his feet firmly planted against a tree, held on like grim death.

Luckily for the Doctor, the snake was too much disgusted with the treatment he had already received, or too intent upon making his escape, to think of turning on his pursuers. But his struggles were tremendous. He coiled himself round the trees, twisted himself into knots, and strained every muscle in his body till they seemed ready to burst through his skin. So great was his strength, that it appeared, once or twice, as if the tail must give way or the Doctor's arms be torn from their sockets.

Whilst this struggle was going on, Charles was busily employed in reloading the rifle.

"Haste you, man! haste you!" gasped the Doctor, nearly black in the face from over-exertion. "Ods, my life, Maister Chairles, if ye dinna be quick and gie him another shot, he'll waur us a' at the hin'er end. He's amaist pou't the airms aff me already. Deil be licket, but I'm thinkin it's the Foul Fiend himsell, in his auld disguise, that we hae grippet. Div ye no find nae smell o' brimstone about him?"

"I rather fancy I do," replied Charles, laughing, as he discharged both barrels into the snake.

Blood gushed copiously from the wounds, and the strength of the snake was perceptibly diminished. He suddenly uncoiled himself from the trees, and turned round, as if with the intention of making an attack. Charles, snatching up the spear, drove it through his head, and pinned him to the ground.

"Hold on now, Doctor," cried he, leaning his whole weight upon the spear to prevent its being withdrawn; "keep his tail fast, so that he may not get a purchase round a tree, and we have him."

The snake writhed about convulsively, but he was now completely paralyzed, his strength was gone. In a few minutes the victory was complete; and Charles and the Doctor returned to the road, dragging along their snake in triumph.

"Bravo, Medico! Welcome the conquering hero! So you've managed to hustle him at last." And Mansfield laughed heartily as the Doctor emerged from the jungle in a perfect fever of heat and excitement, his face laced with streaks of blood, which flowed from innumerable scratches, and his coat literally torn to shreds.

"But I see you have not obtained a bloodless victory. Hang it, Doctor, you have utterly ruined your beauty. You will not be able to show that handsome face of yours among the women for a month to come."

"Ay, I 'm thinkin I 've scarted mysell a wee," replied the Doctor, wiping the blood and perspiration from his face with the sleeve of his coat. "But they 're honourable wounds, Captain. O! man, if ye had seen the grand tulzie we had wi' the rampawgin deevle, it wad just hae putten ye clean out o' conceit wi' Tigre huntin. It was the sarest job that ever I put my hand till. But, O! Captain, it was grand sport."

"I have no doubt it was a very brilliant piece of *shikar*," replied Mansfield, smiling. "But what do you intend to do with your game, now that you have secured it?"

"Do wi' it! Od, man, I 'll take him hame, surely. Na,—I canna do that either, he 's o'er heavy. But I 'll just skin him where he is, and take the skin wi' me."

"No, no, my friend; we can't afford time for that now, the sun is just setting. But, as we are only five miles from camp, you can easily send out to-morrow morning and have him carried home."

The Doctor was reluctantly obliged to agree to this arrangement, and the party proceeded.

Daylight had deserted them before they reached the end of their journey. But the full moon had risen, and shed a flood of silver light over the picturesque jungle encampment, which rejoiced the sight of our wearied travellers, as a sudden opening amongst the trees brought them upon a beautiful natural lawn of velvet turf embosomed in lofty woods, and sloping gently towards the bank of a deep and broad river studded with numerous wooded islands. The snow-white tents, glittering in the moonlight,—the bullocks and baggage ponies picketed under the trees,—the numerous fires, and the groups of natives squatted around them, with their dusky features and picturesque dresses brought out in strong relief by the reflection of the flame, formed altogether a very striking picture, and lent an air of home and comfort to the uninhabited forest.

Our party were quickly seated in the principal tent, around a camp-table sparkling with wax lights, and groaning under a profusion of goodly viands,—amongst which a huge venison pasty, and a wild boar's head, shone conspicuous. Good store of claret was there also,—ruby bright, cold as the mountain spring. And the worthy Doctor's heart leapt for joy, whilst his mouth watered at beholding the unexpected luxury and good living afforded by an Indian Sportsman's camp.

Ample justice was done to the feast, and after a very moderate allowance of wine,—for Mansfield, like all good Sportsmen, was temperate himself and the cause of temperance in others,—our friends retired to rest, prepared to start at daylight on the morrow, with clear heads and well-braced nerves,—two things as necessary to insure success to the Forester as a quick eye and a true rifle.

CHAPTER VII.

BISON SHOOTING.

We left our jungle encampment glittering in the moon-light. The moon hath now set and the forest is shrouded in darkness; but a slight tinge of gray in the eastern sky, and a damp chill in the morning air, announce that day-light is at hand. The distant roar of the prowling tiger, which, at intervals, "had vexed the dull ear of night," is no longer heard, and the silence of the woods is unbroken, save by the melancholy voice of the great horned owl, as he flits past, on muffled wing, like an evil spirit retiring before the approach of day. Heavy wreaths of gray mist slumber on the calm surface of the river, and all nature is hushed in deep repose. The horses, picketed in front of their masters' tents, stand dull and listless, with drooping heads and slouched ears. And the wearied bullocks may be seen reposing in groups, under the shelter of the lofty banyan trees. The only beings which appear possessed of life in the midst of this dreamy scene, are two dusky figures which are brought out in strong relief by the cheerful blaze of a wood fire, over which they are crouching. One is our friend Heels, who, carefully wrapped up in his dark *cumbley*, is busied in preparing a pot of coffee as a morning draught for the Sportsmen. His companion is a strange wild-looking animal, and deserves a more particular description. He is a tall, gaunt figure, and perfectly naked, with the exception of a tattered piece oı blue cotton cloth, which does duty, but very imperfect duty, for a fig leaf. His short woolly hair, flat features, and thick lips, betray an African origin; but his air and manner are very different from what we are accustomed to expect in that persecuted race. He is a *Seedee*, a free inhabitant of the trackless forest, and displays all the lofty bearing, and dignified self-possession, of an independent savage. His woolly pate is slightly sprinkled with gray, but his dark piercing eye is full of fire, and his limbs still display all the muscular power and elasticity of youth. He is sitting cross-legged, with a long matchlock resting across his knees, and is indulging in the luxury of a very primitive species of pipe, formed by rolling up a small quantity of tobacco in a green leaf. He observes a dignified silence, and is evidently regarding the servile occupation of poor Heels with sovereign contempt, as he puffs out huge volumes of smoke, and strokes his mustache with a self-complacent air. He had for several years been in the habit of attending Mansfield as guide in his hunting excursions, and always attached himself to the Camp during his stay in the forest. He had acquired a sufficient knowledge of Hindostanee to make himself understood on all ordinary occasions; and the wonderful sagacity, almost amounting to instinct, which he displayed in following up the trail of wild animals, made him an invaluable addition to a Hunter's camp. He was fully aware of his own importance, dignified himself with the title of *Jemmadar*, or Head Man of his Tribe, and comported himself with becoming dignity. He never condescended to act as guide to the Hunters, except when in pursuit of Bison. It requires great skill and perseverance in following up a trail, to surprise these animals in their wild haunts; and some little nerve and presence of mind to attack them with success when they are found. He was the only man of his Tribe who could reduce the finding and killing of Bison to a certainty. He therefore considered the hunting of them a royal sport, worthy of his superior talents. But if Deer or any inferior game were the object of pursuit, his Son, a boy about twelve years of age, was deputed to attend; the Old Man remarking, with a glance of proud superiority, "The Boy can find Deer."

Mansfield had announced, on the previous evening, that it was his intention to seek for Bison in the morning; and old Kamah was waiting impatiently to lead the Sportsmen into the jungle, whilst the Bison were still feeding and afoot.

"*Hugh!*" exclaimed he, uttering a deep guttural sound, as he pushed Heels, and pointed with an impatient gesture towards the eastern sky, which was fast brightening into day.

"Hah! daylight come?" cried Heels, starting up; "time to call Master:" and wrapping his *cumbley* more tightly around him, he glided into the tent to rouse the sleeping Sportsmen.

In a few minutes Mansfield and Charles made their appearance: the latter had discarded his green hunting-coat and top-boots, and now appeared in a dress better adapted for the jungle; with a hunting-knife in his girdle, a heavy rifle on his shoulder, and all the other accoutrements of a well-equipped *Shikaree.* Kamah rose as they approached, and extended his hand to salute them with the air of an equal. Charles looked with astonishment at this piece of unwonted familiarity on the part of a Native.

"Allow me," said Mansfield, leading up Charles, and obliging him to shake hands with the grinning savage, "allow me to introduce my friend Kamah, the *Jemmadar.* His appearance is certainly not prepossessing, and, like many other illustrious characters, it is his pleasure to affect great simplicity in his dress——"

Here Charles could no longer retain his gravity, but burst into a fit of laughter, and Mansfield was obliged to bite his lips hard, to avoid following his example.

"But, let me tell you, he is a person of no small importance in my camp. He is the best *Shikaree,* and the staunchest hand at following up a trail, in the whole Waliar Jungle. He knows every haunt of the Bison as well as if he had reared them himself. But you will be better able to appreciate his extraordinary talents when you have seen him at work. In the mean time there are just three little cautions which I must beg to impress upon you. Always treat him with marked civility;—never attempt to disturb him when running a trail;—and, above all things, avoid laughing at him. He is as gentle as a lamb when well treated; but his savage nature cannot brook an insult, and if once offended, his revenge is implacable. I have more than once seen the vermin grind his teeth, and handle his knife, on very slight provocation."

This was, of course, said in English, so as not to be understood by their savage friend, who stood showing his white teeth, and looking very much pleased at the formal manner in which he had been introduced, as well as by the accompanying speech, which he, no doubt, thought was uttered in his praise.

"Well, *Jemmadar*," continued Mansfield, now speaking Hindostanee, "can you show us any Bison this morning?"

The *Jemmadar* drew himself up to his full height, and assumed a lofty air.

"Can the shepherd of the plain find the pasture-ground of his flock? Does that vulture," pointing to a black speck which was seen sailing high above the tree tops—"does that vulture require a guide to lead him to the carcase? Follow me; the *Jemmadar* knows where to find his herds."

"Come, Master Charles," said Mansfield, smiling, as he hastily swallowed a cup of coffee; "shoulder your rifle and march. Our swarthy friend is waxing impatient, and if we ruffle the old pagan's temper he will show us no sport to-day."

Charles promptly obeyed the summons; and our two Sportsmen, bringing their rifles to a long trail, followed old Kamah as he stalked into the jungle with rapid strides.

At this early hour, when the morning air is still fresh, and the ground sparkling with dew-drops, the tropical forest seems suddenly to burst into life. The woods resound with the buzzing of innumerable insects. The jungle cock and wild pea-fowl are heard calling to their mates in wild discordant notes. Chattering troops of monkeys frisk amongst the branches overhead, showing their white teeth, and making threatening grimaces at the strange intruders. The startled deer bound across the open vistas of the forest, their bright speckled sides flashing for an instant on the sight, and as suddenly disappearing, like passing meteors. Whilst wandering herds of Bison are now on foot, returning slowly from the open glades, where they have pastured during the night, to the thick covers of bamboo, under the shades of which they find an agreeable shelter from the mid-day sun.

Having penetrated some distance into the forest, the savage guide suddenly slackened his pace, and, making a sign to his companions to keep silent, glided on in front with the stealthy and noiseless tread of a fox, his ears erect to catch the faintest sound, and his lynx-like eye rolling from side to side, now peering into the dark tangled masses of bamboo, and now roving over the ground in search of a fresh track.

"Now," whispered Mansfield, "not another word, as you value the friendship of the *Jemmadar*. Step lightly. Avoid as much as possible treading on the dry twigs which crackle under foot. And mind you do not attempt to fire at any Deer which may cross your path; we can get plenty of them at any time; but the report of a rifle, at present, would be death to our hopes of finding Bison."

"*Hugh!*" exclaimed their guide, suddenly stopping

short, and kneeling down to examine, more carefully, some marks, which his experienced eye had detected amongst the dry leaves and withered herbage. To the less delicate organs of the European, there was nothing particular to be observed, but the *Jemmadar* had evidently made a discovery of importance. After carefully regarding the signs he had observed for some time, he arose with a broad grin of satisfaction on his swarthy features, and merely uttering the word "*Koolgha!*" whilst he held up the fingers of both hands, to denote the number ten, proceeded with a more rapid step, and more confident air, like a hound running breast-high on the scent.

"It's all right now," whispered Mansfield; "the Imp has struck upon a fresh trail, and the Devil himself cannot throw him out, when once he has fairly settled to it; we may, therefore, reckon with certainty on finding Bison at the other end, although it is very uncertain how long we may have to follow it before we come up with them."

Charles smiled incredulously at the idea of any one being able to follow the track of an animal, for miles, over ground where not the slightest vestige of a foot-mark was visible to ordinary eyes; but, at the same time, expressed a hope that they might succeed.

"Look here," said Mansfield, as they approached a dry watercourse, where the fresh footmarks of a herd of Bison were deeply imprinted on the half-baked mud. "You may now satisfy your own senses that our guide is on the right scent. Here, you see, is the fresh trail of ten or a dozen Bison at least; and one of them an old Bull, who will show fight, I'll be bound for him, and put your metal to the test, my hearty, before you take his scalp. But we must push forward, for old Kamah is fuming at this delay."

After following the trail for some miles, at a rapid pace, the *Jemmadar* became sensible, from certain signs which he observed, that the game was not far in advance. He now slackened his pace, and, renewing his signal to observe profound silence, began to creep along the bed of a small watercourse with great caution and circumspection.

"See," whispered Mansfield, as they passed a bank of wet sand, where the trail was distinctly visible, and the water, which still continued to flow into the deeply indented foot-marks, had not yet filled them up—"we are close upon them now. Keep your wits about you, my Boy, and be ready with your rifle, for the old Bull is apt to make a charge, with but scanty warning."

Every faculty of the sagacious Savage was now on the full stretch. He crept along with the air of a Tiger about to spring on his prey: his rolling eye flashed fire; his wide nostrils were distended to the utmost limits, and even his ears appeared to erect themselves, like those of a wild animal. Presently he started, stopped, and, laying his ear close to the ground, listened attentively, then proceeded with more caution than before, stopping and listening, from time to time, till at length it became evident, from the triumphant beam of satisfaction which lighted up his savage features, that he had fully ascertained the position of the enemy. He now stood erect, cast a prying glance around, to make himself master of the locality, held up his hand to ascertain the direction of the wind, and, having apparently satisfied himself that all was right, motioned to his companions to follow his movements. Having scrambled cautiously out of the watercourse, he laid himself flat upon the ground, and, separating the tangled brushwood with one hand, began to worm his way through it, with the gliding motion and subtle cunning of a snake. Mansfield and Charles tried to imitate the serpentine motion of their savage guide, as they best could; but they found their less pliant limbs but ill adapted to this mode of progression, and the noise which they occasionally made in forcing their way through a thorny bush called forth many an angry frown from the *Jemmadar*. Having proceeded in this manner for some hundred yards, they suddenly came upon an opening amongst the bushes; and here a view burst upon the astonished sight of Charles, which made his eyes flash, and sent the blood coursing through his veins like quicksilver. They had gained the edge of a natural clearing in the forest, an open glade about three hundred yards in diameter, clothed with rich green herbage, and shaded by gigantic teak trees, which surrounded it on all sides, stretching their broad-leafed boughs far into the opening.

In the midst of this a herd of fifteen Bison were quietly feeding, perfectly unconscious of the near approach of danger. A mighty Bull, the father of the herd, stalked about amongst the females, with the lordly step of a three-tailed Bashaw in the midst of his seraglio; his ponderous dewlap imparting an air of grave dignity to his appearance, and his sullen eye menacing with destruction the hardy foe who dared to intrude upon his wooded dominions. But Mansfield had tamed as proud as he, and feared not his glance.

A grim smile of satisfaction passed over the harsh features of the *Jemmadar,* as he pointed out the stately herd. Then raising himself cautiously from amongst the long grass, he posted himself behind a large tree, which effectually concealed his person, folded his arms across his chest, and, leaning against the stem, remained cold, still, and motionless as a bronze statue. Every trace of intense excitement which had so lately strung his nerves to the highest pitch, had passed away; and he once more assumed the stoical, passionless air of the haughty Savage. Pointing again towards the Bison, he nodded expressively to his companions, as much as to say, "I have done my duty; there is the game, and now, Gentlemen, let me see what you can do."

Charles, furious with excitement, pitched forward his rifle, and, although his hand shook violently, from anxiety, and the exertions he had made in scrambling through the brushwood, was about to pull the trigger at random, when Mansfield seized his arm with the gripe of a blacksmith's vice, and pulled him down amongst the long grass.

"Are you mad," said he, in a low whisper, "to risk a shot in your present state of excitement? Why, Boy, you are panting like a broken-winded post-horse, and the barrel of your rifle vibrates like a pendulum! I suppose you fancy it 's a drove of *Brinjaree* bullocks we have to deal with. But wait a bit till you have seen the charge of a wounded Bison, and I am much mistaken but you 'll think twice before you risk another shot with an unsteady hand. Here," continued he, pulling Charles behind the stem of a large tree, "get under cover of this, in the first instance; you will find a breastwork somewhat useful before we have done. Now then, sit down till you have recovered breath, and, in the mean time, put fresh caps upon your rifle; I have more than once narrowly escaped death from neglecting this precaution."

Charles, having rested for a few minutes, declared his hand to be as steady as a rock.

"Well then," said Mansfield, rising slowly on one knee, and peeping from behind the large knotty stem which sheltered them, "we shall put your steadiness to the test. Take that cow next you, and mind you aim for the heart, just behind the bend of the elbow; hit her there, and she is your own: go six inches to the right or left, and you must stand by to receive a charge, for charge she will, and the charge of a wounded Bison, let me tell you, is no child's play."

Charles, now perfectly cool, raised his rifle, took a deliberate aim at the nearest Bison, and fired. The enormous brute dropped heavily to the ground, and, uttering one deep groan, expired without a struggle; the ball had passed through her heart.

In the excitement of the moment, Charles was about to raise a shout of triumph, when Mansfield checked him, and pointing to the *Jemmadar*, who had already laid himself flat amongst the long grass, made signs to him to follow his example.

The herd, startled by the report of the rifle, suddenly raised their heads with a loud snort, gazed around them wildly, as if to ascertain from whence it proceeded, and trotting up to their fallen companion, began to snuff at the warm blood. The smell of this excited them to a state of frenzy. They galloped round the open space in wild confusion, kicking their heels in the air, goring at each other with blind fury, and bellowing fearfully, in that deep tremulous tone so expressive of mingled rage and fear. Then, suddenly rallying, they slowly approached, in a body, to the object of their dread, again snuffed at the blood, and again bellowed, and gored, and scampered with more violence than ever.

This wild scene had lasted for some minutes, and Mansfield was beginning to fear that, in the course of their evolutions, the maddened brutes might stumble on their place of concealment; when the *Jemmadar*, clapping his hands to his mouth, gave utterance to a yell, so fearfully wild, so like the voice of a Fiend, that even the Hunters started; and the terrified Bison, uttering one tremendous roar, dashed into the thickest part of the jungle, crashing through the tangled masses of bamboo like a whirlwind.

The old Bull alone stood his ground, lashing his sides with his tail, tearing up the earth, and bellowing with a voice of thunder that made the woods re-echo for miles.

"Our friend is very pugnaciously inclined," remarked Mansfield, indulging in a low chuckle, as he slowly raised his rifle, and brought the sight to bear upon the broad forehead of the Bull, "we must see if a gentle hint from *Clincher* will not bring him to reason."

The report of the rifle was followed by a crash, as if

the ball had struck a plate of iron, and the Bull dropped upon his knees with a surly growl.

The *Jemmadar*, uttering a wild yell, brandished his knife, and bounded forward to despatch him, whilst Mansfield, stepping from behind the shelter of the tree, cheered on the eager Savage with a hearty shout.

But their triumph was premature: the ball had flattened against the massive skull of the animal, and merely stunned him, without inflicting any serious injury. He had regained his legs before the *Jemmadar* could reach him; and now, perfectly mad with rage and pain, rushed with headlong fury upon old Kamah. Quick as thought the active Savage darted behind the nearest tree, and scrambled into the branches with the agility of a monkey. The Bull, disappointed of his intended victim, turned with redoubled fury upon Mansfield. The hardy Hunter, well accustomed to such scenes, and confident of his own coolness and presence of mind, stood by the side of the tree motionless as a statue, his eagle eye steadily fixed upon his mad antagonist, and his rifle on full cock, ready to act as occasion might require: but the weapon was not raised; he had but one barrel remaining, and was determined to reserve it till it could be discharged with deadly effect.

On came the Bull at headlong speed—his tail on end,—his blood-shot eye rolling in the frenzy of madness,—his tongue lolling far out of his mouth,—and the white foam flying in spray from his distended jaws. Mansfield awaited the charge, with perfect coolness, till the furious brute was within a few yards of him, when, stepping behind the shelter of the tree, he allowed the Bull to pass in his headlong career, and, as he did so, discharged the remaining barrel of his rifle into his shoulder. The wounded monster uttered a surly growl, staggered forward about a hundred yards, stumbled, and fell heavily.

Charles, who had been watching Mansfield's movements with breathless anxiety, sprang from behind the tree and levelled his rifle—Mansfield struck down the barrel before he had time to discharge it.

"Gently, Boy, gently," cried he; "wait till he is steady; the brute is tumbling about like a wounded grampus, and it is a hundred to one against hitting him in the right place. Recollect this is our last shot, and it must not be thrown away rashly." As he said this the wounded Bull regained his legs. "Now then, my Boy, be cool; stick close to the tree, and reserve your fire till I tell you."

Mustering his whole remaining strength, the frantic brute fixed his glaring eyes upon the Hunters, and, lowering his head, dashed at them with determined fury. But his shoulder was stiff; the life-blood was ebbing fast, and his sight was bewildered. He stumbled over the trunk of a fallen tree—made one desperate plunge forward—his wounded shoulder failed him—and he rolled over at their feet, making the earth tremble under his enormous weight.

"Now then," shouted Mansfield, "at him, before he can recover his legs. One shot behind the horns, and we have him."

A peal of fiendish laughter followed the report of Charles's rifle, and next instant old *Kamah* was seen clinging to the prostrate body of the Bull, and clutching the hilt of a long hunting-knife, which was buried in his heart.

"He was a gallant brute," said Mansfield, dropping the butt-end of his rifle to the ground, and wiping the big drops of perspiration from his forehead.

CHAPTER VIII.

BEAR SHOOTING.—THE HUNTER'S CAMP, &c.

How great a change has taken place since the Hunters first entered the forest! The sun is now high in the heavens; the fresh morning breeze has died away, giving place to a close, suffocating, steamy air; and all nature seems to be overpowered by the approaching mid-day heat. The stillness of death pervades the woods which so lately swarmed with life. Not a sound is heard to break the solemn silence, save, at long intervals, the tap of a solitary woodpecker, or the dismal wailing cry of the gray monkey, which, heard from a distance, echoing among the hollow arches of the forest, sounds almost unearthly, and, to a superstitious mind, would suggest the idea of some evil spirit of the woods, denouncing woe on the rash intruders whose footsteps have dared to violate the awful solitude of the wilderness.

But we cannot attempt to describe the feelings of wonder and admiration almost amounting to awe, the wild spirit of romance, the ardent love of adventure, with which, in our younger days, we have wandered through the pathless forest, and listened with rapture to the wild voices of the woods, as a lover to the soft sigh of his mistress. No: these feelings are not to be described, nor can they be understood, save by one who has wandered deep into the trackless wilds of an Indian forest, with no companion but his trusty rifle, no guide to direct his steps but the fiery sun which scorches the tree-tops—by one who has seen the prowling Tiger cross his solitary path, and stood, silent and alone, over the prostrate carcass of the vanquished Bison.

We must, therefore, leave our readers to imagine, as they best may, the ideas which are flitting through the brain of our friend Charles, as he sits upon the trunk of that fallen tree, with his head resting on his hand, and gazing vacantly into the dark vista of the forest which lies in front of him. His head is evidently full of poetry; he may be composing verses for aught we know, or perhaps he is only admiring the dancing of the sunbeams, which, streaming through the thick foliage in threads of golden light, chequer the earth with bright fantastic gleams; whilst, over head, the polished green leaves sparkle like emeralds amidst the surrounding gloom. At all events, he is indulging in a day-dream of some sort, and whether the subject thereof be sunbeams or ladies' eyes is no business of ours.

Mansfield is reposing at full length upon the grass, smoking a cheroot, and amusing himself by making a sketch of the fallen Bison—for he is a naturalist as well as a sportsman, and always preserves drawings of rare animals, or specimens of an unusual size which he may happen to meet with.

The *Jemmadar* is squatted at the root of a tree, with his knees doubled up to his chin, puffing out huge volumes of smoke, and apparently unconscious of what is passing around him—for his eyes are half closed, every muscle is relaxed, and his attitude is altogether one of dreamy, listless idleness.—But it is only the repose of the Tiger in ambush: every faculty is on the full stretch; not a sound falls unheeded on his watchful ear; and, from time to time, his breathing is checked and his wide nostrils distended, as if he depended as much on the sense of smell as on any other faculty, for obtaining that information of approaching danger so necessary to the safety of a wandering savage.

"A splendid specimen, indeed!" muttered Mansfield, soliloquizing, as he carefully measured off a tape with which he had previously taken the dimensions of the Bull. "Two full inches higher than any one I have ever met with—and I have seen a few, too; we must take a note of this. Let me see—what day?—ay, fifteenth May—Waliar Jungle—*genus Bos*—variety *Bos Gaurus*—rare animal—history very imperfectly known.—Mem. look him up in Cuvier—large male—height at the shoulder, six feet four—length from nose to insertion of tail, eleven feet—girth of fore-arm, two feet eight—girth of ——"

"*Sunho Sahib!*" exclaimed the *Jemmadar*, suddenly starting from his indolent position, and stretching forward his neck, as if listening attentively to some sound which was not audible to his companions.

"Halloo, old fellow! what's in the wind now?" cried Mansfield, throwing down his note-book, and grasping his rifle.

The *Jemmadar* returned no answer, but continued to listen attentively for a repetition of the sound which had at first arrested his attention; at length, having apparently satisfied himself as to its nature, and the quarter from whence it proceeded, he quietly relapsed into his listless attitude, merely uttering the word "*Reench.*"

"A Bear!" cried Mansfield, hastily shoving his sketching materials into his pocket. "Come, Charles, my boy, we must have his hide before we go to breakfast, hot though it be. What say you?"

"By all manner of means," cried Charles, starting to his feet and shouldering his rifle; "never mind the heat; I'm up to any thing after that brush with the Bison; regularly savage; 'fit to wap my weight in wild cats,' as the Yankees say; so hurrah! and at him. Of course our friend *Kamah* can ferret him out: I shall never presume to doubt his powers in that way again, after witnessing the masterly style in which he brought us up to the Bison."

"You may see by the quiet expression of the old Pagan's features that he has no doubt upon that head himself," replied Mansfield; "but I shall just ask him the question, that we may hear what answer he will make. Here, *Jemmadar;* you heard a Bear just now?"

"*Ho, Sahib.*"

"Shall we we able to get a shot at him, think you?"

"If it is the *Sahib's* pleasure to do so. But, for my own part, I have no quarrel with the Bear at present, for although he does steal a little honey, there is plenty in these woods for both of us."

"Oh! that is a very good excuse," said Mansfield, winking to Charles: "the *Jemmadar* talks like an old woman; he does not know where to find the Bear, and wants to put us off by saying he has no quarrel with him."

"Does the *Sahib* wish to laugh at the beard of old *Kamah?*" replied the savage, with an air of offended dignity. "Is the *Jemmadar* a dog that he should eat dirt, or is the *Sahib* a child, not to know that where the wild bee hangs her nest, there will the Bear be found also? Go, *Sahib*,—try to throw dust in the eyes of the *topee wallahs.*" So saying, the *Jemmadar* turned on his heel, and walked off with a sullen dogged air.

"So much for good example!" cried Charles, bursting into a triumphant laugh. "Do you recollect your good advice to me? 'Mind you always treat him with the utmost respect! Never interfere with him in following up a trail! And, above all things, avoid laughing at him!!' Ha! ha! ha! Capital! I take it, my worthy preceptor has got himself into a scrape, and will find that the *Jemmadar* has turned the joke against him."

"Faith, you may say that," replied Mansfield, with rather a blank look; "I have fairly set the old devil's bristles up, and it will be no easy matter to smooth them down again; however, I must try to coax the vermin into good humour, else, the chances are he will start off and leave us to find our way out of the jungle as we best can: in which case our stomachs are likely to be better acquainted with wild berries than hashed venison for the next two or three days, as I know to my cost. I lost myself in this forest once before, and have no fancy to repeat the experiment."

So saying, Mansfield followed the sulky steps of the *Jemmadar*, in hopes of bringing him to reason, whilst Charles, whose inward man was beginning to wax somewhat importunate for food, and who, consequently, did not altogether relish the idea of a few days' ruralizing in the forest on such primitive fare as wild fruits and muddy water, watched the progress of the conference with no small interest.

The *Jemmadar* was at first implacable; but Mansfield had luckily great influence over him, and, after a long palaver, at length succeeded in pacifying him. A hearty pull out of the brandy flask, which Mansfield always carried in his pocket, but only to be used in cases of emergency, completely restored old *Kamah* to good humour. His harsh features gradually relaxed into a broad grin, as he felt the generous liquor warm his heart, and, extending his bony hand to Mansfield, with an important and somewhat patronizing air, said—

"There is peace between us—Upon my eyes be it! the Bear shall be made to eat the *Sahib's* bullets."

Peace being thus happily restored, no time was lost in proceeding to business. The *Jemmadar* led the way, as usual, advancing directly into the thickest part of the jungle, and occasionally breaking a small branch from the trees, or tying a knot in the long grass to serve as landmarks in guiding him back to the spot where they had killed the Bison.

"*Dekho, Sahib!*" exclaimed *Kamah*, with a broad grin, as they emerged from a thicket of bamboo, and came upon an open space in the forest, in the centre of which stood a teak tree of gigantic proportions. "That is the sort of bait to catch Bears: the *Sahib* will know it when he sees it again," and the old villain chuckled mightily at his own wit, as he pointed to the topmost branches, from whence depended huge semicircular masses of honeycomb several feet in depth, which looked as if it must have required the united labour of many successive generations of bees to have constructed them.

"There," said Mansfield, pointing to the stem of the tree, the bark of which, as high as the branches, was much scratched and torn, as if by the claw of some animal; "there are Master Bruin's marks pretty distinctly visible, and, from the number of them, I should guess he is tolerably punctual in his visits to the *Jemmadar's* bee-hives."

"*Sawmee*," whispered the *Jemmadar*, creeping close up to Mansfield, and touching him on the shoulder; "*dekho, Sahib*," and he pointed eagerly towards the top of the tree. Mansfield followed with his eye the direction indicated; and, there, in the midst of a dense mass of foliage, a small patch of black fur was faintly visible.

"That's our friend, by all that's beautiful!" cried he, rubbing his hands. "Here, Charley, my boy! do you take the first shot, and let us see how cleverly you can knock him off his perch."

"Where is he?" asked Charles, looking up, and shading his eyes with his hand. "I can see nothing."

"There, among that thick mass of leaves at the very top of the tree: do you not observe a small black spot?"

"Ay, ay; now I have it."

Charles raised his rifle slowly and fired. The Bear remained motionless, and the sharp rattle of the bullet as it crashed through the branches left no doubt that it had missed its object.

"Below him," said Mansfield, with great composure, at the same time raising his rifle and firing quickly. This shot was answered by a deep growl, and a convulsive start on the part of the Bear, but he still remained motionless, and showed no symptoms of being wounded.

"Another miss!" cried Charles, in great glee. "I 've still a chance to draw first blood, after all—Hurra!"

"By the beard of the Prophet! I believe you are right," said Mansfield, regarding his rifle with a look of astonishment, such as a keeper might be expected to bestow on a favourite pointer who had suddenly taken a fancy to running in to birds, instead of dropping at shot. "And yet I can hardly believe that *Clincher* would make such an egregious mistake either. I had full six square inches of black fur to fire at, and the range is not above seventy yards. Well, never mind; better luck next time. But, in the mean time, we must get right under the tree to have a view of him, for I see he has shifted his position. That shot was too near to be pleasant, whether it hit him or not. Ha! what 's this?" continued Mansfield, as he looked upwards from the root of the tree, and felt a large warm drop fall upon his forehead. "Blood, as I live! and plenty of it, too. See, it comes pattering down amongst the dry leaves like rain. I thought *Clincher* would hardly play me such a trick as to miss at that distance."

As he said this, a rustling was heard in the branches overhead, and the Bear, sliding from the branch on which he was perched, began slowly and cautiously to descend the tree, turning his head from side to side, showing his teeth in a threatening manner, and growling fiercely at his assailants.

Charles raised his piece, and was about to fire.

"Hold!" cried Mansfield, as he busied himself in reloading the barrel of his rifle which had been discharged; "Fair play, fair play: don't take an ungentlemanlike advantage of poor Bruin; he is a gallant fellow to think of showing fight against such odds, and it is but common civility to let him reach the ground before we proceed to further hostilities. You shall have the first round with him if you only keep quiet and let him get down."

Charles lowered his rifle, and stood watching the clumsy progress of the Bear with great interest. The poor brute had evidently received a severe wound, and moved with great pain and difficulty. Faster and faster pattered the large drops, forming a crimson pool at the foot of the tree. The growl of defiance was changed to a faint moaning cry, half stifled by the blood which now bubbled copiously from his distended jaws; the faintness of death was upon him; he no longer attempted to descend, but clasping his fore-paws firmly round a projecting branch, held on with convulsive energy.

"It 's all over with him," said Mansfield; "give the poor brute another shot, and put him out of pain."

Charles instantly fired: one deep groan was heard; slowly and reluctantly the gigantic fore-paws relaxed their hold.

"Stand from under," shouted Mansfield, and next

moment the enormous black mass descended to the earth with a velocity that made it rebound several feet, effectually extinguishing any spark of life which might have remained.

"A most inglorious victory," said Mansfield, returning his ramrod with an impatient jerk. "But the skin is a good one, which is all that can be said in favour of our exploit. And now, methinks, we had best wend our way homewards, for we are full four miles from camp, and the heat is enough to fry one's brains into an omelette."

"To say nothing of the want of breakfast," continued Charles, whose mouth watered at the very mention of an omelette; I feel as empty as a kettle drum, and hungry enough to eat the hind leg of a donkey without salt—*Allons, mon Capitaine.*"

"Will the *Sahib* not kill another Bear?" asked the *Jemmadar*, with a knowing look, as the two Sportsmen were about to move off.

"To be sure we will," exclaimed both the young men in a breath, "if you will only find him for us."

"*Kamah* can find him," replied the savage, with a confident air. "Follow me."

The *Jemmadar* spoke thus assuredly, from having remarked that the dead Bear was a male, and knowing that, if he followed the trail backwards, there was little doubt that it would lead him to the hiding-place of the female and her cubs.

As good luck would have it, the trail led them in the direction of the camp; a circumstance which induced our two Sportsmen to follow the rapid strides of their conductor with double alacrity. After pursuing a tortuous course, through an almost impenetrable jungle, for upwards of a mile, the trail suddenly ceased on the edge of a small muddy stream, the opposite bank of which rose to a considerable height, and was composed of huge splintered masses of rock piled one upon another in wild confusion.

"We are not far from her now," said Mansfield, cocking both barrels of his rifle, and throwing it across his arm, ready to be used at a moment's notice, whilst old *Kamah* waded across the stream, and hunted about, like a hound at fault, in hopes of finding a continuation of the trail amongst the bare rocks; but their hard surface afforded no vestige of foot-marks even to the experienced eye of the savage.

The indefatigable *Kamah* had climbed more than half way up the rocky bank, hunting with the eagerness of a terrier, and poking his nose into every crevice which afforded the slightest probability of concealing a Bear, when, on turning the angle of a rock, he suddenly started back, and beckoned, with eager gestures, for Mansfield to come across.

At this moment a terrific growl was heard. The *Jemmadar*, casting a hasty glance over his shoulder, sprang, without hesitation, from the dizzy height into the bed of the stream, and ere he reached the water, the infuriated Bear appeared upon the very ledge of rock which he had quitted, giving vent to her impotent rage in a prolonged roar, and glaring with the malignant eye of a baffled fiend, on the intended victim who had so narrowly escaped her jaws.

Quick as thought, Mansfield discharged his unerring rifle, and the Bear, rearing up to her full height, rolled headlong down the rocky steep, falling right over poor *Kamah*, who had not yet had time to scramble out of the water.

The *Jemmadar* had hardly uttered a yell of astonishment, when he found himself firmly clasped in the deadly embrace of the Bear, and felt her hot breath blowing upon his cheek. Twisting his body round, with the agility of a wild cat, he avoided the first grasp which she made at his head; and knowing full well that he had nothing else for it, thrust his naked arm, without hesitation, between her extended jaws, seizing the root of her tongue, with the desperate gripe of a man who is determined that nothing but death shall force him to quit his hold. A deadly struggle now ensued; the two combatants—each equally savage in their own way—rolling over and over, and struggling, like two incarnate fiends, in the midst of the muddy stream, now crimsoned by the blood which flowed copiously from the wounded Bear. And it was well for the *Jemmadar* that she had been wounded, else the contest would have been speedily ended. Mansfield stood for some time anxiously watching their movements, with his forefinger resting on the trigger of his rifle, in hopes that some lucky turn might give him an opportunity of firing into the Bear: and more than once the weapon was raised to his shoulder; but so quick were their evolutions, that he did not dare to risk a shot. For an instant the shaggy hide of the Bear appeared on the surface; and ere it could be well distinguished, its place was supplied by the dusky figure of the savage—his teeth firmly clenched—every sinew in his wiry frame strained almost to cracking—and his blood-shot eyes starting from their sockets, in consequence of the dreadful pressure he endured.

"This will never do," exclaimed Mansfield, hastily throwing down his rifle, and preparing to plunge in the water; but ere he could do so, the blade of old *Kamah's* hunting-knife was seen to flash brightly in the sun, and next moment he started to his feet, with a savage yell of triumph, flourishing the blood-stained weapon round his head, whilst the lifeless body of the Bear floated slowly down the stream—He had just withdrawn it from her heart.

"It was my Fate," said the *Jemmadar*, casting a rueful glance at his arm, which was a good deal mangled by the teeth of the Bear, although, in her wounded state, she had not been able to exert sufficient strength to break the bones: "It was my Fate;" and consoling himself with this reflection, he proceeded to bind up his wounds with a pocket-handkerchief which Charles had given him.

"She must have cubs hereabouts," remarked Mansfield to Charles, after they had dragged the body of the Bear from the stream, and laid it on the bank; "she must have cubs hereabouts, else she would never have made such a desperate attack as she did on the *Jemmadar*. What say you, *Kamah*, are there not young ones in the cave?"

"The *Sahib* hath spoken wisdom," replied the *Jemmadar;* "there are doubtless young bears in the cave—the young devils, the children of an accursed dam, shall not escape my knife!" So saying, and grinding his teeth, the revengeful savage clutched the hilt of his hunting-knife with a determined grasp.

"No, no, Master *Kamah*," cried Charles, checking him; "you shall not kill the poor little wretches. I want a young bear particularly, and I am sure our friend the Doctor would give his ears for one. We must take them alive and carry them into camp."

This measure having been carried, after some opposition from the *Jemmadar*, he was persuaded to go back to the cave to secure the cubs. He soon returned with two little misshapen snarling imps, about the size of terrier dogs, one of which he carried by the nape of the neck in his hand, whilst the other was secured under his arm; and many were the maledictions he bestowed upon them, as they struggled, and scratched, and writhed about, in their vain attempts to free themselves from his iron grasp.

The cubs having been properly secured, and one of them committed to the care of Charles—for the poor *Jemmadar*, with his wounded arm, found his two unruly protégées rather more than he could manage—the party moved off towards their camp, with all the speed which ravenous hunger and the prospect of a good breakfast could inspire.

An hour's scrambling through dense jungle, where the heat and want of air was almost suffocating, brought them in sight of the camp; and poor Charles, now nearly fainting from hunger and fatigue, felt most devoutly thankful as the cheerful scene opened to his view —a scene which formed so striking a contrast to the silent gloom of the forest, giving promise of rest, good cheer, and shelter from the merciless rays of a tropical sun. The white canvass roofs of the tents, sparkling in the sunbeams, and standing out in bold relief against a dark background of forest-trees, looked the very picture of comfort; and the bustle which took place amongst the native servants, as soon as their masters appeared in sight, showed that they anticipated a hasty order for the substantial breakfast which had long awaited their arrival. Under the shade of a widely-spreading Banyan tree, numerous fires sent up their thin spiral columns of blue smoke into the clear atmosphere, indicating the speedy preparation of the mid-day meal of the camp followers, who, enjoying the luxury of a day's relaxation from labour, might be seen swimming, diving, and floundering about in the cool stream of the river, like a flock of wild fowl. The Wives of the Horsekeepers, in their picturesque and gaudy-coloured dresses, squatted in groups around their fires, carefully watching the earthen vessels, which contained their frugal mess of rice: whilst their husbands busied themselves in pouring out and cooling the *gram*, previous to giving it to the noble-looking Arab horses, which, picketed at a short distance, neighed and pawed the ground with impatient eagerness. Groups of bullocks and baggage-ponies strayed about amongst the trees, luxuriating in the rich herbage which the natural lawn afforded; and, in the foreground, in the shallow part of the river, the huge baggage Elephant lay extended, at full length, like an Eastern potentate in his bath, flapping his ponderous ears, and lazily splashing the water about with his trunk; whilst the *Mahout*, kneeling on the top of his unwieldy charge, diligently scrubbed the dark-polished hide of the animal with a rough piece of freestone—a species of shampooing which old "*Anack*" seemed to enjoy mightily, ever and anon expressing his approbation thereof by a complacent grunt, and a more vigorous flap with his ears.

As our party neared the tents, their ears were assailed by the harsh tones of the Doctor's voice, loud in wrath.

"Ye d—d long fushionless gowk, will ye no haud yer grip?" were the first words which reached their ears. "Od's my life, man, can ye no haud on, by the tail, till I pu' the skin o'er his head? If ye let go again, and gar me spoil the specimin, the consequence is, I 'll ding the life out o' ye, ye soft sumph!"

"Suppose Master cut off my head, I never can do this business," replied the squeaking voice of Heels, in a tone of remonstrance. "I poor Matee boy—Master too muchee strong—snake's tail too muchee large—too muchee fat—too muchee slippery make—how can poor black fellow hold him grip?"

"Weel, then, gie me the tail, and tak' ye haud o' the skin, ye poor fushionless cat; and mind ye dinna rive it, or, as fac' as death, I 'll Burke you, and make an anatomical preparation o' your wizen'd carcage."

"Hurra! and walk away with it, my hearties! Pull Doctor, pull Devil?" shouted Mansfield, clapping his hands, and laughing till his sides ached, as he entered the tent, and discovered the Doctor, his gaunt figure very scantily clad in a dirty shirt and a pair of mosquito drawers, holding on, as if his life depended upon it, by the tail of the huge snake he had killed the evening before; his face the colour of a frosty moon, and the big drops of perspiration streaming from his forehead; whilst Heels, grinning like an insane baboon, panted, and strained, and tugged at the skin, which he was attempting to strip off like that of an eel. As the Doctor's evil genius would have it, the tail at this moment slipped through his hands, and he and his black assistant, falling backwards with a violence proportioned to the tremendous exertions they had been making, rolled, head over heels, to opposite sides of the tent. This was too much even for the stoical gravity of the *Jemmadar*, who, opening his leathern jaws, and displaying his formidable array of snow-white teeth, gave vent to an eldrich laugh, which completely drowned the less boisterous mirth of his European companions.

"What, in the name of the foul fiend, gars ye laugh that gait, ye black Pagan?" cried the Doctor, sitting up on the ground, grinning like an ogre, and rubbing the lower part of his back with a ludicrous expression of mingled pain and chagrin. "O, aye, laugh away;—it 's grand sport for you, nae doot: but, by my troth, if you had gotten sic a lick on the *os-coccygis* as I got the noo, I 'm thinking it would gar ye laugh the wrang side o' your mouth; and, faith, it 's wi' the wrang side o' your mouth I 'll gar ye laugh yet, if ance I get a grip o' ye. As true as I 'm leevin, I think it 's knockit off a'thegither," continued the Doctor, feeling the injured part with great delicacy of touch.

"O, the devil a fear of it, Doctor!" said Mansfield, assisting him to rise; "your bones are not so easily broken as all that comes to. Get up, man, and shake yourself; I 've got a patient for you. Poor *Kamah* has been somewhat roughly handled by a Bear, and wants a little of your professional aid to put him to rights."

"Grippit by a Bear!" cried the Doctor, starting to his feet with alacrity, his love for a surgical operation completely getting the better of his angry feelings. "Odd! but that will be an interesting case. Come here, my man, and let me examine you; tak' that clout off your arm—dinna be feared, I 'll no hae recourse to amputation if it can possibly be avoided. But, at the same time, it may be prudent to hae the tools ready, in case they should be required." So saying, the Doctor rummaged out his travelling-case of instruments, which he unrolled and ostentatiously laid upon the table, flanked by the usual accompaniment of sponge, water, lint, bandages, &c. "Noo, then," said he, tucking up his sleeves, and looking very formidably business-like,—after he had felt the edge of his various instruments, and tried them upon the palm of his hand to see if they were in good order; "Sit doon here, my man, and let me examine the wounds. You needna be the least alarmed."

The *Jemmadar*, who had attentively watched the Doctor's proceedings, and evidently did not at all relish the aspect of affairs, bounded back as the Doctor approached, and, glaring at him with the eye of a Tiger at bay, clutched the hilt of his hunting-knife.

"The deevil 's in the bloodthirsty Pagan!" exclaimed the Doctor, perfectly aghast. "Is it gaun to stick me ye are? Weel, weel, tak' your ain way o't," continued he, seeing the *Jemmadar* looked more and more savage; "tak' yere ain gait—dee and be d—d,—for dee ye will

—the limb 'll mortify, ye donnert auld deevil—that 'll be the upshot o't—and a dismal ill-far'd corp ye 'll mak' when ye 're streekit." So saying, the Doctor turned away, and proceeded to pack up his rejected instruments.

The obnoxious apparatus having been removed, Mansfield succeeded in explaining to the *Jemmadar* that the Doctor's intentions were quite harmless; and having, after some trouble, pacified the enraged practitioner, the wounded arm was at length unbound, and the Doctor, —grumbling, however, a good deal as he did so,—proceeded to examine it.

"Humph!" said the Doctor, putting on his spectacles, taking a pinch of snuff, and assuming an air of profound wisdom; "ye 'll condescend to avail yourself of my professional knowledge noo, will ye, ye poor benighted Pagan? Od, it 's weel for you that ye hae sic an easy-tempered man to deal wi'; mony a ane would have seen ye far enough afore they would hae been at the fash o' patching up yere greasy black hide. Whisht, ye cankered deevil, and dinna be girning that gait—faith, if I hae occasion to handle the tools, I 'll gie ye something to girn for, my man! I tell't ye, I 'd gar ye laugh the wrang side o' yere mouth, afore I was done wi' ye. Od, but she 's gi'en ye a gay sair churt," continued the Doctor, as he spunged away the clotted blood; "thae lacerated punctures are bad things, and ill to heal; but I believe there 's nae banes broken, and, I dare say, if mortification does na ensue, we may manage to save the limb, although mony a ane would whip it off at ance, just to save trouble."

Having thus made out the worst case he possibly could,

the Doctor proceeded to wash and clean the wounds, which, after all, were not of so serious a nature as he wished his friends to believe; and having bound up the arm with some simple dressing, and suspended it in a sling, the *Jemmadar* was allowed to retire, evidently delighted at having escaped so easily out of the Doctor's clutches.

"And now," said Mansfield, addressing the Doctor, "if you will be good enough to remove that half-skinned snake, which is an object not at all calculated to improve one's appetite, we will to breakfast. I feel as ravenous as a ground shark, and I see Master Charles is already making play with his knife and fork, so it is time to look out for our share of the rations. I suppose, Doctor, you have had your breakfast long ago."

"Aye," replied the Doctor, casting an amorous glance at the goodly viands which loaded the table, as he assisted Heels in removing the snake—"Aye, I got a bit chack twa hours sin' syne, but I'm gay weel apeteezed again; I'm thinkin' I'll just sit doon and pick another wee bit for company sake. We'll ca' it lunch."

So saying, and wiping his greasy hands in his shirt-sleeves, the Doctor fell to work; and the unwearied industry with which he plied his jaws proved that "the bit chack, twa hours syne," had done but little towards damping his appetite—nor were his companions backward in the fray. Hashed venison, curry, omelette, fresh fish from the river, huge bowls of tea, and goblets of cool claret, disappeared as if by magic. In short, it was a regular Hunter's breakfast, and, by my troth, there was no lack either of appetite or inclination, on the part of the Hunters, to do it ample justice.

"The Lord be thankit for a' his mercies," murmured the Doctor, at length, throwing himself back in his chair, patting his stomach complacently, and proceeding to light a cigar, which he said was good for digestion—"I'm as foo' as a partan."

The Doctor had lighted his cigar, and was sitting, with half-closed eyes, allowing the smoke to escape in thin spiral columns from the corner of his mouth, and thinking what a pity it was that man's gastronomic powers were limited, when he was startled from his reverie by a low, whining cry behind him.

"What's that?" cried he, turning hastily round in his chair, and discovering the two young Bears, who, having been left to their own devices, had crept away and tried to conceal themselves in a remote corner of the tent. "What'na twa queer black things is yon, rowin aboot in that dark corner, for a' the world like twa young imps o' Satan? My certie, they 'r no' very canny like. I wadna say but what they 'r twa familiar spirits belonging to that deevil the *Jemmadar*. I aye thought he lookit gay like a Warlock."

"No, they are my familiar spirits," cried Charles, jumping up, and proceeding to lug the reluctant little savages into the middle of the tent; "I had quite forgotten the unfortunate imps, who must be quite as much in want of food as we were."

"Od's my life, they 'r Bears!" cried the Doctor, in great delight; "*Ursus labiatus*—grand specimins, and just the right size to make pets o'—whar' did ye get them?"

"We caught them in a cave, after having killed their mother," replied Charles, "and I thought they would be well worth the trouble of carrying home. I intend one of them as a present to you, Doctor, if you think it worthy of acceptance: so you may take your choice."

"Warthy o' acceptance! Od, Maister Charles, I wadna' tak' a five pund note for ane o' them. I 'm muckle indebted to you indeed, Sir. Come here to me, ye poor wee hairy tyke," continued the Doctor, putting on his most insinuating look, snapping his fingers, and holding out a saucer of milk towards one of the young Bears. "Come here to me, and I 'll gie you a sup o' milk. I 'm sure your mammy did na' gie ye ony breakfast this morning, for ye look awfu' hungered-like;" but the unmannerly cub turned a deaf ear to the Doctor's gentle importunities. "Hoot, man, come here; what gar's ye look sae dooms stupid-like? div ye no ken the smell o' sweet milk?"

So saying, the Doctor seized the sulky little brute by the nape of the neck, placed him on his knee, and shoving his nose into the saucer, attempted to make him drink, whether he would or not. This was an insult which the independent spirit of young Bruin could not brook; and, accordingly, he made a most determined resistance—growling, scratching, and gnashing his teeth, with a determined courage worthy of his illustrious ancestors. At last he succeeded in fixing his teeth in the worthy Doctor's hand, making the blood start, and extorting an involuntary cry of pain.

"I 'll thraw ye'r neck, ye girnin cankered deevle, that will I," roared the Doctor, starting to his feet, tossing

THE DOCTOR AND HIS [illegible]

his adopted bairn into the middle of the tent, and shaking his wounded hand, as if it had been scalded. "Wha would ha' thought the bit towzy tyke had sae muckle wickedness in it! Od's my life, sma' though it be, it gar'd its teeth play chack like a pair o' hedge sheers; it has amaist nippit ane o' the fingers aff me."

The young Bears having been turned out of the tent in disgrace, and consigned to the care of one of the Horsekeeper's Wives,—who, having half a dozen squalling brats of her own, was supposed to possess some skill in the management of such unruly cubs,—the Doctor patched up his wounded fingers with a piece of adhesive plaster, poured out a fresh bowl of tea, and resumed his cigar.

"That 's true," said he, addressing Mansfield; "I forgot to ask what sport ye had this morning; did ye get ane o' thae muckle Bison beasts ye were speakin' o' yest'reen? I 'm very anxious to see ane of them; for they are, nae doubt, rare animals, and I hae heard sae mony different opinions aboot them, that I 'm just in swithers whether they ought to be classed amongst the Bisontian group, or whether they are only a variety of the wild Buffalo which is found in the jungles of Bengal."

"Well, Doctor, you may soon have your curiosity satisfied on that head. We killed two fine specimens this morning—a male and female—besides a couple of Bears; but to do so, I fear you must accompany *Kamah* and his party when they go to fetch home the game; for the Bison are such unwieldy animals, that it is impossible to carry them off entire. When you see them, I have no doubt you will agree with me that they are true Bison, although a variety quite distinct from the Bison of Europe or North America. You will find a description of the animal—but a very imperfect one—in Cuvier's work, under the name of *Bos Gaurus.* But I see old *Kamah* is already mustering his *Coolies;* so, if you intend to accompany them, you had better order your horse. You can ride well enough till you get into the heavy bamboo jungle, and it is just as well to save an unnecessary walk in the sun."

The Doctor was soon equipped in a white jacket and broad-brimmed straw hat, and bestriding his raw-boned *Cutch* horse, with a goodly-sized umbrella over his head to protect him from the sun, he drove his heels into the lean ribs of his charger, jirked the reins, made a clucking noise with his tongue, and leaning well forward, with his elbows projecting at right angles from his body, started at a shambling trot. The *Jemmadar* and a whole regiment of *Coolies* followed in his wake; some bearing bamboos and ropes to carry home the Bears; whilst others were armed with knives, hatchets, &c., for the purpose of cutting up the Bison.

"Two to one the Doctor gets spilt before he is clear of the camp," cried Charles, laughing heartily at the grotesque appearance of the worthy Doctor, and his raw-boned steed.

"The chances are ten to one in your favour," replied Mansfield; "I can see, by the way the old dromedary carries his ears, that he is in one of his sulky fits this morning: he is not the least inclined to leave the camp, and if he begins to argue the point, the Doctor is pretty sure to get the worst of it. There he goes—I told you so—up with the black flag, and no surrender. Well done, Doctor, hit him again—Hurra!"

The Doctor's charger, as Mansfield predicted, had not advanced above a hundred yards, when he suddenly wheeled round, laid his ears back, clapped his tail between his legs, shook his head with a sulky dogged air, and looked askance at his rider, with his malignant wall-eye, as much as to say, "I'll see you particularly well d—d before I go an inch farther—so do your worst."

"Tak' ye that, 'Smiler,' my man," said the Doctor, suddenly closing his umbrella, and bringing it down on the head of his refractory steed with a force that made it fly in splinters. The amiable 'Smiler' acknowledged the favour by a sulky grunt, and a sidelong kick with one hind leg, after the manner of a vicious cow.

"Hit him again, Doctor—hit him hard—don't be afraid of hurting him—his skull is thick enough;" and the two young men rubbed their hands, and shouted with glee at the prospect of witnessing a well-contested engagement between the Doctor and the pig-headed 'Smiler.'

"Here, my man, give us a lend o' that stick," cried the Doctor, throwing away his broken umbrella, and snatching a heavy male bamboo from one of the *Coolies* ——Whack! down it came upon 'Smiler's' lean flank, making the empty carcass sound like a kettle-drum.

The additional weight of metal told; and, this time, 'Smiler' exerted himself so far as to kick both heels in the air, with a jerk that somewhat discomposed the Doctor's seat.

"Dee'l be in my skin, but I'll ca' the life out o' ye,

ye door deevle," muttered the Doctor, as he once more brandished the bamboo over his head. "'Od, ye 'll try to gang ye'r ain gait, though the Dee'l himsel' should girn in ye'r face;"—Whack. "If ye war drowned,—and Dee'l may care how soon ye come to that,—I 'll wad a sixpence, it 's up the water a body wad need to gang, to look for the ill-faurt carcage o' you. There, tak' that, ye thrawn deevle," and the bamboo descended between 'Smiler's' ears, inflicting a blow that would have felled any other horse to the ground. But it only seemed to rouse the dormant energies of that proud-spirited steed: his wall-eye flashed fire, he snorted indignantly; and, rearing upon his hind-legs, made a desperate plunge forward.

This unwonted feat of activity, on the part of 'Smiler,' completely unshipped the Doctor, who was pitched clean out of the saddle; but, determined to regain his seat, if possible, he remained clinging with his long legs entwined round the horse's neck, and holding on vigorously by the ears. The Doctor made a desperate effort to right himself; for one moment the victory appeared doubtful; and the spectators watched the issue of the struggle with breathless impatience;—He 's up again:—No!—that last kick has turned the scale of victory, and the discomfited Doctor lies sprawling in the dust.

"Are you hurt?" said Charles, running up to him, and kindly assisting him to rise; for he was really sorry for the poor Doctor, although he could not help laughing till the tears ran down his cheeks—no one ever can on such an occasion;—"I hope you are not the worse for your fall."

"Deevle a bit," cried the Doctor, jumping up and wiping the blood from his nose, the bold outline of which was a good deal disfigured by the fall—"deevle a bit—he has flattened my neb a wee; but, by my troth, I 'll gar him rue the day he did it."

So saying, the Doctor grasped the reins; sprang into the saddle, with an agility quite surprising in one of his ungainly make; and plied the bamboo so vigorously about the ears of his refractory steed, that the unfortunate 'Smiler' was glad, for peace-sake, to turn his head the right way, and shamble off at his best pace.

"Faith, 'Smiler,' my man, ye got the worst o' that tuilzie, I 'm thinkin," said the Doctor, tucking the bamboo under his arm, and smiling complacently, as he refreshed himself after his labours with a huge pinch of snuff.

CHAPTER IX.

A WET NIGHT UNDER CANVASS.

The sun has already set, and the short twilight of the tropics is fast darkening into night. An unnatural silence pervades the forest. The close air of the woods is more dense and oppressive than usual, and the heat is almost suffocating.

Our three friends are seated in front of the principal tent, smoking their cigars; their hunting dresses have been exchanged for that truly oriental dishabille of slippers and musquito-trousers; they appear languid and oppressed by the unnatural heat of the atmosphere, and their shirts are thrown open, to woo the passing zephyr, as they sit smoking in profound silence. Even the dumb animals appear to feel the overpowering influence of the electric fluid with which the atmosphere is surcharged. The horses, with drooping ears, hang listlessly over their untasted food. The dozing bullocks have forgotten to ruminate. The birds have already flown for shelter to the densest thickets of the forest. And Nature awaits, in silent awe, the coming storm.

"We are going to have a dirty night of it," said Mansfield, after regarding the appearance of the sky for some minutes.

" Faith, you may say that," replied the Doctor, starting from a half doze ; " and it is high time we were getting the tents secured, else we shall hae them aboot our lugs before day-light. Whare the deevil are a' thae lazy loons o' Lascars? they might hae thocht of bushing the tent-pegs afore this time. Od, the hale camp appears to be in a dwam, kye, and horses, and a'—*Chuprassee bolow!*" continued he, bestowing a kick on the ribs of our friend Heels, who, rolled up in his *cumbley*, was snoring right lustily between the walls of the tent.

" *Abba!* " muttered Heels, turning on his side, with a grunt, and again snoring louder than ever.

" *Chuprassee bolow!* " with another kick, more earnestly bestowed than the former.

" *Sahib!* " cried Heels, sitting up and rubbing his eyes.

" *Chuprassee bolow!* " roared the Doctor, shaking Heels till he was thoroughly awake.

" *Ho, Sahib!* " yawned Heels, and, leisurely gathering up his *cumbley*, he shuffled off to rouse the tent-pitchers and Lascars.

In a few minutes a dozen busy hands were employed in bushing the tent-pegs, digging trenches round the tent, and taking all the necessary precautions to secure the camp against the effects of a tropical thunderstorm.

" What a fuss you old Indians make about a shower of rain ! " remarked Charles, laughing as he watched the eager haste with which the Lascars worked : " these fellows remind me of a ship's crew shortening sail in a hurry when a white squall is expected."

"And, with all their hurry, they will not have done their work much too soon either," replied Mansfield; "for here it comes, with a vengeance. You will have a fine opportunity now of seeing what an Indian shower is, my lad. And if you have the luck to get a wet tent blown about your ears to-night, which I think exceedingly probable, you will recollect the appearance of a thunder-cloud the next time you see it, I'll be bound."

As he said this, Charles felt a cold damp air come stealing over his face. And now comes sweeping from afar a low mysterious muttering sound, like the distant roar of troubled waters. The atmosphere is suddenly filled with that peculiar smell of newly-wet earth, which is the sure forerunner of a tropical storm. Dry leaves, bits of straw, and other light substances are caught up, and whirled into air, with a quick spiral motion, as if by the action of innumerable little whirlwinds, although, as yet, not a breath of air is stirring. A dense mass of inky clouds rises above the tree-tops, with a rapidity that shows the mighty power of the tempest, by which it is driven on, and the faint twilight is suddenly quenched in the darkness of midnight. And now a bright flash of livid fire shoots from out the gloomy mass, blasting the spectators' sight with its unearthly splendour—and the vault of heaven is rent asunder—and the Earth trembles, as she listens with awe to the chiding voice of angry thunder.

And hark!—at that signal, the howling spirits of the tempest have been loosed, and come sweeping through the woods on a thousand whistling wings, rejoicing in their strength:—and the forest bows low, and groans aloud in agony, as the hurricane host sweeps by:—and the aged trees toss abroad their gigantic limbs, and lash the air with frantic gestures, as if in the madness of fear they were striving to uproot themselves, and to flee from the coming wrath of the mighty Spirit that rides upon the whirlwind:—and the rain descends in unbroken sheets of water that appear to threaten the earth with a second deluge:—and the crash of uprooted trees is mingled with the awful pealing of the thunder:—and the air is filled with wild unearthly sounds, as if legions of evil spirits were mingling in the fray:—and strange misshapen forms seem to flit amongst the trees, revelling in the work of destruction, as the wild scene is for an instant revealed to sight by the livid glare of forked lightning, and again shrouded in more than midnight darkness.

"The whole universe must be tumbling into chaos," was the idea which flashed across the mind of Charles as he stood amidst the war of elements, and gazed in stupified wonder.

Reader, if thou art a lover of the sublime in nature—if thou art anxious to be impressed with a due sense of the Omnipotence of thy Creator—go, look upon the tropical storm, as it sweeps howling through the wilderness—and tremble, like Charles, at thine own insignificance!

But the Doctor had been too long in India, and had witnessed too many thunder-storms, to understand the feeling which prompted Charles to gratify his love of the sublime at the expense of his bodily comforts.

"Come in by,"—cried he, from the interior of the

tent, where he had already snugly ensconced himself behind the dinner-table. "Come in by, Maister Charles, and dinna be standing there glowrin' frae you, like a demented poet. The deevil 's in the laddy, has he gaen daft a'thegither, or is he dazed by the thunner, or what 's gaen wrang wi' him, that he stands there in a pour of rain that 's fit to wash the sark aff his back? for a' the world like a drooket craw on an auld fayle dyke, and him ha'in' a good dry tent at his back, and a prime haunch of venison smoking on the table; and the kettle blawin' out steam like the boiler of a twa hundred horse-power engine; and that bonny bit bottle of real Glenlivat smiling in his face, fit to seduce a vara Saunt. Hoot fie!—Come in by, ye poor demented cratur, and dinna be catching your death o' cauld there.—Ye 'll be laid up wi' jungle fever, the morn, as sure as my name 's Mc. Phee—or may be ye 'll be blinded by the lightning, and that would be a bonny-like story to tell to your winsome cousin, Miss Kate, when we gang back to the Hills. Come in by, my man, to ye'r denner, and never ye fash yer thum' aboot the war o' the elements, as thae poor, silly, half-starved, bits of poets ca' it:—just let them abe, and let them fecht it out their ain gate; they 'll ca' through fine, without'n your help; and, whichever gets the best o't, we are sure to hae a gran' day for the Deer-shooting the morn.—Oh, man! but that 's prime juicy meat,"—continued he, licking his lips, and eyeing the noble haunch, in which Mansfield had just made the first cut—"A wee bit mair o' the fat, if ye please, Captain, and another spoonfu' o' the jeely—ay, that 'll do fine."

And the Doctor, regardless of the storm which raged without, fell to, with an earnestness of purpose that would have done credit to the appetite of a half-starved Ogre.

"Well, Charles, my boy, what think you of an Indian shower now?"—asked Mansfield, as Charles entered the tent, dripping like a River God:—"that is something like a squall, is it not?—the breaking out of the monsoon, amongst the western *Ghats*, is a sight worth seeing, we flatter ourselves."

"It is indeed,"—replied Charles—"about the grandest sight I ever beheld. I have often heard it talked of before, but never could have pictured to myself anything half so sublime, so awful—it——"

"Talking o' the grand works o' nature"—interrupted the Doctor, with his mouth well filled, and keeping his eyes steadily fixed on his plate,—"talking o' the grand works of nature, Maister Charles, allow me to recommend to your favourable notice that haunch o' venison; that's what I ca' a grand specimin o' combined nature and art,—a majestic hint quarter o' a maist sublime Buck—and just roasted to the very minutest fraction of a turn.—Another slice, if you please, Captain!"

"Faith you appear to think so, friend Mc.Phee, if one may judge by the hole you have made in it already," replied Charles, pulling in a chair:—"'By the beard of the Prophet!' as my worthy Uncle would say, one must needs look sharp when you come to close quarters with a joint, else they are like to have bare bones to pick. Manners, you old cannibal, manners—why you don't mean to say you want another slice already!"——

"Truth do I, Maister Charles—and what's mair, I'm

no going to let you sit down to denner in that weet sark, to get a fit o' the ague, and gie me the trouble o' makin' you well again.—Na, na!—just gang in atween the wa's o' the tent, like a man, and put dry clothes on you,—Heels has got them a' ready—and I 'll keep a prime bit o' the venison for you; I 'll no let the Captain eat it a', although he is such a deevle o' a twist. Captain, I 'll tak' a wee bit mair from you, just to keep you in countenance, for I see ye 'r no' done yet."

"Will you, by Jove!—the devil 's in your maw, Doctor,"—cried Charles, who, although perhaps a little the worse for his pretty cousin's blue eyes, had not by any means allowed his appetite to go the same way as his heart, and off he bounded to change his wet clothes with all convenient speed.

Charles having made a hearty dinner—for man's powers are limited, and the Doctor, in spite of himself, had been obliged to desist before he had more than half finished the haunch—the cloth was removed, and a bottle of claret, with the unusual accompaniments of hot water, sugar, and a bottle of real Highland whisky, were placed upon the table.

"Noo, then, lads," cried the Doctor, lighting a cigar, and rubbing his hands with glee. "Noo, then, for a cozie night, in spite of the wind and the rain. Heels, ye black sinner, tie up the tent door, and keep the wind out, it 's enough to gie an alligator the lumbago."

"Hullo, Doctor!—what 's all this?" exclaimed Mansfield, in astonishment.

"Aha, lads!—there 's something to warm the cockles of your heart. I hae been sair stinted in my drink, since I left the Hills, wi' you and your temperate habits, Captain—and your lang-winded preaching about cool heads, and steady hands:—that 's a' very weel for you crack rifle shots, but it doesna' agree wi' my constitution; and, by my troth, I maun hae my ain way this weet night. There 's a bottle o' the right sort, that never paid sixpence to the Excise—bless it 's sonsie wame!—and hot water enough to plot a pig, and a' the rest o' the materials; and so, Captain, dear, just pitch that sour trash o' claret to the dogs—fiech!—it gar's me grue to look at it—and mak' yoursel' a good stiff tumbler, like a man. Here 's 'The Lasses—God bless them!'—I 'm sure you 'll drink that toast, Maister Charles, if the ague has na got a grip o' you already, and frozen the blood in your veins."

"Not, by any means, a bad move," replied Mansfield and Charles in a breath, as they filled their glasses, for the night was really cold enough to make a little hot stuff mighty palatable, at least between the canvass walls of a wet tent. "Here 's your toast, with right good will—'The Lasses—God bless them!'"

"Weel done, Captain! Od, I see ye mak' it gae an' stiff, like mysel'. I dinna' misdoubt but what there 's some o' the right stuff in you yet, ye mahogany-faced auld sinner, in spite o' the puritanical look ye put on whiles, when I propose takin' a second tumbler. I daresay noo, Captain," continued the Doctor, draining his glass, and proceeding to replenish it, "I daresay ye think I 'm mair given to drink than a professional man like me ought to be, because I 'm, whiles, a wee funny in my cups; but I assure you, Sir, I 'm the maist temperate man leevin', by ordinar.—Hout, Maister Charles, man, tak' up your glass, you 'r far ahint.—It 's no' the love o' drink, Sir; no, no—your health, Captain:—it is the conviviality o' the thing I enjoy—the conviviality, Sir—no' the liquor, by no manner of means. Did you ever hear tell o' the man and his cow, Sir?"

"No, never," replied Mansfield, smiling.

"Weel, then, Captain, I'll tell you the story, for it 's a good illustration o' my subject. Hout, fie! I have drouned the miller. Just rax me the bottle, Maister Charles, till I put in a wee drap mair o' the speerit. Weel, gentlemen, as I was saying, about the man and his cow. There was a cousin o' mine, by the name o' Jock Mc.Phee, that was married on a sister o' the Minister of our parish. And the Minister, honest man, on the strength o' this, thought himsel' in duty bound to take a special charge of my cousin Jock's morals: for, although no' muckle waur than his neighbours, Jock was a gae throughother cheel when he got a drap in his head. So, ae day, after Jock had been at a neighbour's wedding, and had gotten a glass o'er much, the Minister yoket to, to flyte him about the drink, and he was unco' hard upon poor Jock, and misca'd him terrible; and at last, says he, 'Just look at your cow there, John,' says he—'look at her, honest beast, she gangs to the water, when she 's dry, and slokens her thirst, and comes back, douce and sonsie, to the byre, but she never drinks more than what does her good, or makes a beast o' hersel', like *some folk*. And is na' it a crying shame to see you, a Christian man, wi' a soul to be saved, having less sense and discretion than the beasts that perish? Are ye no' ashamed, Sir, to do the like, and you Good-brother to a Minister?'

"'Indeed, then, Sir, what you say is o'er true,' replied Jock, scarting his lug, and looking a wee foolish; 'but it's no' the love o' liquor, Sir, it's the good company—it's the good company, Sir, and naething else that leads me astray. There's my cow, hummled Bess, as your Honour says, a sonsie weel-conditioned beast, she tak's her drink, and comes hame quiet and peaceable without makin' a spectacle o' hersel'. But, O, Sir, if a neighbour's cow was to come the other side o' the water, and sit down on her hunkers, and say, 'Here's to ye, Bess!' od, Sir, as true as death, she wad just sit and drink there till she was *blind fou!!*'"

"Bravo, Doctor!" shouted Mansfield, "a right good story, and well told. You have earned your glass of grog honestly to-night," and Mansfield and Charles laughed till their sides ached.

"Haich! haich! haich!" roared the Doctor, at the same time helping himself to a little more of the *mountain dew.* "Haich! haich! It aye gars me laugh when I think o' poor Jock and the Minister. O, man! but this is grand stuff to cheer a body's heart, and gar his tongue wag.—Here's wishing speedy promotion to you, Captain, and a good Wife to you, Maister Charles,"—and the Doctor winked his eye, with a maudlin expression, and tried to look knowing, as he buried his muzzle in the tumbler.

"Now, Mansfield," said Charles, "it is your turn. Suppose you fulfil the promise you made this morning, and give us the particulars of the two extraordinary runs you had lately, on that wonderful little horse Challenger."

"Riding down a Wolf and an Antelope, you mean?"

"Exactly—"

"I shall do so with great pleasure, provided you do not accuse me of boasting; for I confess I am not a little vain of Challenger's exploits. You are aware that the feat of riding down an Antelope has always been considered impracticable, and spearing a Wolf on horseback, as next to an impossibility.—I have often seen the experiment tried, but never knew it to succeed before, except in one instance, when the Wolf happened to be gorged with food. In my case, however, the Wolf was as lank as a greyhound,—all I have ever heard of the untiring gallop, and extraordinary bottom of these animals, was equalled by this one,—and nothing but the condition, and high blood of my horse, carried him through so severe a run.—I was riding out one evening, for exercise, carrying a spear in my hand, as usual, when I suddenly came upon a large male Wolf. Challenger being in the highest possible condition, and very fresh, I thought a gallop would do him good, and accordingly laid in to the Wolf, rather for the sake of having some object in view, than with any idea of riding him down. However, after a gallop of a mile both horse and rider became interested in the chase.—I remembered that Challenger had never yet met his equal in the hunting field—his blood was now fairly up—and, on the impulse of the moment, I resolved to let him try his metal against the gaunt long-legged devil, who was going along before me at an easy lobbing gallop, which, without any apparent exertion on his part, kept my horse pretty nearly at the top of his speed. I now laid in to him in earnest, over a fine open piece of country, easy to cross, except where it was occasionally cut up by *nullahs*. For the first hour the Wolf kept up the same pace, a long lobbing gallop, without exhibiting any symptoms of fatigue,—but after that he began to run short, twisting and turning, to throw me out—stopping in the bottom of *nullahs*, till I had jumped over, and then returning as he had come—and practising all sorts of cunning tricks to shake me off. When the horse was at his haunches, he would suddenly throw himself flat on the ground, and allow me to pass, thus gaining ground before I could turn; and as a last resource, when his dry tongue, white with foam, was hanging from his parched jaws, he took to the water in a tank, where I speared him to death. He was fairly done—so dead beat that he could not even bite the bamboo when the spear was driven through his body. The chase lasted for two hours and five minutes, —a pretty good trial of wind and bottom, you will allow. I had dismounted, and was standing at my horse's side, loosening the girths, when he suddenly began to snort and tremble, as if alarmed at something on the edge of the tank. I looked over his back to see what it was, when, to my astonishment, I observed the *bund*, or embankment, lined with Wolves, sitting on their haunches, and watching my proceedings, whilst others were hurrying to the spot from all quarters. Where they came from I cannot conceive, for I had not observed one during the run. The sun having set, and the Wolves appearing rather pugnacious, I thought it prudent to decamp before they came to extremities; so mounted and rode off, leaving them masters of the field. They followed for some distance, but did not attempt to attack me, and I got home, sometime in the course of the night, without further adventure."

"And was not poor Challenger the worse for his tremendous gallop?"—asked Charles.

"Not a bit.—He fed well, and appeared as fresh as ever next morning. It was the spurt after the Antelope that so nearly killed him—I did not think he would ever get the better of that day's work."

"Come, let 's have the Antelope,"—exclaimed Charles, drawing his chair closer to that of Mansfield.

"Here 's your health and sang, Captain," murmured the Doctor, rousing himself from a nap, and replenishing his glass—"Was it a sang, or a story?—I 'm no very sure—but never mind, it 's a' the same in Greek."

"Thank you, Doctor—your good health!" replied Mansfield smiling. And the Doctor, taking a long pull at the whisky punch, relapsed into his dozing fit.

"It was some days after my adventure with the Wolf,"—continued Mansfield—"and whilst I was still flushed with victory, that I determined upon attempting the still more difficult task of riding down an Antelope.

"I sallied forth to the black plain, little Challenger arching his neck proudly, and bounding under me in the exuberance of his spirit. It was in a very different mood that he returned, poor fellow.—I soon found a fine solitary black Buck; and laid in to him while he was concealed by a rising ground—thus gaining a long way, before he heard the clatter of hoofs, and went his best. The ground was beautiful, and we flew across the plain at racing speed. But, for the first mile, this was not fast enough to press the Buck,—bounding along before me, like some winged creature, whilst the horse, straining every nerve, could hardly keep him in sight. Occasionally some Labourer, in a cotton field, made the Antelope swerve from his line, and then, by cutting off an angle, I was enabled to gain a little;—yet a few dashing bounds, as I approached, sent him further off than ever. These exertions, however, began to tell at last—he ran shorter, and appeared undecided as to his line of country—advantages for the pursuer which I seized on at every turn—and, by pressing him to do his utmost over stony ground, I found that his strength was getting gradually reduced. Challenger was still going collected, and I nursed his remaining powers with anxious care, giving him a sob, with a hard pull at his head, whenever we crossed a field of black soil.

"We had now gone, as the crow flies, seven miles, and the Buck was getting weaker every moment. We came in sight of a distant herd, feeding on the top of a small hill. This appeared to give him fresh courage, and he exerted himself to reach them with renewed speed. It was the flickering of the flame ere it expires—I knew the symptoms well—his tail began to shake—he carried his head low—and instead of bounding forward, and covering his stretch, he appeared to fall shorter at every stroke. The hill was gained—now, my good little horse, press him and he dies!—It was as I expected. The steep ascent choked the panting Antelope, and he dropped, completely exhausted, ten paces in front, at the very moment that poor little Challenger came to a dead halt, reeling under me with fatigue. Having dismounted, and put the Antelope out of pain with my hunting knife, Challenger became the object of my care, and I must confess his appearance rather frightened me—flanks heaving—forelegs tottering—tail quivering—and every symptom of extreme distress. I turned his head to the wind, and loosened his girths. He lay down by the fallen Buck—and then I cursed my cruelty, in pressing the noble spirit of my game little Arab, till he sank at my feet. But I cannot pull up when once in chase.

"The hope of running into my game, at every stride, and the fear of losing, what a few hundred yards further might gain, always prevents my giving in, while a chance remains. I feel an indescribable longing to come up with any animal—even a hare—if once I have laid in to him, and reflection and remorse come only when it is too late. This time, however, I had not to reproach myself with riding poor Challenger to death. He gradually recovered,—in half an hour he was able to walk home, where you may be sure he was well taken care of—and in a few days was as fresh as ever. The distance ridden was nine miles, in a direct line, without including turns. And, if it be *the pace that kills*, this was far enough and fast enough to burst anything that ever was foaled. I need not say how much the gallant little horse has risen in my estimation since that day's work—I would not part with him for his weight in gold!

"And now, Master Charles, having complied with your

request, and performed the part of my own—or rather my horse's—trumpeter, methinks we had better turn in; for I perceive our friend Mc.Phee is waxing drowsy, and I intend to sound the *reveillie* by times to-morrow—what say you, Doctor?"

"Hoot fie, no!" replied the Doctor, who was fast verging towards a state of inebriation. "It 's but early in the night yet. Wha cares for hours?—hours were made for slaves!—Hurra! Na, na! Sit ye down, lads—sit ye down, and I 'll sing you a sang—a sang wi' a grand chorus til 't; and mind, ye maun a' join in when I tell you. Whisht, noo!" and the Doctor, forthwith, cleared his pipes, and struck up, in a voice that rivalled the howling of the wind without—

"'O Willie brew'd a peck o' maut,
And Rab and Allan cam to pree;
Three blither hearts, that lee-lang night,
Ye wadna' find in Christendee.'

"Chorus, now, lads!

"'For, we are na' fou, we 're no' that fou;
But just a drappie in our e'e;
The cock may craw, the day may daw,
But we will taste the barley bree.'

"Hoot! Maister Charles, sing up, man—dinna be blate!

"'Here are we met, three merry boys—
Three merry boys, I trow are we;
And many a night——'"

Here the Doctor's melody was interrupted by a gust of wind, more furious than the rest, which tore up several of the tent-pegs, and made the loosened canvass flap violently.—Mansfield and Charles jumped from their seats.

"Hoot, fie! never mind the wind, lads; there 's nae danger,"—exclaimed the Doctor, who had now become exceedingly pot-valiant, and had no idea of being interrupted in his song by any such trifle:—"Heels, ye' lazy deevle; gang and drive in thae tent-pegs, will you?—Where was I again—eh?—I dinna mind. Weel, never heed, we 'll just begin at the beginning, that 's the surest way no' to lose any o't.

"'O Willie brew'd——'"

But, before the first line was finished, crash came the tent-pole right across the table, demolishing candles, bottles, and glasses; and our unfortunate revellers found themselves grovelling on the earth, in utter darkness, and more than half smothered in the wet folds of the tent; whilst the loosened ropes, with the tent-pegs still attached to them, flapped, and whistled, and banged about their ears, threatening to fracture their skulls, if they were fortunate enough to escape suffocation.

"The Lord preserve us frae a' Bogles and Warricowes, and other mischancy things!"—roared the Doctor, who, half stupified by what he had drank, and completely deprived of his little remaining sense by the suddenness of the catastrophe, could not, by any means, account for his present very uncomfortable situation.—"The Lord preserve us, what 's a' this?—What 's this?—what 's this? It 's surely a judgment come upon me for drinkin' illicit whisky and singin' profane sangs. O dear! O dear! O meeserable sinner that I am, I 'll surely get my paiks noo, for I verily believe that Auld Clootie himsel', and a' his imps, are playing their cantraips upon me. Will nae charitable Christian lend a hand to get out o' this damnable brulziement?—the Lord forgie me for sweerin'.—O, Maister Charles! O, Heels, ye black-a-vic'd Pagan! Oh! oh! oh!"—and the unfortunate Doctor roared aloud, in agony of spirit, as he scrambled about, amongst the broken fragments of bottles and glasses, and entangled himself more and more amongst the complicated folds of wet canvass in which he was enveloped.

Mansfield and Charles, who had their wits about them, had already scrambled clear of the wreck, but were so convulsed with laughter, that, for some minutes, they were incapable of rendering any aid to the miserable Doctor, who continued to struggle, and howl, and pant for breath, like a dog tied up in a wet sack.

At length, however, with the assistance of the Lascars, he was extricated from the ruins of the tent, and stood, shivering and stupified, in the pelting rain.

"Preserve me! but this is an awfu' nicht,"—muttered he to himself, when he had partially recovered his senses —"There 's something no cannie in 't, I 'm thinkin'. I 'll awa to my bed—And the bottle o' Glenlivat no finished—and me in the middle o' my very best sang—and—and—and——Ou ay, I see how it is—I see fine how it is—it 's just a judgment on me for drinkin' illicit whisky and singin' profane sangs,—poor sinfu' creature that I am! But, thanks be to Goodness, I 'm no fou—Na, na! I 'm no fou—I ken the road to my tent fine." And so the Doctor continued to soliloquize, as he reeled about in his vain endeavours to steer a direct course to his own tent.

"By mine honour, friend Mc.Phee, thou art thankful for small mercies," cried Mansfield, laughing immoderately at the worthy Doctor's expression of thankfulness for *not being fou.*

"But there 's surely something gaen wrang wi' my legs the nicht—I maun hae hurted them some way in yon stramash. Here, Heels, my man, gie us a haud o' your airm, for I 'm sair hurted, and no fit to gang my lane. Haud up, ye stammerin' deevle," cried he, clutching the grinning varlet by the shoulder. "Can ye no walk steady, you mislear'd Pagan? Haud up, I say. Ye 've been drinkin', Sir—ye 've been drinkin'—ye need na try to deceive me—I ken it fine by the way ye walk—ye 've been drinkin', ye besotted beast. I 'll report you to your maister in the morning, and gar him gie you a good thrashing. I—I—I wonder, Sir, ye 're no ashamed to make sic a spectacle o' yoursel' and me in the face o' the hale camp. It 's dis—dis—dis—reputable, Heels—it 's highly disreputable. If there 's a vice on earth, Heels, that I dislike mair than anither, it 's drunk—drunk—drunkenness!" And here the Doctor's voice became inaudible, as he pursued his tortuous course towards his sleeping tent.

We are, reluctantly, obliged to confess that our worthy and much respected friend, Mc.Phee, was *drunk* —not exactly drunk according to the definition given by an Irish friend of ours, who said that he always considered a man sober till he saw him *trying to light his pipe at the pump*—The Doctor was not quite so far gone as this—But that he was considerably *disguised in liquor* we have not the conscience to deny.

Reader, hast thou ever, in the course of thy travels, witnessed the breaking-up of a tropical thunder-storm at the approach of day—when the eastern sky is streaked with purple and gold, and the heavens, in that quarter, are cloudless to the zenith, and studded with fading stars, winking as if exhausted by their long night's vigil.—And the cool, balmy, morning air, kisses thy bronzed cheek like a smiling infant just awakened from sleep.—And the tempest-torn trees, loaded with sparkling rain-drops, like frightened women smiling through their tears, sigh forth their gratitude to the rising sun, at whose glorious presence the gloomy spirit of the storm unwillingly retires—his sable host, as they roll away, slow and majestic, into the far west, growling forth their indignation in muttered thunder.—And the refreshed earth sends up a grateful incense to Heaven.—And the timid birds who have all night long cowered, trembling, amidst the gloomy recesses of the forest, come forth singing their morning-hymn of thanksgiving—and the jungle-cock, like a blustering bully, struts amongst his admiring females, crowing defiance—and, on the naked branches of some blasted tree, at the edge of the forest, a family of vultures, like a hoard of wandering gipsies drying their rags, sit, with drooping wings, preparing to bask themselves in the grateful sunshine—their high shoulders, downcast look, and ruffled plumage giving them, at once, an air of poverty, cunning, and abject humility—and, from out the bosky thickets of feathery bamboo, comes, stealing on the ear, the gentle cooing of the turtle-dove, as he pours forth his very soul in amorous vows of love and constancy.—And the air is filled with joyous insects, and gaudy-coloured butterflies, which have been suddenly called into life by the electric fluid—and even the creeping things appear to claim their share of enjoyment—and Nature smiles as she looks upon the happiness of her children?

It was on such a glorious morning as this, after a *wet night*, in every sense of the word, that the cheerful notes of Mansfield's bugle roused the poor Doctor from feverish sleep and troubled dreams, to the humiliating consciousness of having made a beast of himself. What a sad contrast does his flushed cheek, and parched lips, and fevered blood, present to the cool, fresh, smiling face of Nature!

Oh man! proud man! thou who wert formed in God's own image, how hast thou degraded thyself by the sensual gratification of thy appetites!

But, of this day's adventures, anon.

CHAPTER X.

AN EVENTFUL DAY IN THE JUNGLE.

"I BELIEVE it wasna' the real Glenlivat, after a'," exclaimed the Doctor, as he sallied from his tent with the feeble and undecided step and nervous tremor of a man who has just been roused from a drunken slumber. "I believe it wasna' the real Glenlivat, after a', for I hae a deevle o' a sare head after it this morning. Good morrow to ye, lads," continued he, addressing Mansfield and Charles, who, with their rifles ready loaded, were lounging in front of the tents and sipping their coffee. "This is a grand fresh morning after the rain."

"Ah! good morrow to you, Doctor," exclaimed Mansfield, smiling. "Glad to see you so alert. Talking of *freshness*, it strikes me you were tolerably *fresh* last night. How do you feel this morning? coppers rather hot—eh?"

"Hoot, fie!" replied the Doctor, looking half ashamed and half pawky—for we must do the poor Doctor the justice to say that he was not by any means a hardened sinner, nor habitually addicted to the use of strong waters, although, when the temptation offered of a bottle of Glenlivat, and a neighbour's cow sitting on the other side of the water, to cry, "Here 's to you, Meg," he sometimes indulged a little more freely than was good for him. "Hoot, fie, Captain, keep your thumb upon that—keep your thumb upon that. Od's my life, if auld Lorimer gats a haud o' that story, to say nothing o' Miss Kate, I'll never hear the last o't. I maun confess I'm no just mysel' this morning. But I'm thinkin' the whisky wasna' as good as it ought to hae been, for we didna' take such a dooms big drink, after a'; the bottle wasna' finished, if I mind right."

"Is not this a glorious change from the storm of last night?" remarked Charles, good-naturedly trying to turn the conversation, for he saw that Mansfield was bent upon bullying the poor Doctor, who, although he tried to put the best face he could upon the matter, was evidently ashamed of himself. "Who that looks now upon the smiling face of Nature would believe her capable of giving way to such ungovernable bursts of fury as the one she favoured us with last night?"

"Like a spoilt beauty," remarked Mansfield, "who goes to bed in a towering rage because she fancies her charms have been slighted, cries herself to sleep, and awakes next morning, all smiles, to laugh at her own folly, and to be more admired than ever."

"Or like a bairn on a Sabath morning," suggested the Doctor, "who, after having his face weel scrubbit wi' brown sape and a rough tawel, and alarming the hale house wi' his eldritch skirling, begins to nicher and laugh at the sight o' his new corduroy breeks wi' plenty o' brass buttons on them—they 'r may be his first—and fairly burst out into a hearty guffaw, when he keeks at his ain shining red face and weel sleekit hair in a cogfu o' clean water. You see, Dame Nature has been taking a sly keek at hersel' this morning in the water down-by, and in spite o' hersel' she canna' but smile, through her tears, at the sight o' her ain bonny weel-washed face."

"Bravo, Doctor! quite poetical, I declare; the Glenlivat has inspired you. But we must not stand talking here, the sun is already up: we should have been off long ago, only we thought you intended to accompany us to-day, as it is the last we shall be able to spend in the forest."

"And so I do intend to gang wi' you. What the deevle else do you think would trail me out o' my warm bed at this unchristian-like hour o' the morning? But, that 's true, I hae forgotten my weapon. Here, Heels, my man, just run into the tent, and bring out my fusee, auld 'Mons Meg,' and the bag o' swanshot ye 'll find lying aside her."

"Why, my dear Doctor," exclaimed Mansfield, regarding, with a smile, the worthy Doctor's very unsportsmanlike dress, consisting of his eternal broad-brimmed hat, and an old red jacket, which, on the strength of a damp morning, he had substituted for his usual one of dirty white jean. "Why, you don't mean to say you intend to take the field in such a dress as that? You look, to use one of your own expressions, 'exactly like a potato bogle;' you are enough to scare all the game within a mile of you, and, if we fall in with a herd of Bison, the Lord have mercy on your miserable carcase!—they 'll hunt you to the world's end. And there you are again, with that infernal fusee, and your handful of grit-shot. O Doctor! Doctor! will you never learn to handle a rifle like a man? I wish we had the old Governor here to keep you in order."

"By my troth, he keepit me in order enough when I was on the Hills, and a bony-like job he gar't me make o't, wi' his lang-winded lectures about projectiles, and parabolic curves, and sights, and elevations, and friction, and attraction, and deevle kens how many mair jaw-breaking terms. Na, na, nane o' your confounded lectures on natural philosophy, nane o' your new-fangled pernickety weapons for me. A good wide-bored fusee, like 'Mons Meg,' for my money—ane that lets a crack like a six-pounder, and spreads the lead the breadth o' a barn-door;—that is the weapon for real execution, and sae ye 'll see afore the day 's done," continued the Doctor, as he rammed down a huge fid of brown paper by way of wadding, returned the ramrod, and carefully hammered the well-worn flint with a key which he took from his pocket. "I 'll warrant the auld jade no' to miss fire this time, and, my certie, it 's no' for want of pouther and lead, if she doesna' do execution."

"Faith, you may say that," replied Mansfield, much amused at the Doctor's warlike demonstrations. "If your shot fails it will not be for want of ammunition, you may take your oath. You have given the old jade, as you call her, a sufficient dose of that, and I have no hesitation in predicting that she will do execution, but whether on the carcase of the Deer, or the head of her confiding master, appears to me exceedingly problematical. I suspect you will find her somewhat like your friend 'Smiler,' when overcharged with Bengal *gram*, as she is with powder, rather prone to kick up her heels, and apt to give her master a bloody nose."

"Weel, weel, never ye fash your thumb about that,

Captain; but show me the Deer, and, I 'll be cation, ye dinna want for a haunch of venison the morn to your dinner. Where 's that deevle's-bucky the *Jemmadar?* Stir your stumps, ye auld Pagan, the sun has been up this half-hour." So saying, the Doctor shouldered Mons Meg with a confident air, and strode off, whistling "Johny Cope" right lustily.

Our friends had proceeded some distance into the jungle, the *Jemmadar* leading, as usual, and our three Sportsmen following his steps in single file, when Charles, who was the last of the party, happened to spy the head and antlers of a noble spotted Buck, about a hundred yards from their path, cautiously peering over a thick patch of high grass which they had just passed.

The fact of his having made this discovery, after the lynx-eyed *Kamah* had passed it unobserved, was of itself a great triumph to the ambitious young Sportsman, and his heart palpitated with anxiety as he halted and silently raised his rifle, for he felt that his character was at stake. Resting the barrel against the stem of a tree, the fine-drawn sight was brought to bear upon the glittering eye of his victim—for one instant the ponderous rifle remained as steady as if fixed in a vice—light as the delicate touch of a lady was the gradual pressure of the fore-finger on the finely-balanced trigger. Bravely done, my young Forest Ranger, there must be death in that shot. The sharp crack of the rifle makes the woods ring, the ragged bullet speeds hissing through the air, and the antlered head disappears amongst the long grass as if by magic—Hurra!

Charles had already pulled off his cap, and opened his

lips to give the death halloo with due emphasis, when a whole herd of Deer burst from the thicket of long grass, headed, apparently, by the very Buck at which he had fired, and dashed across the path with the speed of lightning.

"Deuce take the rifle!" exclaimed Charles, pettishly, dashing his cap to the ground, and, in the excitement of the moment, quite forgetting that his rifle had a second barrel which might still do execution.

Mansfield, although taken by surprise, turned on his heel with the coolness of an old Sportsman, and pitched forward his heavy rifle, the piece exploding at the very instant it dropped steadily into the hollow of his hand—so truly did hand and eye act in concert—and the leading Buck, bounding convulsively from the ground, fell heavily forward: without removing the rifle from his shoulder, the deadly weapon was brought to bear upon another of the herd, and the second barrel was discharged as rapidly as the first. The soft *thud* of the bullet announced that it had taken effect, and a fat Doe stumbled to her knees, but immediately recovering herself, disappeared amongst the jungle with her companions.

"We shall have blood upon that trail," said Mansfield, quietly, as he dropped the butt-end of his rifle to the ground, and proceeded to reload it with great composure. "But what on earth is the matter with you?" continued he, turning round and discovering the Doctor squatting on the ground, and holding a pocket handkerchief to his nose, which was bleeding profusely. "I thought old Meg made more noise than usual. I hope she has not burst?"

"Na, na!" replied the Doctor; "there 's nae fear o' her burstin': but, O man, she 's just a perfect deevle to kick. Od's my life, she dang me heels over head like a kale-runt; ane might as weel hae gotten a kick frae a coach-horse. But how mony o' the Deer is down? I 'll warrant she made a grand stramash amang them, for she spreads the lead fine, by ordinar."

"Why, I believe there is but one down, this round," replied Mansfield; "and I think you will find he bears my mark. But, as I predicted, Mons Meg has done some execution. Your nose, Doctor, will vouch for her powers, in one way; and here is an unfortunate young tree which she has doomed to a premature death, by blowing away more than half the trunk. By my faith, you may well say that such a charge *o' grit-shot* would have made a fine *stramash*, if it had gone in the right direction. But never mind, Doctor, better luck next time; so get up, and give old Meg another chance."

"Od, man, I maun confess that yon was an awfu' gleed shot," said the Doctor, scratching his head, and regarding the shattered sapling with a comical grin, as he still sat, wiping the blood from his nose. "I begin to think, Captain, I 'm no just that good wi' the gun either. It maun be my ain faut, for I ken Meg aye kills, if she 's handen straight. The fact o' the matter is, there was a *pretty man* spoilt, when they made a Doctor o' me, as the auld Heeland Carle said to his son."

"What is the story of the Highlander and his son?" asked Charles, who was always delighted to catch the Doctor in a story-telling humour.

I 'll tell you that, Maister Charles," replied the

Doctor, as he proceeded to charge Mons Meg with a more moderate allowance of powder. "There was, ance, a grim auld Carle, lived in the Isle of Mull, and he had three sons. The two eldest were awfu' big, strong-made cheels, in fact, perfect giants, and deevles for fechtin. But the youngest, who was of ordinary stature, and, consequently, looked down apon as a dwarf in his own family, was a quiet, peaceable lad, and mair given to his books, than the use of the dirk or the claymore. And so, the auld Carle, who despised everything in the shape o' book-learning, and considered fighting and cattle lifting to be the chief end o' man, determined to bring him up for the Church, because, as he said, he wasna' fit for anything better. Weel, ae day, when the young lad was sitting at his books, and the two auld anes were up amang the hills, looking for a Deer, a neighbour's Bull, an unco cross-tempered beast, happened to stray into the Good-man's bit of arable land, and, when he noticed him, he was just dancing mad, for he was gae short in the temper, at any rate, and he roars out to his son, who was ben the house, reading his books, 'Get up,' says he, 'ye saft sumph, throw by thae trash o' books, and gang and turn that Bull out o' the corn, do you no' see he 's makin a perfect hash o't?' So the lad he throws by his book, and grips his staff, and runs out fou gleg to turn the Bull. But the Bull was a dour deevle, and wadna' thole to be thwarted; and so, when he seed the lad coming at him, wi' the staff in his hand, to drive him out o' the corn, he sets up a roar, and at him like mad. But the douce canie lad, wi' a' his book-learning, had a stout heart o' his ain, when he was put upon his metal.

And, instead o' fleein', as the auld Carle his father expected, he stood up manfully, and watched the motions o' the Bull wi' an eye like a gled; and just as the beast was at the stickin' o' him, he jinket to ae side, as souple as a wild cat, and grippit him by the horn, and gied him a twist that cowpet him on his back, as though he had been a year-auld stirk, and then he yoket to, wi' the staff he had in his hand, and, by my troth, he laid on, wi' such good will, that the Bull was fain to gather himsel' up, and run for it. And the auld Carle, who had been standing at the door, watching him, was just astonished and delighted to see so much of the man in his youngest son, whom he always considered a poor, soft, useless sumph—and he runs to meet him, wi' the tear in his ee', and throws his arms about his neck, and cries out, in Gaelic, 'Ochon! ochon! it was me that spoilt the pretty man when I set you to turning the leaves, instead of handling the claymore.'"

"Come, Doctor," cried Mansfield, "we have no time to listen to your old stories, just now; you must keep them for after dinner. And you, Master Charles, are a pretty fellow for a Sportsman, to stand gossiping there, instead of breaking up your Deer. Recollect, we are like to have a long, and a hot chase after the wounded Doe, before we get her; and get her we must, before we do anything else; for I consider it a most unsportsman-like proceeding, to look for fresh game, as long as one has a bloody trail to follow."

"*My* Deer!" exclaimed Charles, in astonishment. "Why, that was my Buck that you killed. I ought to have killed him, I grant you, for I never took a steadier aim in my life; but the leading Buck, which you dropped, at the first shot, is the one I fired at—I can swear to his horns."

"Why, my dear boy," exclaimed Mansfield, laughing, "do you suppose there is but one Buck in the forest with such a head? I can swear you killed him, although my back was turned at the time, and hit him in the head too. There is no mistaking the crashing sound of a bullet when it strikes upon bone, and so you will discover, when you have had a little more experience. Just go and look at the spot where you fired at him, and if you do not find the Buck, with an ounce of lead in his skull, then do I renounce all claim to knowledge in woodcraft."

Charles, without answering a word, dashed into the long grass, with the eagerness of a young hound, and his shout of triumph, as he stumbled over the carcase of the Buck, announced that he had not been disappointed.

"Od, man, but that's the best beast I've seen this mony a day!" exclaimed the Doctor, feeling the well-covered ribs of the Deer, with the scientific touch of a Highland drover, and admiring the depth of fat on the brisket, as the *Jemmadar* proceeded in the operation of cutting up the animal, "he's as fat as a four-year-old wether."

"Just like you, Doctor," cried Mansfield, "always thinking of that ungodly maw of yours, which, Heaven knows, would be ill enough supplied, if Mons Meg were the only caterer to its wants. Look at the head, man, instead of feasting your eyes on the fat morsels. There is a shot worthy of the best *Shikaree* in the country; a ball right through his eye at full a hundred yards. If I could only get you to handle a rifle, and make such a shot as that, I should have some hopes of you."

"Troth, then, it 's no' an ill shot," replied the Doctor; "the laddy has a quick eye, and a steady hand, and if you dinna look sharp, Captain, he 'll be fit to brag you at your ain weapon, afore you 'r a month older. But as to Mons Meg, she 's a good auld trusty servant, and I'm no' goin' to part wi' her, for a' that 's come and gane yet, so ye may just let that flea stick to the wa'."

"Well, well, Doctor, so be it—I see you are utterly incorrigible; and now to find the wounded Doe. Charles, my boy, do you take the lead, and let us see how you can follow up a trail. Here is the spot where she made the first stumble, and you may see by the manner in which the blood has spouted, that there is some large vein cut. The poor beast cannot have run far in that state—Forward!"

Charles, proud of being intrusted with the important office of tracker, started off at a round pace; the large drops of blood which marked the course of the poor animal rendering the task a sufficiently easy one; whilst the *Jemmadar,* who considered so conspicuous a trail as quite unworthy of his talents, followed in rear of the party, occasionally breaking a small twig, or tying a knot in the long grass, to serve as landmarks to guide him on his return, to fetch home the venison which had been left behind.

In this manner the trail was followed for upwards of a mile, through tangled masses of bamboo, and Tigrish-looking patches of long grass, which reached far above their heads, and where the skulls and half-picked bones of Deer showed that the tyrant of the forest had occasionally selected them for his lair.. But Charles was too much excited by the chase to think of danger, and persevered in a direct course, regardless of the poor Doctor, who remonstrated loudly against tempting Providence by venturing into such mischancy-looking places; and more than once started, and changed colour, as the rustling of a lizard amongst the long grass, or the melancholy howl of a gray monkey, "frightened him out of his propriety."

"Oh, Captain Mansfield!" exclaimed he at last—"I wish you would speak to that daft laddy, and no' let him trail us ony further, through such awfu' like places—it 's just a perfect tempting o' Providence.—I tell you, Sir, we 'll be made Tiger's meat o' before we get out—I see their tracks here, back and forret, as thick as rabbits in a warren. Od, Sir, it 's surely an unchristian-like act to gar a decent body risk his precious life in such uncannie bits as this, for the sake o' a wounded Deer."

"Forward! forward!" shouted Mansfield, turning a deaf ear to the Doctor's lamentations, for he had remarked that the drops of blood, which had latterly been few and far between, now became larger, and had assumed a frothy appearance,—a sure sign that the wounded animal is nearly exhausted. "Forward, Charles, my boy! we are close upon her now." But his shout was answered by a surly growl, not ten yards in front of them, and the whole party stopped dead, as if electrified by that fearful sound.

"A Tiger, by heavens!" muttered Mansfield, setting his teeth hard and cocking both barrels of his rifle.

"*Ho Sahib, bagh hie!*" remarked the *Jemmadar*, looking as unconcerned as if it had only been a dog.

"I told you how it would be," roared the Doctor, turning short round and preparing for a hasty retreat.

"Hold, madman!" cried Mansfield in a voice of thunder, seizing him by the collar, and dragging him back to his side—"Do you wish to bring the Tiger upon us? If we turn our backs to him, we are dead men. Our only chance is to keep our eyes steadily fixed on the spot where he lies, and be ready to pour in a volley if he attempts to charge. But if we put a bold face on it, the chances are he will slip off quietly. Look at Charles, how manfully he stands his ground. I wonder you are not ashamed to show less nerve than a boy of his age. Here, stand by my side, and be ready with Mons Meg, she is like to do us yeoman's service, amongst this long grass. Hang it, man, don't look so blue upon it; I have been in many a harder pinch than this, and got clear after all."

But although Mansfield talked thus encouragingly to rouse the Doctor's drooping courage, his flashing eye, distended nostril, and compressed lips, showed that he considered it no child's play, but an affair of life and death—one of those desperate scrapes which the hardy Forester must sometimes expect to fall into, but which it requires all his skill and steadiness of nerve to get well out of.

"*Kamah*," said he, in a low, deep-toned voice, still

keeping his eye steadily fixed on the spot where he supposed the Tiger to be, and grasping his rifle more firmly —" *Kamah*, keep a good look out, and try if you can mark him amongst the grass.—Steady, my lads !" whispered he, setting his teeth and holding his breath, as another deep growl was heard, accompanied by that impatient switching of the tail which too certainly denotes an inclination to charge. " He is determined to fight, I see, and there is nothing for it, but a well-directed volley.—But, as you value your lives, stir not, and reserve your fire till you can see him."

The Doctor's teeth chattered, and a cold perspiration broke out upon his forehead at this unwelcome announcement: Charles, too, looked a little paler than usual, but his hand was steady, his eye quailed not, and the firm, though compressed expression of his mouth, showed that he was prepared to act like a man, when called upon to do so.

" *Dekko Sahib!* " whispered the *Jemmadar*, his fierce eye flashing fire, as he gently touched Mansfield on the shoulder, and pointed eagerly towards the spot from whence the sound proceeded.

Mansfield strained his eyes in vain, to discover the object which had attracted the attention of the savage.

A low rustling sound was heard amongst the long grass, as if the Tiger were creeping cautiously forward, so as to bring himself within springing distance of his victims. It was a moment of fearful suspense; but Mansfield never altered a muscle of his countenance—his courage appeared to rise, as the danger became more imminent.

The rustling sound ceased, and the ominous switching of the tail was again heard.

"Now for it, lads! death or victory!" said Mansfield, in a low firm tone of voice, his proud lip curling haughtily as he drew himself up to his full height, and half raised the rifle to his shoulder.—"Be steady, and don't throw your shots away; there is life or death in every ounce of lead.—Ha!"—at this critical moment, he caught a hasty glimpse of the Tiger's malignant green eye as he lowered his head for the fatal spring. Like a flash of lightning, the trusty rifle poured forth its deadly contents. A roar—a bound—and the stricken monster rolled gasping at their feet, with a two-ounce ball buried in his skull.

"*Wallah! wallah!*" shouted the *Jemmadar*, with uplifted hands, for once startled out of his stoical self-possession, by the suddenness of the catastrophe.

Charles and the Doctor stood as if petrified, gazing on the fallen Tiger, and still grasping their weapons firmly, as if they expected him again to rise.

"Od's my life, he 's no' dead yet!" roared the Doctor, bounding back some paces, as the dying Tiger gasped painfully for breath.

"Well, Doctor, what is Mons Meg about?" replied Mansfield, smiling; "why don't you give him a dose of the *grit-shot?*"

The Doctor raised his piece with a trembling hand, and pulled the trigger:—the thundering report of Mons Meg made the woods ring—the Tiger gathered up his limbs with a convulsive start, and then stretched them out, quivering in the last agonies, whilst the frothy blood bubbled from his mouth and nostrils.

The Doctor, as if scared at his own temerity, threw down his gun, and, jumping behind Mansfield, peeped cautiously over his shoulder.

"Od, I believe the grit-shot has settled him at last," cried he, rising on tiptoe, and clutching Mansfield's shoulder in an agony of nervous excitement—"he's just about gone!—Od, there's another awfu' gape though—Mercy on us! what gruesome teeth—there's another! Ha!—ha! that's the last—hurra! hurra!—he's dead!" and the Doctor began dancing, and snapping his fingers, and laughing with a sort of hysterical giggle, as if the sudden revulsion of feeling from mortal terror to excessive joy, had been too much for him, and had actually turned his brain.

Charles, who had stood all the time perfectly motionless, with his forefinger resting on the trigger of his rifle, allowed the weapon to drop mechanically into the hollow of his arm, and grasping Mansfield's hand, wrung it hard, as he mentally returned thanks to the Almighty for their providential escape. His nerves had been strung to the highest pitch of excitement, and his heart was too full to speak.

"You have behaved gallantly, my boy!" said Mansfield, heartily returning the pressure of his hand: "the steadiness and presence of mind you have shown on this occasion, would have done credit to the oldest Sportsman in India, and with a few months' more training, I would not wish for a stauncher hand to back me in a case of emergency.—Come, Doctor," continued he, turning towards our medical friend, who still continued his gambols—"don't be ridiculous, but thank God for being in a whole skin, and load your weapon. This is no place to stand twirling our thumbs with empty barrels."

Whilst the Sportsmen re-loaded their rifles, *Kamah* went ferreting about amongst the long grass from whence the Tiger had sprung, and now returned, dragging after him the carcase of the wounded Doe, her head being crushed, and exhibiting evident marks of a Tiger's paw.

"Ah! this accounts for his facing us as he did," said Mansfield, stooping down to examine the head of the Deer, "for in general, a jungle Tiger, who is not in the habit of seeing men, is glad to steal away unobserved. The brute must have just struck down the wounded Deer, and was too hungry to abandon his prey without making a fight for it. However, that is all well over now, so let us be thankful, and get out of this infernal long grass with as little delay as possible; there may be more of the family here yet for all we know."

"Od preserve us, Captain! dinna be speakin' that way—it 's enough to fright a body out o' his wits. Haste ye, lads, haste ye, we 'll awa hame as fast as we can, and if you ever catch me plouthering through long grass again, you may cut my lugs aff." So saying, the Doctor shouldered his fusee, and began to force his way through the tangled grass with desperate energy.

Having gained the open ground, a council of war was held, and, as the sun was already high, it was agreed, much to the Doctor's relief, that the party should return to breakfast, and send out their *Coolies* for the game.

"The Lord be thanked for all His mercies!" exclaimed the Doctor, fervently, when this plan was decided upon.

But, alas! short-sighted mortal, thou art not yet at home. Little dost thou know of the many dangers which beset the path of the *Forest Ranger*.

"Come, Doctor, cheer up, man," cried Mansfield, after they had proceeded some distance in silence; "you look as melancholy as a gib-cat, or a man who is kept by an undertaker to let out at funerals. What with the Glenlivat last night, and the Tiger this morning, your brains appear to be addled."

"Hoot, Captain, dinna' say nae more about the Glenlivat, I have had nae luck since that confounded black bottle was put upon the table, and my head is just throughother with it to-day. Faith, you may say that a man wad need a cool head, and a steady hand, afore he yokes to this jungle work; it's just a perfect tempting o' Providence; and, if once I get safe back to the tents, by my troth, you may whistle on your thumb long enough afore you catch me at it again. But, Heaven save us!—what 's that?" shouted the Doctor, springing behind Mansfield, and seizing him by the arms, as a tremendous crash was heard amongst the bamboos, accompanied by a shrill scream, like the sound of a cracked trumpet,

"*Huttee! Huttee!*" shouted the *Jemmadar*, darting behind the shelter of a tree, and beckoning the others to follow his example.

"Down! down, for your lives!" exclaimed Mansfield, in an audible whisper, at the same time crouching behind a tree, and cocking his rifle. "This must be the far-famed solitary Elephant, which has been committing such ravages of late on the edge of the Forest; and, if we can manage to kill him, it will be a glorious victory."

The Doctor groaned aloud, in agony of spirit.

"Now, lads, mind what you are about, and if you only behave steadily, the day is our own. Keep perfectly still till he shows himself:—when I whistle he will lower his head to listen from whence the sound comes—take a steady aim at the hollow in his forehead, just above the insertion of the trunk, and, when I whistle a second time, fire together. But take care that you only fire one barrel, reserve the other and dash off, two to the right and two to the left, so that if he does not fall, he may find a clear space to make his first rush. They are stupid, short-sighted animals, and if you keep quiet, we shall probably have time to re-load before he discovers us; at all events we shall have our second barrels ready. Now, mind these directions; and you, Doctor, do, like a good fellow, try to keep your wits about you: everything depends upon our steadiness, and the slightest mistake may cost us our lives."

"The Lord have mercy on us! This is awfu' work!" groaned the poor Doctor, casting a rueful glance at his favourite Mons Meg.

There was a moment of breathless silence. Another fearful crash was heard, and the gigantic brute, bursting into the open space, brandished aloft his ponderous trunk, like a Knight entering the lists to defy all comers, and screamed forth his shrill note of defiance. He was a stupendous animal, a perfect mountain of flesh, full twelve feet high, with enormous tusks, and his little, twinkling, red eye, glared with the fire of madness.

Flourishing his trunk about, he snuffed the tainted air, and his scream of rage, as he stamped upon the ground, announced that he was aware of the close proximity of his enemies, although he had not yet decided in which direction to make his headlong charge.

"Now, lads, steady, and reserve your fire till the proper time."

Mansfield gave a low whistle.

The Elephant started, cocked his ears, and bent down his head in the attitude of listening. He was just in the right position, and Mansfield was in the act of raising his rifle, when, crack went Mons Meg, with a report like a six-pounder, and the Doctor, throwing down his weapon, took to his heels, roaring lustily that the monster was after him. The poor Doctor's nerves had got the better of him, and, by an involuntary twitch of his forefingers, he had pulled the trigger when he least expected it.

Mansfield and Charles fired, and both balls took effect in the head of the Elephant, making the blood flow copiously; but being discharged almost at random, and not planted in the correct spot, they only acted as stimulants to his rage. Uttering a shrill scream, he dashed madly forward, his mouth wide open, his tail on end, and his trunk upraised, to crush all which opposed his headlong career.

Mansfield and Charles darted to one side, and fled for shelter behind the stem of a large teak tree. But the poor Doctor, whose senses were completely bewildered, ran blindly forward, and his red jacket, being much too conspicuous an object to escape the notice of the enraged Elephant, his fate appeared inevitable.

In vain did the panting wretch twist, and turn, and dodge amongst the trees, like a hunted jackal. The destroyer was close at his heels, following every turn with the perseverance of mortal hate. His strength was failing fast, and the fearful chase appeared to be drawing to a close. The trunk of the Elephant was already stretched forward to grasp him, when he made a sudden turn; the Elephant overshot his mark, and, for one moment, was at fault, apparently uncertain in which direction his victim had fled. The Doctor, seeing his advantage, began, with all diligence, to climb the tree behind which he had sheltered himself. He was already several feet from the ground, and his arm was outstretched to grasp a branch which would have raised him to a place of safety, when the Elephant, catching a hasty glimpse of him, dashed forward with redoubled fury, twisted his trunk round his legs, hurled him to the ground, rushed upon him, as he lay, stunned and bleeding, and, kneeling down, drove at him, furiously, with his enormous tusks, burying them up to the very root.

At this moment, Mansfield, who had followed the chase, dodging cautiously from tree to tree, in hopes that some lucky turn might give him a steady shot at the Elephant's head, came in sight of the bloody scene.

"The Lord have mercy on his soul, for he is beyond the aid of man!" exclaimed he, dropping the butt-end of his rifle to the ground, and leaning against a tree, sick and giddy at the ghastly sight.

The Elephant rose from his knees, picked up the body of the unfortunate Doctor in his trunk, tossed it to a short distance, and stood gazing on his victim, with flaming eyes, as if gathering fresh breath, before he rushed at him again, to finish the work of death, by trampling him with his feet.

"By Heavens you shall not complete your bloody work!" muttered Mansfield, grinding his teeth, and raising his rifle, with a steadiness of hand which never forsook him, even in the most desperate situations. The deadly bullet sped true to the mark, entering the eye, and burying itself in the brain of the Elephant. The gigantic brute uttered one shrill scream of mingled rage and pain, and, sinking slowly to the ground, rolled over like a falling tower.

Charles, followed by the *Jemmadar*, now came running to the scene of action, and, by way of making sure, discharged both barrels into the head of the Elephant; but he moved not, Mansfield's shot had done the work effectually.

"And so there is an end of poor Mc.Phee," said Mansfield, casting a melancholy look on the breathless body of the poor Doctor, as it lay at his feet, covered with blood and dust. "I feel a sad remorse of conscience for having persuaded the poor fellow to join in a dangerous sport for which he was so ill adapted. But it is worse than useless to make vain lamentations now. *Kamah*, do you cut a few stout bamboos; we must prepare something in the shape of a litter to carry home the body." And Mansfield proceeded, instinctively, to re-load his rifle, whilst his proud lip quivered, and the unbidden tear started to his eye, for, with all his haughty exterior, he had the soft heart of a woman. Charles, completely overcome by the scene, threw himself at the root of a tree, and buried his face in his hands. And even the savage features of the *Jemmadar* were softened into something like pity, as he stood, with folded arms, gazing on the work of destruction.

"By Heavens, he still breathes!" cried Mansfield, dashing his rifle to the ground, and flying to raise the head of the poor Doctor, as a faint groan reached his ear. "This is indeed miraculous!"—and hastily tearing open the jacket, he discovered, to his infinite joy, that, although his face was deadly pale, and his clothes smeared with blood and dirt, the Doctor's body was perfectly uninjured.

It appeared that the Elephant, blinded, probably, by the blood which flowed from the wounds in his forehead, had missed his aim, and instead of transfixing his victim, as he intended, had buried his tusks in the ground, on each side of his body, thus holding him down, as if within the prongs of an enormous pitchfork, and, of course, covering him with the blood which flowed from his own wounds. In short, the Doctor, in spite of his ghastly and blood-stained figure, had escaped with no other injury than being stunned and severely bruised by the first toss. A strong dose of brandy, which Mansfield poured down his throat, soon revived him, and so far restored his spirits that he was enabled to examine the head of his fallen enemy, and discovered, to his immeasurable satisfaction, that some straggling drops of the *grit-shot* had actually taken effect.

"Faith, Meg, my woman," said he, apostrophizing the old fusee, which the *Jemmadar* had picked up and restored to him, "you have had a tight morning's work of it, and, by my troth, it will be long enough afore ye hae the like again, at least in my company. Captain, a wee drap mair out o' your bottle, if you please, for I feel a kind o' fainting about my heart. But, stout or faint, it will ne'er forget the gude turn ye hae done me this day. Here is your health, and my blessing be upon you and your trusty weapon!"

So saying, the Doctor gulped down his brandy, while the big tears of gratitude dimmed his eye, and, finding himself wonderfully refreshed, limped off toward the camp, supported by his two young companions.

CHAPTER XI.

THE NIGHT MARCH.

"WELL, Doctor, how fares it with you?" asked Mansfield, pulling aside the canvass door, and thrusting his head into the Doctor's tent, about three hours before daylight, on the morning after the memorable Elephant-hunt, which had so nearly proved fatal to poor Mc. Phee.

"Wha 's yon?" muttered the Doctor, with a grunt like a sick bear; partially opening his eyes, and suddenly closing them again, to exclude the light of the lantern which Mansfield carried in his hand. "What ails you, you misleer'd loon, to gang stavin' about the camp at this time o' night, wi' your cutty sark, and your lang spauls o' legs, and your bit bowet in your hand, for a' the world like the troubled speerit o' a departed tinkler, walking the earth in search o' his breeks? If you canna' sleep yoursel', Sir, I wish ye would find some other place to play your cantraips in, and no disturb the rest o' honest folk, that want to sleep." And the Doctor, turning his back upon the unwelcome intruder with a stifled groan, and a catching of the breath, which showed that the effort cost him considerable pain, drew the bedclothes over his head, and settled himself as if determined to answer no further question.

"I beg your pardon, my dear Doctor, for disturbing you," replied Mansfield, smiling at the poor Doctor's crusty humour. "I merely came to inquire after your health, and to ask whether you are well enough to undertake a march this morning, for we have a long way to go, and it is high time for us to think of striking the camp, if we are to move."

"Umph!" grunted the Doctor, tucking his knees up to his chin, and pulling the bedclothes farther over his head with an impatient jerk, as he felt the cold air creeping round the walls of the tent.

"But I see you are still in great pain, and am afraid you must be more seriously injured than you at first supposed. Come, man, let me look at you. I suspect you ought to lose a little blood, or, at all events, a repetition of the hot fomentation you applied last night, might help to relieve you. Shall I call Heels, and desire him to prepare some hot water?"

"Where the deil did you learn the doctoring trade, may I ask?" growled the Doctor, thrusting his black muzzle from under the bedclothes, and looking askance at Mansfield over his shoulder: "do you suppose, Sir, that I took out my degree at the College of Edinburgh for nathing? or that I am soft enough to lie here, and let mysel' be sticket, and plotted wi' hot water, like an auld soo, by a daft, harumscarum, throughother, bletherin' loon o' a Sodger, that has nae mair knowledge o' the noble science of pharmacy than my Granny?—and no that same—for she, honest woman, had some skill o' the rhumatis, and was no' an ill *Howdy*, at a pinch.—Awa! out o' that, I say, and dinna fash me nae mair wi' your havers, for I 'm just perfect ramfeezled and disjaskit for want o' rest."

"Well, well, Doctor," said Mansfield, striving to suppress a laugh, as he approached the bed, and patted the Doctor gently on the shoulder, "don't be so sulky about it, you old Bear; there is no necessity for your moving, unless you like it; so keep yourself quiet, and try to sleep. I shall call you when breakfast is ready, and hope to find your temper improved, as well as your bodily ailments. Adieu, my old boy, and pleasant dreams to you."

"Come back here, Captain," cried the Doctor, poking his head from under the clothes, and extending his long bony hand towards Mansfield, who was about to retire. —"Come back here, I tell you, and shake hands with me. Hoot, fie, Sir! what ails you to be in sic a dooms hurry? I thought ye might hae kent better than to hae taken a cankered body at his word, yon way."

"Well, old Sulky," said Mansfield, returning, and taking the Doctor's hand in his, "what is the matter now?"

"You maun excuse me," said the poor Doctor, squeezing his hand affectionately; "you maun excuse me, Sir, for being a wee bit cankered ways this morning. Ye ken, Sir, I 'm gae short in the temper at the best o' times; and I 'm so sair birzed and churted, that, between that and the want o' rest, I 'm just a wee bit mair cantankerous than ordinar. It was an ill-done thing,—it was an unco ill-done thing in me, Sir, to speak sae short to you, to whom I owe my life. But I hope you 'll excuse me, Captain, and believe that I 'm no ungratefu', although the pain has made me a wee crabbit like."

"No, no, my dear Doctor," said Mansfield, returning the pressure of his hand. "I know your honest heart too well to suspect you of ingratitude; and a little fretfulness is excusable in one who has passed a sleepless night of suffering; so pray, do not make yourself uneasy about it, but keep quiet; and, if you can only get a few hours' sleep, I have no doubt you will awake in such a good humour, that a child might play with you."

"Thank you, thank you, Captain," said the Doctor, squeezing his hand hard;—"It 's o'er good o' you to forgie me sae easily, and I 'm just ashamed of mysel' for giving way to pain, and lying here, girning like an auld wife. I believe it 's best for me to rise after a', for I canna sleep; and, as there are nae bones broken, the exercise o' riding, and a good sweat, will, maybe, do me good.—Heels, ye black sinner!—Heels, I say! bring me my clothes." So saying, the Doctor, with one mighty effort, and one fearful grunt, kicked his long legs out of bed, and sat upright.

Mansfield, after trying in vain to dissuade him from his purpose—for the Doctor was as obstinate as a mule when once he got a crotchet in his head—lighted a candle from his lantern, and departed to rouse the camp, leaving the Doctor to be dressed by Heels, who was striving, as gently as possible, to insinuate his battered limbs into the legs and sleeves of his garments. This operation, however, was not completed without extorting sundry groans and curses from the irritable patient, who, between the twitches of pain, might be heard muttering, between his clenched teeth,

"D—n the muckle black beast! I believe he has yerkit every bane in my body out o' its place; but I will hae my ain way, in spite o' him. I will rise, though the Deil should girn in my face."

It is not yet within three hours of daylight; but the moon, although sinking towards the western horizon, and now partially concealed by the waving tree-tops, still sheds a broken light upon the drowsy camp, chequering the dew-bespangled grass with strange fantastic shadows, and ever-changing spots of sparkling light. The wandering night-wind sighs through the Forest, wafting to the ear the melancholy murmur of the lonely river, as, in solitary grandeur, it glides along its dark mysterious course, far, far away into the unknown wilderness. But no sound of life is there—no living thing is seen to move in that sequestered spot. The white-robed figures of the natives, stretched at full length upon the ground, look like sheeted corpses in the cold moonlight. Silence reigns within the tents, and the death-like calm, which pervades the whole scene, tends to impress the mind of the beholder with a solemn feeling of awe, as if he gazed upon a spot which, once indeed, had teemed with life, but over which the cold breath of the destroying angel had passed, during the silent watches of the night, leaving the forest winds, as they howled through the wilderness, to sing the dirges of the unburied dead.

But hark!—the cheerful notes of a bugle rise full and clear upon the still air, rousing the startled echoes, which slumbered deep amidst the gloomy arches of the Forest; and, at that joyous sound, the slumbering camp, which so lately presented an image of death, suddenly bursts into life, as if aroused from its trance by the mighty voice of a magician. The active Lascars are already busy in knocking up the tent-pegs; their wildly-chanted song keeping time to the rapid stroke of their mallets. The Horse-keepers bestir themselves to rub down and saddle their masters' steeds; the proud animals snorting and pawing the ground, as if impatient of their long rest, and eager for the chase. A confused jingling of bells, mingled with the grunting of camels, and the faint lowing of oxen, announce that the beasts of burden are also on the move. The dusky figures of the native servants may be seen flitting about like evil spirits, and jostling each other, in eager haste to pack up and despatch their masters' baggage. Groups of women and children, shivering in the cold morning air, crouch closely around the numerous fires, for which the old litter of the horses has furnished them a ready material: — their gaudy-coloured dresses, picturesque figures, and graceful attitudes, now thrown out in strong relief against the dark background of trees, and again shrouded in comparative darkness, as the expiring fire, occasionally replenished by a handful of straw or dry leaves, suddenly sends up a bright sheet of bickering flame, and again subsides into a dull red glow. Here the kneeling form of a camel is distinctly seen by the light of a neighbouring fire, gnashing his long tusks, and threatening, with out-stretched neck, the busy natives who are employed in arranging his load; and there the gigantic form of the stately Elephant may be faintly traced, advancing slowly from amidst the surrounding darkness, like a moving tower. Whilst, from the remoter clumps of trees, where the deepened gloom renders the actors of the busy scene invisible, the wild song of the Camel-drivers, intermixed with hearty maledictions denounced against the ancestors of some restive brute, which unwillingly submits itself to be accoutred for the march, come faintly borne on the night wind. Old *Kamah* is the only one of the busy throng who appears unoccupied, as he leans against the stem of a tree, smoking a cheroot, and bearing in his hand a flaming torch, with which, in the capacity of guide, he has prepared himself, to direct the steps of the travellers through the dark paths of the Forest, as well as to scare any wild animal which may happen to cross their path during the hour of darkness which must intervene between the setting of the moon and the appearance of daylight.

In little more than an hour from the time the signal for moving had been given, every tent was struck, and the last camel loaded. And Mansfield, who maintained a sort of military discipline in his hunting camp, having remained to see the latest straggler quit the ground, our three friends mounted their horses, and, turning their backs upon the deserted camp-ground, struck into the Forest by a different path from the one by which they had arrived; it being their intention to return to the Hills by a circuitous route, through the plains, where Mansfield expected to fall in with wild Hog and Antelope.

The moon had by this time set; and, notwithstanding the light of the torch which old *Kamah* carried in front, the horsemen found some difficulty in preventing their horses from falling in the rugged path, along which, in spite of the deepened gloom, occasioned by the overhanging trees, their savage guide pursued his onward course, with a steadiness of purpose, and swiftness of foot, which appeared almost miraculous.

A little more than an hour's riding sufficed to carry them through the denser part of the Forest, which was traversed almost in silence; the constant attention necessary to prevent their horses from stumbling over roots of trees, and other impediments, keeping them too fully occupied to admit of much conversation; neither did they encounter any of the savage denizens of the Forest, although, more than once, a suspicious rustling among the branches made the poor Doctor's heart rise to his throat, and forced upon his recollection, with fearful distinctness, all the ghastly tales he had ever heard of night attacks from Tigers and wild Elephants.

The first gray tints of morning were beginning to appear, as they emerged from the dense bamboo jungle, and entered a romantic valley, flanked by lofty hills, wooded almost to the top, and terminating in abrupt rocky crags, which reared their gray and thunder-riven summits to the clouds.

And now streaks of purple and gold are spreading gradually over the Eastern sky, against which is traced the fine bold outline of the mountain, which appears to rise perpendicularly from the path, like a wall of black marble; but darkness still broods over the valley, and the silence of night is unbroken, save by the distant sound of falling water, or the wild plaintive cry of a stray plover.

"The Lord be about us! what na eldrich skirl is yon?" whispered the Doctor, seizing Charles's arm with a convulsive grasp, as the silence was suddenly broken by an unearthly voice, apparently amongst the rocks above, uttering a loud and sudden *Waugh O! Waugh O!* followed by a half-suppressed scream, as of a person in the act of being strangled. "Oh! Maister Charles, hear to that—what can it be? It is surely something no canny."

Waugh O! Waugh O! replied that wild mysterious voice, so close, that it appeared to the Doctor to be shrieking in his very ears—then an awful pause, and again the wailing cry was heard, but at so great a distance, that it appeared to proceed from some wandering spirit of darkness, flitting from place to place with more than mortal speed.

"Why, I really do not know what to make of it," replied Charles: "I should take it to be the voice of some wild animal, probably a Hyena, only that I am puzzled to account for the sudden and noiseless manner in which it moves from place to place."

"Na! na! Maister Charles, there is something no just so canny as a wild beast there, take my word for it. But we had better ride on and ask the Captain; for if we bide here any longer, it will, maybe, come and grip us in the dark." So saying, the Doctor clapped spurs to his horse, and cantered after Mansfield, who had now got some distance ahead.

"Heard what?" asked Mansfield, smiling at the

anxious manner with which the Doctor inquired whether he had "heard *yon*."—"Do you mean the Owl?"

"The Hoolet, Sir?"

"Yes, just the *Hoolet*, as you call it; for I can assure you the savage cry you heard just now, although I confess it sounds rather unearthly, is nothing more than the cry of the great horned Owl. Often and often, during my rambles in the Forest, have I been warned of the approach of day by that same ghostly watchman, and well do I know his ugly voice."

"A Hoolet! a Hoolet!" cried the Doctor. "Od, Sir, do you think to mak a fool o' me, and gar me believe that sic an unearthly skirl as yon, came frae the throat of a Hoolet, or ony other bird that ever was clockit? Na, na, Sir! I 'll no believe the like o' yon—you maun no hae heerd it right. That sound was na uttered by ony craiter o' this world, and sae some o' us will find to our cost ere lang."

"What the Devil do you suppose it is then?" asked Mansfield impatiently.

"Whist, Captain! speak laich, for ony sake," whispered the Doctor, drawing closer to him, and seizing him by the arm. "It 's the *Banshee*, Sir—it 's the *Banshee*, as sure as I 'm a miserable sinner; and tak my word for 't, nae good ever comes o' hearing her ill-omened wail. A Hoolet, indeed! Na, na, that 's nae Hoolet!" and the Doctor shook his head mournfully; for although a sensible man in other respects, he had never been able entirely to divest himself of the superstitious ideas which had been instilled into his mind, almost with his mother's milk, and like many of his countrymen, in the same sphere of life, fully believed in the existence of that harbinger of death, the *Banshee.*

"Well, well, Doctor," replied Mansfield, laughing, "you, being a Scotchman, ought to know more about the *Banshee* than I do; but if that be she, I can only say, her style of singing does but little credit to the country from whence she comes."

"She was na singing—she was greetin',"—replied the Doctor, with great *naïveté.*

"Well, laughing or greeting, she has a cursed ugly voice of her own. But hark ye, Doctor," continued Mansfield, unslinging his rifle, and carefully examining the caps by the light of the torch, to satisfy himself that they had not been injured by the damp—"you had better not lag so far behind as you did just now, for the *Jemmadar* tells me this ravine is dreadfully infested by Tigers; and if we fall in with one of these fly-by-night gentlemen, retiring to his lair with an empty stomach, you will find it rather a more serious business than hearing the *Banshee*, although you appear to think that bad enough."

"Bad enough, bad enough, indeed," muttered the poor Doctor, plying the spurs vigorously, and urging the unwilling Smiler into a trot.

The party had proceeded about a quarter of a mile, and had reached a turn in the road, which being overhung by a dense mass of trees, was so intensely dark, that, without the assistance of the torch, the horsemen could not have seen their own length in front of them, when the Doctor's horse, which as usual had fallen behind the rest, suddenly stopped short, and, uttering a loud snort, began to tremble violently, as if overcome by mortal fear.

"Captain! Captain!" shouted the Doctor, plying his stick furiously in the vain attempt to make Smiler move, "Oh, Captain, for ony sake come here!—the beast surely sees something uncanny, for he 'll no stir an inch, in spite o' me!"—and again a shower of blows descended upon poor Smiler's sounding ribs.

Mansfield and Charles, who were a little in advance, immediately pulled up; but ere they could turn their horses' heads, a terrific roar was heard—a crash—a wild scream of agony—and the ill-starred Doctor, with his struggling horse, were borne to the earth by some heavy body, which, flashing for an instant in the torch-light, darted from the bank above with the velocity of a thunderbolt.

It was too dark to distinguish objects on the ground; but it was evident, from the violent struggle which ensued, and the piteous moaning of the poor horse, that he was trying to free himself from the grasp of some powerful animal.

"*Bagh! Bagh!*" shouted the *Jemmadar*, hurling his torch in the direction from whence the sound proceeded.

"Here, *Kamah*, hold this beast," cried Mansfield, jumping from his terrified horse, and throwing the reins to the *Jemmadar;* as, by the faint light of the expiring torch, he discovered a Panther clinging to the prostrate body of the horse, with his teeth and claws firmly fixed in the throat of the dying animal, who had now almost ceased to struggle, and drew his breath in thick gasping sobs, as the throttling savage, with a malignant growl of

THE DEATH OF SNIDER.

satisfaction, sucked the warm blood from his ebbing veins.

"This is a bad light," said Mansfield, shaking his head, and recovering the rifle, which he had brought to his shoulder, the flame of the torch having sunk so low, as to render surrounding objects almost invisible. "I wish to Heaven it would blaze up again, and allow me to see whereabouts the poor Doctor lies, for I have as good a chance of hitting him as the Panther, if I risk a shot in the dark. Ha! that will do."

A sudden gust of wind fanned the expiring torch into a bright flame, lighting up the ghastly scene with more brilliancy than ever. The Panther, startled by the sudden light, quitted his hold of the horse, and grinning fiercely, shrunk into a crouching attitude, as if prepared to spring on his assailant.

"Now, then, you snarling devil!" muttered Mansfield, laying his cheek against the stock of his rifle, with as much cool deliberation as if he were about to fire at a mark; but ere he had brought the fine-drawn sight to bear upon its object, a convulsive kick from the dying horse struck the fiery end of the torch, and sent it flying among the bushes.—The air was filled with a shower of glittering sparks—and again all was darkness.

"A spear! a spear!" shouted Mansfield, mad with disappointment, throwing aside his rifle, and snatching at a spear which Charles carried in his hand. "Quick, man, before he moves! I can pin him to the ground where he lies.—Ha! who fired that shot?"

A bright flash—a sharp report—the whistle of a

bullet—and then a gasping bubbling sound, was heard, as of an animal stifling in his own blood.

"Hurra!" shouted the Doctor, from amidst the gloom; the unexpected but welcome cheer coming to the ears of his companions like a voice from the dead. "Hurra, lads! he 's dead, he 's dead!—Come here, some o' you. For ony sake, come here and help me to get my leg out frae below the horse, for it 's amaist smashed. This way, this way! ye needna be 'feard; I 've dang the life out o' him fairly.

"What do you think of the auld Doctor, noo?" exclaimed Mc.Phee, brandishing, with a triumphant air, a huge horse-pistol, as Mansfield and Charles busied themselves in extricating him from the dead horse. "Was na that weel done, Captain?—Easy! easy wi' me, lads, for I 'm that sair birzed wi' yesterday's work, that I canna thole to be touched, amaist. Wasna that weel done, I say, Sir? Od, ye hae often laughed at my old Grandfaither's pistol, but I telt you it would come to use some day or other, and sae it has, at last. O, man, but I 'm stiff!" continued he, as he got upon his legs, with the assistance of his two companions, and seated himself on a bank.

"By Heavens, it was well done!" exclaimed Mansfield, grasping the Doctor's hand with enthusiasm; for he was really attached to the worthy man, and his heart was filled with gratitude to Heaven for his wonderful escape, and admiration of the unwonted spirit he displayed on the occasion. "Well done, and coolly, as any thing I ever saw. Why, Doctor, you have come out quite in a new character—a very dare-devil;—but, as you say, it was fortunate for you, and, indeed, for all of us, that you had the old pistol at hand, and presence of mind to use it; for, to tell you the truth, when the light was extinguished, I began to have rather unpleasant forebodings, as to the termination of our adventure."

"Faith, ye may say that," replied the Doctor: "I was sae dumb-foundered, and taken by surprise at first, when I found mysel' sprawling on the ground, like a cripple puddock, and heard the worry, worry o' the bloodthirsty deevle, as he rugged and rived at poor Smiler's throat, that I just gied mysel' up for lost—and, then that awfu' cry we heard the now came into my mind.—Ye needna laugh, Sir, for I tell ye there was something no canny in that cry.—And I thought my hour was come, and then I prayed for mercy on my sinfu' soul. —And wi' that, I appeared to get new strength and courage.—And then I minded o' the auld pistol I had put in the holster; and the wee drap Heeland blood I hae in my veins began to boil.—And, says I to mysel', 'D—n you, for a muckle girnin cat! I'm a match for ye yet!'—And, wi' that, I lifted mysel' cannily on my elbow, and whippit the pistol out o' the holster, and clappit it to his lug, and dang the life out o' him afore he had time to wink. Ha! ha! Captain, you see there is some good stuff in the auld Doctor yet; although I maun confess, my nerves rather got the better o' me yesterday. But that was a' the effects o' the Glenlivat, ye ken—Eh, Captain?"—and the worthy Doctor grinned, and rubbed his hands with evident satisfaction.

"Tut, tut! never mind what happened yesterday," said Mansfield, encouragingly; "you have behaved like a man this morning, at all events, and so 'let byganes be byganes,' as you say yourself. But are you not hurt?—I am sure you got a terrible roll."

"Hoot, fie, no!" replied the Doctor, "I came down in a fine saft place, amang the lang grass. But I'm so cursedly warped in the back, after yesterday's toolzie, that the shake I got has just put me a wee through-other, and gart me feel faint-like about the heart. Maister Charles, if ye will just be good enough to look in the other holster, and gie me a wee bit flask ye'll find there, I think a drap out o' it will maybe do me good. The horse-pistol has done us a good turn already, and now we'll try what effect the pocket-pistol will hae—Ha! ha! ha! Captain."—Here the Doctor chuckled, and poked Mansfield facetiously in the ribs, "You see I'm an old soldier, and aye march with twa pistols—ane for my enemies, and anither for my friends. Here, Sir, tak a sup o't—it will warm your heart this cold morning."

The dew having fallen so heavily during the night, as almost to wet through their thin clothing, neither Mansfield nor Charles made any objection to the Doctor's proposal; and Charles, who was blessed with a youthful appetite, that never failed him under any circumstances, having produced some biscuits and a piece of cold venison, from the holsters of his saddle, our three friends seated themselves on the grass; and the energy with which the worthy Doctor applied himself to gnawing the bones, after having whetted his appetite by a hearty pull at his pocket-pistol, proved that, however stiff his other joints might be, his jaws, at least, had escaped uninjured.

Day had, in the mean time, been rushing on with that rapidity peculiar to a tropical climate, where light succeeds darkness almost instantaneously; and, ere their hasty meal was finished, nature burst into life; and the glorious sun, rising in fiery splendour, poured a flood of golden light into that sequestered valley—The gloomy mountain-pass, which, an hour before, in the darkness and silence of night, appeared a fitting haunt for prowling beasts and birds of evil omen, now smiling in all the luxuriant beauty of oriental scenery. The woods, sparkling with dewdrops, festooned with beautiful flowering creepers, and echoing to the tender cooing of turtle-doves; birds of gorgeous plumage, wheeling, in joyous gambles, amongst the lofty tree-tops; the balmy morning air, loaded with perfume, and breathing melody,—all conspired to soothe and calm the ruffled spirits, to soften one's very nature, and make the most careless observer, in his inmost heart, acknowledge and worship the Almighty Power, which had given birth to so much beauty.

"What a Heavenly scene is this!" exclaimed Charles, after gazing for some minutes in silent admiration.

"It is, indeed, a Heavenly scene," replied Mansfield; "and yet how treacherous are its beauties!—How strange the thought, that this lovely spot should be the chosen haunt of wild beasts—its perfumed atmosphere a compound of deadly vapours;—looking an earthly Paradise, yet teeming with pestilence and death, like a lovely woman, with the exterior of an angel, cherishing a demon in her heart! Methinks a group of dancing wood-nymphs would form an appropriate foreground to such a picture; and yet, behold the stern reality—A band of armed men—a naked savage, but one degree removed from the beasts that perish!—mangled carcasses—death in its most ghastly form—and the steam of reeking gore, ascending to Heaven, mingled with the incense of flowers! How forcibly doth such a contrast as this bring to one's recollection the melancholy truth, that fallen man has brought sin and death into the world!"

"Indeed, Sir, what you say is o'er true. It's just a mischancy bit, this same glen; and, bonny though it be, I wish we were well out o' it; for, after what we hae heard this blessed morning, it were a mere tempting o' Providence to bide here ony longer. And, Oh, Sir," casting a rueful glance at the mangled remains of poor Smiler, "is it no a sair sight to look at that poor beast lying cold and stiff there, and the bonny green grass steepit in his blood, and the sun shining sae bright, and the bit birdies singing sae blythe and happy, as if there was nae such thing as death in the world? And it would be just the same, though you or me were lying there in his place.—Poor Smiler—poor Smiler; ye were a good honest beast, although a wee short in the temper, like myself. But you and me will never cast out nae mair." And the poor Doctor, drawing the back of his large hand across his eyes, pulled a flint and steel from his pocket, and proceeded to strike a light for his cheroot, humming, as he did so, a melancholy Scotch ditty.

"Well, Doctor, you certainly are an unlucky dog in some things," said Charles, smiling at the Doctor's rueful countenance; "and I must say that, of late, you have come in for monkey's allowance, or worse; but if you do get into scrapes, it must be allowed you have a wonderful knack of getting out of them again. Just look back to the last four and twenty hours: within that short space of time, you have been at the killing of a Tiger on foot; you have had an Elephant playing at pitch-and-hustle with your unfortunate carcass; and taken the scalp of a Panther, single-handed. And here you are, resting on your laurels, and smoking a cigar, as if nothing had happened—a trifle battered, to be sure, and minus your old horse, but covered with glory, and having a trophy in that Panther-skin, which will, no doubt, be preserved by the next ten generations of Mc.Phees, as a memento of their illustrious ancestor. Come, come, my dear Doctor, cheer up, and do not look so miserable about it; for, after all, you have much to be thankful for."

"Aye, Maister Charles, what you say is very true. I hae, indeed, much to be thankfu' for; and I trust I am no ungratefu' for the providential way in which my life has been spared. But, foolish though it be, I canna look at that poor beast, without feeling as if I had lost an auld and trusty friend." And the Doctor began to puff his cheroot furiously, as if annoyed with himself for being possessed of a good heart.

The baggage and followers had by this time come up, and the dead Panther having been placed upon the Elephant, a fresh horse was saddled for the Doctor.

The *Jemmadar* was dismissed with a handsome present of ammunition and tobacco; and, leaving the remains of poor Smiler to become a prey to the Vultures, the three Horsemen cantered off at a round pace, in hopes of reaching the village where they intended to halt, before the heat of the day had become oppressive.

The poor Doctor was so disconcerted by the loss of his faithful steed, that he did not recover his wonted spirits for the rest of that day; and, after having tried in vain to convince his companions that the mysterious voice, which they attributed to an Owl, was a supernatural warning of poor Smiler's tragical end, he gave up the point, and rode on, smoking his cheroot in moody silence. But, from that day to this, he never exhibits the Panther's skin, or tells the story of the Night March, without assuring his hearers that, "as true as death," he heard the *Banshee*.

CHAPTER XII.

THE HALT.

The blazing Indian sun was already high in the Heavens, and the reflected heat, from the scorched earth, was becoming painfully oppressive, ere our three Horsemen came in sight of the sequestered village, where they intended to halt for the day. The cool tank, near which it was situated, reflected brightly from its glassy surface, the struggling sunbeams which found their way through the dense grove of tamarind and Indian fig trees, by which it was overshadowed; promising to the wearied traveller the grateful luxuries of deep shade and a refreshing bath. The panting steeds, which, for the last hour, had been plodding along the deep sandy road, with drooping heads and languid steps, pricked their ears, expanded their wide nostrils, parched with heat and clogged with fine particles of sand; and, uttering a low neigh of satisfaction, started off at a lively canter, towards the welcome halting-place.

"The Lord be thanked!" exclaimed the Doctor, throwing himself from the saddle the moment he entered the grove, and stretching his gaunt limbs at full length under the shade of a tamarind-tree.

"The Lord be thanked! this day's work is over, any how," — and pulling a flint and steel from his hunting-pouch, he struck a light, applied the tinder to a formidably large Trichinopoly cheroot, which he had already deposited in the corner of his mouth; pulled the peak of his cap well over his face, folded his arms on his chest, and, closing his eyes, abandoned himself to the full enjoyment of the narcotic weed. "Hech, Sirs, but this is real luxury! Ye may talk o' the luxury o' a cigar to warm your nose on a frosty night, or a merescham pipe of old canaster, to keep the fog out o' a body's lungs on a misty morning, but gie me a shady tree, and a good long Trinchinopoly, after a twenty miles march, in an Indian sun. That 's the real luxury —that 's the thing to soothe the tingling nerves, and check the boiling o' the fevered blood, and fill a body's head wi' pleasant thoughts, and gar him feel as though he were in Paradise. Hech, Sirs, it 's fine,—it 's just a perfect cordial—"

"I am glad to see you looking so comfortable, my old boy," said Mansfield, as he loosened the girths, and removed the bridle from the head of his smoking horse. "I was afraid you would be completely knocked up, for it has been a long and a hot march, to say nothing of your adventure with the Panther; but, if we may judge by appearances, you seem to be in a fair way of recovering—"

"Hoot fie! what for no?" grunted the Doctor, without unclosing his eyes. "I 'm no' just that far through yet—Na, na, lad, it 's no' the rattling cart that coups the soonest; there 's a heap o' life in me yet, for a' that 's come and gane. That brulzie I had with the Elephant yesterday has gart the banes rattle in my skin a wee; and, as I telt you afore, I 'm a trifle warped in the back; but I 'm no going to coup the creels on you yet—na, na, I 'm finely noo—I 'm finely noo. Yon hot ride has done me a hantle o' good, although I maun confess it wasna the pleasantest remedy in the world. O man, but them sheroots are prime tobaccy. Will ye try ane, Captain?"

"Not now, thank you," replied Mansfield, as he busied himself in adjusting a halter round his horse's neck, and fastened him to the stem of a tree. "I must rub down poor little Challenger first, for he is steaming with heat, and I would not have him get a stroke of the land-wind for ten times his value. No, my beauty, I should never be able to mount myself so well again," continued Mansfield, patting affectionately the arched neck of the beautiful creature, whose fleetness had gained for him the *spear of honour* in many a well-contested field, and whose glossy gray skin was now changed to purple, by excessive heat and perspiration. The sagacious animal turned his head, as if he understood the compliment paid him, and gently rubbed his soft velvet muzzle against his master's bronzed cheek. "Ay, Chally, boy, give me a kiss; you and I have had many a hard day's work together, and shall have many more, please Fate, if care and good grooming be of any avail. Quiet, you little Tiger,—quiet, I say,—you are as full of tricks as a young monkey."

"Od, Captain, but that 's a fine canny beast o' yours," said the Doctor, raising himself lazily on one elbow. "Smiler, poor beast—he 's deed and gone now—Smiler and me were gae good friends, too, when our tempers warna out o' order; but, at the best o' times, I wadna like to play wi' him yon way. Na, na, he wasna to be compared to your horse, Captain."

"I should think not!" replied Mansfield, smiling at the simplicity of the Doctor, in attempting to draw a comparison between the defunct Smiler and his favourite Challenger.

"They say in Scotland, Sir, that a good man is good to his beast, and if that be true, you maun be an unco good man, and I as ill a ane; for there are you and Maister Charles, strapping away at your horses like two regular bred *Gorah-wallahs*, while I am lying here, at my ease, and that poor beast, you were good enough to gie me the loan o', standing reeking there, like a half-slockened lime-kiln. I 'm no' very good at the grooming, Sir, I 'm fear'd, but I 'll try what I can do."

"No, no, never mind, Doctor," replied Mansfield, "he is a hardy old fellow that, and well used to it; just loosen his girths, and throw your cloak over his loins, and there is no fear of him. See, here comes the *Cotwall*, so, if you wish to make yourself useful, you had better speak to him, and try to procure some forage for the horses, and some materials for our *tiffin*, for, it strikes me, we shall be quite ready for it by the time the servants arrive with the *cowrie-baskets*. Mind, Doctor, plenty of eggs, a fowl or two, and, I think, after this long march, we must treat our followers to a sheep."

"Aye, aye, Captain, let me alone for looking after the victualling department! I 'll take care that we have plenty. De'il hae me, if ever I seed the like o' yon!" continued the Doctor, as the *Cotwall* approached, shuffling along in his embroidered yellow slippers; his ample robes floating in the breeze, and twirling his mustache with that self-sufficient swaggering air, which your good Mussulman, particularly if he be a man in authority, thinks it necessary to assume, when about to address an inferior, or even an equal. "Just see to the airs the long, blackaviced, tinker-like, slouch o' a fellow is putting on. I 'm thinkin' he mistakes us for a parcel o' travelling half-caste Apothecaries; and, by my troth, we 're black enough, and dirty enough, to pass for any thing. Aye, I see fine what he would be at; he 's going to come the big man o'er us. Ha! ha! I 'll hae some fun with this birky."—Then, in a tone of command,—"*Idder aou*, you *Cotwall*."

The *Cotwall* advanced, twirling his mustache, with a supercilious grin, and stared the Doctor full in the face.

"Weel, Maister *Cotwall*, what vivars may this village o' yours afford? It looks gae poor like, I maun confess; but I suppose ye can get us a wheen eggs, and a howtawdy and a pickle strae for the naigs—eh?"

The *Cotwall* smiled a grim smile, but made no answer.

"What are ye girnin' at, ye black Pagan?" growled the Doctor, "hae ye nae English?"

"Engliss?" replied the *Cotwall*, with an impudent stare, "Engliss? O iss, Sar, Engliss I can speak very proper. Suppose Faringee man speak Engliss, that time I understand."

"Faringee man! Speak English! De'il be in his black skin, he takes me for a Portuguese cook, and says I canna speak English!"

Mansfield and Charles, who were watching the scene

with much interest, laughed till their sides ached, but did not attempt to spoil sport by interfering.

"Chickens!—Eggs!—Strae for the horses!" shouted the Doctor, at the very top of his voice. "That's plain English, I'm sure; do ye understand me now?"

"*Wah! wah!*" exclaimed the *Cotwall*, raising his eyebrows with a look of intelligence, "chickens!—yeggees!—abbah! now I understand. Suppose Faringee man give *buckshish* preshent—that time I make *in*quiry."

"Give present, indeed! Troth, my man, ye'r no' blate! What should I see in your ill-faurt face to gie you a present, ye muckle Malabar soo,—eh? when ye ken it's your duty to provide travellers wi' what they want, and to be ceevil to them into the bargain. Be off now, and get what I want directly, afore ye set my birse up, else I'll kick you, like a fut-ba', frae this to the bazarr, and back again. Start, I say!" and the Doctor raised his foot, as if about to carry his threat into effect.

"*Wah! wah!*—what for Faringee man make so much *bobbery*—eh?" replied the *Cotwall*, in an angry tone, but, at the same time, retiring a few paces, and looking rather aghast at the Doctor's warlike demonstrations. "Suppose Master speak civil word, that time I do Master's business." And, turning towards the village, with a less consequential strut than he had assumed at first, the *Cotwall* shuffled off, in no very amiable mood, to execute the Doctor's commands.

"Od's my life, things are come to a pretty pass indeed, when an M.D. o' the College of Edinburgh is taken for a half-caste Apothecary, or a Portuguese cook, bearded by a lousy *Cotwall*, and telt, to his very face, that he canna speak English!"—and the Doctor, uttering a surly grunt, threw himself once more at the root of the tree, and began to puff furiously at his cheroot.

"Well, Doctor, have you settled it at last?" cried Charles, laughing mischievously, and rather anxious to encourage the feud than otherwise. "I must say the fellow used you with but scant ceremony. I do believe he takes you for a half-caste in earnest."

"Never ye mind," replied the Doctor, rather sulkily; "strap away at your horse, Maister Charles, and let me alane to settle the *Cotwall;* I 'll gar him open his een, afore I 've done wi' him, else my name is no' Mc.Phee."

The *Cotwall* returned, before the Doctor's cheroot was finished, followed by two crouching villagers, one carrying in his hand a couple of half-starved, consumptive-looking chickens, and the other bending under a huge bundle of dirty litter. This, the *Cotwall* asserted, was the best the village afforded, and in a bullying tone demanded, not only double the price of the articles, but a present for his own trouble in procuring them.

The Doctor's blood began to boil, for he had a horror of being imposed upon by any one, and more particularly by a native: but, curbing his wrath, by a strong effort, he asked quietly why there were no eggs.

"Yegges, Sar!" replied the *Cotwall*, with an impudent grin—for the Doctor's quiet manner had inspired the bully with fresh confidence. "Yegges, no can find—this very poor village, Sar—cicken, in this village, no can make yeggees—look, Sar!"—pointing to the two wretched specimens of the *Gallinæ*, which were fluttering in the bony grasp of the no less wretched villager;

"that cicken too muchie tin—how can that cicken make yeggees—eh?"

The sneering tone, in which this was said, was too much for the Doctor's forbearance.

"De'il be in my skin, but I 'll learn you better manners, afore we part!" cried he, starting to his feet, and seizing the *Cotwall* by the beard. "How dare you stand there, girning in a Gentleman's face, ye lang-legged ne'er-do-weel. Is it no enough, that ye hae been rapping out lee upon lee, for the last ten minutes, till ye are amaist black in the face, without yokin at the hinnerend, to laugh at your ain wit—eh, you misleer'd loon?" Here the Doctor gave the unfortunate *Cotwall's* beard a tremendous shake, extorting a yell of agony from that dignified personage, and inspiring the timid natives, who accompanied him, with such mortal fear, that they dropped their loads, and fled for their lives.

"Will you ever presume to insult a Gentleman again?" shouted the Doctor, giving him another shake, that made his teeth rattle in his head. "Will you, you black sinner?"

"*Ne, Sahib!—Allah, Allah!*" shrieked the trembling *Cotwall.*

"Aha, my fine fellow! I thought I would make you open your eyes afore I was done wi' you. Do you think the hens will lay any eggs now, ye leein tyke? Will they, ye limb o' Satan—eh?" Here another tremendous shake.

"*Ne Sahib!* Master make pardon this one time—I very bad man—plenty lie I tell.—Master please to let go my beard, that time I make plenty yeggees come—plenty yeggees—I tell true word."

"Weel then, see that ye do so, and be quick about it. And I say!—just try if ye can persuade the hens to look a wee thing fatter at the same time—Do ye hear?" So saying, the Doctor relaxed his hold of the *Cotwall's* beard, and, spinning him round, gave him a shove, which projected him several yards on his way towards the village.

The crest-fallen Functionary, right glad to make his escape, shuffled off with great precipitation, till he thought himself at a safe distance, when he stopped, adjusted his disordered robes, stroked his insulted beard, to assure himself that it still adhered to his chin, and giving his mustache a fierce twirl, as he faced round towards the Doctor, spat upon the ground in token of insult and defiance.

"Ha! my lad, is that the way o't? Just bide there, till I get a grip o' your goat's beard again,"—and the Doctor, jumping once more to his feet, made a furious rush forward. But the *Cotwall*, like a yelping cur, who perceives that a stone is about to be flung at his head, turned tail, without further warning; and, starting off at a pace, which must have occasioned no little surprise in those accustomed to his usual stately official strut, never stopped till he found himself safely within the walls of the village.

"Hurra! here comes the *Peon*, with the *cowrie-baskets*, at last," cried Charles, rubbing his hands with glee, at the prospect of a good breakfast, as a tall, handsome-looking *Peon* approached, followed by two naked *Coolies*, covered with dust and perspiration, each balancing across his shoulder an elastic bamboo, from either end of which was suspended a circular rattan basket with a conical top, covered with green oilcloth, and secured by a brass padlock.

The wearied *Coolies*, having deposited their loads at the root of a tree, with a deep grunt, expressive of the relief they felt in so doing, rubbed their aching shoulders, and, approaching Mansfield in a crouching posture, with the palms of their hands brought together, and raised to their foreheads, in the attitude of supplication, patted their empty stomachs,—which had been drawn in for the occasion, till they nearly touched the back-bone,—in the most expressive manner. Mansfield, who perfectly understood their signals, smiled good-naturedly, and promised, that in consideration of the long march, a couple of sheep should be distributed amongst them, as soon as the other followers came up. At this joyful intelligence, the wrinkled stomachs immediately resumed their natural form ; all the fatigues of the march were forgotten ; and the poor simple-hearted creatures—to whom a good meal of animal food was an event in their lives—after making a number of the most profound *salaams,* bounded off to refresh themselves by a dip in the cool tank, and to prepare their primitive cooking apparatus for the promised feast.

" Now then, if we could only get a good fat hen to brander, and a wheen eggs to make an omelet, I 'm thinkin', wi' the help o' these cold vivars, and twa or three bottles o' this light claret, we may manage to make an indifferently-good breakfast, or *tiffin* rather ; for I 'm thinkin' the day has ta'en the turn afore now." So said the Doctor, half soliloquizing and licking his lips, as he busied himself in unpacking the contents of the *cowrie-baskets*, consisting of a cold buffalo's hump, a tongue or two, biscuits, rice, and other eatables; together with a goodly store of French claret, Hodson's ale, and brandy.

"Methinks you may do that same, with great safety, friend Æsculapius," said Mansfield, tapping him on the shoulder; "and say grace afterwards, with a clear conscience, provided you have breath enough left to do so, after lining your stomach with the many good things you have been enumerating. Why, man, here is a breakfast fit for a Prince, all ready to your hand—cold meat, biscuits, beer, claret! What would you have more?"

"Hoot fie, Sir; would ye hae us feed upon cauld junk, like ignorant Pagans, after sic a march as this, and us in the midst o' plenty? Na, na, Sir, I hae nae intention o' offending my stamach that way. We munna want the brandered hen, or the omelet, on no account. Let abe that tongue, Captain," continued the Doctor, as Mansfield was about to help himself to a slice, with his hunting-knife. "Let it abe, I say—mind, Sir, we are no' in the jungles now, and we maun study manners a little. Ye hae appointed me Clerk o' the kitchen, for the present, and I maun insist on feeding you like a Gentleman, whether ye will or no."

"Far be it from me, most sapient Doctor, to dispute your authority," replied Mansfield. "You shall order the time and manner of my feeding, as appears unto you most fitting, and shall have eggs and fowls to your heart's content, if it only be for the sake of bringing that fellow the *Cotwall* to his senses. I shall slip

Ayapah at him—I suspect the sight of a *Peon's* belt and silver badge coming from his friends, the travelling Apothecaries, will astonish him a little. Here, Ayapah!"

"*Sahib*," answered Ayapah—the tall handsome-looking *Peon* before mentioned—stepping up to Mansfield, making a respectful *salaam*, and remaining as steady as a Soldier on parade.

"Ayapah!" said Mansfield, speaking in Hindoostanee, "put on your belt again—go to the village, and bring me the *Cotwall*, by the ears."

"*Jo hookum, Sahib!*" replied Ayapah, without altering a muscle. And facing to the right-about, he marched away with a most soldier-like air.

"Had I told that fellow, Ayapah, to bring the *Cotwall's* head instead of his whole person, he would have gone upon his mission with equal coolness, and obeyed me to the letter," said Mansfield, smiling. "Ayapah!"—

"*Sahib!*"

"I have changed my mind about the *Cotwall*—you need not bring him by the ears. Just say I want him, and see that he comes."

"*Bhot Atcha, Sahib,*" replied Ayapah, making his *salaam* with the same imperturbable gravity, and marching off again with the same stately pace.

Ayapah soon returned, followed by the *Cotwall*, cringing like a rated hound. The *Peon's* belt of office had acted like a talisman. A single glance was sufficient to open the eyes of the astonished Functionary. Those whom he had foolishly taken for half-caste Apothecaries, and whom he fancied he might bully with impunity, turned out to be *Burrah Sahibs!*—real *Burrah Sahibs*

—there could be no doubt of the fact; for their *Peon* wore an embroidered shoulder-belt, and a silver badge. Such visiters seldom honoured his village by their presence. Had he only been commonly civil, he might have reckoned, with tolerable certainty, on a handsome present. But he had insulted them, and instead of receiving a present, was nigh having the beard torn off his chin. Oh! Mustapha! Mustapha!—what dirt hast thou been eating!

The *Cotwall's* cringing civility now became even more disgusting than his former insolence had been. The wretch grovelled in the dust. There was nothing good enough for their Excellencies—the *Burrah Sahibs*—Clean straw came tumbling in by waggon-loads—Hens laid eggs by word of command—The starved chickens were suddenly transformed into well-fed capons.—And a troop of Dancing-girls, dark-eyed Houries, from the neighbouring Pagoda, were sent for to charm their Highnesses into good humour, by their bewitching smiles and graceful movements.—Every man, woman, and child in the village, were the bounden slaves of their Mightinesses; and of these, the most devoted was Mustapha himself, who, not contented with exhausting his whole vocabulary of highflown Oriental compliments, made an ostentatious display of his disinterested zeal in their service, by banging the ears of an unfortunate *Ryot*, with the heel of his slipper, and calling him a cheating rascal, for daring to ask half the price for clean straw and fat capons, which he himself had demanded, half an hour before, for dirty litter and starved chickens.

In short, the amiable Mustapha spared no pains to make himself agreeable, and gain "Master's favour." But the *Burrah Sahib* was inflexible, and no *buckshish* was forthcoming. Mansfield turned a deaf ear to all his highflown compliments; and, after reading him a lecture on the impropriety of attempting to impose upon unfortunate Half-castes; and assuring him that the first time he heard of his being uncivil to any traveller, of any rank whatever, he would report his conduct to the Collector of the district, and have him removed from his situation; he dismissed him with merely the price of the things he had provided, whilst a handsome present was given to the Dancing-girls and other Natives.

This was touching the avaricious *Cotwall* in the right place. Had Mansfield broken a stick over his head, and given him a few rupees to buy a plaster withal, he had pocketed the affront with thanks. But to see his inferiors pocketing their rupees, whilst he, the Great Man, was sent away disgraced and empty-handed, was gall and wormwood to his grasping spirit.—As the Doctor remarked with a chuckle—

"It was touching the life o' the niggardly craiter—his heart's blood—the very marrow o' his banes."

The Doctor's culinary operations now progressed rapidly, and the good cheer he provided was done ample justice to by his hungry companions, after they had refreshed themselves by a change of dress, and a swim in the cool tank.

The tents arrived and were pitched. The *Shikaree* of the village was summoned to an audience, and reported that the surrounding country abounded with wild Hog, and that amongst them was a certain Boar of gigantic size, which had, for years, been the terror of the *Ryots*, and had laughed at the beards of the most skilful *Shikarees;* but which, he had no doubt, would fall beneath the invincible spear of his Highness—the terror and destroyer of wild beasts.

Scouts were despatched in all directions to gain intelligence of the mighty Boar. A goodly band of *Coolies* were ordered to be in attendance by to-morrow's dawn. A couple of sheep were killed, and distributed amongst the happy camp-followers; fires blazed in all directions; earthen pots boiled and bubbled; the light-hearted Natives, calculating on the morrow as a day of rest, abandoned themselves to all the joys of feasting and merriment; and, long after midnight, happy voices might be heard, chanting wild Hindoostanee airs to the simple accompaniment of the *zittar* or the *tom-tom.*

CHAPTER XIII.

BOAR-HUNTING.

"I DECLARE it is nearly ten o'clock! The sun is already hot enough to broil one's brains into an omelette, and still no sign of our Scouts returning."

So said Charles, pulling out his watch, and returning it to his pocket with an impatient gesture, as he sat, lounging indolently under the fly of the tent, the *kunnauts* of which were raised, and supported on bamboos, to act as a verandah, and to admit of a free circulation of air.

A substantial breakfast had already been disposed of. The horses had been visited, to ascertain that their feet were in good order after yesterday's march; that they had been well groomed, and that no water had been given them. Saddles, bridles, girths, and stirrup-leathers, had been carefully overhauled. Spear-heads had been sharpened to the last degree of keenness; and our three Nimrods having now nothing further to occupy their attention, were waiting, in a feverish state of impatience, for the return of the Scouts, who had been despatched, on the previous evening, to gain intelligence of the famous Boar.

The dense shade of the overhanging trees, tempered the heat of the land-wind, which sighed through the grove, rendering it cool and refreshing. But the straggling sunbeams, which here and there darted through the dense foliage, dancing and sparkling on the glassy surface of the tank, with intense, almost painful brilliancy; the glimpses of the open country, which were caught through the stems of the trees, showing the parched earth glowing like heated copper, and the tall palm-trees twisting and twining like gigantic snakes, in the fiery haze, bore ample testimony to the scorching heat of the tropical sun which blazed overhead.

A hundred *Coolies*—almost as wild-looking as the animals for which they were to beat—all nearly naked, and many of them armed with rusty matchlocks, hunting-spears, or wood-knives, were lounging about in picturesque groups under the shade of the trees. The old baggage Elephant, wearied with his long march, stood dozing listlessly under the shadow of a widely-spreading Banian, and fanning himself with the feathery branch of a palm-tree, to protect his skin from the stings of the buzzing insects which swarmed around him. And a group of smiling *Natch-girls,* encouraged to repeat their visit, by the handsome present of the previous day; and now, having their charms set off to the best advantage, by all the glittering finery of Indian Belles, with large gold rings depending from their noses, their necks loaded with jewels, massive silver bangles encircling their slender, well-turned, ankles; their braided hair, decked with wreaths of the sweet-smelling *Maugree*, and their silken robes filling the air with the perfume of sandal-wood, were twining their graceful figures in the dance, and darting the most bewitching glances from their large voluptuous dark eyes, in the vain hope of charming the impatient Sportsmen, whose minds, however, were too fully occupied by floating visions of panting steeds, blood-stained spears, and foaming Boars, to be captivated by the charms of the fascinating Syrens.

The Doctor was lounging indolently in an arm-chair, with a cheroot in his mouth, as usual, twirling his thumbs, and nodding his head approvingly, as any particularly graceful movement of the *Natch-girls* happened to meet with his approbation; and Mansfield was amusing himself by giving a finishing touch to the keen edge of his favourite Hog-spear, on a fine hone; when Charles, who was by far the most impatient and watchful of the party, started from his seat, with an exulting shout, which brought the performance of the *Natch-girls* to an abrupt conclusion.

"Hurra! here come our Scouts, at last!"

The *Natch-girls*, startled by the sudden exclamation, shrunk aside, and made way for two panting *Shikarees*, covered with dust and perspiration, who, advancing at a long, easy, wolf-like trot, and, halting in front of the tent, announced with a profound *salaam*, that a large *sounder* of Hog, headed by the far-famed Boar, had been marked down, amongst the Hills, a few miles from camp.

"Boot and saddle! spurs and spears! and hurra for the man that first draws blood from the old Boar!" shouted Mansfield, starting to his feet, and brandishing aloft his light elastic spear—a faultless male bamboo from the jungles of the Concan, about ten feet long, tough as whalebone, and tapering away beautifully to the smaller end, where it terminated in a keen glittering blade, about the size and shape of a laurel-leaf—a blade which had reeked with the blood of many a grisly Boar.

"*Gorah lao!*" was now the cry; and, in less than five minutes, three snorting steeds, accoutred for the field, were pawing the ground impatiently, in front of the tent.

Mansfield's favourite hunter, Challenger, was the very model of a perfect Arab; a light iron-gray, with broad expanded forehead, deep jowl, fine tapering muzzle, wide nostrils, and beautifully-placed ears; his thin withers, well-placed shoulder, round carcass, compact joints, and long, sloping, muscular quarters, gave promise of uncommon strength and fleetness; whilst a full dark eye, mild as that of the Gazelle, but beaming with the latent fire and indomitable courage of a true son of the desert, belied him much, if his endurance were not equal to his speed. In short, his figure was perfect symmetry, with the exception of his legs, which, although perfectly sound, were sorely disfigured by many a bruise and deep unsightly scar. Such blemishes would have given great offence to an English eye; but, to one accustomed to the headlong pace at which the Indian Hog-hunter urges his horse over the rocky hills, and through the thorny jungles of the Deccan, those honourable wounds, the inevitable portion of every good horse, who has carried a good rider, excited no surprise, and but little regret.

Charles's horse, Lightning, a bright chestnut, had also sprung from Araby's best blood; but his clean, unblemished, wiry limbs, showed that he, like his master, had seen but little service in the field; whilst his fiery eye, restless ears, and fretful movements, together with the unusually long-cheeked bit, with which his bridle was furnished, led one to suspect, that his temper, like that of most horses of his colour, was somewhat of the hottest.

The horse provided for the Doctor, was a strong, short-legged, serviceable-looking hack; exhibiting somewhat less breeding, and less appearance of speed than his companions, whilst the deep hollows over his eyes, together with his subdued manner, looked as if age, and hard service, had somewhat tempered the fire of his youth. But this was no disadvantage in the eyes of the Doctor, who, although a keen Sportsman, had never been remarkable for desperate riding; and, provided he kept the chase in view, and came up in time to blood his spear before the Boar had actually drawn his last breath, it was a matter of very little importance to him, who took the first spear; the "*spear* of *honour*" he never would allow it to be, for, as he very justly remarked, the dangerous part of the sport often began after that had been taken.

The Sportsmen now mounted, without loss of time, and rode out of the grove, followed by their respective Horsekeepers, and the whole party of Beaters. Not a cloud appeared in the whole wide expanse of deep blue sky, to veil the splendour of the tropical sun, which shot down his vertical rays with an intensity of heat, that threatened to penetrate to the brain, even through the thick hunting-caps, and damp towels, which the Sportsmen had provided, to protect their heads. A silence, deep as that of midnight, pervaded the land: for nature was faint with heat, and every living thing had sought shelter from the merciless glare of an Indian noon, save the hardy Hog-hunters, and the ever-ravening Vulture, which, soaring at an immense height, almost beyond the reach of human vision, swept through the air in wide extended circles, seeking his obscene food in the very eye of the blazing sun.

An hour's easy riding brought them to the place where the Hogs were said to be marked down; it was a rocky hill, thinly clothed with stunted brushwood, and rising abruptly from a bare stony plain intersected by numerous dry *nullahs* or watercourses, and dotted, in the extreme distance, with clumps of palm-trees, and fields of sugar-cane, to which the Hogs were in the habit of resorting to feed during the night.

Having ascertained the nature of the position, by a rapid glance of his experienced eye, Mansfield issued the necessary orders to his Beaters, and then desired Charles and the Doctor to follow him to a small clump of date-trees, near the foot of the hill, where they, and their horses, might lie in ambush, till the Hogs were roused.

Having carefully concealed themselves amongst the trees, and ascertained that neither they, nor their horses, were visible from the hill-side, the riders dismounted, and waited with breathless impatience for the first joyous shout of the Beaters. Charles's heart beat almost audibly as he peeped through the leafy screen which concealed them, expecting every moment to hear the yell, which announced the finding of the mighty Boar, and to see the grisly monster dash headlong down the rocky steep. But half an hour had elapsed, during which the deep silence was unbroken, and the excited feelings of the young Sportsman were beginning to subside into something very like disappointment, when a distant shout came faintly on his ear, from the opposite side of the hill. Mansfield, who had been smoking his cigar, and chatting carelessly with the Doctor, started at the well-known sound. A grim smile curled his lip, and fire flashed from his kindling eye, as he bounded to his feet, grasped his spear, and sprang into the saddle.

"Now, lads, mount!" said he, settling himself firmly in his seat, and grasping the reins. "Mount, and be ready; we shall have him afoot directly."

The others mounted in haste, and fixed their longing eyes on the side of the opposite hill, whilst every nerve tingled, with an almost sickening sensation of wild excitement.

"I see him! I see him!" said Charles in an eager whisper; at the same time tightening his reins, and closing his heels, with an involuntary jerk, which made the impatient Lightning snort and rear.

"For Heaven's sake, Charles! keep that fidgetty brute of yours quiet," replied Mansfield, in a chiding tone, as the gigantic Boar was seen to rise slowly from his solitary lair on the hill-side, shaking his gray hide like a roused Lion, and turning his head to listen to the approaching shouts of his pursuers. "Steady, steady—not a move till I give the word, 'ride,' and then you may knock the fire out of master Lightning as soon as you like. That Boar will try his metal both in running and fighting, else I'm mistaken."

The Beaters were, by this time, coming over the crest of the hill; and the Boar, apparently satisfied that his enemies were advancing in too great force for him to attempt resistance, began to steal away through the brushwood, stopping occasionally to listen, as if debating with himself, whether to make for the plain, and trust to his speed for safety, or to turn, and charge gallantly amongst his pursuers.

Charles, in the excitement of the moment, was several times on the point of raising a shout to inform the Beaters that the Boar was afoot, and to urge them forward; but a glance from Mansfield's frowning eye immediately checked him.

The ground now becoming more open, the Boar increased his pace to a shambling trot; and, the eager Beaters having at the same moment caught sight of him, a wild unearthly yell arose, as if a whole legion of devils were at his heels. The chafed brute stood for one moment with upraised bristles, churning the white foam between his jaws; then, uttering a short, angry grunt, that seemed to announce his desperate determination of trying his speed across the plain, he dashed down the hill, and disappeared in the brushwood.

"Now we have him! Now for a glorious burst!" exclaimed Mansfield, grasping his spear more firmly, and shortening his reins, in the hope of seeing the mighty Boar burst gallantly from the belt of low jungle which skirted the foot of the hill. But no Boar appeared, and Mansfield was about to give vent to his feelings in a very unseemly oath, when a thick patch of brushwood, immediately below the Beaters, appeared in violent motion, and, next moment, a whole *sounder* of Hog burst from the cover, and came scrambling down the hill; their round black backs rising and falling in quick succession, like a shoal of porpoises tumbling along the face of a giant wave. The excited Beaters redoubled their yells, and the terrified animals, dashing at once through the belt of jungle, took to the open ground without hesitation.

"Ride!" shouted Mansfield, in a voice clear as a trumpet-sound. And at that thrilling cry, the three Horsemen, darting from their concealment, like lightning from a thunder-cloud, urged their snorting hunters across the plain at the very top of their speed.

Charles's hot-blooded chestnut went tearing along with his head and tail in the air, and the bit in his teeth, as if determined that nothing should stop him till he was brought up, by running his head against a stone wall, or till he succeeded in breaking his own neck, or that of his rider, in one of the numerous ravines which lay so opportunely in the way. But this was no time to argue the point with a runaway horse, and Charles let him go to his heart's content.

The Doctor followed at a less headlong pace; but, to do him justice, he plied the spurs, and made the old horse do his best.

"Now Charles, my boy—now for the spear of honour!" cried Mansfield, as he and Charles rode neck and neck, at a racing pace, over the most terrific ground. "We are tolerably well matched as to speed, I see; and, if you can draw first blood, to dim the lustre of your maiden spear, you shall bear the palm, and welcome; but, by the Prophet! you must ride for it."

"Hurra! here goes for first blood then!" cried

Charles in an exulting tone, at the same time shaking the reins, and driving the spurs into his fiery horse, already mad with excitement and lathered with foam, whilst the more temperate Challenger, although urged to his utmost speed, had hardly turned a hair.

Hurra! hurra! away they scour like Falcons darting on their prey; the hard-baked earth ringing like metal beneath their horses' iron-shod hoofs, and a long train of dust rising like smoke behind them.

Although the two horses were, in fact, well matched as to speed, Charles's light weight soon began to tell, in favour of his horse Lightning, who gradually crept ahead of his antagonist, till, by the time they had got within a hundred yards of the Hog, he was nearly half that distance in advance.

"Shall I try it?" exclaimed Charles, looking over his shoulder, and addressing Mansfield, as the leading Boar, much to his astonishment, bounded, with the agility of an antelope, over a yawning ravine, which happened to cross his path—a dry watercourse, with rocky, half-decayed banks, which looked as if they would crumble into dust under the light foot of a fawn, and as break-neck-looking a place, as the most desperate horseman would care to ride at.

"Ay, ay! go along!" replied Mansfield. "A good horse can always follow where a Boar leaps, but keep his head straight, and rattle him at it, as if you were in earnest; for, by mine honour, it is not a place that will improve on acquaintance."

Charles, who was just in the mood to ride at the Styx, if it had come in his way, drove in the spurs, and went at the leap with the heart of a Lion; but, just as he reached the brink, his violent brute of a horse, who had hitherto gone with his head in the air, and his mouth wide open, as if he neither knew nor cared whether there was any impediment in his way or not, suddenly swerved, and wheeling round, with a loud snort, dashed off at right angles.

The well-trained Challenger, on the contrary, accustomed to Mansfield's resolute manner of riding, and knowing, from experience, that it was in vain for him to refuse any thing at which he was put, cocked his ears, gathered his hind-legs well under him, and quickening his stroke, as he approached the ravine, cleared it in beautiful style, although the decayed rock, from which he sprung, gave way, just as his hind-feet quitted it, and rolled thundering to the bottom of the *nullah*.

Charles had, by this time, succeeded in turning his horse, and putting him once more at the leap, with his head held straight, and the spurs goring his sides, the snorting brute went at it like a charging Tiger, bounding high into the air, and clearing the ravine by several feet.

The race for the first spear was now resumed in earnest, Charles straining every nerve to recover lost ground, and come up with Mansfield, who, having singled out the largest Boar, was now pressing hard upon his haunches; the angry brute, with foaming jaws and flaming eyes, uttering, from time to time, a short savage grunt, and swerving from side to side, to avoid the deadly thrust of the spear, which quivered, like a sunbeam, within a few inches of his heaving flanks.

Charles was now nearly alongside of Mansfield, and

gaining upon him at every stride. Both horses were beginning to show symptoms of distress; but the gallant little Challenger still answered to the spur, and by one desperate bound, brought Mansfield almost within spear's length of the Boar. A long reach will do it now—and a grim smile of triumph passed over Mansfield's swarthy cheek, as he leaned over his horse's neck, and made a desperate lunge at the flying Boar. He has it!—No! it was an inch too short.—Another stride will do it.—Again the trusty Challenger bounded to the spur—again the spear was poised for the fatal thrust—another second, and the glittering blade would have been quenched in blood; when the Boar made a short turn to the right, and dashed across Charles's horse. The terrified animal made a bound to clear the Hog, and as he did so, Charles thrust his spear awkwardly forward, without aim or direction; the point, however, went true to its destination, and passing through the Boar's brawny shoulder, buried itself in the earth. The horse, at the same instant, stumbled over the wounded Boar, and came to the ground with a tremendous crash, depositing his rider in the position of a spread eagle, some ten yards beyond him, and shivering the tough bamboo shaft of the spear in a thousand pieces. But the spear of honour has been fairly won, and who cares for broken bones! Hurra!

The wounded Boar scrambled to his feet, with the splintered lance still sticking in his flesh, and uttering a savage grunt, was about to rush upon the prostrate Hunter, when Mansfield, coming up at speed, speared him through the heart, and rolled him over in the bloody sand as if struck by a flash of lightning.

Whilst Mansfield and Charles were thus engaged, the Doctor was not idle. Following in the wake of his companions, he had fallen in with a little half-grown Hog, technically termed a *Squeaker*, which, having been unable to keep up with the rest of the *sounder*, now appeared in a fair way of falling a victim to the Doctor's prowess, although he still made a good race with the old horse across the plain.

Charles, having gathered himself up, and ascertained that neither he nor his horse were materially injured by their fall, was heartily congratulated by Mansfield on his good fortune in taking the spear of honour; and the two young men, having loosened the girths of their smoking hunters, now awaited, with much interest, the issue of the struggle between the Doctor and the unfortunate *Squeaker*.

"Ha! ha! ha! a goodly sight. By mine honour, a goodly sight!" exclaimed Mansfield, doffing his heavy hunting-cap, and wiping the perspiration from his forehead, whilst his sides shook with laughter at the strange grotesque figure which the Doctor exhibited. "Behold a second Don Quixote! The Knight of La Mancha himself turned Hog-hunter! Heavens and earth, how he rides! some evil spirit hath surely possessed him. Ha! ha! ha! Rare—oh, rare!"

Leaning well forward, with his lance couched, like a Knight of old riding a tilt, and rattling his old horse over the stones, at a terrific pace, on came the Doctor in a cloud of dust: his elbows projecting at right angles from his body; his trousers, which were guiltless of straps, rolled up, by the friction of the saddle, nearly to the knees; and his long, loose-jointed legs, bloody with spurring, banging against his horse's sides, at every bound, as if, from the knee downwards, they were perfectly unconnected with the rest of his body, and were merely ingenious machines, suspended from the saddle, to act as stimulants to the animal's speed. His broad-brimmed straw hat had, long ago, parted company with his head, but being attached to his buttonhole by a piece of ribbon, now flapped and fluttered in the wind behind him. His gaunt features, which, during the last few days, had been scorched to a fiery red, by the action of the sun, now glowed like a mask of heated copper, the big drops of perspiration, which fell in a copious shower upon his horse's mane, appearing actually to hiss and boil as they rolled over it. In short, his figure was, altogether, as perfectly grotesque, as any thing can well be imagined; and the effect of the scene was not a little heightened when, on a nearer approach, the traces of intense excitement became visible on his countenance; his eyes rolling wildly, his teeth firmly clenched, like the jaws of a rat-trap, and his parched lips trembling with eagerness, as he wheeled his snorting horse from side to side, making desperate but vain attempts to strike the active animal, which now, nearly exhausted, had begun to double amongst the bushes, like a hunted hare.

"Well done, Doctor! Well done, Piggy! Gallantly thrust! Beautifully doubled!" cried the two young men, clapping their hands, and shouting with all the eagerness of spectators at a well-contested race. But the Doctor was much too intent upon securing his prey, to pay any attention to their exclamations, and went on spurring, and poking, and panting, and grinning, with desperate energy. At length, after many fruitless attempts, and being more than once nearly unhorsed, by digging the point of his spear into the ground, his efforts were crowned with success. A lucky thrust transfixed the panting *Squeaker*, and the worthy Doctor, brandishing his spear, gave vent to as hearty a shout of triumph, as if it had been dyed in the blood of a second Cretan Boar.

"Now, Gentlemen," said Mansfield, as the Doctor dismounted, lighted his ever ready cigar, and seated himself on a stone, "I shall give you five minutes to let your nags recover their wind after this little spurt, and then we must have another beat for the Great Boar. This is mere child's play to the work we shall have, if we can only get him to break cover."

"Child's play ca' ye it?" exclaimed the Doctor, rubbing his aching limbs, and shifting his seat uneasily. "My certie, it may be sae; but I'll tell ye this, Captain, they maun be gae strong tykes o' bairns that play at it. Just look at that poor beast," pointing to the old horse; "see to him, the way his tail is shaking, and his knees trembling, and his flanks heaving like a pair o' smithy bellows. Troth, Sir, I'm thinking it was nae bairn's play for him, nor for me neither, and far less for that poor wee forajaskit looking deevle," pointing to the bleeding carcase of the little Pig which lay at his feet. "Hech, Sirs!" continued he, in a moralizing tone—for the excitement of the chase having subsided, he began to view his victory in a less pleasing light, and his tender heart smote him, for having hunted the unfortunate *Squeaker* to death, with such ruthless perseverance. "Hech, Sirs! to think o' me, at my respectable time o' life, rampaging across the country, after thae twa daft Laddies, riding fit to brain mysel', and amaist foundering a good naig; and a' for what? To hae the honour o' sticking a Soo! and no a respectable sized Soo even, far less a Boar; but just a poor meeserable bit grise, that it 's a perfect sin and disgrace for ony respectable man to take the life o'. Weel, weel, they say there are nae fules like auld fules, and I believe it 's o'er true." And having arrived at this comfortable conclusion, the worthy Doctor went on mopping his face, and puffing his cigar, with the air of a philosopher.

As soon as the horses had pretty well recovered their wind, the Sportsmen remounted, and rode slowly back towards the hill, from whence the *sounder* of Hog had been driven. The Beaters had already assembled on the plain, leaving a few experienced *Shikarees*, perched upon commanding eminences, to prevent the possibility of the old Boar, which had not yet broken cover, from stealing away unobserved. Mansfield had just selected a tough and well-poised spear, from amongst the spare weapons carried by his Horsekeeper, and was explaining to Charles the proper manner of holding it, showing him how the other had been broken in consequence of his stiff manner of carrying the weapon, tucked under his arm, like the lance of a dragoon, instead of being lightly poised in the right hand; when a shout from one of the lookout men attracted his attention, and, on looking up, he beheld a Native perched upon a pinnacle of rock, waving his *puggarie*, and pointing, with eager gestures, down the side of the hill, opposite to where they stood.

"By Heavens he 's off!" exclaimed Mansfield, putting spurs to his horse, and starting at a hand gallop. "Follow me, Gentlemen; but do not press your horses too hard at first, we shall want all the wind they can spare, when we get to the other side of the hill."

The belt of jungle, which skirted the base of the hill, obliged the Horsemen to make a considerable detour, and, by the time they reached the opposite side, the crafty old Boar, who had availed himself of a quiet moment to steal away, as he fancied, unobserved, now appeared a mere speck on the surface of the plain, making direct for another rocky hill, about two miles distant.

"Now, my lads, go along," cried Mansfield, giving Challenger his head, and urging him at once to the top of his speed. "He has got a tremendous start, and nothing but hard riding will avail us now; for, if he once gains yonder hill, our horses, blown as they must be, will stand but little chance of bringing him to action."

The Boar, finding himself hitherto unpursued, had been cantering along, at an easy pace, so that his pursuers gained upon him rapidly at first; but, no sooner did he hear the clatter of hoofs behind him, than he turned half round, as if some faint idea of doing battle had crossed his mind, and then, uttering a savage grunt, bounded off at a pace, which, had he been able to maintain it for any length of time, would have rendered pursuit hopeless.

"Now is the time to press him," cried Mansfield, urging his willing horse to still greater exertions, although the poor brute was already straining every nerve to the uttermost. "If we can only keep him at this pace, for another half-mile, we shall force the sulky brute to show fight, whether he will or no; and then, Charles, my boy, we shall have a first spear worth contending for."

They were now nearing the hill fast, and, as they approached it, the ground over which they rode, neck and girth, at such headlong speed, assumed every moment a more terrific appearance. In fact, it appeared almost miraculous that horses should be able to cross it at all; for, independently of the yawning ravines, and rocks, and thorny bushes which impeded their progress, the ground was so completely broken up by holes and fissures, just sufficiently concealed, by stunted grass, to prevent the rider seeing them, till his horse was in the act of flying over them, that even at a foot pace, a horseman would have found some difficulty in picking his steps over it. Still, they pressed forward with undiminished ardour, and, save a few desperate stumbles, no accident had yet occnrred.

The Boar was evidently sinking fast, and the Horsemen gaining upon him. Mansfield was already sufficiently near to mark the malignant twinkle of his little gray eye, as he glanced suspiciously over his shoulder, measuring the distance, and calculating whether he had better turn upon his pursuers, or make one more desperate effort to gain the shelter of the hill. But still the foaming brute kept beyond the reach of his spear.

"The Devil take him, he'll beat us, after all," exclaimed Mansfield, driving the spurs madly into the flanks of his gasping horse, lifting him with both hands, and throwing him bodily forward—his heart smote him as he did so, for, even in the wild excitement of that moment, he could feel the gallant brute reeling under him with fatigue.

"Bravely done, my trusty Challenger," cried Mansfield, in an exulting tone. "One more such stride, and the spear is mine."

True to the last, the high-spirited creature once more answered to the spur; but it was like the last bound of a wounded Deer. He stumbled, his trembling limbs gave way under him, and horse and rider rolled upon the ground. Next moment the Boar had reached the goal; and now, considering himself safe from further pursuit, began slowly to scramble up the rugged ascent, his lolling tongue, foaming jaws, and staggering gait, bearing ample testimony to the severity of the chase.

Charles, whose once fiery horse was now so effectually blown, that he no longer answered to the spur, except by a faint groan, seeing that the case was desperate, raised himself in the stirrups, and hurled his spear after the Boar; but the weapon fell harmless amongst the rocks, and the excited Boy, throwing himself from his reeling horse, stamped upon the ground with rage and vexation.

Reader, hast thou ever chased a goodly Boar over the scorching plains, and rocky hills of the Deccan, till thy blood boiled, and thy brain reeled, and thy best horse sunk under thy weight? Hast thou ever, at the very moment when thy thirsty spear quivered over his brawny back—yea, even as the death halloo was rising to thy lips—seen the foaming brute dash into thorny jungle, or gain the sanctuary of inaccessible rocks? Hast thou ever seen him thus laugh at thy beard, whilst thou stoodest gnawing thy finger-ends in impotent wrath? If thou hast, but not unless, thou mayest be able to form some faint idea of our young Hog-hunter's feelings, as he watched the slow progress of the panting Boar; fancying that he could almost have overtaken him on foot, and yet knowing full well, that he was effectually beyond his reach. It was the very torment of Tantalus.—Losing a Fox is bad—Missing a Stag of ten, with both barrels of thine own favourite rifle—particularly if thou hast stalked him for the best part of a hot August day before getting the shot—is worse. But to be baffled by an old gray Boar, with tusks nine inches long, after having foundered thy best Hunter, and imbibed a sufficient quantity of caloric to keep all the juices in thy body up to the boiling point for the next twenty-four hours, is—is——. Discreet Reader, we leave thee, in the fulness of thy imagination, to fill up the blank, with any epithet thou thinkest most appropriate; if a Hog-hunter, thou wilt be at no loss; if not, we would venture to recommend something rather energetic.

"Well, there is an end of it, I suppose; for the Devil himself would hardly attempt to face that pile of rocks," said Charles, in a desponding tone, as he withdrew his longing eyes from the Boar, and addressed Mansfield, who, having replaced his battered hunting-cap, and shaken the dust from his clothes, was carefully examining Challenger's knees, to ascertain what damage they had sustained in the fall.

"It is bad riding-ground enough," replied he, coolly; "but we must try it.—The Boar is all but done for, and if we can only keep him in view, and force him to cross the hill, we shall make short work of it in the plain beyond. Just keep your eye upon him, in the mean time, and see that he does not give us the slip again."

The well-conditioned horses, although effectually blown by the severity of the first burst, soon recovered their wind, and the Horsemen, remounting, began to climb the steep ascent, picking their steps with difficulty, and clambering amongst rocks and loose stones, where it appeared hardly possible, even for a goat, to find secure footing. Yet the hardy and sure-footed little Arabs persevered. And, after a toilsome scramble, the Hunters succeeded in driving the Boar over the crest of the hill, and had the satisfaction of seeing him fairly on his way towards the plain.

Here Mansfield reined up his horse for a moment, to let him recover breath; while he glanced his keen eye around, to discover the most practicable place for making a descent. Then, sitting well back, and grasping the reins firmly, he put spurs to his horse, and dashed, at speed, down the rocky hill-side; which, although much less precipitous than the one they had ascended, was still sufficiently so, to have scared any other horseman than a desperate Hog-hunter, with his blood, as we said before, at the boiling point; and even for him to attempt it, on a tired horse, appeared little short of madness. At least so thought our friend the Doctor, who, having made the circuit of the hill, now appeared on the plain below, going along at a steady canter, and watching the progress of the reckless Horsemen, with fear and trembling.

"Od's my life, but that 's awfu'!" muttered he, pulling up and clasping his hands convulsively, as Charles's horse made a desperate stumble, but was cleverly recovered by the steady hand, and good nerve, of his rider. "That Mansfield is just a perfect Deevle incarnate when his blood is up. He'll never rest till he makes that Laddy Charles as ill as himsel', if he doesna break his neck and his ain too afore they get to the bottom o' that brae, as it 's my opinion he will do. Lord sake! there 's another awfu' stammer! They 'll surely be brained."

But, in spite of the Doctor's evil forebodings, the two Horsemen reached the plain in safety, not a hundred yards from the Boar's haunches; and the gallant Mc.Phee, fired by the sight, and forgetting in a moment all his prudent caution, dashed in the spurs and joined in the chase, with as much eagerness as if he had no neck to break.

The Doctor's horse, being comparatively fresh, now managed to keep pace with his companions; and the three Horsemen were riding abreast as the hunted Boar approached a deep and wide stream with precipitous banks. This, the Doctor fancied, must either bring him to bay or force him to alter his course; which, in consequence of a bend in the river, would have the effect of bringing him to close quarters.—An idea suddenly flashed across his mind that, by making a desperate rush at this auspicious moment, he might immortalize himself by taking the spear of honour from the renowned Mansfield. Fired by this magnificent thought, the excited Mc.Phee darted in the spurs, brandished his spear, and uttered a war-whoop, that made the old horse bound under him, as if he had been electrified. But to his astonishment, the Boar, instead of turning, plunged from the high bank without ever looking behind him; and—oh! horror!—his two wild companions, far from hesitating, only urged on their horses to the desperate leap with redoubled fury.

"Stop! ye incarnate Deevles!" roared the Doctor, striving desperately, but in vain, either to stop or turn his horse, for he was wedged in between the other two; and the hard-mouthed old hunter he bestrode, excited to madness by the recollections of former glory, was not to be stopped by the power of man. "Stop, ye Deevle's buckies—stop, ye misleer'd loons. Is it going to drown yoursels and me ye are, like the herd o' swine possessed by evil speerits?—Stop! I say—stop! —I canna soum! I canna soum!—I 'll surely be drowned!—I 'll ——" Here the Doctor's exclamations were lost in a faint bubbling cry, as his unmanageable horse plunged with the others, over head and ears, into the middle of the stream; and by the time he returned to the surface, he was so nearly suffocated, that he could only give vent to his outraged feelings in strange inarticulate sounds. Mansfield, hearing the coughing, and spluttering of the poor Doctor behind him, turned half round, with the intention of going to his assistance; but, seeing that he still clung to his horse, and that the animal was swimming strongly, he called out to him to hold on by the mane and fear nothing; and slipping himself out of the saddle to relieve his favourite horse, he swam by his side, supporting his head with one hand, and cheering him with his voice.

The Boar reached the opposite bank before the Horsemen were half-way across, shook the water from his dripping hide, and casting one malignant glance at his pursuers, trotted on sulkily for a short distance; then, as if aware that any further attempt at flight, over the wide expanse of plain which lay before him, would only be wasting his energies to no purpose, he wheeled suddenly round, erected his bristles, and stood resolutely at bay.

Mansfield at this moment emerged from the water, dripping like a River-God; and, seeing the warlike position assumed by the enemy, he uttered a shout of triumph, put spurs to his steaming horse, and charged him at speed—which, by the way, gentle Reader, is the only safe manner of approaching a Boar at bay. The savage brute having now made up his mind to fight to the death, uttered a fierce grunt, and dashed forward to meet him. Mansfield's well-directed spear entered his chest, and passed out behind the shoulder; but, in spite of the severity of the wound, he still rushed forward, shattered the bamboo, and dashing under the belly of the unflinching Challenger, before Mansfield had time to wheel out of the way, succeeded in inflicting a deep and deadly gash, from which the bowels protruded in a shocking manner.

Charles now dashed forward to despatch the wounded monster; but such was his strength and ferocity, that he rose staggering from the ground, rushed at the horse, knocked his fore-legs from under him, and rolled him over, inflicting a cut across the shank-bones as clean as if it had been done by a razor.

While he yet stood tottering, and meditating further mischief, the Doctor dashed up to him in gallant style, and shouting at the top of his voice,

"That 's second spear, ony how!" plunged the glittering blade into his heart.

The frantic brute made one desperate effort to bite through the tough bamboo; but in that effort a stream of black blood, mingled with foam, gushed from his mouth; and uttering one shrill scream, in the weakness of expiring nature, he sank slowly to the ground, and died.

Loud and long was the death halloo, with which the exulting Doctor proclaimed his victory. But poor Mansfield had not the heart to join in it. For him, the victory had been too dearly purchased. Sitting on the ground, with the head of his dying horse resting on his knees, he watched his glazing eye, and quivering limbs, with the solicitude of a mother hanging over a sick child. The faithful and beautiful creature had been his companion in camp and in quarters, in battle and in the Hunting-field, ever since he was a colt; he had shared his master's tent, and fed from his master's hand, and exhibited towards him all the affection of a dog. Smile not then, gentle Reader, nor call it weakness, when we tell thee that a tear rolled down the weather-beaten cheek of the hardy Soldier, as his highly-prized and almost faultless steed, fixing his large mild eye upon his face, stretched forth his stiffening limbs, and sighed forth his last breath in a deep groan.

"He has died nobly," cried Mansfield, starting to his feet and dashing the unbidden tear from his eye. "But never shall I forget the day that has cost me the life of my incomparable Challenger."

CHAPTER XIV.

THE MAN-EATER.

On the banks of the river Cauvery stands one of those mean-looking villages, which occur, at intervals of a few miles, throughout the greater part of the Mysore country. A small mud fort, long since dismantled, and now almost concealed by jungle, overlooked a sluggish stream, whose dark waters lazily licked the crumbling walls. The snow-white egret and the stately crane waded amongst the shallows, with their long necks outstretched, in attitudes of intense watchfulness. The scaly alligator lay basking on the half-covered sandbanks; and the Brahminey kite hovered above the reeds, uttering its querulous note, as its bright chestnut wings quivered in the level beams of the setting sun. Herds of sluggish buffaloes, their bare black hides plastered with mud, were slowly returning from their pasture, a sunburnt urchin perched upon the back of the most docile, shouting at the top of his voice a wild recitativo, addressed to his charge, who responded by deep surly grunts. The shrill cry of the wild peacock, perched npon the ruined battlements of the fort, was answered by his mate from the rank thicket underneath. And the soft cooing of the turtle-dove whispered among the mango-leaves. As evening advanced, the huge vampire-bats, which hung in clusters suspended by their hinder claws from the drooping branches of the banyan-trees, dropped, one by one, and glided silently away in search of food. Labourers, with their black blankets hanging over their shoulders, came in straggling parties from the fields, driving their bullocks before them: and the women returned from the wells in picturesque groups, each supporting with one hand an earthen jar of antique form, gracefully balanced on her head; whilst the jingling sounds of the bangles which encircled their ancles, made music to their light elastic step. Such was the peaceful scene, as evening closed upon that lonely village.

But at intervals, a wild startling shout would come booming on the breeze, and ere its falling notes had died away, the cry was taken up, and continued from an opposite quarter. This was the *Shikar*-cry of the Mysore woodsman; and, to an Indian Sportsman, told its tale. A jungle village on the banks of a river, is generally haunted by a Tiger; if there be a ruined fort, overgrown with grass and brushwood, such probability is much increased—and whenever the woodcutter returns hurriedly at sunset, shouting that ominous holla, the chances are, that a Tiger dogs his steps.

The sun had set, and the shades of night were fast approaching, as Rung Row, the venerated Priest of the village, strode along the banks of the river to a convenient spot for making his evening ablutions. He returned with dignified condescension the salutations humbly offered by each *Ryot* whom he met, and proceeded on, wrapped in his own meditations. Little thought the proud Brahmin, as he pondered over the probable success of his last project in priestly craft, that he was not doomed to reap its fruits.

At a winding of the river, less than a quarter of a mile from the village, was a little bay, sheltered from observation by some aloe bushes. The water was not too deep; and soft sand, pleasant for the foot to tread, shelved gradually into a clear pool.

"Here shall I enjoy a refreshing bath," thought the luxurious Priest, "and then shall the antelope-eyed Luxshmee welcome me to her arms."

Having no clothes to encumber him, save a cotton wrapper round his loins, the devout worshipper of *Vishnoo* waded at once into the stream, muttering a prayer at every step, and commenced the important ceremony of ablution, by pouring water, from a small brass vessel, over his shaven crown and well-oiled skin.

What rustle was that?—The Brahmin's ears heard not, they were stunned by the cold stream that poured over them. His eyes, too, were closed, else would he have seen two bright green orbs, glaring fiercely upon him, through the branches of an aloe-bush at his side. His hour had come, for the famous Man-eater of *Shikarpoor* was upon his trail. Her eye had rested on her victim, and she thirsted for his blood. Her grim head was cautiously thrust through the bushes, and the striped monster issued from her lair with stealthy tread. Dragging her belly along the sand, her tail switching impatiently, her ears laid flat upon her neck, and her whiskered lips drawn back, so as to expose her formidable array of tusks, she crept silently to the brink of the water, there, gathering herself together, she glared for one moment on the devoted wretch, like a triumphant fiend, and bounding forward, threw herself upon him with a roar, which thrilled through his guilty soul, and drowned the death-shriek which he uttered in his agony. —Struggle there was none—the paw of the Tigress fell like a bar of iron upon his skull, crushing it to the brain, and her powerful teeth met in his throat. Death was almost instantaneous.—A senseless body hung quivering in her grasp, as she turned to the shore, but she still shook it with ferocious energy, and buried her tusks deeper still, as it throbbed at the last convulsive gasp.

This fearful death had been the fate of many a poor *Ryot* and Woodcutter belonging to the village, for the Tigress had haunted it during several months. Their fate created little sensation—they were only *Soodras;* but when a herd-boy, who had witnessed this tragedy, ran to the village, screaming, *Bhag! Bhag!* and announced that the Man-eater was supping on the holy carcass of a Brahmin Priest, the holy brotherhood were roused from their apathy into a state of keen excitement. Women ran about beating their breasts, and howling their national lament, and the village resounded with the dismal cries of *Wha! Wha! Bhag! Bhag!*

After a decent indulgence in strenuous demonstrations of grief, the *Ameldar* despatched a *Peon* to summon *Bhurmah*, the principal *Shikaree* of the village. In a few minutes he was dragged by the officious policeman, as if he were a criminal, into the great man's presence, and abused, with that despotic disregard of right and wrong, which ever accompanies an Asiatic's possession of power.

Bhurmah was one of the most noted *Shikarees* of that province; his whole life had been spent in watching beasts of prey; but the dreaded Tigress of *Shikarpoor* had as yet baffled him; and now that she had killed a Brahmin, it followed, according to a Brahmin's reasoning, that poor *Bhurmah*, together with all his kindred, but more especially those of the female line, were every thing that is odious in a Brahmin's eyes. Having been duly apprized of these fair inferences, resulting from a Priest having been eaten, he was commanded, upon pain of an *Ameldar's* displeasure, to produce the head of the Tigress before she committed further sacrilege.

"It is an order!" answered the submissive Hindoo, shouldering the long matchlock on which he had leaned during this satisfactory audience. And the man who wore three medals on his breast, rewards for gallantry in his many conflicts with Tigers, retired cowering from the presence of an effeminate Brahmin, without a word of reply to the most insulting and unjust abuse.

Bhurmah, a poor *Shikaree*, and Mansfield, a British Officer, were very different persons, and very different was the style in which the *Ameldar* addressed them.

As soon as he had vented his wrath upon the inferior, the administrator of justice penned a flowery letter to his superior, the English *Burrah Sahib*, of whose arrival in a neighbouring village he had that day been informed.

Having described the sad event in glowing language, he proceeded to beg that "the mighty warrior, the great and powerful Lord, in whose hands a Lion was as a mouse, would be graciously pleased to extend the shadow of his protection over his devoted slaves, and come with his Elephant and death-dealing weapon, to rid them of the destroyer of their peace."

Before sunset next day, Mansfield and Charles, attended by the trusty *Ayapah*, were galloping along a path which led to *Shikarpoor*. The Doctor, whose battered frame had not yet recovered from the effects of the previous day's adventures, had remained behind, intending to follow them at a more sober pace next morning. Their road lay, for some miles, through a bamboo jungle, the outskirts of the Wynaad Forest, and as the day declined, the faster did they ply their bloody spurs.

There were mementoes enough on that silent road, to warn the traveller not to linger after the sun had set. Heaps of stones, raised by the passers-by to mark the spot where some ill-starred wretch had been killed by a Tiger, presented themselves in many a gloomy spot, and as the riders passed each of these sad memorials, the foaming Arabs were pushed on at renewed speed—it would not do to be benighted here.

The open country was gained, the lofty pinnacle of the village pagoda was seen towering above the trees, and, ere another mile was passed, the riders had pulled up their smoking horses in the midst of the bazaar, and were surrounded by a host of natives, all *salaam*ing with true Oriental obsequiousness, and thrusting into their hands the offerings of fruit, without which it would be presumptuous to approach a superior. They were the authorities of the village, sleek, well-fed Brahmins, each vying with the other in the favour of his welcome, and prayers for the invincible warrior's prosperity.

All this must be submitted to; and, although Mansfield fidgeted in his saddle, he was too well-bred to show his annoyance. He returned their *salaams*, answered their compliments, pocketed as much of the fruit as he could, and insisted on the *Ameldar* remounting his little ambling pony, from which, in his humility, he had dismounted. With this gracious order the smooth-faced Brahmin complied, after a decent show of resistance, and was forthwith embedded in a crimson cushion, which, with its complicated trappings, smothered the little punchy steed, so as to leave little visible, save a white head, and a pink tail that swept the ground.

A band of native musicians, armed with terrible instruments of discord, struck up a barbarous piece of music, that might have shattered the nerves of a Highland bagpiper. Armed *Peons* cleared the way—the mob shouted, and the cavalcade proceeded. Charles was delighted with the bustle and novelty of the scene; but poor Mansfield, who had long ago been disgusted with the barbarous pageantry and fulsome flattery of native dignitaries, most devoutly wished the obsequious *Ameldar* and his shouting myrmidons at the Devil.

It would have been amusing to a stranger to contrast the dusty, wayworn figure of the European, to whom all these honours were paid, with the spotless white robes, gaudy turbans, and magnificent shawls, of his fawning flatterers. His shooting-jacket, which had once been green, was now indeed a garment of many colours. His hunting-cap, bruised and battered out of all shape, matched it well; and brown cord breeches, met by deerskin gaiters, completed the attire of the weather-beaten, sun-dried Sportsman, who rode on with Quixotic gravity, surrounded by a staring if not an admiring throng. Thus escorted—the noble Arab which he rode alone denoting his rank—Mansfield was conducted, in a sort of triumphant procession, to a garden on the banks of the river, where a tent was pitched for his reception. The Elephant, just arrived, was refreshing itself in the stream, and a party of *Coolies* were cooking their messes, to recruit themselves after their march. Here the Brahmins asked permission to take their leave—a boon most willingly granted—and Mansfield was left to a conference more congenial to his taste. They were no sooner gone, than he threw aside his coat, kicked off his gaiters, dropped into an arm-chair, and inhaling a long whiff from the *hookah*, placed at his side by a venerable Mussulman, damned the whole fraternity of Brahmins for a set of hypocritical scoundrels, and despatched *Ayapah* to summon *Bhurmah* the *Shikaree.*

* * * * *

It was not yet light enough to distinguish objects clearly, when Mansfield was roused by his attendant announcing that the dawn had come, and that the people were ready. A sleepy voice answered,

"Order the gray horse and the chestnut pony to be saddled. Take the rifles and ammunition, and go to the jungle where *Bhurmah* lost the trail yesterday. Order the *Mahout* to start with the Elephant immediately, and see that there is a bundle of rockets in the *howdah*. I shall be with you before you reach the ground."

The interval between the first faint dawn, and the bright glare which immediately precedes sunrise, in the tropics, is brief. By the time the two Sportsmen were mounted, there was sufficient light to enable them to pick out the Elephant's tracks, guided by which, they overtook the party, as *Bhurmah* was leading the way into a Tigrish-looking valley, the bright verdure of which contrasted strongly with the brown tints of the surrounding country. A ravine, which was never dried up in the hottest weather, ran through it, and discharged itself into a tank at one extremity, where the cover was thickest. On that side, the jungle ended abruptly in a plain, where Hog might be ridden, so free was it from brushwood. On this, the valley contracted gradually towards the hills, till it became the mere bed of a little mountain-stream.

"I carried it thus far, *Sahib*, by sunset yesterday," said the *Shikaree*, pointing to the impression of four huge paws in the soft bed of the ravine.

Mansfield, dismounting, stooped over the trail, and examined it for a few seconds attentively, whilst the Natives awaited his opinion in silence. Having satisfied himself, he sat down, and with an air of serious gravity, commenced the following dialogue with *Bhurmah*:

"She was in no hurry when she took that line. A hurried step would not leave so smooth a trail."

"No, *Sahib*, she had travelled three *coss* before she crossed the hills, in the gray of the morning, and she would come in here quietly, before the sun was hot. The trail was long cold when I ran it up to this jungle."

"You have been on her trail before. Is this one of her favourite haunts?"

"I have marked her into it more than once," answered the old man. "But who can tell where a wandering Tigress will lie down to-morrow, although you have found her bed warm to-day? She is seldom more than twelve hours in one place, and the death-lament may now be singing ten *coss* off, for the man she killed last night. I have lived in the jungles now more than thirty years, and the people have not called me *Bhagmar* without a cause, but this Tigress has always proved too cunning for me."

"Aye, but you are the man, *Bhurmah*, who is destined to run her down," interrupted Mansfield, who thoroughly understood native character, and observed that the old *Shikaree's* want of confidence had thrown a damp over the spirits of the rest. "It is you, and you only, that shall bring her to bay. I was told it in a dream."

At this announcement, every face brightened, and every doubt of success vanished.

"Well, *Sahib*, your words must be true," replied *Bhurmah*, stroking his long white mustache, with a look of gratified vanity; "and as such is my fate, I shall follow her to the world's end. May dogs defile her grave!—my only Son fell under her accursed paws, and I suppose I shall die by a Tiger, too, when my hour comes. But who can escape his fate?"

"Very true, my fine fellow; but your fate is to get

another medal, for ridding the country of this incarnate Devil—so, let us to work. You say that you found no track leading from the east side into the jungle, so now try the outskirts to the westward with your people, while I follow the trail along this ravine with the Elephant, and mind you get into trees the moment you hear me holla—I am sure she is here."

While the Natives, fifteen in number, examined the edges of the cover, Mansfield and Charles, mounted on the Elephant, searched the bed of the ravine: following the foot-prints until they were lost on rocky soil. After making several fruitless casts to recover the trail, they rejoined the Natives, who had also failed in hitting on any fresh track. A brief consultation was held, and the result was *Bhurmah* declaring his conviction that the Tigress lay concealed in the cover.

Mansfield, therefore, ordered every man, except *Ayapah*, who would accompany him on the Elephant, to take up a position, by which all points might be guarded. And, as a further precaution, a native horseman was posted on an eminence, commanding a clear view, with orders not to lose sight of the Tigress if she broke away.

These arrangements having been made, the stately Elephant advanced, at the word of command, crashing his way through the yielding branches as a ship tosses the opening waves from her side. His progress was slow, for the utmost exertions of the *Mahout* were required to force him through some parts of the thicket, where masses of prickly shrubs bristled against him, and tough creepers matted the bushes into a compact barrier, which threw back the immense animal at every rush he made to beat them down. Some hours were spent in this arduous search. The heat was becoming intense; the Elephant growing sulky, and the *Mahout* muttering to himself broken sentences, expressive of impatience; even *Ayapah* relaxed in the diligent scrutiny with which he had examined each tuft of grass. But the leader persevered in his usual patient manner, never passing a bush until it was thoroughly beaten, although no trace had as yet been found to cheer them. Once, indeed, the Elephant trumpeted, and a rustle was heard in front. The rifles were raised, and the eyes of the Sportsmen eagerly fixed upon the moving bushes; but Mansfield's weapon was quietly replaced, and Charles's suddenly snatched from his hand, as the shaggy hide of a Bear brushed through the underwood. Charles opened his eyes in astonishment, at being thus unceremoniously disarmed, and turned upon Mansfield in no very amiable mood. But the old Sportsman met his angry glance with a quiet smile.

"Come Charley, my boy," said he, returning the rifle, "do not be angry. 'T is very annoying, I grant you, to be deprived of so tempting a shot; but I really could not afford to lose the Tigress, after all the trouble she has given us, for the sake of a Bear, which we can find at any time. You have no idea what skulking brutes these Man-eaters are; they never show fight unless they are driven to it; and this old devil has become so cunning, from being frequently hunted, that the report of a rifle would send her off to her strong hold among the hills, if she be within hearing."

One corner of the valley, in which were some withered brambles, overgrown by high spear-grass, was yet untried. To this the wearied Elephant was advancing with unwilling steps, when a monkey, which had been quietly watching their proceedings, was observed to spring from tree to tree, looking down, grinning, and chattering, with every mark of violent agitation, while the long grass waved below him.

"Look, *Sahib!*" cried *Ayapah*, from the back of the *howdah*.

"Push on the Elephant to his utmost," shouted Mansfield in a voice of thunder; "she is there and is making off."

The sagacious brute knew well that his game was near. His eye glistened, and flapping his ears, he rushed forward with his trunk curled in the air.

"There is the trail!" exclaimed *Ayapah*, pointing to a fresh impression of paws on the side of the ravine.

"Shall I cross?" asked the *Mahout*, looking over his shoulder.

"Over, quick," was the reply. "She is away! Hark to that holla!"

While he spoke, a piercing yell proclaimed a view; and then arose the wild *Shikar* cry, in full chorus, causing every nerve to thrill with excitement. The goaded Elephant scrambled across the ravine, and threaded his way to the point where shouts of *Bhag* announced that the Tigress was approaching. The jungle rang with the cry, and it was returned in echoes from the hills. Earnest exertions were making to hem her in; but she had been hunted before, and would not be stopped. The directing signal from the scouts was still forward, and, before the Elephant had forced a passage through the jungle, a *Shikaree*, watching the plain, waved his turban, and uttered the well-known whoop, which announced that she had broken cover.

"Confound her for a cunning devil!" muttered Mansfield, "she has beaten us, and is off to the hills."

Charles, who had been standing up in the *howdah*, trembling with eagerness, and stamping impatiently with his feet, as if by doing so he could drive the Elephant faster, dropped his rifle, and sank back into his seat with a blank look of disappointment.

They had now reached the open plain, and there was the *Sewar*, on whom all their hopes of marking the game depended; his arms and legs going like a windmill in fits, screwing along his old spavined mare, in apparently hot pursuit of the flying Tigress. He might safely have done his best, for there was little fear of a native horseman overtaking a wandering Man-eater across a hilly country. But, to make "certainty more sure," he pulled yet harder than he spurred; and the consequence was, a pace admirably adapted for raising a cloud of dust. Of course, as he intended, the Tigress disappeared over the brow of a hill, well in advance, and he returned faster than he went, brandishing his spear manfully, as if he really had intended to use it. Without slacking his speed, he galloped up to the Elephant, all in a foam, and pulling the poor old mare on her haunches, by a tug that wellnigh broke her jaw, blustered out a confused account of his own amazing zeal, and hints of what he would have done had the Tigress not fled before him. "*Inshallah!* she did not wait till my spear could reach her—she fled like a bird before a hawk!"

"It is well for you that she did so," replied Mansfield, drily. "You appeared to have your mare tolerably well in hand too. But did you mark the Tigress? Was she in sight when you gained the top of the hill?"

"What could your slave do?" replied the *Sewar*, looking rather crest-fallen. "Could he outstrip the wind?"

This unsatisfactory reply spoke volumes. Mansfield turned from him in disgust, and, addressing his followers, urged the necessity of pressing on at once, and endeavouring to hit her trail.

"That fellow has been of little service as a marker," he added; "but we may track her up again; she has not gone far. A hundred rupees to the man who strikes her trail, and runs it to her lair!"

Money will do any thing with a Native. The wearied, dispirited *Shikarees* roused themselves at the sound of rupees, and the chase recommenced.

From the point where the Tigress was lost, they scattered themselves over the country, inspecting the soil with earnest gaze, as if searching for treasure. Some time elapsed without any discovery being made. At last a young villager who had been examining a sheep-track, stopped short, and gave the signal of success. All ran eagerly to the spot, crowding round a foot-mark, which certainly was that of a Tiger.

"Look at it, *Bhurmah*," said Mansfield, uncertain how to act.

The veteran gave it a single glance, and turning away with a look of contempt, declared the marks to be three days old.

An assurance coming from such authority, admitted of no dispute, and the search was resumed.

As when a puppy, opening on a false scent, brings around him some babblers, who bustle about, whimpering and lashing their spotted sides with their feathery tails; an old hound raises his head, and joins them for a moment; but, detecting the error at the first sniff, leaves them with disdain to make his own cast; so *Bhurmah*, his long white mustache giving him an air of peculiar sagacity, struck off from his less experienced companions, and, as if guided by some unerring instinct, proceeded straight in a line, which brought him to a little mountain-stream. Into this he dived, and, for some time, disappeared; then, raising his head above the bank, sent back a thrilling halloo, which was answered by a shout of triumph from the rest of the human pack.

"Hark to *Bhurmah!*" shouted Mansfield. "That signal can be depended upon. Bravo! old fellow; you deserve another medal, and shall have it."

On joining him, he was found inspecting the margin of a small pool.

"She has stopped here to drink, and cannot be far ahead; for the sun has not yet dried the moisture from her foot-prints."

This was addressed by Mansfield to his *Peon*, *Ayapah*, who, jealous that another should excel, began to doubt before he had deigned to look. The old *Shikaree* listened in silence, and with a smile of triumph, to the acknowledgment, which, after a careful examination of the spot, the *Peon* was obliged to make, that they were now on the true scent.

The new trail was followed up rapidly, each step eliciting some cheering remark, as to its distinctness. It had been found upon the summit of the hills, where a considerable extent of table-land intervened before the country beyond became visible. Over this the *Shikarees* proceeded at a long trot without a check, till the plain lay stretched beneath them. A flock of goats was feeding amongst the rocks on the mountain side, watched by a shepherd, who sat motionless, like a bronzed figure, on the heated rocks. The little gray fox basked in the sun, heedless of his proximity ; and the wolf passed by at a lazy trot, lolling out his tongue, and hanging his slouching head as if indifferent to the presence of man. Ranges of naked rocks encircling a plain of barren sand, like a vast amphitheatre, met the eye on every side. The scanty vegetation was scorched into a uniform sunburnt tint, and the few sickly date-trees which reared their stunted heads in the midst of the wilderness, only served to heighten the appearance of desolation. There is something peculiarly wild in such a scene. A sky without a cloud, a plain without a spot of verdure cracked into gaping fissures, and the sun, like a ball of burnished metal, blazing over its nakedness. No smoke to mark the site of a single hut ; no trace of man, save that solitary goatherd, passing his life amongst the beasts of the desert, and they not fearing him.

So far the party had pursued the wandering Tigress by her trail. The nature of the chase was now altered.

While the Natives stood clustered together at fault, having lost the track among stones, Mansfield was looking around, considering where they would probably bring her to bay, when his quick eye perceived the goats to start, and scramble in confusion up the rocks.

"My rifle, *Ayapah*; there she goes!"

It was indeed the hunted Tigress once more in view. Charles threw forward his rifle, and fired without a moment's hesitation, although the Tigress was nearly three hundred yards distant. But the bullet fell far short of its intended mark.

"That is rather too long a range for accurate shooting, Master Charles," said Mansfield, "we must push on and get nearer. She can never keep up that pace under such a sun."

"*Sahib*, if an old man may speak," interrupted *Bhurmah*, "it will be better to remain quiet. She is making straight for her house—that ravine below us. There she will lay up. I have followed her trail into it before now."

"I dare say you are right," replied Mansfield, watching the Tigress with his glass. "She is nearly blown. Aye, now she looks back—I can see her jaws wide open, her tongue is hanging a foot out of her mouth, and is as white as her teeth. We have her now, she has disappeared under the bank. Her race is run, and she must stand to bay. But, oh! for two hours more of daylight!" he added, looking at the lengthening shadows on the plain.

"It is a strong hold she has chosen," observed *Bhurmah*. "I have seen a Tiger hold out for a whole day against three Elephants in that very place, and you may be sure the Man-eater of *Shikarpoor* knows the strongest part."

"She shall not beat us," exclaimed Mansfield, rising and motioning to the *Mahout*. "She shall not beat us, if we should be forced to burn her in her lair. Come on!"

"The bushes are green," quietly observed *Bhurmah*.

In that remark there was much meaning, as the sequel proved.

By the time the indefatigable band had surrounded their game, the sun was gilding the hill tops with its setting rays. Not a moment was lost. *Bhurmah* mounted the *howdah* that he might guide the *Mahout* at once to the spot where he expected to find the Tigress, for he knew every inch of the ground, and, on this occasion, he was not mistaken. The experienced *Shikaree* brought the Elephant under a clump of bauble bushes which grew upon a high ledge of almost perpendicular rock. Farther progress was impossible. Pointing upwards to an opening in the grass, through which a heavy animal had evidently passed, he said,

"There is her den!" A low growl from the centre of the bushes confirmed his accuracy.

She had chosen her strong hold admirably. It was protected, in front, by a mountain-stream, and backed by a perpendicular rock, which projected over it so as to shelter it from above. Mansfield looked in vain for a path where the Elephant might find footing. There was none. A man might have reached the den by climbing; but certain death would have been the fate of him who dared to approach the watchful Tigress. One chance of success still remained, and it was adopted. The Elephant having been withdrawn, Mansfield and Charles posted themselves on a rock, sufficiently high to protect them from the Tigress, in the event of her bolting, and directed the people to bombard her position with rockets from the opposite height. But all was ineffectual. Showers of rockets lighted up the gloomy chasm, and ignited the thin grass along its edges, but it quickly consumed, without spreading to the bushes in which she lay: they were green and would not burn.

When the whole stock of combustibles had been exhausted, rocks were hurled down, and volleys of matchlocks fired; but the only result was an occasional surly growl; and the party, wearied, and dispirited by their fruitless efforts, were unwillingly obliged to retire, it having become too dark for further operations.

For three whole days the same party traversed the country without finding a mark, or hearing any intelligence of the dreaded Tigress. But she was pursued by men who had sworn that she should die, and the ardour of their search was not relaxed.

On the morning of the fourth day, whilst *Bhurmah* and his men were trying some covert in the neighbourhood, two herd-boys sat watching their Buffaloes, in that valley where the pursuit had first commenced. They cared little about Tigers; for they knew that the old Bull of their herd would protect them while they kept at his side. And now that the great Man-eater had been driven from the neighbourhood, there was nothing to fear. Thus unsuspicious of danger the boys sauntered along, picking berries, and amusing themselves with childish sports, till they had wandered a considerable distance from their protectors.

Alas! the destroyer was at hand. She had crept from bush to bush, so silently, that her heavy breathing first gave warning of her approach. The hindermost child turned round, his heart beating with a vague presentiment of danger. The fierce eye of the Tigress met his. He uttered a scream of terror, and shrieked the fearful name of *Bhag!* The sound had scarcely passed his lips, when the terrible roar of the monster shook the earth, and his small bones crackled between her jaws. The other boy fled to the nearest tree, into which he climbed, with the agility of a monkey; from thence he saw the Tigress toss her prey over her shoulder, and trot back, growling, to the jungle. As soon as she was out of sight he hurried to the village to give the alarm; and, in less than an hour, Mansfield and his followers, guided by the little herd-boy, were on their way to the fatal spot.

It was a sight to make a woman weep, to see that poor trembling child standing with the tears rolling down his cheeks, over the scene of the late tragedy.

The ground was spattered with the blood and brains of his brother; and as he told his melancholy tale, a cold shudder ran through his little frame, and choked his feeble voice, each time that his downcast gaze fell upon the horrible traces.

Mansfield drew a rough hand across his eyes, as he ordered the Elephant to kneel, in a voice that faltered.

"Ask that boy, one of you," said he, addressing a *Peon*, "if he would like to come with me, on the Elephant, and see that cursed Tigress die."

The man whom he addressed stared; and a murmur of amazement ran around, at an offer so little in conformity with a Native's idea of becoming dignity. To mount a naked outcast boy upon the same Elephant with an English *Burrah Sahib!* The idea was almost sacrilegious. But the honest, manly heart of Mansfield knew no such petty pride, and he repeated his orders in a tone which admitted of no remonstrance, whilst he cast a look of kindness on the poor despised child, whose large black eyes were fixed upon him, with a look of stupified amazement. He was reluctantly obeyed: Charles had taken his seat, and Mansfield was about to follow, when the Elephant, tired of kneeling so long on hard ground, gave utterance to his annoyance, by an angry roar.

Before the Elephant had time to rise, the Buffaloes, which had been quietly grazing round the edge of the jungle, raised their heads, snorted, and rushed in a body towards one point, bellowing furiously.

"*Bhag! Bhag!*" shrieked the terrified child, cowering down into the bottom of the *howdah*.

"By Heavens, it is!" cried Mansfield, springing to the ground. "She has taken the alarm already.—The large rifle, quick!"

Ayapah thrust it into his hand. Setting the third sight, for a long shot, he stretched back one leg, and slowly raised the heavy weapon to his eye, his finger feeling the trigger, with a pressure so gradual, that the barrel seemed to pour forth its contents, spontaneously, at the instant it rested motionless.

"That hit her!" he calmly observed, as he dropped the discharged weapon into the hollow of his arm, and stood for a moment to watch the effect of the shot.

The Tigress, who was stealing along, at a distance of full two hundred yards, uttered a short angry roar, and dropped on her knees. When she rose, one fore-leg hung dangling from her shoulder, and in this crippled state, she slunk into cover, pursued by the Buffaloes, bellowing at her haunches.

A murmur of admiration ran around the bystanders at this exhibition of skill, which so far exceeded what the majority thought possible, that it seemed more than human, and made them look upon the successful marksman almost in the light of a Demi-god. Even old *Bhurmah* could hardly believe his senses, when he heard the soft *thud* of the bullet, and saw the animal drop, at a distance so far beyond the range of his own trusty matchlock. And the poor little herd-boy clasped his hands together, and his large eyes glistened with tears of gratitude when the joyful shout announced that his dreaded enemy was disabled from flight, and her death certain.

Without noticing the admiration which his skilful shot had occasioned, Mansfield reloaded his rifle with scrupulous exactness, and took his seat in the *howdah* beside Charles, with the wondering herd-boy between them. Old *Bhurmah* climbed up on the Elephant's crupper to insure being in at the death, and the stately animal marched up to the final encounter.

Drops of blood guided them to the bush in which the wounded Tigress lay. The heavy foot of the advancing Elephant shook the ground. She raised her head, laid back her ears savagely, and ceased licking the blood from her shattered shoulder. Mansfield cautioned Charles to be ready, but not to fire in a hurry, as he would wait for him to take the first shot. They were now near enough to observe the bush agitated, as if she was collecting herself for a rush, and a low growl gave forth its warning. Old *Bhurmah* danced about like a maniac, one hand grasping the back of the *howdah* to support himself, the other brandishing his sword; and his long white mustache, which curled up to his eyes, giving him a look of ferocity almost equal to that of the Tigress. The sagacious Elephant twisted his trunk up to be out of harm's way, and advanced cautiously another step. A louder growl increased to a short hoarse roar.

"Keep him steady now,—she is coming," said Mansfield, addressing the *Mahout* with perfect coolness. Charles held his breath, and his eyes seemed as if starting from his head with excitement, as he cocked both barrels of his rifle, and half raised it to his shoulder.

"No hurry, boy; take her coolly," said Mansfield.

The branches crashed—a brindled mass gleamed through them—and the Tigress sprang forth. Her flaming eye gazed wildly around, then settled on her foes. Every hair in her body stood erect—her tail lashed her painted sides, and her flanks heaved laboriously, as if almost suffocated with rage. Uttering a deep growl, she arched her back and lowered her head for a spring.

"Now!" Quick as lightning followed the flash of the rifle, both barrels being discharged almost simultaneously, and the Tigress staggered back with two balls in her chest. She recovered her footing, and was in the act of bounding forward to the charge, when a shot from Mansfield's unerring rifle entered her brain. She dropped from her proud attitude, and the famous Man-eater of *Shikarpoor* lay gasping in a pool of blood, which gushed from a ragged hole between her eyes.

Whilst *Ayapah* busied himself in the important operation of singeing the whiskers of the dead Tigress, the overjoyed Natives crowded around rending the air with shouts, and invoking blessings on the head of the *Burrah Sahib*, the invincible slayer of wild beasts, whose powerful hand had rid the country of this dreadful scourge.

Mansfield and Charles reloaded their rifles, and, guided by the keen eye of old *Bhurmah*, followed the back trail to examine the lair of the famous Man-eater. They now forced their way through the tangled brushwood without fear of danger; and, in the heart of a thick clump of bauble bushes, soon found the half-devoured remains of the unfortunate herd-boy. On a further search, many more ghastly traces were found of the dreaded monster's fearful devastation. Human bones, and human bones alone—for, of late, she had confined herself exclusively to man-eating—lay scattered about in various directions; and one there was, which, more than all the others, smote the heart of Charles with a feeling of deadly sickness. It was a mangled and disjointed skeleton; but the long silken tresses of a Woman still hung in tangled masses from the grinning skull; and silver *bangles*, once the cherished ornaments of female beauty, now encircled bleached and marrowless bones. What a fearful mockery of human vanity was this! And, oh! what dreadful pangs had racked those fleshless bones! What maddening thoughts may not have flitted through that now senseless skull! What wild shrieks of despair may not have been uttered by those mouldering jaws, ere the trembling spirit took its flight! How many unavailing tears have been shed for the untimely, perhaps unknown fate of her, who, now a loathsome skeleton, may once have been the smiling Beauty of the village!—perhaps a beloved Wife!—perhaps the widowed Mother of children!—helpless, friendless children, who now look in vain for the fond smile of maternal tenderness, in the cold eyes of strangers; and, with feeble voices, call upon the name of her who loved them.

Reader, if thou hast ever assisted in slaying a Man-eater; if thou hast ever gazed on such a scene as this, thou wilt doubtless have felt, as Charles did, something more than a Hunter's triumph at the successful termination of thy labours; and thy heart will have swelled with a grateful consciousness of having been an instrument in the hands of Providence, to deliver thy helpless fellow-creatures from one of the most dreadful scourges by which the human race is persecuted—a confirmed Man-eater.

CHAPTER XV.

THE SACRED VILLAGE.

Before daylight, on the morning after the successful encounter with the Man-eater, Mansfield and Charles, accompanied by the Doctor, who had joined them on the previous evening, were making the best of their way, across a wide extent of barren plain, towards the sacred island of Seevasamoodrum. Here they intended to halt for a day, on their way home, to visit the celebrated falls of the Cauvary. The country over which they travelled being of that uninteresting character which affords neither fine scenery nor any prospect of adventure, beyond a chance shot at an antelope or a bustard, Mansfield beguiled the tedium of a long march by giving his companions a description of the Island and the falls. This our Readers will perhaps pardon us for repeating, in as few words as possible, to save explanation hereafter.

Seevasamoodrum, one of the small islands of the river Cauvary, affords an object of interest to the antiquary, as having been the site of the ancient and sacred city of Gungah Parah. It is now almost a wilderness, overgrown with high jungle grass, and forest trees; the only traces of its former splendour which now remain being the ruins of two or three Pagodas, with fragments of ancient sculpture, half buried in the earth. It is also interesting to the admirer of Nature, from the beauty of its scenery, and the magnificent falls which the river forms on either side of it; and to the Sportsman, as being a favourite haunt of Tigers and other wild animals.

The Island still retains its sacred character, and a few modern Pagodas have sprung up among the ruins, like suckers from a decayed root, affording shelter to a nest of lazy Brahmin Priests, its only inhabitants. It is the property of a petty *Jagheerdar* named Rhamaswamy, who, from having been head servant to a European Gentleman, has gradually amassed a fortune, and raised himself to a situation of some importance. Whether he came by his wealth honestly or otherwise, does not appear. But, at all events, he has shown his gratitude to those from whom he derived it, by erecting upon the Island a handsome, well-furnished house, the hospitable doors of which are ever open to his European friends. An establishment of servants, and a palanquin, are also kept. And, to particular friends, the key of a well-stocked cellar is generally offered, although few trespass so far upon his hospitality as to make use of it.

The larger branch of the river, which flows on the western side of the island, forms the fall called "*Gungan Jooki*," or the "Leap of Gungah." The corresponding fall, on the eastern side, is called "*Bir Jooki*," from *Bir*, a banyan-tree. The legend from which the falls derive their names, is as follows. It is a translation from an ancient Hindoo MS. preserved in one of the Pagodas of Seevasamoodrum.

"Gungah Raj, King of Seevasamoodrum, had a servant, whose name was Humpah. This man conceived a violent desire to eat at the table of Gungah Raj. But being of low caste, his doing so would, according to the religion of the Hindoos, have been considered an abominable pollution. His wish was at length gratified in the following extraordinary manner.

"As Humpah one day wandered along the bank of the river in a melancholy mood, thinking how he might possibly accomplish the object of his wishes, he met a young woman, bearing upon her head a pitcher of milk. The woman addressed Humpah, and demanded the cause of his melancholy. He, being ashamed, refused to tell her. But the woman was a sorceress, and not only informed him that she was aware of his desires, but promised, on certain conditions, that they should be gratified. Humpah having agreed to her terms, she procured a young *bir*, or banyan-tree, which had grown under the shade of a large tree of the same species. From this young shoot she prepared a certain ointment, with which she directed Humpah to anoint his forehead. Upon doing so, he immediately became invisible; and by means of this charm, was enabled, for the space of twelve years, not only to partake of the luxuries of Gungah Raj's table, but to participate in all the other pleasures which the Rajah enjoyed. At length Gungah Raj fell sick, but had no apparent disease to account for his altered appearance. He consulted the Divinity, who informed him that his sickness was occasioned by an inmate of his house, and directed him to mix some very hot ingredients in the dishes that were sent to table, by which means the offender would be discovered. This was accordingly done; and Humpah, by eating of the hot preparation, was thrown into such a profuse perspiration, that the charmed ointment was washed from his forehead, and he became visible. Humpah fell dead before the Rajah as they sat at meat.

"Gungah Raj applied to the Brahmins to know by what means he might be cleansed from the pollution he had sustained. They replied, that nothing but death could wipe away the stain; and Gungah, with his favourite Wife, resolved to destroy themselves by leaping down the cataract. The Rajah having mounted a spirited horse, and placed his Wife behind him, galloped furiously towards the precipice. The noble animal took the leap boldly; but, instead of plunging into the gulf below, alighted in safety on the opposite bank. A herdsman seeing this, and being aware of the Rajah's determination, came up, and advised him to blindfold the animal. The Rajah accordingly took off his turban, and having bound it over the eyes of his horse, leaped down the precipice with his Wife, and so perished."

We may here remark that the distance, from bank to bank, said to have been cleared by the Rajah's Charger, is *upwards* of *a thousand feet!* The sceptical Traveller would be apt to doubt the authenticity of this part of the legend, were it not that the foot-prints of a horse, deeply indented in the solid rock, still remain to mark the exact spot where the Rajah alighted.—Who can doubt *such evidence as this*, supported, as it is, by the authority of *an ancient Hindoo MS.* and the solemn asseverations of a whole Village of *Brahmin Priests?*

The fall on the other side of the Island is called *Bir Jooki*, in commemoration of the banyan-tree, from which the charm was prepared. The ancient tree under which the charmed plant is said to have grown, is still to be seen near the bridge.

Nothing particularly worthy of notice occurred during the march, and three hours of hard riding brought our travellers to the village of Bulkawaddy, on the banks of the Cauvary, from whence, to reach the Island, it was necessary to cross a branch of the river in basket-boats. Here they were met by Mr. M—, a very intelligent half-caste, who acted as overseer of Rhamaswamy's property, and did the honours to his guests in the absence of the old Gentleman, who resided at Mysore, and seldom visited the Island himself. Mr. M— having been apprized of their intended visit, by a messenger despatched on the previous evening, had a large basket-boat in waiting, to ferry the party across the river. Charles, who had never before seen one of these antediluvian-looking craft, was not a little astonished, on reaching the bank of the river, to behold nothing but a huge circular wicker-basket, roughly covered with hides, and manned by two naked boatmen, each provided with a long bamboo pole instead of a paddle.

The stream was rapid, and the sharp-pointed rocks which shot up in all directions above the surface of the troubled waters, threatened destruction to the rash mortals who dared to brave the fury of the torrent in so frail, and apparently unmanageable a machine, as a circular basket propelled by poles. Charles, however, seeing that Mansfield jumped in without hesitation, and that even the Doctor showed but slight symptoms of fear, took his place, and said nothing, till he saw the

Horsekeepers leading the horses down the bank, as if with the intention of embarking them also.

This was a proceeding which he could not by any means understand, much less admire, and perching himself upon the edge of the boat, to keep his legs out of harm's way, he asked Mansfield, with a look of astonishment, how he proposed stowing the horses.

Mansfield laughed heartily at the idea of embarking three fiery horses in a frail basket-boat, and explained that he only intended to take them in tow, and make them swim. To accomplish this, in so rapid a stream, and with so many impediments in their course, appeared to Charles little less difficult than embarking them at once. But, although he fully expected to be forced to swim for his life, before they reached the opposite side, he put the best face he could upon the matter, and looked on in silence.

The Horsekeepers having removed the saddles and bridles, and fastened a rope round the neck of each horse, jumped into the basket-boat, and holding the end of the rope, called to their respective charges to follow them. The sagacious animals reluctantly obeyed, snorting and pawing, as they gradually waded into the water, till it suddenly deepened, and they were obliged to betake themselves to swimming. Once fairly afloat, the horses were pulled up close to the edge of the basket, and the Horsekeepers, holding the rope in one hand, caressed the heads of their favourites with the other, whilst they strove to encourage them by every term of endearment, which the fondest nurse could have lavished on a frightened child.

It is beautiful to witness the mutual attachment which exists between an Indian groom—than whom there is no better groom in the world—and his horse; and enough to make an Englishman blush for his country, when he thinks of the barbarous treatment, which even the best-guided horses sometimes meet with among his more civilized brethren. But this is a digression, and one for which English grooms, at least, and perhaps English *steeple-chasers*, will hardly thank us. Well! no matter—it is a short one—and if it happen to meet the eye of those worthies—an honour we hardly dare to hope for—they may revenge themselves by calling the *Forest Ranger* an "Old Fogy," which will be no great matter either: so let us return to our subject.

One vigorous push sufficed to launch the frail bark, with her living cargo and appendages, from the sheltered nook where she lay, into the angry flood; and sent her sweeping along with fearful rapidity, amidst rocks, and shoals, and quicksands. The raging waters hissed, and roared, and boiled; the horses snorted; the boatmen shouted; and all appeared a scene of wild confusion; whilst to add to the horror of a novice in such matters, the scaly snout of a hungry alligator would ever and anon thrust itself above water, as if to remind the unfortunate occupants of the whirling basket, that an upset in such company, would probably be attended with more serious consequences than a wet jacket. The quick eyes and nervous arms of the practised boatmen, however, carried them safe through all difficulties.

They had just escaped, by something like a miracle, from being dashed to pieces on a pointed rock, and had got into the strength of a rapid which appeared to be hurrying them towards inevitable destruction in a boiling whirlpool, when by a dexterous push, given at the right moment, the frail bark was diverted from her course, and even Mansfield drew his breath more freely, as he perceived that she had been caught up by a smooth current of back-water, and was gliding swiftly and steadily towards the bank.

"Weel, weel; thanks be to goodness we 'r no' born to be drowned; although some o' us may be spared to stretch a tow yet: and that 's a comfortable reflection." So said the Doctor, now breaking silence for the first time, and diving into his capacious pocket, in search of his snuff-mull.

"Which do you call a comfortable reflection, Doctor?" said Mansfield, laughing. "The certainty of our not being born to be drowned, or the probability of some of us living to be hanged—eh?"

"Whist noo, Captain, wi' your ill-timed jokes," replied the Doctor, cramming a huge pinch of snuff up his nostrils, and trying to look grave in spite of a strong inclination to laugh. "Be thankfu' that ye are in a dry skin, my man, and dinna be o'er sure it 's no' yoursel' that has the hangman's mark on him—ye hae an awfu' hempy look whiles—and, by my troth, I hae seen as likely a lad come to an ill end."

Having landed in safety, the dripping, half-drowned horses were rubbed down and saddled, and the travellers, remounting, rode on slowly towards the village.

It was a lovely morning. The sun, although bright, even for an Indian sun, had not yet been sufficiently long above the horizon to render the heat oppressive. The balmy morning air had still all the freshness and elasticity of youth. The dewdrops hung, like liquid diamonds, from the long pendant branches of the stately palm-trees, which bent gracefully over the wimpling river, as if lost in admiration of their own beautiful forms. On the opposite bank, the picturesque huts of the village, half-concealed amidst a grove of venerable trees, with the richly-carved Pagoda rearing its head proudly in the midst, were brightly reflected from the surface of a deep still pool of the river. And on the strand, and in the water, were numberless groups of Natives, adding beauty to the scene, by every variety of graceful drapery and picturesque colouring. In a sequestered nook, at cautious distance from the contaminating presence of his less holy brethren, a devout Brahmin performed with scrupulous exactness the prescribed number of priestly ablutions, muttering as he did so his pharisaical prayers. And, on the bank above, a *Fakire*—a Mahometan devotee—naked as at the day of his birth—for your devout *Fakire* does not condescend to the common decencies of life—lay extended at full length upon his back, with his long tangled locks, which shears had never dared to violate, carefully spread out to dry. He also offered up his morning prayers, and ever as he told a bead, he cast a look of proud contempt on the benighted Pagan, who, in the plenitude of his ignorance, shaved his head and clothed his body. Here a group of laughing Girls disported themselves, like bathing Nymphs, amidst the sparkling water, whilst their companions, who had not yet completed their morning task, came and went, balancing elegantly-formed jars on their still more graceful heads; their silken robes filling the air with the perfume of sandal-wood, and the heavy silver *bangles*, which encircled their ankles, making music to their light elastic steps. There, a professional water-carrier, like an overloaded beast of burden, plodded along under the weight of his well-filled leathern bag, regardless of all, save the speedy completion of his laborious duty. In one corner of the bay a group of industrious fishermen plied their trade, casting their circular nets with skilful hand. And in another, a warlike band of Mysore horsemen, armed to the teeth, and soiled with dust, looked upon the gay scene in stern silence, whilst their wearied steeds eagerly plunged their muzzles into the stream, and swallowed copious draughts of the refreshing beverage which had not blessed their sight for many a weary mile.

The stately adjutant, his ponderous bill reposing on his breast, with a look of dignified importance, stalked fearless amidst the crowd. And the sacred monkeys, presuming on the sanctity of their character, frisked and bounded among the branches overhead; now descending to levy their accustomed tribute from the fruit-basket of a passing Brahmin; and now insulting, with curiously abstruse grimaces, the profane vulgar, who dared to pass them by unnoticed.

It was altogether such a scene as a painter would love to study, or a poet to dream of—a scene all life, and beauty, and apparent happiness. Who could look upon the fair face of Nature on such a morning as this, and call himself an atheist? Or what gloomy philosopher would dare to say that this is not a fair world—a world formed for happiness?

The heavens smile—the earth smiles—the glad waters smile, as they flow along their sunny course, through evergreen woods and flowery meadows.—The beasts of the field feed, and are thankful—the birds of the air sing for gladness—the very insects which live but for a day, sipping the dew of Heaven, and dancing in the sunbeams, are grateful for their short hours of happiness: and yet Man, Man alone of all God's creatures, looks with a jaundiced eye upon the beautiful works of Nature, and says there is no God! or if there be, that he is a God to be feared, not loved. Why is this? So thought Charles as he gazed upon the scene in silent admiration. An answer was at hand.

Hark to that strain of barbarous music! Behold that far-winding procession approaching from the sacred village of the Hindoo! Mark that group of dancing Girls—the fairest, yet most dissolute of their sex—singing the praises of their demon God! The gorgeous car elaborately carved with the most obscene figures, bearing aloft the hideous Idol of their worship! The crowd of frantic devotees dancing and shouting with the air of maniacs as they draw him along, and ready to throw themselves, a willing sacrifice, beneath the wheels of his chariot. See the crafty Priests decking the carved Image with garlands, and chanting his praises to excite his benighted worshippers to still more frantic deeds of superstition. Look upon this—a religious ceremony—contrast it with the beautiful simplicity of Nature, and wonder no longer that man is discontented—miserable!

To one sunk in such depths of ignorance, the voice of Nature will call unheard, the light of truth will shine unseen, leaving his darkened mind heedless as the mountain air, through which the eagle's wing hath passed.

Charles turned with horror from the disgusting pageant, and spurred in haste after his companions.

A short ride brought our travellers to the village; their way lying through cultivated fields of rice, cotton, and indigo, intermixed with patches of that graceful plant, the Palma Christi, from which castor oil—the common lamp-oil of the lower classes in India—is prepared. Passing through deserted streets—for the whole male population of the village had poured forth to swell the procession of their Idol—and stopping for a moment to admire the beautiful architecture of the Pagoda, guarded by a gigantic image of the sacred Cow, elaborately carved in black marble, they came upon an open space beyond the village, and found themselves in front of a handsome *bungalow*, built in the European style. Under a lofty portico, supported by *chunam* pillars, a band of obsequious native servants, in flowing robes and crimson turbans, stood ready to receive them; and a fantastically-dressed trumpeter, bearing a huge serpent-shaped instrument, decorated with a fringe of Tigers' tails, brayed forth a deafening welcome.

Charles, who had not been prepared for anything on so grand a scale, was struck dumb with admiration; and his astonishment was not a little increased when, on entering the house, they were ushered into a lofty apartment, richly carpeted, the walls covered with the most expensive English prints, intermixed with oil paintings of Rhamaswamy and his family; the furniture being of the best European manufacture, and the tables covered with china, *or-molu* clocks, and other little ornaments, which one would expect to find in a Lady's boudoir, rather than in the house of a Native.

Having given his visiters time to admire the decorations, and particularly solicited their attention to a highly-coloured, but villanously-executed painting of their absent host, Mr. M— conducted them to the next room, where a breakfast-table was prepared in the European style, besides being loaded with a profusion of the rarest tropical fruits; and having shown the travellers to their respective bath-rooms, the polite *major-domo* took his leave for the present, leaving them to refresh themselves after the fatigues of their journey.

"Weel, here 's long life to Rhamaswamy!" exclaimed the Doctor, laying aside his knife and fork, and proceeding to wash down a most substantial breakfast with a goblet of cool claret. "He is a gentleman every inch o' him, in spite o' his name; and, by my troth, he kens how to make himsel' comfortable, there 's nae doubt o' that, for there 's no a better keepit house than this in a' Madras."

"You do injustice to the hospitality of our worthy host," said Mansfield; "he never inhabits this house himself, it is kept up entirely for the accommodation of his European friends; and when he visits the Island, he takes up his abode in one of the neighbouring Brahmin's houses, living upon the frugal fare of the most abstemious Hindoo."

"Weel, weel! mair 's the pity," replied the Doctor,

availing himself of the opportunity to fill another bumper of claret. "But it only proves him to be mair o' a gentleman than ever; so here 's to him again, honest man, and may grace be given him to quit eating cauld rice, and betake himsel to the mair Christianlike vivers o' het beefsteaks, and weel corket claret."

Breakfast being finished, our friends lighted their cheroots and sallied forth on foot to visit the great fall of *Gungan Jooki*. Mr. M— attended to act as *cicerone*, and the trusty *Ayapah*, who considered himself an indispensable appendage to his Master, followed at a respectful distance. He was armed to the teeth, as usual, for he loved his weapons as a woman loves her ornaments, and on his shoulder he bore Mansfield's ever-ready rifle. This was the weapon which he respected above all others—no profane hand ever dared to touch it—and the worthy *Ayapah* never threw it across his shoulder, even on the most pacific occasion, without assuming a look of determination, which might have struck awe even to the heart of a Tiger.

The branch of the river which forms the great fall of *Gungan Jooki* is divided into two streams, just at the point where it throws itself over the precipice, by a small island without a name. We used, in our younger days, to call it Tiger Island, from the circumstance of our having encountered, and narrowly escaped being devoured by a whole family of these amiable animals the very first time we set foot upon it—and so Tiger Island let it be. The appearance of an island in such a situation, tottering, as it were, on the brink of destruction, is very striking. It gives one the idea of its having been floated down the river, and accidentally stopped by some impediment, just as it reached the brink of the cataract. The river, which for some distance above the island flows along with a gentle current, here assumes a new character; the divided streams, as if irritated by their abrupt separation, sweep furiously along their rocky channels, fretting like parted lovers, till having reached the brink of the precipice which forms the fall, they hail their approaching union with a shout of triumph, and throwing themselves headlong from a height of nearly three hundred feet, are again united. The ever-glowing rainbow, which floats upon the spray, forms their bridal wreath, and Echo sings a marriage-hymn amidst the rocks and caverns of the surrounding mountains. It is a song of thunder—fit music for such giant lovers.

CHAPTER XVI.

TIGER HUNTING AT THE FALLS OF THE CAUVARY.

WE left our three friends, attended by Mr. M——, and the trusty *Ayapah*, on their way to visit the great fall of *Bir Jooki*. We have already, in our last chapter, inflicted upon our readers a translation of the Hindoo legend, from which this fall derives its name. We have also attempted to present them with a faint outline of the river, and Tiger Island. We must now try to describe the fall itself. But, being aware that the subject is one considerably beyond our powers, we feel ourselves in honour bound to forewarn our gentle Reader of the fact; and to beg, if he have the slightest objection to a bad description of fine scenery, that he will be kind enough to skip over the next few pages, and either take our word for it that *Bir Jooki*, in spite of its barbarous name, is one of the grandest falls in the world, or, if that be not sufficient, let him, after having applied to us for a letter of introduction to our friend Ramaswamy, take his passage in the first ship bound for Madras, hire a palanquin, with twelve bearers, and a *Mussaulchee*—make the best of his way to the Island of Seevasamoodrum, and judge for himself.

After walking about a mile, the party struck into the low belt of jungle, which skirted, and concealed the river; and, descending by a rugged path, suddenly emerged upon a smooth platform of rock, directly facing the principal fall, and about a hundred feet above the level of the basin, into which the cataract discharged itself. On their left, and so close to their position, that the rock on which they stood trembled as if shaken by an earthquake, one branch of the river came bounding from ledge to ledge of rock, forming a succession of roaring cataracts, and hurrying along, in its headlong course, huge masses of rock, the crash of which might be heard, even amidst the din of raging waters. Directly opposite, the great fall rushed in one unbroken sheet of water, over a perpendicular cliff, nearly three hundred feet in height, and was lost in the cloud of spray, which, rising from the dark abyss, like steam from a boiling caldron, rolled away in light eddying wreaths, along the sides of the surrounding mountains.

So stupendous a scene, bursting suddenly upon the beholder, is almost overpowering. The steady, unceasing, irresistible, rush of the eternal waters—giving one the idea, more than any other object in nature, of unlimited power—the fearful turmoil, unseen though heard, in the fathomless gulf below, the dull monotonous roar, the mysterious cloud of vapour, all tend to bewilder the senses. The head swims, the sight is dazzled, the ear is stunned, all the faculties appear to be paralyzed. Man feels his own insignificance, and the proudest gazes for a moment in awe-struck silence.

Even the Doctor held his breath, and the remains of

his beloved cheroot, not yet half consumed, dropped unheeded from his lips.

Mansfield, folding his arms upon his chest, gazed upon the bewildering scene, with the same calm and apparently unmoved expression, which his noble features ever wore, even in moments of the greatest excitement; but the flashing of his dark eye showed that lofty thoughts were swelling in his bosom.

Charles, also, stood for some moments in silence, till, overpowered by the rush of poetical images which crowded upon his mind, he sprang forward to the very edge of the precipice, and throwing his arms aloft, like a young eagle spreading its wings for flight, shouted, at the very top of his voice, the following beautiful lines from "Childe Harold:"—

"The roar of waters! from the headlong height,
Velino cleaves the wave-worn precipice;
The fall of waters! rapid as the light,
The flashing mass foams, shaking the abyss,
The hell of waters! where they howl and hiss,
And boil in endless torture; while the sweat
Of their great agony, wrung out from this
Their Phlegethon, curls round the rocks of jet
That gird the gulf around, in pitiless horror set.

And mounts in spray the skies, and thence again
Returns in an unceasing shower, which round,
With its unemptied cloud of gentle rain,
Is an eternal April to the ground,
Making it all one emerald:—how profound
The gulf! and how the giant element
From rock to rock leaps with delirious bound,
Crushing the cliffs, which, downward worn and rent
With his fierce footsteps, yield in chasms a fearful vent.

To the broad column which rolls on, and shows
More like the fountain of an infant sea
Torn from the womb of mountains by the throes
Of a new world, than only thus to be
Parent of rivers, which flow gushingly,
With many windings through the vale :—Look back !
Lo ! where it comes like an eternity,
As if to sweep down all things in its track,
Charming the eye with dread,—a matchless cataract.

Horribly beautiful ! but on the verge,
From side to side, beneath the glittering morn,
An iris sits amidst the infernal surge,
Like Hope upon a death-bed, and, unworn
Its steady dyes, while all around is torn
By the distracted waters, bears serene
Its brilliant hues with all their beams unshorn :
Resembling, 'mid the torture of the scene,
Love watching madness with unalterable mien."

"Whew!" the Doctor gave a long whistle, turned on his heel, picked up the stump of his cheroot, replaced it in the corner of his mouth, seated himself on a stone, puffed out a huge volume of smoke, and winking at Mansfield, tapped his forehead significantly with his forefinger, thereby implying that he had serious misgivings as to the perfect sanity of "The laddie, Maister Charles."

Standing, as he did, on the brink of a precipice, his arms outstretched, his flowing locks drenched by the heavy spray which fell around him, and shouting at the top of his voice, as if declaiming to the spirits of the flood, the excited appearance of our young friend was such as might have induced a commonplace, unimaginative mind, to coincide in the Doctor's opinion. But

Mansfield, although a bit of a stoic in externals, was an enthusiast at heart, and liked to see enthusiasm in others. He remembered the day when he would have acted as Charles did, and a benevolent smile played around his mouth, a responsive chord vibrated in his heart, as he witnessed this natural burst of feeling in his young companion.

"A good and apt quotation, boy," said he, tapping Charles on the shoulder, "and one I had almost forgotten. I thank you for reminding me of it. If you are ever asked for a description of the Falls of Gungah, you cannot do better than repeat these very lines. But your eyes have been so intently riveted upon that 'Hell of waters,' as your friend Byron has it, that you have not yet beheld half the beauties of the scene. Look upwards, above the cloud of spray, hanging, as it were, between Heaven and earth, with what an air of dignified composure that beauteous island, glowing in all the splendour of tropical vegetation, sits like a Queen, smiling amidst the war of elements. And here, to the right, see that narrow gorge, throughout which the foaming torrent, lashed to madness in this boiling whirlpool, bounds with such frantic speed, like a hunted Lion, bursting through the toils. Cast your eyes around, mark the grandeur of the hills, by which we are surrounded—children of an earthquake—their hoary heads, scathed by the fires of heaven, bleached by the storms of a thousand ages, piercing the clouds; their rugged fronts frowning defiance to the spirits of the tempest; proud and unyielding, as at the day of their birth. See the graceful feathery bamboo, cowering from the blast, and clinging for protection to their iron sides. The deep scarlet flowers of the rhododendron, glowing like gems, upon the rugged breast of that moss-grown rock. The swift-winged paroquets darting among the branches of that lofty teak-tree—The—Ha! what was that?"

Mansfield stopped short, in the midst of his rhapsody, and, bending forward, listened eagerly for a repetition of the sound which had attracted his attention. Again it was heard, even amidst the din of rushing waters, and this time there could be no mistake. It was the short barking cry of the spotted deer, and, apparently, close at hand. Charles fixed his eyes upon Mansfield's face, with an inquiring look, as if he expected some explanation of so strange a circumstance. But Mansfield, whose quick ear immediately recognized the well-known signal of an Indian *Shikaree*, bounded forward, without uttering a word, and, snatching the proffered rifle from the hand of *Ayapah*, followed with his eye the direction of his finger, as he pointed eagerly towards the bottom of a deep ravine, which flanked their position, and whispered the exciting word—*Bhag*.

Mansfield's rifle was thrown hastily forward, as a bramble-bush, immediately below him, was seen to rustle, and a solitary monkey, which sat grinning, like an evil spirit, in a dark nook of the glen, began to spring from rock to rock, filling the air with hideous screams. Swift as lightning a brindled mass glided, like a huge snake, across an open space in the bushes, and again disappeared in the dense thicket which filled the bottom of the ravine. The report of the rifle bellowed among the rocky caverns, as if a twelve-pounder had been discharged, and the narrow chasm was filled with a dense cloud of smoke. But no angry roar answered to the shot; and when the sulphury vapour rolled away, the blue mark of the bullet, which had flattened upon a stone, in the dry watercourse below, convinced Mansfield that, for once, a Tiger had been too quick for him.

"Away with you, son of a slave!" cried he, turning upon the unfortunate *Ayapah,* for want of some more fitting object upon which to vent his wrath,—"why do you stand gaping there like an old woman, as if you had never seen a Tiger missed before? Off with you, I say, to the top of the hill, and mark him."

Ayapah turned, without answering a word, and dashed into the jungle—next moment he was seen perched amongst the highest branches of a tree, which crowned a hill, and commanded a full view of every outlet from the ravine. But Mansfield waited, in vain, for a signal that the Tiger had appeared. *Ayapah* remained motionless as a vulture watching his prey.

"He does not intend to show himself, I find," observed Mansfield, throwing his rifle carelessly into the hollow of his arm. "As my friend *Ayapah* would say, he has no fancy to eat bullets; but we must force him a little. Mr. M——, I believe you have some good *Shikarees* in your village."

"Yes, Sar," replied the half-caste, with alacrity. "Plenty *Shikarees* got—plenty nets got. Suppose I give order, in one half-hour plenty *Shikar* Men attend Master's pleasure. That very bad Tiger, Sar—two mans he eat last week. Suppose Master kill that Tiger, that thing make black man's heart glad. He very much ceremony make—plenty cocoa-nut, plenty *jaggary* he give to *Swamy*."

"Ha! another Man-eater. By the hump of the Holy Camel we are in luck. And nets too, you say. I am glad of that, it is the most effectual way of securing a Tiger in such jungly ground. The sooner, then, you can get the *Shikarees*, and the nets, the better. And, hark ye, Mr. M——, if you can manage to procure a few rockets, at the same time, I shall feel obliged—it will save much trouble in beating him up. I shall leave *Ayapah* here, to watch the ravine, and, in the mean time, I would propose that we adjourn to the *bungalow*, and have some *tiffin*, to give us strength for the encounter."

"What new species of *shikar* is this?" asked Charles, with a look of wonder. "Do you really mean to say that you intend to catch the Tiger in a net!—to bag him like a rabbit?"

"Ay," replied Mansfield, smiling, "and to spear him too, when he *is* bagged. How like you the idea, boy, of spearing a Tiger on foot? It will be something to talk of, when you get back to the Hills."

Charles appeared rather startled by this proposal, but said nothing.

The Doctor sprang to his feet, shoved his hands deep into his pockets, and stood staring at Mansfield with a look of utter bewilderment.

"Spear a Tiger!" The words dropped from his lips as slowly as if he had stopped to weigh each individual syllable. "Spear a Tiger! The Lord forgie ye, Captain. I aye thought ye had a bee in your bonnet; but now I am satisfied ye are just fit for Bedlam. Spear a Tiger indeed! Did ony leevin' mortal ever hear the like!" So saying, the Doctor turned on his heel, and marched off, whistling the old Scotch tune of "The Devil among the Tailors."

"Our friend the Doctor does not appear to relish the idea of spearing a Tiger," said Mansfield, indulging in a quiet laugh; "but, I can assure you, it may be done, and is done, constantly, in some parts of India. However, you shall see, and judge for yourself. It will, at all events, be something new, and I think you will allow it to be the most exciting style of sport you have yet seen."

The Sportsmen had hardly finished their *tiffin*, ere a clamorous beating of *tomtoms*, and blowing of horns, announced that the *Shikarees* had arrived. Mansfield and Charles started to their feet, at the welcome sound, —thrust their hunting-knives into their belts,—snatched up their rifles, and sallied forth to inspect and arrange their forces. Even the Doctor, whose blood had been warmed with generous wine, shared in the enthusiasm of the moment. Shouldering his favourite weapon, *Mons Meg*, he crammed his broad-brimmed hat fiercely over his eyes—swallowed a glass of brandy-and-water, to strengthen his nerves,—and swearing, by the "Piper of war!" that he would not be outdone by "ony young birkie o' them a'," struck up the warlike tune of "Johnny Cope," and strode after his companions, with the air of a man, determined to do or die.

On the steps of the portico, they were received with a profound *salaam*, by the *Cotwall*, or head policeman of the village, in his holiday robes. The quaintly-dressed trumpeter gave forth a deafening blast, from his gigantic instrument, streaming with Tigers' tails, the hard-earned trophies of many a bloody field. A confused clatter of *tomtoms* rent the air; and the assembled multitude prostrated themselves before the *Burrah Sahib*, whose fame as a Tiger-killer had reached even to the banks of the Cauvary.

The *Cotwall*, in a flowing speech, complimented Mansfield on his exploits, calling him, "the Lion of Mysore—the Invincible—the Open-handed,"—here he looked out of the corner of his eye to see whether this last compliment was likely to produce the desired effect upon Mansfield's purse-strings; and concluded by expressing a hope that the arrangements he had made, might meet with the approbation of his Magnificence.

His Magnificence, who, instead of attending to the *Cotwall's* elaborate speech, had been counting the number of the beaters, and scanning the features of the *Shikarees*, with the eye of a connoisseur, expressed his entire satisfaction; and, slipping a pagoda into the extended hand of the delighted *Cotwall*, informed him that he was at liberty to make his *salaam*, and take leave.

The *Cotwall* had done his duty, and well deserved the present bestowed upon him. In front of the crowd, leaning on their long matchlocks, stood four *Shikarees* of the real fighting caste—long-legged, wiry, hard-featured, hairy-muzzled, devil-me-care-looking fellows—such as a Yankee would say, at the first glance, were "fit to flog their weight in wild cats." Behind them,

MUSTERING FORCES FOR A TIGER HUNT.

some dozen naked *Coolies* tottered under the weight of the hunting-nets, or toils. And beyond them again, appeared the whole male population of the village, liberally provided with *tomtoms,* horns, and other noisy instruments, from which, from time to time, issued diabolical notes of discord, expressive of eagerness, and overflowing valour. Mansfield having ascertained that all the necessary preparations had been made, the procession moved off in good order to the scene of action.

On arriving at the ground, *Ayapah* was found still sitting patiently at his post; and from him the welcome intelligence was obtained that the Tiger had not yet moved.

The *Shikarees,* who appeared perfectly to understand their business, bustled about with great activity, and, in a wonderfully short space of time, the toils were pitched, and the Tiger's lair so effectually surrounded that it appeared impossible for him to escape. But how was this done? some of our Readers may ask—we must try to explain.

The toils are huge nets, made in the same manner as those used for fishing, only that they are formed of stronger cord, nearly as thick as the little finger, and with meshes large enough to admit a man's head. The ground having been first carefully examined, poles, about ten feet long, pointed at one end, and having a notch at the top, are driven into the ground at regular intervals, across every outlet by which it appears possible for an animal to escape. Upon these the toils, or nets, are suspended, like a curtain, with the upper rope resting in the notch on the top of the pole. This is so slightly fixed, that the moment a large animal rushes against the net, it becomes disengaged, the net falls over the animal, and in his struggles to escape he becomes so entangled in the meshes, that the Hunters, who lie in ambush at a short distance, and who, in general, are only armed with spears, have time to run in and despatch him before he can extricate himself.

Every thing being arranged, a council of war was held, to decide finally, whether the bold experiment of attacking the Tiger with spears should be attempted. The Doctor remonstrated loudly; but the *éclat* of such an adventure was a temptation not to be resisted. It was voted decidedly unsportsmanlike to shoot a Tiger after he had been netted—it was taking an ungentlemanlike advantage of him.—In short, the Doctor's objections were over-ruled, and the measure carried, with great applause from Charles, and a grim smile of satisfaction on the part of *Ayapah*.

Two strong, broad-bladed, hunting-spears having been provided, Mansfield and Charles laid aside their rifles, and, armed with these more primitive weapons, posted themselves at some distance from each other, so as to command the only two outlets from the ravine, by which it appeared probable that the Tiger would attempt to escape. The more prudent Doctor, having no idea of risking his valuable life in any such wild adventure, climbed, with the assistance of *Ayapah*, into a neighbouring tree, and lighting his cheroot, nestled himself among the branches, to witness the coming strife in safety and comfort.

For some time after they had taken their positions,

all remained quiet—not a leaf stirred—no sound was heard, save the dull, hoarse, monotonous roar of the cataract, which, mellowed by the intervening woods, only served to increase the feeling of lifeless solitude, imparted by the perfect stillness of all else around, to the silent lairs of the watchful Sportsmen.

The Doctor's patience, and his cheroot, were both wellnigh exhausted. Charles, in spite of himself, was beginning to feel that disagreeable, cold, creeping, nervous sensation, which is not fear, but which will occasionally steal over the stoutest heart in such a situation; it is a feeling which any of my readers who have happened to lead a forlorn hope, or have stood upon a frigate's deck, during the few minutes of portentous silence which precede the first broadside, may perhaps remember. Even Mansfield was beginning to handle his spear in a fidgety manner, and to think, with peculiar affection, of his trusty rifle, when a distant shout came swelling on the breeze, and all ideas, save those of victory, vanished.

Nearer, and nearer came that cheering sound. The air was filled with wild discordant cries—the rocky sides of the ravine echoed to the clatter of a hundred *tomtoms*. Now is heard the rushing sound of the lively rockets, as they dart, like hissing snakes, among the tangled bushes—and now the angry voice of the hunted Tiger, as he starts indignant from his lair, and roars defiance to his foes.

Every nerve was braced, and the blood rushed like lightning through the veins of the excited Sportsmen, as that sound reached their ears. The shouting of the beaters was redoubled—a shower of rockets swept the ravine like a storm of fire,—and the Tiger, rushing at once from his concealment, dashed, with tremendous bounds, towards the pass which Charles commanded. He had approached within ten yards of the nets, when he suddenly stopped, having probably observed the impediment, and stood in an attitude of indecision, lashing his tail from side to side, and uttering a low savage growl. Charles, in conformity with the directions he had received from Mansfield, immediately stepped from his concealment, and, bringing his spear down to the charging position, advanced steadily towards the frail barrier, which formed his only defence against the expected charge of his formidable antagonist. It was a moment of fearful interest; and the Doctor, who from his perch commanded a full view of the scene, felt the blood curdling in his veins. But Charles, although he felt a peculiar tingling of the nerves, and a slight palpitation of the heart, bore himself gallantly.

No sooner did the Tiger perceive his intended victim, than his whole appearance was altered. His green eyes glared savagely—his ears were laid flat back upon his neck—the hair upon his back stood erect,—and, crouching close to the ground, he crept swiftly towards the nets. Having got sufficiently near, he uttered a tremendous roar, and springing forward with a lashing bound, threw himself against the net with a force that threatened to carry every thing before it. But the tough cordage yielded to the shock without sustaining any injury,—the upper rope became disengaged,—the net fell together in a heap—and the enraged monster was instantly enveloped in a complicated mass of network, from which, in spite of his frantic efforts, he found it impossible to disengage himself.

So furious was the onset of the Tiger, and so apparently frail the defence opposed to it, that Charles had not sufficient command of nerve to stand his ground; —he made an involuntary spring backward, stumbled, and fell.

The Doctor, seeing the desperate rush of the Tiger, accompanied by a roar that made his heart sink within him, and perceiving through a cloud of dust, that the net was, apparently, demolished, and his young friend down, immediately jumped to the conclusion that he must be in the Tiger's jaws. His first impulse was to shout to Mansfield for help, which he did right lustily; his next to slide from his perch, with a reckless haste that considerably injured the appearance of his nether garments; to snatch up his fusee, and hurry to the rescue, invoking maledictions on the man who first invented the desperate amusement of spearing Tigers on foot.

But, ere he could reach the scene of action, Charles had recovered his footing, picked up his spear, and driven it deep into the chest of the Tiger. The previous struggles of the powerful animal were those of a cat, compared to the frantic efforts which he now made to reach his pigmy antagonist. His eyes glowed like live coals—foam, mingled with blood, flew in spray from his distended jaws—he roared—he gnashed his teeth—he tore up the earth—he twisted and turned with the agility of a wild cat. By dint of gnawing, he had so far succeeded in destroying the net, that his head protruded; but still the complicated folds entangled his limbs and paralyzed his efforts. Charles, although tremendously knocked about, clung manfully to his weapon, and exerted his utmost strength to force it through the monster's body and pin him to the ground. At length the Tiger succeeded in grasping the shaft with his powerful jaws, and, by one vigorous shake, snapped the tough ash-pole as if it had been a reed. Charles, although partially disarmed, still retained sufficient courage and presence of mind to make the best use of what remained of his weapon, and so gain time till assistance arrived; he had never quitted his hold of the spear-shaft, and, with this, he showered such a volley of blows upon the Tiger's head, as partially to stupify him, and thereby impede his efforts to disengage himself.

The Doctor, whose courage had failed him, the moment he perceived Charles on foot again, had all this time remained at a respectful distance, dancing about like a maniac, brandishing "*Mons Meg*," and shouting to Charles "to haud out o' the gate till he got a rattle at the brute wi' the grit-shot." But Charles, who expected no aid from any one but Mansfield, was much too busily engaged in preventing the Tiger from getting clear of the nets, to pay any attention to his exclamations, and continued to thrash away with his heavy ash pole like a young Hercules. The Tiger's efforts, however, instead of diminishing, only seemed to increase. He gnawed, and tore, and plunged, with the fury of desperation. Mesh after mesh of the strong network gradually gave way. He had already succeeded in liberating one fore-paw as well as his haed, and it was but too evident that a few more vigorous struggles must set him free. At this critical moment, Mansfield came bounding over the rocks, and, uttering a hearty cheer of encouragement to Charles, drove his spear deep into the body of the Tiger. Instead of attempting to hold the animal down, as Charles had done, he instantly withdrew the weapon, and repeated his thrusts with such strength and rapidity, that in spite of a desperate resistance on the part of the Tiger, he was speedily covered with wounds, and bleeding at every pore. The rapid loss of blood had perceptibly diminished his strength—his shrill roar was changed to a hoarse bubbling growl—the victory was all but gained—when, with one tremendous blow of his gigantic fore-paw, he snapped the shaft of the spear in two, leaving the iron head sticking in his own body, and bringing down the butt-end of the shaft with such violence upon Mansfield's head, that he fell backwards, stunned and insensible.

The case was now indeed a desperate one. Poor Charles, although his courage failed not, was so much exhausted by his previous exertions, that his blows fell harmless as those of a child, and it was evident that he could not much longer maintain the unequal contest. Most heartily did he now wish for his trusty rifle, and loudly did he call upon the Doctor for assistance.

The Tiger, weakened though he was by loss of blood, had by this time so far succeeded in destroying the net, that his head and shoulders were at liberty. One struggle more, and he was free, to wreak a fearful vengeance on his foes—to quench his burning thirst in their blood. A hellish fire shot from his eyes, and his whiskered lips curled into a grin of ineffable malignity as he gathered himself together for a decisive spring. It was madness to oppose him longer. Charles, upbraiding the Doctor for a cold-blooded poltroon, turned to fly; but, in doing so, he stumbled over his prostrate companion, and fell heavily.

Doctor! Doctor! where is your manhood? Will you allow your gallant young companion to be miserably mangled before your eyes?—No!—The latent spark of fire which lurked in the blood of his Celtic ancestor, is at length roused. He utters a war-cry—he rushes boldly between the infuriated Tiger and his prostrate victims,—*Mons Meg* pours forth her deadly contents, —and the monster, in the very act of springing rolls dead at his feet, with two ounces of "grit-shot" in his brain. Hurrah!!

"What think ye o' the grit-shot now, Captain?" exclaimed the Doctor, pointing with an air of triumph to the dead Tiger, as soon as Mansfield had sufficiently recovered from the stunning effects of the blow, to understand how narrowly he had escaped destruction. "There are waur things than a fusee and grit-shot, at a pinch, I 'm thinkin'. That plan o' yours, o' spearin' Tigers, is a' very weel, for ance in a way; but, by my troth, lads, ye had better no *make a practice o't.*"

This was a sentiment in which the two young Sportsmen perfectly concurred. They had got a lesson which made them heartily repent of their folly. And, after returning thanks for their Providential escape, and bestowing abundant praise on the Doctor for his timely aid, they both vowed, solemnly, never more to engage in so foolhardy an adventure.

Great were the rejoicings that night in the Sacred Village, and many were the good jokes cracked by the worthy Doctor over a bottle of *Glenlivat*, which he insisted on draining in honour of his victory.

We have heard it hinted, that towards the "sma' hours," the Doctor was seen pursuing rather a tortuous course towards his bedroom, under the guidance of his friend Heels; but this we believe to be a calumny. At all events, it was the proudest day in the worthy Doctor's life; and, to this hour, his favourite story after dinner is, "The daft-like Tiger-hunt, wi' thae twa wild *Birkies*, at the Falls of the Cauvary."

CHAPTER XVII.

THE HUNTERS' RETURN; AND A LITTLE LOVE-MAKING.

LOVE-MAKING! Love-making! Ha! ha! Fair Reader, does it not make thee laugh to see the weather-beaten, sun-dried Old Forester thus deliberately announcing that he is about to attempt a love scene—to dash headlong into a description of that all-powerful passion which our quaint friend, Burton, describes as "*a fire in a fire; the quintessence of fire,*"—backing his assertion by the following fearful description of an unfortunate youth, who died for love, and was dissected in the presence of Empedocles, the philosopher:—

"*His heart was combust, his liver smoakie, his lungs dried up, insomuch that he verily believed his soul was either sod or rosted, through the vehemency of love's fire.*"

There, young Ladies!—there 's a pretty fiery subject for an old fellow of three score and ten to handle! "He 'll burn his fingers," you will say. That, between you and ourselves, we think very probable; but, having followed our young friend, Charles, so far through the dangers of the wilderness, we are loath to desert him, now that he is in a fair way of having his soul either "*sod or rosted,*" by the bright eyes of his pretty Cousin.

No, no ; we must stand by him, even at the risk of burning our fingers. But, before we re-introduce the dangerous little beauty, we must see how it fares with our male friends, whom we left at the Falls of the Cauvary, and who are now on their way back to Ootacamund.

"So ends our jungle campaign for the present," said Mansfield, throwing the reins upon the neck of his smoking horse, and removing his heavy hunting-cap, to let the cool mountain-air fan his throbbing temples, as the Hunters, after a hot and rapid ride, of some twenty miles, emerged from the dense jungle which encircles the Neilgherry Hills, and commenced the toilsome but beautiful ascent which leads to their summit. "Away with the spear and the rifle for a season; and now, Charley, my boy, for Ladies' eyes and love-ditties! Ha! have I guessed your thoughts?"

Charles, whose eyes had been riveted on the cloud-capped summits of the mountains ever since they became visible, and whose thoughts were, at that moment, many miles in advance of his body, felt the conscious blood mount into his cheeks.

"Nay, nay, never be ashamed to own it, boy. I have seen a little of the world in my day, and never yet have I met with a real good soldier, a forward rider, or a stanch Deer-stalker, who had not a soft corner in his heart for 'The Angels of the Creation.' What say you, Doctor, is it not so?"

"By my troth, Captain, ye never said a truer word," replied the Doctor. "I ken weel what it is to hae a soft heart, an o'er soft heart for the Lasses—bless their sweet faces.—Hech, Sirs! hech, Sirs! it 's just a slavish passion, yon love,"—and the Doctor heaved a deep sigh, and turned up the whites of his eyes, as if overwhelmed by a torrent of tender recollections.

"What! Bully Doctor," exclaimed Mansfield, laughing, "art thou, too, a victim to the tender passion? By the darts of Cupid! I would as soon have expected to see a Brahmin Priest turn rope-dancer, as to find our sapient Leech acting the love-sick Swain. Why, thou burly Scot, I fancied if thou hadst a soft corner in thy heart at all, thy weakness was for a haunch of venison, or a bottle of Glenlivat, rather than the Ladies. But come, Doctor, confess:—who is the enslaver of thy tender heart? 'Tell me, in sadness, whom she is you love?' Her name—her name, I pray."

"Whist, Captain," said the Doctor, with a look of mock gravity, "and dinna be speakin' about things ye dinna understand. Ye hae nae mair idea o' what true love is, ye stony-hearted Deevle, than that black Pagan, Heels; and ye would just like to make sport o' Maister Charles and me, because we hae the feelings o' Christian men. But you needna expect us to pleasure you that far: so ye may just quit wi' your daffin. And now, lads, that ye hae minded me o't, I maun beg o' you no to crack nae mair o' your jokes about the Glenlivat. It's a' very weel in the jungles. But in civilized society, Gentlemen, I beg to remind you that it 's no' good manners. In fact, it 's just enough to ruin a respectable man's character; and gar folk believe, that he is nae better than a poor drunken body, like my auld Grand Uncle, the Laird o' Bonniemoon,—rest his soul, honest man! And ye ken weel that 's no' my case—for, although

I like a glass o' het toddy as weel as my neighbours, and although we have had twa or three cantie nights thegether, yet ye maun baith allow that ye hae never seen me rightly fou yet—"

"Oh! oh! Doctor!"

"Aye! ye may cry 'oh! oh!' But I'll uphaud it that ye hae never seen me right fou yet, although I'll no deny but what I hae, anes or twice, been a wee thing hearty and chatty like."

"Well, Doctor," replied Mansfield, laughing, "we'll not dispute the point. You shall have the best possible character for sobriety, and we shall not crack any more jokes about the Glenlivat. But, in return, pray give us a definition of what you consider being fou, that we may know, in future, at what particular stage of *obfuscation* a cannie Scot may, with propriety, be termed drunk."

"Weel, Gentlemen," said the Doctor, looking wise, and taking a pinch of snuff, "that's rather a kittle question to answer, for ye maun ken there is a great diversity of opeenion on that subject. Some say that a man is sober as long as he can stand upon his legs. An Ireish friend o' mine—a fire-eating, hard-drinking Captain of dragoons—anes declared to me, on his honour as a soldier and a jontleman, that he would never allow any friend of his to be called drunk, till he saw him trying to light his pipe at the pump. And others there be—men of learning and respectability too—who are of opinion that a man has every right to consider himself sober as long as he can lie flat on his back, without holding by the ground. For my own part, I am a moderate person, and would allow that a man was fou, without being just sae far through as ony o' these. But, with your leave, Gentlemen, I 'll tell you a story, about the Laird o' Bonniemoon, that will, maybe, gar you laugh, and will, at any rate, be a good illustration of what I ca' being fou."

"Do, do, Doctor," exclaimed both the young men, delighted at the prospect of having one of the Doctor's good stories to beguile the tedium of the long ascent.

"Weel then, Gentlemen, ye maun ken that the Laird of Bonniemoon was gae fond o' his bottle—in short, just a poor drunken body, as I said afore. On one occasion the Laird was asked to dine with Lord R—, a neighbour of his, and his Lordship, being weel acquainted with the Laird's dislike to sma' drinks, ordered a bottle o' cherry brandy to be set down afore him, after dinner, instead of port, which he always drank in preference to claret, when nothing better was to be got. The Laird he thought this fine heartsome stuff, and on he went, filling his glass like the rest, and telling his cracks, and ever, the mair he drank, the mair he praised his Lordship's port. It was fine, full-bodied wine, and lay weel upon the stamach, no' like that puisonsome stuff, claret, that gar't a body feel as if he had swallowed a nest of puddocks. Weel, Gentlemen, the Laird had finished ae bottle o' cherry brandy—or, as his Lordship called it, his particular port—and had just tossed off a glass of the second bottle, which he declared to be even better than the first, when his old confidential servant, Watty, came stavin into the room, and making his best boo, announced that the Laird's horse was at the door.

"'Get out o' that, ye fause loon,' cried the Laird,

pooin' aff his wig and flinging it at Watty's head. 'Div ye no' see, ye blethering brute, that I 'm just beginning my second bottle?'

"'But, maister,' said Watty, scartin his lug, 'it 's amaist twall o'clock!'

"'Weel! what though it be?' said the Laird, turning up his glass with drunken gravity, while the rest of the company were like to split their sides with laughing at him and Watty. 'It canna be ony later, my man, so just rax me my wig, and let the naig bide a wee.'

"Weel, Gentlemen, it was a cauld frosty night, and Watty soon tired o kicking his heels at the front door; so, in a wee while, back he comes, and says he,

"'Maister, maister, it 's amaist one o'clock!'

"'Weel, Watty,' says the Laird, wi' a hiccup—for he was far through by this time,—'it will no' be ony earlier, Watty, my man, and that 's a comfort, so you may just rest yourself a wee while longer, till I finish my bottle. A fou wame makes a stiff back, ye ken.'

"Watty was by this time just dancing mad; so, after waiting another half-hour, back he comes, in an awfu' hurry, and says he,

"'Laird, Laird, as true as death, the sun's rising!'

"'Weel, Watty,' says the Laird, looking awfu' wise, and trying wi' baith hands to fill his glass, 'let him rise, my man, let him rise—he has farther to gang the day than either you or me, Watty.'

"This answer fairly dumfoundered poor Watty, and he gave it up in despair. But at last the bottle was finished: the Laird was lifted into the saddle, and off he rode in high glee, thinkin' a' the time, the moon was the sun, and that he had fine daylight for his journey.

"'Hech! Watty, my man,' says the Laird, patting his stomach, and speaking awfu' thick, 'we waurna the waur o' that second bottle this frasty marning.'

"'Faith,' says Watty, blawing his fingers, and looking as blue as a partan, 'your honour is, maybe, no' the waur o't, but fient a hait is my wame the better; I wish it was.'

"Weel, on they rade, fou cannily, the Laird gripping hard at the horse's mane, and rolling about like a bow o' meal; for the cauld air was beginning to gar the speerits tell on him.

"At last they came to a wee bit burn that crossed the road; and the Laird's horse being pretty well used to having his own way, stopped short, and put down his head to take a drink. This had the effect of making the poor Laird lose his balance, and away he went over the horse's ears into the very middle o' the burn. The Laird, honest man, had just sense enough to hear the splash, and to ken that something was wrong; but he was that fou, that Deevle a bit did he ever suspect it was himsel'.

"'Watty,' says he, sitting up in the middle o' the burn, and stammering out the words with great difficulty, 'Watty, my man, there is surely something tumbled in the burn, Watty.'

"'Faith, your Honour may say that,' replied Watty, like to whamble off his horse with laughing, 'for it's just yoursel', Laird!'

"'Hout fie, no, Watty!' cried the Laird, with a

hiccup between every word; 'it surely canna be me, Watty, for *I'm here!*'

"Now, Gentlemen," continued the Doctor, "here is a case in which I would allow a man to be fou, although he had neither lost his speech nor the use of his limbs."

"Why, yes, Doctor," said Mansfield, laughing, "I think when a man is so far gone, that he tumbles into the water without being conscious of it, one may fairly be allowed to pronounce him *fou*. But proceed, proceed, I long to hear how Watty behaved on the occasion."

"Troth, Sir, he just behaved as any other douce, sober, serving-man would hae done on a like occasion. After having had his laugh out—for he wasna fit to get off his horse till he had done that—he trailed his master out of the water, laid him on the bank to dry, and set off to look after the Laird's hat and wig, which had been carried off by the burn; for Watty was valet as well as groom, and had a great respect for the Laird's best sabath-day wig. After some trouble he succeeded in cleeking them up with the crook of his umbrella, and restored them to his master.

"The Laird being fou, as aforesaid, very naturally clapped on his wig wrong side foremost; but, fou though he was, he was aware that it didna fit him; so he tore it off in a rage, and flung it at Watty's head, saying, with a look o' great disgust,

"'That 's no' my wig, Watty; that 's no' my wig, ye fause loon; I 'll no' wear that wig!'

"'Troth, then,' said Watty, quietly picking up the wig, and wiping it with the sleeve of his coat, 'your

Honour maun just be doin wi't the night, for there 's nae waul o' wigs in *this* burn.'

" Ha, ha, ha! he was an awfu' droll chap that Watty."

But enough of the Doctor and his Grand Uncle, the Laird. We must now leave the travellers and return to our fair friend, the pretty Kate, whom we have so long and so shamefully neglected.

Kate was an only child, and the darling of her father; she was consequently a spoilt child—at least so far spoilt as her naturally amiable disposition would admit of. She also had the misfortune to lose her mother early in life, and although every justice had been done to her in the way of education, although she was highly accomplished, and her manners in general perfectly ladylike, still there was wanting that indescribable something, which a gentle mother's constant care and good example can alone impart. She was high-minded, generous, affectionate, and naturally gentle; but she was wilful, overapt to be hurried away by the impulse of the moment, and impatient of control; and yet, withal, so open-hearted, so ready to confess her little faults, and so anxious to make amends, where she fancied she had given offence, or hurt the feelings of another, that the most austere could hardly have found it in their heart to be angry with her. Having no female companion, she naturally associated much with her father, accompanying him in his wildest mountain rambles, and sometimes even following him to the Hunting-field.

She had thus, almost imperceptibly, acquired a romantic turn of mind, a love of adventure, a promptness and decision of character, which, however praiseworthy it might have been in one of the rougher sex, would, in these refined times, be thought hardly becoming in so young a Lady, for she was not yet seventeen. But to counterbalance these little defects in her character, there was so much good sense, so much tenderness of heart, and refinement of feeling, that those who knew her best, learned at last to love her very faults, if faults they may be called, which were only virtues run wild for want of proper cultivation.

We give this little sketch of Kate's character in hopes that our Fair Readers, if they have occasion to find fault with her, will make some allowance for her peculiar situation, and do so in the spirit of charity.

It was on a lovely evening, just as the sun had dipped behind the western mountains, that the pretty Kate sat at an open window which commanded an extensive view of the lake and surrounding country; her usually gay and animated features were clouded by a look of sadness, and one sparkling drop trembled on the long silken lashes which shaded her deep blue eye. She appeared to be watching the fading tints of purple and gold which streaked the western sky, and her thoughts might well be supposed to tend Heavenward, were it not that, from time to time, the vacant look with which she gazed upon the clouds, was exchanged for an eager and expectant glance along the dusty road, leading to the pass by which travellers ascend to the hills from the Mysore Country.

Had one been curious enough to inquire what her occupation had been, previous to her falling into her present reverie, a letter in the hand-writing of her Cousin

Charles, which lay open on her lap, might have answered the question. How would his young heart have bounded with love and joy, had Charles seen that fair Girl press the unconscious paper to her lips, and marked the big tear which dropped from her quivering eyelid, and blotted his own name! The letter had arrived that morning, by a swift-footed messenger, whom Charles had despatched to announce to his Uncle that the Hunting-party would return in time for dinner.

Kate had snatched up the precious billet which her father had thrown carelessly aside; and after giving the necessary directions for the accommodation of her Cousin and his companions, had flown to her own room to read and re-read the kind messages to her which it contained, and to watch with eager eyes for the appearance of the expected Horsemen.

But why in tears, fair Kate?

Alas! that morning's post had brought other and less welcome tidings. The *Madras Gazette* announced that, in consequence of a dispute with a neighbouring Rajah, Charles's regiment was in daily expectation of an order to take the field, and the same post had brought a long, misshapen, official letter—a thing hateful ever to fond mothers and love-sick maids—addressed to her Cousin, sealed with the royal arms, and having the ominous words "War Office—O.H.M. Service," printed in large, unfeeling, Commander-in-Chief-looking characters on the reverse side. This it was which had dimmed the lustre of the pretty Kate's laughing eyes. But why? we must ask once more. Why? because Charles was her Cousin, to be sure; and because they had now lived together for nearly three months—and ridden together—and walked together among the hills—and picked wild strawberries—and gathered flowers—and read poetry—and taken sketches—and sung duets together. And because Charles was so useful in leading her pony over all the bad steps which she had to cross in her mountain rides—and because he tuned her guitar so much better than any one else—and mended her pens so well—and copied music so nicely—and held the skeins of silk so patiently while she wound them off, and never grumbled though they were ever so much tangled—and was altogether so good-natured and so useful—and—and—in short, it was very natural that she should miss him when he was gone. One is always sorry to part with one's Cousin, you know; but it does not follow, because one is sorry, that one must be in love with one's Cousin! Of course not!

It was somewhat in this manner that Kate reasoned with herself, as she once more kissed the letter, and dropped one more large tear upon the well-conned page.

But was it possible that Charles could really be in love with her? She hoped not, poor fellow, for his own sake—and, as she mentally expressed this wish, she felt a flutter at her heart that gave her thoughts the lie. She knew, indeed, that he pretended to be rather fond of her, and appeared to be happier in her society than any where else; and now that she thought of it, she remembered that he always coloured a little, and squeezed her hand a little, when they met after a short absence—and once, indeed, he had gone as far as to tell her that he loved her better than any of his other cousins. But then he was only a boy, who did not know his own mind; and besides, even supposing he did love her a little, he would soon learn to forget her when he returned to his regiment; so she need not be unhappy upon that score.

By the time she had arrived at this comfortable conclusion, she found it necessary to have recourse to her pocket-handkerchief.

The last streak of daylight had faded from the sky, and our fair warder, unable longer to distinguish objects at any distance, was about to close the window, with a heavy sigh of disappointment, when the distant clatter of horses' hoofs reached her ear, and next moment her quick eye detected, even amidst the deepening gloom, the well-known form of her Cousin, as he spurred ahead of his companions, and urged his snorting horse up the steep ascent which led to the door. Hastily wiping the tears from her eyes, she thrust the crumpled letter into her bosom, and, with a bounding heart, hurried down stairs to welcome her Cousin.

Whether Charles met with as cordial a reception as he expected, we know not—nor is it any business of ours to inquire. But that pawky loon, the Doctor, who had followed him more closely than he expected or wished, used frequently afterwards to quiz him on the subject, remarking, that he 'thought their jungle campaign had done Maister Charles a hantle o' good, for he wasna near-hand sae *blate* as he used to be wi' his bonnie Cousin.'

Mansfield also declared that the Young Lady met him with a flushed cheek and a pouting lip, which led him to suspect that friend Charles had been somewhat less bashful at meeting than his fair Cousin bargained for. But, as we said before, this is no business of ours.

"Welcome! Lads—welcome!" exclaimed old Lorimer, as he shuffled down stairs in his dressing-gown and slippers, and extended both hands to each of the young men in succession. "Bones of my ancestors! my dear boys, I'm right glad to see you once more safe at home. And you, Bully Doctor, what would life be worth without the *Burrah Hakim Sahib?* I have had a fit of the gout, and been as dull as a gib-cat ever since you left me. Never handled a rifle since—hardly breathed the air of Heaven. That confounded fellow, Doctor Henbane, stopped my grog too. The Devil fly away with him for a pottering quack—eh! Bully Doctor? A d—d blunder-headed, quack-salving, son of a sea-cook! Wouldn't trust him to physic a sick Bear—eh? No, I knew you wouldn't. Old Ishmail eating his fingers off for want of something better to do—dogs threatened with melancholy madness—all wrong—all at sixes and sevens; but never mind, we'll soon set things to rights again, now that I've got you back. Give us your hand again, Charley, my boy—give us your hand,—right glad to see you looking something like a *Jungle Wallah* at last. Shaken yourself clear of the green coat and cords, I see. Found that cords and top-boots didn't answer in the jungles—eh? Got that little dash of mother's milk burnt out of your cheeks too. Mansfield has taught you how to handle a rifle, no doubt.—Eh, Mansfield? Well! well! we shall see—we shall see. And you, Bully Doctor, what have you been doing? How many *Anthropophagi* have you sent to the shades, 'wi' a nieve-fou o' grit-shot in their wame,' eh? But, hang it, man, what is the matter with you? You are as stiff in the joints as an old post-horse. Getting rheumatic in your old age, Doctor—eh? or had a fall perhaps. Ay, ay—I see, I see—that old brute, Smiler, came down with you—rolled over you, I'll be bound—those shambling brutes always do—told you long ago how it would be, if you persisted in riding such a Dromedary."

"Whist, Sir!" exclaimed the Doctor, quite affected by the recollection of his poor old horse's tragical fate. "Whist, Sir! and dinna be misca'in' the poor auld beast, he's—"

"Ay, ay! poor beast—I see, I see," exclaimed the garrulous old Gentleman, interrupting the Doctor in the midst of his sentence; "we'll hear all about it presently. But, in the mean time, go and dress, lads, for dinner is waiting." So saying, and pushing his friends before him, the old Gentleman, in the joy of his heart, continued to laugh and talk without allowing any one else to edge in a word, till he had fairly deposited each in his own dressing-room.

Old Lorimer was fond of good living as well as of good sport. He took almost as much interest in his kitchen and his cellar, as he did in his kennel or his stables; and, being a civilian of high rank, his princely salary enabled him to establish and maintain his character as the best dinner-giver in the Madras Presidency. Next to Ishmail Khan, the black Portuguese cook was looked upon as the most important personage in the establishment. Old Lorimer had given directions that a feast, in his very best style, should be prepared in honour of the Hunters' return; and the native artiste had, on this occasion, exerted himself to produce a *burrah khanah*, worthy of his great talents. His preparations for so small a party, were somewhat too profuse to be quite in accordance with our modern ideas of good taste. They were such as might have done credit to the hospitable board of a Baronial hall; and yet the dressing of the dishes argued a degree of culinary skill on the part of the cook, which would have gained for him immortal honour even at a modern civic feast. Fish there was none, because neither the lake nor the brawling streams of the Neilgherry Hills produce any, and fish is too perishable a commodity to bear carriage in such a climate as that of India. But if a profusion of every other delicacy which the country afforded, could make amends for this deficiency, the most fastidious gourmand would have found no just cause of complaint.

Turtle-soup and venison, a turkey from the Conkan, supported by a burly ham from Yorkshire, wild-boar chops, and marrow-bones of the great Rusa Deer; a steaming dish of all-blaze—that inimitable Indian compound of all the most delicate game-birds, curiously blended with piquant sauce, and the hottest spices—a variety of exquisite *curries* and *pillaws*, and a profusion of cunningly-devised sweetmeats; mangoes from Goa; grapes and apples from Bangalore; oranges from the sunny gardens of Laulpette; and the rarest preserves from China;—all appeared in succession, and were washed down with wine that would have done credit to the cup of Ganymede. Nor were any of those accessories wanting, which, although apparently of trifling importance in themselves, are so necessary to the comfort of those who understand and value real luxury. A blazing fire—ay!—a fire, for even within eleven degrees of the equator, a fire becomes a luxury at the elevation of eight thousand feet above the level of the sea—luxurious arm-chairs, snow-white damask, sparkling crystal, a profusion of wax lights, and a host of well-trained servants, in scarlet turbans and sashes, and flowing robes edged with gold lace—all were perfect of their kind—nothing was forgotten, which the most devoted follower of Epicurus could have desired.

Mansfield, indeed, cared little for such luxuries; but, even to the most indifferent, there is something pleasing in the sudden transition from the hardship and fatigue of a jungle campaign, to the perfect repose and comfort of so well-regulated an establishment as that of old Lorimer. The worthy Doctor, who fully appreciated good living, and who, after having been subjected, for a time, to the comparatively hard fare of a Hunter's camp, now saw realized the most voluptuous dreams of his hungry imagination, was in Elysium. Charles and his Fair Cousin were as happy in each other's society, as the unwelcome intelligence received that morning would permit them to be. Old Lorimer was happy because he saw his guests were so; and, in short, a more cheerful or contented little party were never met around the hospitable board.

The conversation naturally turned upon the late adventures of the jungle party, and many a laugh there was, at the expense of the worthy Doctor, who, in the fulness of his heart,—and of his stomach,—enjoyed the fun as much as any one, adding zest to the jokes against himself, by his quaint sayings and pithy Scotch proverbs.

But, interesting as the conversation proved to those engaged in it, it would hardly be so to the Reader who has already followed our friends in their wanderings. We shall, therefore, pass over the dinner in silence, merely remarking that Kate, who remained at table as long as she could, with any degree of propriety, appeared as deeply interested in the various moving accidents of jungle warfare as any of the Sportsmen, and listened, with a double portion of interest, whenever her Cousin happened to be the hero of the tale.

Charles had no taste for late sitting after dinner, and the feeling that this was, probably, the last opportunity he might have of enjoying a *tête-à-tête* with his Fair Cousin, made him, on the present occasion, doubly anxious to escape from the carouse which his Uncle's comfortable arrangement of a horseshoe-table, and chairs round the fire, appeared to indicate. But, like most young men of his age, he had an insurmountable dread of ridicule. Conscious as he was of a fidgety impatience, and feeling himself unable to join in the conversation, with a proper degree of interest, he fancied the eyes of all—but particularly of his pawky friend, the Doctor, of whose satirical powers he had the utmost dread—were watching his every movement; although he might easily have perceived that the honest Doctor was much too agreeably employed, in discussing a magnum of claret, and narrating his own exploits, to waste a thought upon him, or his intentions. Charles, therefore, kept his seat, —although the seducing notes of a guitar, faintly heard in the next room, made it to him a seat of thorns,—and passed the bottle manfully, till the second magnum having been produced, and Mc.Phee having just commenced an elaborate description of the Hog-hunt, in which he had signalized himself by spearing the old Boar, he availed himself of the opportunity to make a dash at the door, and succeeded in effecting his escape, under cover of one of the Doctor's boisterous peals of laughter.

On entering the drawing-room, Charles found his Cousin seated on a sofa, and hanging pensively over her guitar; she had just concluded a little Spanish air, a particular favourite of his, and one of those which he had copied for her; and his heart beat quicker, as the thought flashed across his mind that her present pensive attitude might, in some way, be connected with the train of ideas which that air was calculated to arouse. Her back was towards him as he entered. His approaching footstep made Kate start, and turn hastily round, and a slight blush suffused her cheek, as she discovered the intruder to be her Cousin;—there was an undried tear, too, upon her cheek;—but why she blushed, or why the tear was there, she hardly dared to ask. And why Charles felt a certain degree of nervous awkwardness in her presence he could not exactly tell, for Kate and he had hitherto been on the most intimate footing of *cousinly* affection,—which, by the way, Young Ladies, is a very dangerous sort of intimacy, and a slippery footing, to say the best of it;—yet certain it was that he did feel like an intruder; and equally true was it that the conscious blush, and the tell-tale tear, were but too distinctly visible on the soft cheek of the blooming Kate.

There is an old Scottish proverb, that "a blate cat makes a proud mouse," and in this instance it was verified. Kate's spirits began to rise the moment she perceived her Cousin's embarrassment; one glance was sufficient to convince her that the bashful youth was at her mercy; and, with that assurance, her self-possession, and the love of tormenting, instantly returned. The timid blush forsook her cheek, and an arch smile played around the corners of her mouth, as she demurely raised her eyes, and inquired of Charles, with an air of great solicitude, whether he did not feel over-fatigued by his ride.

"Over-fatigued!" exclaimed Charles, looking up in his turn, and fixing his eyes upon his Cousin's face, with a look of the most perfect *naïveté*, "what on earth, Kate, should make you think of my being over-fatigued this evening, of all evenings in the year? Why, we only rode some five-and-thirty miles altogether!"

"I crave your pardon, Gentle Cousin," replied Kate, bending over her guitar to conceal a smile which this unsophisticated answer called forth. "I forgot that you were now no longer a *Griffin*, but a seasoned Forester, whose iron frame knows not fatigue. But your having left the other Gentlemen so early, added to your jaded looks, made me feel quite anxious about your health."

"And cannot my Fair Cousin think of any better

reason than that of over-fatigue to account for my leaving the dining-room so early?" replied Charles, now beginning to act on the defensive. "Has she so mean an opinion of her own powers as to suppose that any one with a soul for music could act the part of the deaf adder, with such notes as those I heard just now ringing in his ears?"

"A very prettily-turned compliment, as times go," interrupted Kate. "A delicate mode of insinuating, that your highly accomplished, very musical Cousin, is a charmer. Divine thought! But, Master Adder, as you have taken the trouble of proving to me that you are not deaf, I must avail myself of the opportunity to din into your ears, for the hundred and fiftieth time, that your highly-accomplished and musical Cousin knows too well the value of such empty compliments, to be in the slightest degree flattered by them. She is somewhat fastidious in her taste, and if you have nothing better to offer than the commonplace assurance of her being a charmer, capable of seducing wild beasts from their food, you had better not attempt to act the part of flatterer."

"Flatterer! ah, Kate, you know too well how dear to me are the witching notes of that sweet voice, to believe, in your heart, that I am capable of insulting your good sense by empty flattery."

"Why, this is worse and worse," replied Kate, laughing. "Flattery upon flattery, almost amounting to love-making! Is this all the thanks I get for the interest I have taken in your education? I sent you to the jungles on purpose to make a man of you—to give you an opportunity of performing deeds of valour worthy of my smiles—I expected to see you return a mighty Hunter, a terror to wild beasts, a fearless rider of the 'tempest-footed' Arab. And lo!—unworthy that thou art—you come back upon my hands, a very carpet-knight, a silken-tongued flatterer, a retailer of unmeaning compliments, and, I have no doubt, a would-be lady-killer. Away, away—thou shalt no longer be Knight of mine."

"Come, come, Fair Cousin," replied Charles, laughing in his turn, "you are over-hasty in your judgment; you forget that love and war go hand in hand—the boldest Knight is ever the most enthusiastic in praise of his mistress—and therefore, reasoning from analogy, the very fact of my having so far improved in the art of flattery, as to pay compliments which, you yourself allow, almost amount to love-making, is rather an argument in favour of my having improved also in the art of woodcraft, which every one allows to be a species of warfare. If further proof be wanting of my prowess, I have grim trophies enough to lay at the feet of my peerless Cousin, for which I hope to be rewarded with one of her most gracious smiles. But a truce, dear Kate, I pray you, to this bantering, I am haunted by visions of the many bright hours which have fleeted by so swiftly—alas, how much too swiftly!—since first we met under this happy roof; and the recollection that this is the last evening that we shall spend together for many a long day, hangs like a weight around my heart. When we shall meet again, Kate, Heaven only knows! but let us at least part friends—say that I may still wear your colours in my cap, and let me be happy in the belief that, when we are far apart, the gentle Kate will sometimes bestow a kind thought on her unworthy Cousin."

Kate was about to reply in her former bantering style, but an imploring glance from her Cousin smote her heart; she extended her hand kindly towards him; and her bright eye was dimmed with moisture, as she said in a tone of deeper feeling, than any one would have expected from her,

"Pardon me, dear Charles, I am a foolish, giddy girl, and had almost forgotten that unfortunate official letter, else I should never have thought of tormenting you; but with all my faults I am not ungrateful, and it would be ingratitude on my part, were I to forget the kind, good-natured Cousin, who for the last three months has borne so patiently with all the wild caprices of a foolish girl. It is hard to say when we shall meet again; but, meet when we may, it shall always be with pleasure on my part; and in the mean time believe, that if your giddy Cousin Kate is steady in nothing else, she can be steady in her friendship."

Charles only replied by seizing the proffered hand of his Cousin, and pressing it to his lips. His heart was too full to speak.

There was an awkward silence for some minutes, during which Kate, who had forgotten to withdraw her hand from the grasp of her Cousin, sat with downcast eyes, as if absorbed in studying the elaborately-traced pattern of the Persian rug, on which her fairy foot reposed.

"I dare say you will think me very foolish, Kate,"

said Charles, trying to smile, and hastily dashing a tear from his eye; "but the idea of leaving you to-morrow has quite unmanned me. I did not know, till now, how hard it would be to part."

Charles perceived that the little hand which still reposed in his, trembled slightly; but Kate was not one of those whose nerves are easily upset, and she instantly rallied.

"No," replied she, looking up, and speaking with somewhat of her usual gaiety, "I shall not call you foolish, nor shall I be prudish enough—or prudent enough, if you like it better—to deny, that the regret at parting will be mutual. But at the same time, I must say, that I think you have allowed your imagination to run away with you, and are trying to persuade yourself that parting with a Cousin—a very agreeable Cousin we shall allow her to be, for the sake of argument—is a much more tragical business than you will find it in reality. You certainly have had the advantage of being sent into this wicked world some twelve months before me, but in spite of this advantage, I suspect I know more of the ways of the world—or the ways of the heart, at all events—than you do. Listen, then, with becoming respect, to my prophetic words—You will leave this to-morrow, vowing that Cousin Kate is an Angel of light, and, that parting with her has torn your very heart-strings asunder; you will eat no dinner, and will probably amuse yourself the greater part of the night in writing a sonnet to her eyebrow; after three days' march you will recover your appetite, and although you still allow Cousin Kate to be a very charming creature, you will begin to have serious misgivings as to the possibility of living on one of her smiles for more than a week; by the time you have attended two or three balls at Bangalore, Cousin Kate will have dwindled down into a really nice girl! and the last roll of the big drum as you march to take the field, will scatter to the four winds of Heaven, any few romantic ideas, which, in your mind, may still be associated with the name of Kate."

"Kate! dearest Kate!" exclaimed Charles, clasping her hand in both of his, and squeezing it passionately to his heart, "this levity is cruel. Forget you! By all that 's bright, I might as soon forget that the sun shines in heaven! Forget you! Oh, Kate, Kate! if you only knew how deeply, how indelibly, your image is impressed upon my very heart's core—if you had ever known what real love was, you would not talk thus lightly of forgetting."

Kate had, probably, quite as good an idea of true love as her impassioned Cousin; but she was gifted with a little more prudence; and if she entertained towards him any feelings of a warmer nature than those of cousinly affection, she had too much good sense to intrust her secret to the keeping of a wild lad of eighteen, whom she had only known for three months, and whom she might not again see for years. It would be soon enough to do so, if, at their next meeting, she found his love had stood the test of time and absence.

"Charles! Charles! this is folly," exclaimed the blushing girl, hastily withdrawing her hand, and rising from her seat.

But Charles was not thus to be repulsed; he sprung to her side, and again seizing her hand, attempted to lead her back to her seat.

"Stay, dearest Kate!" exclaimed he, with passionate energy, "do not leave me thus—only hear me say how deeply, how devotedly I love you—only allow me to—"

Whether Charles would have succeeded in urging his pretty Cousin to listen further to his suit, we know not; for at this interesting moment the deep voice of old Lorimer was heard, humming a snatch of his favourite Hunting-song, as he crossed the hall on his way from the dining-room.

Poor Kate, who, in her present agitated state, would gladly have escaped to the privacy of her own room, but who had no means of doing so, save by the door at which her father was about to enter, darted across the room, and, seating herself at the piano, began to play violently; whilst Charles remained standing opposite the sofa, looking very much like a fool, and heartily wishing his worthy Uncle and his boon companions at the bottom of the Red Sea.

"Ah! you young dog—you gave us the slip, did you?" exclaimed the jolly old Gentleman, laying his hand playfully on the shoulder of his nephew. "You young hands are sad fellows for shirking the bottle nowadays. Such proceedings would not have been tolerated in my time. But perhaps you are in the right after all. Boys should keep their heads cool—young blood is hot enough without the stimulant of overmuch wine—and so I dare say you have been more rationally employed than your seniors. I see Kate, like a good girl, has been amusing you with some of her new waltzes. Does she not play them with spirit? Bravo, my girl—you are excelling yourself to night!"

Poor Kate, hardly knowing what she did, was banging the instrument most unmercifully, and, in her agitation, making the most egregious mistakes; but fortunately the old Gentleman had not a very refined ear for music, and as long as she made plenty of noise, and galloped over the notes, at what he called a slashing pace, he fancied her performance perfect.

"Amusing him, quoth he!" whispered the Doctor, who, with his usual sagacity, saw at a glance how matters stood, and could not resist the temptation to indulge in a little quizzing. "By my troth, Maister Charles, I 'm thinking it 's you hae been amusing the Young Leddy, else I 'm far mista'en. And ye maun hae frighted her too, ye wild birkie; just see to her, poor thing, the awfu' raised look she has, and the way she 's dingin the very life out o' that unfortunate piane. Hoot fie, Maister Charles—and you sae douce like, too. But it 's just the way o' the world. Learn the cat to the kirn, and she 'll aye be lickin. Let ane o' you smooth-faced blate-lookin chiels, anes learn the way to blaw in a Lassy's lug, and deil a muckle peace will you gie her ever after."

Charles, who knew from experience that it was in vain to bandy words with the Doctor when he was in one of his quizzical humours, made his escape across the room, and entered into conversation with his Uncle regarding his intended departure on the morrow.

"Going to-morrow, you young dog!" exclaimed old Lorimer. "The deuce a bit of it. Why, man, we have settled to beat the Orange Valley—the most beautiful spot on the Neilgherry Hills—not been disturbed this season—a regular preserve; as full of game as ever it can hold. And Kate is to be of the party, too—she is wild to see this Valley of which she has heard so much, and I promised long ago to take her the first time we went there. She will be quite in despair if she has not Cousin Charles to help her pony over the bad steps—eh, Kate? is it not so?"

Charles cast an inquiring glance towards his blushing Cousin, and felt that one look of encouragement from her, would almost induce him to turn deserter for her sake; but she took no notice of her father's remark; so he replied,

"You know, my dear Uncle, nothing would give me so much pleasure as to make one of your party, but I have received an order to join immediately, and—"

"Well, I know you have!" cried the impatient old Gentleman, "and right sorry I was to hear it. But what of that? They expect you to march, I suppose, and not to travel in a balloon!"

"Why, yes," replied Charles, "as I am ordered to carry my bullocks and camp-equipage along with me, I conclude that they intend me to march by the regular stages."

"Well, then, in Heaven's name, start your bullocks and tents—to-night if you like—but go yourself you shall not. I shall have bearers posted for you. You shall have my palanquin to travel in; and even supposing your people to have four or five days' start of you, you would find no difficulty in overtaking them, so you need not be afraid to spare a couple of days for the Orange Valley."

This reasoning was unanswerable. Charles thanked his Uncle warmly for his kindness, and, with a wonderfully good grace, made up his mind to spend two more days on the Neilgherry Hills.

CHAPTER XVIII.

THE ORANGE VALLEY.

The Orange Valley! There is perfume in the very name! Our old heart warms, and a delicious languor steals over our senses, as we recal to mind the silent, balmy, incense-breathing morn when first we trod the flowery shades of that enchanting spot. Armed as we were to the teeth, and bent on slaughter, we felt as if we profaned the scene by our unhallowed presence. It seemed to us the abode of peace and innocence; a place for young lovers to walk hand in hand, culling the golden fruit, and twining into bridal wreaths the snow-white blossoms, which made the very air love-sick with their fragrance. It was not for such as we—the blood-stained weather-beaten Hunter.

Such were the thoughts which flitted through our brain as we wended our solitary way through this wilderness of sweets. And were it not that at the root of an orange-tree we discovered the mangled carcass of a Deer, with the fresh foot-prints of a Tiger leading therefrom, there is a fearful probability that the Old Forest Ranger might, in the softness of his heart, have thrown aside his rifle, betaken himself to a straw-hat and pastoral crook, fastened bunches of green ribbon to his knees, and devoted the remainder of his life to piping lovelorn ditties in praise of some cruel, stony-hearted Shepherdess. But the well-known print of the Tiger's royal paw recalled our manhood, and rescued us from the puling life of an Arcadian Shepherd. We were once more in our element. We hugged our trusty rifle, thanking our good stars that it was no pastoral crook. And as we loosened our hunting-knife in its sheath, we felt that we loved the sweet spot all the better, now that we had a right to explore its beauties with the free step and roving eye of a Hunter.

It was at the lower end of this beautiful Valley, which derives its name from the dense jungle of wild orange and lime-trees with which it is clothed, that the party from Ootacamund had pitched their tents. It was late on the previous evening before they had reached their ground; the march had been a rough and a weary one; and although the Eastern sky was fast brightening, and the Jungle-cock crowing merrily, there were not as yet any signs of life within the camp. The canvass walls hung damp and heavy with the dews of night. The wearied Horses stood dozing at their pickets, carefully enveloped in thick woollen clothing, which extended over the head and ears in the form of a hood. The Deer, as they descended the hill-side to seek their fragrant bed among the orange-groves, stopped to gaze on the unwonted sight of human habitations; and the prowling Tiger, as he returned with sulky steps to his solitary lair, cast many a wistful glance towards the baggage bullocks, from which he had been scared during the night by the smell of fire and the neighbourhood of man. The cry of the great black Monkey was heard among the woods like the voice of a laughing Satyr. The industrious Woodpecker, like a sober mechanic, plied his noisy trade; and the winking Owl, like a drowsy reveller returning from his nightly carouse, answered with a hoot of drunken merriment, as if in derision of his early-rising neighbour. The hungry Vulture, anticipating the feast which, before sunset, would be prepared for him by the hand of man, wheeled about over the camp in wide gyrations. The joyous Paroquets—gay-coated, light-hearted varlets—darted about on rapid wing, screaming with delight at the prospect of a new day of thoughtless merriment. All nature was in motion, save the sleeping inmates of the Hunters' camp.

Charles, who, lover-like, had slept but little, was first afoot; and his impatient summons speedily called forth a host of yawning native servants, looking wofully out of their element in the cold bracing air of the Hills, and creeping about with a sort of paralytic motion, like half-*dazed* flies in the end of autumn. The camp fires, however, were soon replenished; and by the time the Doctor had finished his toilet, his naturally good appetite had been whetted to a pitch of wolf-like keenness by the savoury steams of curry and ragout which were wafted to his tent on the wings of the sharp morning air. In less than an hour the Gentlemen of the party had discussed a substantial breakfast, and were assembled in front of the mess-tent, smoking their cheroots, and examining their weapons, to see that all was in good order for a grand field-day. The horses were accoutred, the beaters assembled, and old Ishmail already in the saddle, smiling complacently, and remonstrating with his impatient hounds—a band of veterans, scarred with many a glorious wound—which crowded around him, gazing up in his face, and whining as if to reproach their venerable leader with his unusual want of activity.

But there was one tent, larger and more commodious than the others, the curtain of which had not yet been withdrawn; a Horsekeeper, bearing in his hand a silver-mounted *chowrie*, was leading up and down, in front of it, a handsome ambling Atcheen pony, accoutred with a side-saddle; and on this tent Charles kept his eyes fixed with all the devotion of a good Mussulman gazing on the Tomb of the Prophet.

The patience of old Lorimer was wellnigh exhausted, and even Mansfield was beginning to get fidgety, when the canvass door of the tent was at length drawn aside by a smiling *Ayah,* and the blooming Kate, in all the pride of youthful loveliness, came bounding forward to crave forgiveness of her Father for her unusual want of punctuality. There was a beaming smile of happiness on her young face, a look of confiding love in her deep blue eye, which would have melted a far sterner heart than that of her fond Father. The meditated words of reproof died upon his lips, the frown vanished from his brow, as a cloud upon the hill-side melts before the rising sun. He kissed his daughter's cheek affectionately, and, calling her a lazy monkey, desired her to jump upon her pony.

Need it be said with what alacrity Charles hastened to help his Fair Cousin to her saddle; how he gently squeezed her hand in doing so; how close he rode by her side, and how often he dismounted in the dirtiest parts of the road to lead her pony over a difficult pass, or a stony watercourse? No! The discerning Reader will imagine all this. And were we to inform him of the very kindly manner in which all these little attentions were received by the gentle Kate, we rather think he would agree with us, that the Doctor was not very far from the truth, when he remarked to Mansfield that "Yon loon was garrin' the bit Lassie's heart to thaw like snaw aff a dyke."

They had nearly reached the head of the valley, when Kate was roused from a pleasing reverie, by hearing the distant sound of her Father's bugle calling together the stragglers; and she became aware that, during an interesting discussion with her Cousin, they had fallen nearly half a mile in rear of their companions. A conscious blush suffused her cheek, and without waiting for another word, she applied the whip smartly to the flank of her willing pony, who, not being accustomed to such rough usage, started off at a pace which, on so rough a path as the one they travelled, appeared even to Charles somewhat venturesome. And so the result proved it to be; for, on turning a sharp angle, where the path was overgrown with slippery grass, the pony's legs flew from under him, and poor "Douce Davie"—for so he was called—came heavily to the ground, throwing his rider against a bank, and nearly rolling over her. Charles felt his heart sink within him, as he pulled up his horse with a jerk that nearly broke the poor animal's jaw, just in time to avoid riding over his Cousin. Trembling in every limb, he threw himself from his horse, and hastened to raise his beloved Kâte; but, ere he could do so, the spirited Girl had regained her feet, seized her pony's bridle, and was ready to remount. Her cheek was paler than usual, and Charles felt that her delicate hand trembled; but her innate courage had not deserted her. Her eye was bright as ever; and, although her bloodless lips showed that she had sustained a severe shock, she replied with one of her sweetest smiles to the anxious inquiries of her Cousin, assuring him that she was not in the slightest degree hurt. Her only anxiety, after having ascertained that "Douce Davie's" knees were uninjured, was to remount as quickly as possible, and to exact a promise from her Cousin, that he would not mention the accident to her Father, lest he should be over anxious about her in future. Charles, more charmed than ever at her spirited conduct, lifted her gently into the saddle, and the light-hearted Girl, smiling her thanks, cantered off as gay and fearless as ever.

"So much for good *caste*," thought Charles, as he followed at a hand canter along the narrow path. "How often have I seen a great hulking Lass, with bones and sinews like a man, who, after such a fall as this, would have sat for half an hour, wiping her gooseberry eyes with a crumpled pocket handkerchief, redolent of apples, and sobbing forth her unalterable determination never again to trust her precious person upon horseback! whilst this delicate creature, all grace, gentleness, and refinement, exhibits a degree of courage and self-possession worthy of a hero. It is the *caste* that tells—the lightning in her blood which prevents it from stagnating round her heart like the muddy stream which flows in the veins of a plebeian." (O, fie, Mr. Charles! How can you venture, in this age of Liberty and Equality, to insult the Majesty of the people by drawing such odious comparisons?)

By the time Charles and his Cousin had overtaken the party, Ishmail, with his dogs and beaters, had already moved off to the point from whence the beat was to commence; and old Lorimer was pointing out to Mansfield the different passes where the guns ought to be posted.

"There," said he, addressing Mansfield, and pointing to the opposite side of the valley, "do you see that rhododendron-tree, covered with scarlet flowers, overhanging a mass of gray rock? Well, that is the best pass, and must be defended by the best man. Do you take it; you will find a Deer-track just below, which will lead you across the valley. And now to your post—you have some distance to go, and will hardly reach it before the hounds are in cover. And how are we to dispose of *you*, Young Lady?" continued he, addressing his Daughter, who at this moment rode up, followed by Charles.

"I think I had better go a little further up the hill, Papa," replied Kate, "where I shall be out of your way, and at the same time have a good view of your proceedings. I have brought my drawing materials, and can amuse myself very well by taking a sketch of this beautiful valley."

"No, no, dear," replied her Father, smiling; "picturesque as you and Douce Davie would be on the hill-side, you would form rather too conspicuous an object in the landscape, and might prevent the game from breaking cover. As you have come out in the character of a Huntress, you must go through with it, and betake yourself to a place of concealment as we do."

"What! am I to shoulder a rifle and defend a pass, Papa?" asked Kate, with one of her bewitching smiles.

"Not yet, my pretty Recruit," replied the old Gentleman, patting her shoulder affectionately. "We shall excuse you from bearing arms this time, in consideration of your only mounting guard as a supernumerary. But I shall expect you to be so far a good *Shikaree*, as to keep your mouth shut and your eyes open. I shall look out for a safe place for you as soon as I have posted the guns."

"If you will put my Fair Cousin under my charge, Sir," said Charles, eagerly, "I promise to take the utmost care of her, and shall do my best to teach her her duty as a Huntress."

"Well, so be it, boy. Take her with you, and keep her quiet if you can. But mind, if she spoils your sport, it is your own fault."

"Will my gentle Cousin deign to accept of my unworthy services as her trusty squire?" exclaimed Charles, springing gaily from his horse, and extending his hands to assist the Young Lady in dismounting.

The blushing Kate was about to decline her Cousin's offer on the score of her being troublesome, and in his way. But the imploring look he gave her, and the thought that this would be the last day they might spend together for a long, long time, caused her to relent. She placed her hands in his with a confiding look that went to his very heart's core, and springing lightly to the ground, the young couple walked off, arm-in-arm, to take possession of the pass assigned to them.

"And so may ye gang linket thegether for the rest o' ye'r days," thought the kind-hearted Doctor, as he followed the retiring figures with a look of fond admiration; "for ye are twa as bonny and as winsome young things as a man would wish to see in a simmer's day. And there 's true love atween you, or I 'm far mista'en.

"And where will ye be pleased to put me and *Mons Meg*, Sir," continued the Doctor, turning to old Lorimer, who was giving directions to have the horses removed out of sight. "I hae gi'en the auld lass an extra fingar's depth o' pouther ever since the day she killed the Tiger; and she 's that proud, Sir, she lets a crack would amaist deeve ye, and is fit to fright the life out o' ony ordinary beast, let abee killin' him. Odd, Sir, it will just do your heart good to hear auld *Meg* speak to them. She 's a Deevle, Sir, when she 's angred; and rattles the grit-shot about their lugs in a style that 's just perfectly amazin'!"

"I crave your pardon, my worthy friend," replied Lorimer, smiling, "I had almost overlooked you in my hurry. But I have not forgotten the late exploits of your trusty fusee, and have retained a pass for you, where the range being short, I think her good qualities as a thrower of *grit-shot* may be displayed to advantage. It is not above a hundred yards from hence; so come along, and I shall post you before I take up my own position."

"And ye 'll no hae nae objections to the grit-shot then —will ye, Sir?"

"No, you incorrigible old poacher, no," replied old Lorimer, laughing outright at the comical look with which the Doctor accompanied his last question. "You may cram what barbarous missiles you like into that antediluvian-looking weapon of yours; but only do not ask me to stand godfather to her atrocities, for it goes against my conscience."

"Thank you, Sir; you are a handsome man, and a good Christian," replied the Doctor, shouldering his fusee and stepping off, left foot foremost, to the tune of "Johnnie Cope," a favourite air, which the Doctor always whistled when he felt himself unusually valiant.

Reader, have you ever been in love?—Start not, Gentle Lady, at our home question, it is only intended for the male sex. Have you ever sat by the side of her who inspired that love, in some romantic spot, far, far away in the woods, with the summer sun smiling in the deep blue sky, and green boughs waving over head, and the clear rill bubbling at your feet, and the distant hills sleeping in the sunshine; and listened to the sweet voice of the thrush and the hum of the wandering bee, and the drowsy murmur of insects, intoxicated with the perfume of flowers? And have you not at such a moment experienced a delightful, dreamy, indescribable sensation of happiness, not of this earth—a feeling unknown to the inmates of the glittering ball-room, or the sumptuous banquet-hall—a silent communion of soul, expressed by looks, far more eloquent than words—a twining together of the heart-strings—a charm—a spell—a something which you feel that a single word would dissipate? If so, you will be able to imagine the feelings of Charles as he sat by the side of his beloved Kate, on a sloping bank of velvet turf, sufficiently far up on the hill-side to command an extensive view of the beautiful valley which lay extended at their feet.

The position occupied by Charles and his Cousin was backed by a perpendicular rock of considerable height, overgrown with moss and creeping shrubs. An orange-tree of goodly size stretched forth its fragrant boughs to shelter them from the heat of the sun, and all around them sprung up a thicket of beautiful flowering shrubs, forming a screen sufficient to conceal them; but, at the same time, affording a clear view, through the openings among the branches, of any animal which might pass within range of their post, as well as of the general scenery of the valley.

Charles was sitting with one rifle resting across his knees, and another lying by his side, now gazing into the expressive blue eyes of his Cousin, and now casting a rapid glance towards the head of the valley, from whence he expected the hounds and beaters to approach; for, much as he was in love, he did not forget his late training in the jungles, which had taught him to make good use of his eyes and ears, even when his thoughts were most abstracted.

Kate, with her drawing implements lying idly beside her, leant her back against the stem of the orange-tree, and fixed her eyes upon the beautiful scene before her, as if absorbed in deep and pleasing thought.

It was one of those warm, still, dreamy days, when Nature appears to slumber in the sunshine. No sound was heard save the dull, mysterious roar of a distant waterfall, far up among the wild hills at the head of the valley: not a leaf stirred—no living thing was seen. There was something almost awful in the deep silence, and yet it harmonized well with the feelings of the young lovers, soothed as they were into a state of pleasing languor, by the relaxing heat, and the overpowering perfume of orange-blossom, with which the air was loaded. Their hearts were full to overflowing, and they sat for some time in thoughtful silence, before either could find words to express the feelings of admiration and happiness which almost overwhelmed them.

Kate was the first to break silence.

"Oh! what a beautiful world is this!" she exclaimed, clasping her hands together, and turning towards Charles, with her expressive eyes swimming in moisture. "How grateful ought we to be when we think that this glorious sun, this perfumed air, those smiling woods, and purple mountains, have all been given to us, with health and strength to enjoy them; and yet, in the bustle of the world, how seldom do we put the proper value upon these manifold sources of happiness and innocent enjoyment which are open to all mankind. Oh! how sincerely do I pity those whose hearts have become callous to the beautiful works of Nature!"

"It is indeed a fair world, dearest Kate," replied Charles, with much feeling. "I have always been a lover of Nature; but never have I so fully appreciated her beauties as I do at this moment. I feel as if I viewed every object in a new light and through a happier medium than I have ever done before. Are you philosopher enough, dear Kate, to tell me the reason why?"

Kate's heart whispered to her the true reason, and although a downcast eye and blushing cheek formed the only answer to her Cousin's question, they spoke more eloquently than words could have done.

"It is because we were never intended to enjoy happiness alone," whispered Charles, laying his hand gently upon that of his blushing Cousin; "Say, dearest Kate, is it not so?"

Kate felt the conscious blood mounting with double rapidity to her face and neck, at this rather home question; but she was spared the embarrassment of replying to it, for, before she could do so, the first joyous shout of the beaters, as they dashed into cover, arose from among the hills at the head of the valley; and, for the first time, it grated harshly on the ears of Charles.

However, the spell was broken. That shout reminded Charles that the Orange Valley, with all its beauty and fragrance, was no longer a place for whispering lovers; it had now become an arena, in which the most formidable beasts of the forest might be encountered, and where all the energies of man must be called into action. He felt like a sentinel who had been caught napping on his post; and hastily snatching up his rifle, he placed himself so as to command a better view of the open ground in front of his position.

Even the gentle Kate became excited as the hounds now opened on the scent, and the deep-toned pack came sweeping down the valley, their voices now muffled by intervening woods, and again rising full and clear upon the still air.

Nearer and nearer came the yelling pack, their onward

course marked by the flights of peacock and jungle-fowl, which rose before them like pheasants in a preserve; and as they approached, it became evident that the game, whatever it might be, was running directly towards the pass which Charles commanded.

It was only now that Charles, whose thoughts had been somewhat bewildered, bethought himself of the danger to which Kate might be exposed, in the event of the animal, which was now on foot, proving to be a beast of prey.

There was no time to be lost; so, laying down his rifle, he seized the astonished Girl by the arm, and stammering out an apology for his apparent rudeness, hurried her, with very little ceremony, up a rugged path, leading to the top of the rock which backed their position; and having there bestowed her in a place which appeared free from danger, and cautioned her to keep as quiet as possible, he hastened back to his post.

Charles had hardly regained his pass, when a crashing sound was heard, as if some heavy animal was forcing its way through the tangled brushwood, about three hundred yards on one side of his position.

This was the moment of real excitement; for who could tell, unless he were better skilled in the art of woodcraft than was our friend Charles, what animal he might be called upon to encounter? It might only be a Deer, or a Wild Hog; but it might with equal probability be a Bear, a Panther, or a Tiger.

Whatever it might be, Charles was prepared to give it a warm reception. Cocking both barrels of his rifle, he crouched more closely behind his leafy screen, and waited with breathless anxiety for the moment when the animal should break cover. Again the crashing sound was heard, followed by a dead pause—then a loud snort—a furious rush—a bound—and a noble Stag, followed by three Hinds, burst through the opposing brushwood—halted for one moment—gazed wildly round—snuffed the air—laid back their large ears to catch the yell of their pursuers—and uttering a wild snort, started off again at the top of their speed towards the hills.

Charles, waiting till the Stag was directly abreast of his position, and not more than twenty yards from him, raised his rifle, and fired. He had already measured with longing eyes the wide-spreading antlers of the noble brute, little inferior in size to an American Moose-deer, and felt confident that this shot must make the prize his own. But whether it was that his hand shook from over anxiety, or whether the consciousness that his Fair Cousin was watching his proceedings, had any thing to do with it, we know not: yet certain it is, that the Stag, instead of falling, only tossed his head disdainfully, and making a higher bound than usual, pursued his course with unabated speed.

Kate, who had watched the effect of the shot with trembling anxiety, felt her heart relieved as she saw the beautiful creatures bounding away unharmed; her enthusiasm completely got the better of her; and starting to her feet with an exclamation of joy, she waved her pocket-handkerchief as if to cheer on the graceful fugitives.

Charles, mad with vexation, discharged a second and a third shot in rapid succession; but all with the same result. The bullets rebounding from the hard ground, went spinning and whistling through the woods, as if in derision of the unsteady hand that fired them; and the Deer, after a few more bounds, were lost to view behind the shoulder of the hill.

It has a plaguy unpleasant twang with it, Gentle Reader, that same whistle of a stray bullet, whether it be discharged from your own weapon, or from that of a short-sighted friend, who happens to fire in your direction.

"So much for showing off!" thought Charles, as he dropped the discharged weapon into the hollow of his arm, with a blank look of disappointment.

"You have not hurt any of them—have you?" asked Kate, peeping over the edge of the rock on which she was perched.

"No," replied Charles, in no very cheerful tone; "not a hair ruffled."

"Oh! I am so glad!" exclaimed Kate, joyfully. "It would have made me quite miserable to have seen you kill one of those beautiful creatures."

"Thank you, my gentle Cousin," replied Charles, smiling. "But I doubt whether your Father will be equally well pleased with my performance, particularly if I allow the hounds to get away after the Deer. Ha! here they come! I must manage to stop them, whatever happens, else I shall get a proper roasting."

So saying, he snatched up a whip which he had fortunately kept by him—and which, by the way, he was just in the humour to use with effect—and rushing in front of the hounds, he succeeded, after some difficulty, in flogging them off the scent.

This accomplished, and the sulky pack having been recalled by the sound of Ishmail's bugle, Charles felt that he could now face his Uncle with a better grace, and returned to his post, determined, if possible, to acquit himself better on the next occasion.

He had not to wait long before the hounds were again in full cry, and running in different directions—the pack having divided in pursuit of the different sorts of game with which the valley abounded. The rifles, too, now began to play their parts, and several shots were heard in the direction of Mansfield's pass, as well as that of old Lorimer. The beaters, encouraged by the sound of fire-arms, and the prospect of a plentiful supply of venison, redoubled their shouts. The hounds bayed more savagely, yells of pain occasionally mingling with their deep-toned notes; and the smiling groves of that beautiful valley rung with wild discordant sounds, which ill accorded with the character of its scenery.

To Kate, whose feelings had been wound up to the highest pitch of romantic sensibility, the sudden transition from sentimental solitude to this scene of rude excitement was painful; and appeared to her like a profanation of the beautiful spot.

Charles, on the contrary, felt his blood warm as the uproar increased—he longed for an opportunity of wiping out his late disgrace in the blood of some formidable antagonist, worthy of his overflowing valour; and, for the time being, all recollection of his late sentimental fit was lost among thick-coming fancies of desperate encounters with grizzly Bears and brindled Tigers.

O man, hard-hearted man! how different is thy love from the love of woman!

But what has become of the Doctor all this time? we have not heard the voice of old *Meg;* he must surely have fallen asleep, or smoked himself into a fit of apoplexy. So thought Charles, as the storm of men and dogs swept down the valley in the direction of the Doctor's pass.

"Ha! there she goes at last—there is no mistaking her voice!" exclaimed Charles, as a report was heard, like that of a six-pounder, followed by a savage roar, and desperate shouts for aid.

Now then, Master Charles! now is the time to distinguish yourself! To the rescue—to the rescue, if you be a man!

Charles was noways backward. Starting at once to his feet, and calling to his Cousin not on any account to leave her place of safety, he sent before him a shout of encouragement to the poor Doctor, who was evidently in urgent need of assistance, and rushed towards the spot from whence the cries proceeded, bounding over the rocks and bushes like a young Stag.

On reaching the Doctor's pass, Charles found poor Mc.Phee very much out of breath, and in a profuse perspiration—his hat off, his clothes torn and soiled with dust, and in his hand the shattered remains of his favourite fusee, the stock of which was broken, and the barrel sadly bruised and dented.

"May the De'el pick your banes, and make whistles o' them for his bairns, ye old black-avized besom," muttered the Doctor between his clenched teeth, as he carefully examined the different fragments of his sorely injured weapon.

"Hollo, Doctor! who are you maledizing so fearfully?" exclaimed Charles, unable to contain his laughter, on beholding the mingled expression of anger and distress depicted on the poor Doctor's long, sallow face.

"She 's just perfectly ruined," growled the Doctor, continuing his soliloquy, without taking any notice of Charles; "the stock in twa halves, the barrel cloured as flat as my loof, and the lock—De'el be in her skin—the lock 's gone a'thegither!! Hech, Sirs!—poor auld *Meg!*—I 'm fairly by wi' you at last:" here he dropped the remains of his fusee, and shook his head mournfully. "Ye 'll never mair fire a nieve-fou o' grit-shot or take the life o' man or beast."

"What on earth has happened to you, Doctor?" exclaimed Charles, still laughing immoderately. "You look as if you had seen the Brownie."

"Brownie, indeed! By my troth, lad, gin Brownie be as fashious a neighbour as the old Deevle that came my gate, it maun be ill biding in a'e house wi' him. See to the way she left my firelock, the mislear'd limmer, no' to mention the riving o' my coat, and a terrible ill-fa'urd hole in my breeks. See to that, Maister Charles! What way can I appear before Miss Kate, or any other Leddy, sicken a daft-like figure?"

So saying, the Doctor faced round, and exhibited a terrible rent in his nether garment, which the short round jacket which he wore for the sake of coolness, rendered painfully conspicuous.

There was something so irresistibly ludicrous in the

poor Doctor's appearance, that Charles nearly rolled upon the ground with laughter; and so infectious was his mirth, that the good-humoured Doctor, who had a strong sense of the ridiculous, and never could resist a joke, even at his own expense, at length burst forth into one of his most hearty guffaws.

"But, my dear Doctor," gasped Charles, as soon as he recovered breath enough to articulate, "how did this happen? Who or what has maltreated you in this abominable manner?"

"There is ane o' her kind, at ony rate," replied the Doctor, pointing with rather a triumphant air to the carcass of a young Bear, not much larger than a terrier dog, which lay at some distance among the bushes. "I hae rid the world o' ane o' the mischancie Deevles; and gin it be as ill-natured a craiter as the mither o't, it was a weel done turn."

"Ha! a young Bear," exclaimed Charles, turning over the animal with his foot, "and a terrible dose of grit-shot you have given him, poor thing; he is nearly blown to pieces. But what has become of the old one?"

"She may hae gane to Bamf for a' I ken or care," replied the Doctor, "and glad enough I was to get quit o' her. But wherever she be, I 'm thinkin' she 's gotten a taste o' the grit-shot that will keep her skin hot enough for a day or two—and Deevle mend her."

"Wounded, is she? How did that happen? I heard but one shot."

"I 'll tell you that, lad," replied the Doctor, deliberately tapping the lid of his snuff-mull. "You see,

I was just sitting at my pass, and taking a blow o' my cheroot, and basking in the sun, and winking for a' the world like an auld ram-cat in the ingle nook; and what wi' the heat, and the bonny smell o' the orange flowers, and a' that, I was just in a kind o' waking dream like, and was beginning to think o' some o' my old sweethearts, and the bonny summer days when I hae set aside them in the sweet birk woods o' cannie Scotland, and—"

"In short, you were half asleep, Doctor," interrupted Charles.

"Asleep, say you!—and me thinking o' my sweet-hearts! O Maister Charles! Maister Charles! I wonder to hear you say the like, and your bonny Cousin, Miss Kate, sae near at hand;" here the Doctor took a huge pinch of snuff, and fixed his eyes upon the face of his young companion, with one of his most penetrating looks.

"Well, well," replied Charles, becoming rather fidgety at the turn the conversation had taken, "we shall not discuss that point at present. But tell me, I pray you, about the Bear, for, if she be wounded, it is high time we were upon her trail."

"That 's true," replied the Doctor. "Well, as I wa' saying, I was sitting at my pass, and thinking o' my old sweethearts, and the like o' that, when a' at ance I heard a terrible stramash among the bushes, and then a wild growl, just at my very lug. Up I jumps, wi' the fusee in my hand, and my heart in my mouth, and out came a muckle brute o' a Bear, wi' that wee towsie tyke sitting on her back, as conceity as you please, and haudin' the grip, like grim death, wi' his claws. The auld Bear, as soon as she seed me, she up wi' her birse, and shows her muckle white teeth, and girns at me like a perfect cannibal; and the wee Deevle he sets up his birse too, and snaps his bit teeth, and tries to girn like the mither o't, wi' a queer auld-farrant look that amaist gart me laugh; although, to tell the blessed truth, Maister Charles, I thought it nae laughing sport. Well, there was naething else for it, so I lets drive at them wi' the grit-shot, thinking to ding them baith at ance. I killed the sma' ane dead enough; but the auld one, she lets a roar that amaist deeved me, and at me she comes like a Tigre. I was that frighted, Sir, I didna ken what to do; but in despair I just held out the muzzle o' the fusee to fend her off, and I believe that saved my life; for she gripped it atween her teeth, dang me o'er on the braid o' my back, and off she set, trailing me through the bushes like a tethered stick; for some way or other I never let go the grip I had o' the stock. I was that stupified I hae nae recollection what happened after this, till I found mysel' sticking in the middle o' a brier bush, wi' my breeks rived the way you see, and poor old *Meg* smashed in bits—De'el be in her skin that did it."

"A most unpleasant adventure, truly," replied Charles, "and quite enough to make a Saint swear. But come, Doctor. Faint heart never won fair lady, or black bear either; so let us to work, and see if we cannot follow her up, for I perceive the hounds are not upon her track; she leaves a pretty conspicuous trail; and see, here is blood upon it! Hurrah! we shall make her pay for this yet!"

So saying, Charles, who during his late excursion in the jungle had acquired considerable skill in the art of following a trail, started in pursuit of the wounded Bear. The Doctor, with no great stomach for the sport, but fearing to be left alone in his present unarmed state, followed close to his heels, brandishing the barrel of his fusee, the only weapon which now remained to him.

They soon cleared the jungle, and found the track running along the side of the hill, in the direction of the rock upon which Kate had been left.

"I fear she is not so badly wounded as all this blood would lead one to suppose," remarked Charles, "else she would hardly venture to face the open country in this manner."

"She has na' tried to lift the brae, however," replied the Doctor, "although there 's strong cover on the other side, that she would be keen enough to get to, if she were fit. I 'm thinking she 's no' far afore us, and that we 'll find her in the first wee bit burn. They aye make for the water when they 're sore hurted."

"Well, keep your eyes about you," answered Charles, "whilst I follow the track, and try if you can view her. Ha! what was that? By Heaven! it is Kate's voice!" exclaimed he, as he cast his eyes towards the rock upon which he had left his Cousin, and caught the graceful outline of her figure against the sky, standing in the attitude of an inspired Priestess, and waving a handerchief, as if beckoning them towards her.

"I canna hear what she says," remarked the Doctor, who had been holding his hands on each side of his head, to catch the sound more distinctly, "but I 'm thinkin' she sees something."

"Forward! forward for your life!" shouted Charles, making a spring like a Tiger, as his quick eye detected the shaggy form of the Bear, slowly emerging from a small watercourse, within little more than two hundred yards of the rock upon which his Cousin stood. "She is making for the rock!"

This was indeed the case. The wounded Bear, unable or unwilling to face the extent of open ground which lay between her and the next wooded ravine, appeared bent upon dislodging Kate, and occupying her position, and the great start she had of her pursuers, rendered it but too probable that she would succeed in doing so. It now became a question of speed between Charles and the wounded Bear, and desperate were the efforts he made to overtake her. But although the animal was so far crippled by her wounds as to enable Charles to gain upon her, yet the farther they advanced, the more evident it became, that in spite of his utmost exertions, the Bear must reach the goal, not only before him, but almost before he was within shot of her.

In the mean time, Kate, unconscious of the danger which threatened her, was watching the chase with intense interest, and cheering on her Cousin in pursuit of the flying foe.

Charles felt a sickness at his heart, as the fearful idea flashed across his mind, that the sweet voice which now urged him forward, might, a few minutes hence, be gasping forth its last convulsive sob in the strangling embrace of the enraged Bear. The very precaution he had taken to insure the safety of his beloved Cousin, would now prove her destruction. He had placed her upon the top of a high rock, to which there was but one mode of access, a narrow and intricate path among the bushes; it was but too probable that this stronghold was well known to the savage brute of which he was in chase; and the pass once occupied by her, all means of retreat were cut off to poor Kate. There was madness in the thought. Charles ground his teeth together in agony; and although the violence of his previous exertion had already caused the blood to gush from his nostrils, he still attempted to press forward with increased speed.

But the case was now hopeless. The Bear was already within ten yards of the foot of the rock, whilst the distance between her and her pursuer was still upwards of a hundred. A well directed rifle bullet now appeared to Charles the only thing that could save the life of his unconscious Cousin; and Oh! how fervently did he pray, poor fellow, that hand and eye might prove true in this, his hour of need. Halting at once, and dropping on one knee, he raie d the rifle to his shoulder, took a long aim, and fired. Is she down? Alas, no! Who could direct a rifle truly after such a run! The hand which supported the long barrel trembled like an aspen leaf, the bullet flew far wide of the mark; and, ere the second barrel could be discharged, the Bear had disappeared among the thick brushwood which covered the side of the rock.

"O Kate! my beloved Kate!" exclaimed Charles, starting to his feet, and again rushing wildly forward, without waiting to reload.

By the time Charles reached the foot of the rock, the Bear had already accomplished more than two thirds of the ascent; and in a few seconds more, poor Kate, who was still unconscious of danger, would have been clasped in the deadly embrace of her paws.

"What is the matter, dear Charles?" exclaimed Kate, who having rushed eagerly towards the edge of the rock on the approach of her Cousin, now started back in horror on beholding his exhausted appearance, and the blood which, flowing from his nostrils, had dyed his clothes in front of a crimson colour.

"Stand back, dearest, stand back! Your life depends upon it!" exclaimed Charles, keeping his eye steadily fixed upon the Bear, and slowly raising his rifle.

Kate, terrified by the wild energy of her Cousin's manner, shrunk back without uttering a word, and the next moment the sharp report of the rifle was answered by a savage roar, which proved that the shot had taken effect.

The wounded Bear now turned open-mouthed upon her pursuer, and rushed furiously down the steep pathway to attack him.

Charles, who felt a load removed from his heart now that the rage of the animal was turned against himself, threw aside his rifle—both barrels of which had been discharged—drew his hunting knife, and coolly awaited the attack.

So furious was the onset of the Bear, that although Charles drove his hunting-knife up to the hilt in her body, he was borne to the ground with sufficient violence to be completely stunned, and deprived of the power of motion.

[illegible] LAST VICTORY

Oh! how bitterly did poor Kate now repent of having taken part in a sport so ill suited to her sex! and how solemnly did she vow never more to be guilty of such folly, when she beheld her gallant Cousin, after having risked his life in her defence, lying helpless and insensible beneath the enormous weight of the dying Bear, who, in her last efforts at revenge, was savagely gnawing and lacerating his unresisting arm!

Kate's first impulse was to scream loudly for assistance; her next—brave girl—to rush wildly down the rugged path, in hopes that even her feeble arm might be of some avail in rescuing her Cousin.

But, fortunately for poor Charles, there was more efficient, though not more willing aid at hand. The Doctor, who had been left far behind in the chase, now came rushing up, panting most furiously, and flourishing round his head the heavy barrel of his fusee.

"Hurrah! there 's a death-blow in auld *Meg* yet!" exclaimed he, heaving up his uncouth weapon to the full extent of his muscular arms, and bringing it down upon the head of the Bear, with a crash that made the eyes start from their sockets, and sent her rolling over on her back, with her stiffened limbs quivering in the air.

"Hech! tak' ye that, ye Deevle's buckie," muttered the Doctor, as he repeated the blow, to make the work of death more certain, at the same time inhaling his breath with a short energetic *Pech*, "and weel hae ye earned it, for by my troth ye hae gane near to kill as bonny a lad as ever stepped in shoe-leather.

"But there 's life in him yet, and sma' thanks to you

for it," continued the Doctor, as he raised the head of his young companion, and found that he still breathed.

"Is he alive?" exclaimed Kate, who had stood gazing on this scene of blood, pale and motionless as a marble statue.

"Indeed is he, Miss Kate, bless your bonny face, and like to do well enough, after I hae ta'en a drap blood fra' him," replied the Doctor, fumbling about in his numerous pockets to find his lancet.

"Thank Heaven!" exclaimed the poor Girl, fervently, "Thank Heaven!" and clasping her hands together, she sank down, fainting, by the side of her Cousin.

CHAPTER XIX.

A PARTING WORD FROM THE OLD FOREST RANGER.

Lady, thou art weary of our savage tales—we can see it in thy languid eye, although thy kind heart will not permit thee to hurt the feelings of the poor Old Forester, by telling him to withdraw. We are becoming garrulous in our old age, and although we have endeavoured to render our descriptions of jungle-warfare more fit for Lady's bower, by introducing some scraps of sentiment, and feeble sketches of the glowing Eastern scenery which many long years ago made an indelible impression on our youthful mind, yet we feel that our subject is, at best, one but ill adapted to a Lady's ear.

Our conscience tells us that we have already trespassed over-long on thy patience, and we blush to think of the many tales of blood and strife in which we must have done violence to thy gentle nature. But we are not ungrateful, Lady.—We fully appreciate thy condescension in having so long borne with the idle *clavers* of a garrulous old man.—We thank thee from our inmost heart; and if thou wilt only grant us thy indulgence for a few minutes longer, whilst we dispose of poor Kate and her Cousin Charles, whom we left in rather a sorry plight, we shall, with thy gracious permission, make our respectful obeisance, and retire.

A little cold water soon restored Kate ; but it was very different with poor Charles. He had fallen with the back of his head against a stone, and had received so severe a contusion, that in spite of copious bleeding and cold applications, it was many hours before he returned to consciousness, and then only to fall into a raging fever, which was not a little augmented by the severe wounds he had received from the teeth of the Bear.

This untoward accident brought the day's sport to an abrupt conclusion ; and next morning the party started on their return to Ootacamund.

Charles travelled in his Cousin's palanquin, whilst she rode by his side, watching him with the utmost assiduity, and stopping the bearers from time to time, to moisten his parched lips, or to arrange, with gentle care, the pillows which supported his aching head.

The unfortunate termination of their expedition had cast a gloom over the spirits of the party, and their journey was dull enough—neither did any thing occur, worthy of notice, with the exception of one little incident, which, being illustrative of the manners of those interesting people, the *Todahs*, we may here mention.

Kate had desired the bearers to halt near a *Todah* village, to procure a draught of cold water for her Cousin—this was speedily furnished by the kind-hearted creatures in one of their cleanest vessels; and whilst Charles greedily swallowed the refreshing beverage, the women and children crowded round the travellers, laughing and talking in their usual frank, goodhumoured manner, examining with great marks of astonishment the various parts of Kate's dress, and asking innumerable questions, which Kate, being ignorant of their language, could only reply to by smiling kindly, and patting the heads of the children. But there was one woman, a pretty, interesting young creature, apparently not more than eighteen or nineteen years of age, who took no share in the noisy conversation, but sat apart from the others, wrapped up in the ample folds of her mantle, and watching, with a look of melancholy interest, the childish gambols of a fine boy of about two years of age, who frisked about the green, now gazing in wonder at the strangers, and now flying, half in fear and half in play, to the protection of his mother's arms.

It was evident, from her appearance, that she was soon again to become a mother; and there was altogether something so interesting in her appearance, that Kate, whose heart was ever ready to sympathize in the grief of others, begged of one of the bearers to inquire why it was she looked so sad.

On being addressed, the poor Girl raised her large expressive eyes from the ground, and fixed them upon the face of the speaker with a vacant stare, as if her thoughts had been so much abstracted, that she did not at first understand the import of the question; but on its being repeated in rather an impatient tone, she slowly withdrew the folds of her mantle, pointed to her hair, which, instead of flowing in ringlets like that of her companions, was cropped close to her head, and clasping her child to her breast, burst into a passionate flood of tears.

Kate did all in her power to soothe and comfort her;

but, even with the assistance of some little trinkets which she gave her, it was some time before she was sufficiently composed to express her thanks.

It was only now that Kate became aware of the custom which prevails among the *Todah* women of cutting off their hair as a token of grief, on the occasion of their becoming widows.

This young creature had lost her favourite husband, only a few days before, which accounted for her sudden burst of grief, and the expressive manner in which she pointed to her shorn locks as an explanation of it.

You will smile, gentle Reader, at the idea of a poor savage woman mourning so deeply for the death of a *favourite* husband. But they have warm hearts, these *Todah* women, and a natural refinement of feeling, in spite of their barbarous custom of indulging in a plurality of husbands.

The injuries which Charles had received confined him to his room for some weeks after his return to Ootacamund; and instead of joining his regiment at the time he purposed, he was obliged to forward a sick certificate signed by Doctor Mc.Phee.

This respite he would, at any other time, have considered cheaply purchased, even at the expense of his wounds; but now that his regiment was in daily expectation of an order to take the field against the Maharattahs, the ardent spirit of the young Soldier could ill brook the confinement of a sick-room; and even the pleasure he derived from the constant society of his beloved Cousin, hardly enabled him to submit to it with becoming patience.

Every one knows how patiently, how devotedly, how like a "ministering Angel," a fond woman watches by the sick-bed of one she loves—and we can no longer conceal the truth, that Kate's grateful heart returned her Cousin's love, perhaps with interest. We shall therefore beg of the sagacious Reader to imagine the many long, weary, sleepless nights which poor Kate passed during the time her Cousin remained in a state of fever and delirium; how, when he became convalescent, she cheered and soothed him with the witching notes of her voice and her guitar; how on such occasions our friend Charles's protestations of eternal gratitude to his Fair Cousin, gradually warmed into protestations of eternal love; how the gentle Kate could not find it in her heart to hurt the feelings of him who had all but sacrificed his life in her defence, and who even now remained feeble and enervated from the effects of his wounds, by frowning on his suit: and, in short, how Master Charles prosecuted his wooing with such good success, that the wounds in his heart were healed before the wounds in his body.

The Doctor's prophecy was fulfilled. "Charles had gart the bit Lassy's heart to melt like snaw off a dyke;" and even before the day of his departure, poor Kate was constrained to own that Cousin Charles was all the world to her.

So far all was well. But there still remained another outwork to be carried, in the person of Uncle Lorimer; and well Charles knew that he must expect to find the Old Gentleman's heart somewhat more strongly fortified than that of his fair Daughter. However, the experiment must be tried; so one fine morning, after he had talked the Governor into good humour, by praising his hounds and admiring his rifles, Charles ventured to broach the subject next his heart; and with very little circumlocution—for he knew that to be a thing which his Uncle detested above all others—he somewhat bluntly craved the honour of being promoted from the rank of Nephew to that of Son-in-law.

Old Lorimer, who was at the moment handling one of his favourite rifles, and giving Charles a minute account of some extraordinary shot he had made with it, suddenly dropped the butt-end of the weapon to the ground, as if he had been electrified, faced round, stared Charles full in the face, and finally burst into an immoderate fit of laughter.

"Marry my Kate! Ha! ha! ha! Bones of my ancestors, but this is a mad world! Marry my Kate indeed! Why she is hardly out of the nursery—you have not quite shaken yourself clear of your mother's apron-strings—and yet, forsooth, you must begin to talk of love! Get along, you precocious young rascal, and do not let me hear again of your putting such absurd ideas into the Girl's head. Love and marriage—Ha! ha! ha! by mine honour, it is enough to make an honest man break the rim of his stomach with laughter, to hear children talk in this manner!"

The worthy Gentleman forgot that although his Nephew and Daughter were children in his estimation, the former had nearly arrived at the respectable age of nineteen, and that the latter was only one year younger; and that although their thinking of marriage at that age might be imprudent, still it was natural enough that something very like love should have sprung up between two young creatures thrown so much together as they had been for the last two or three months, and that it was entirely his own fault if he had been so blind as not to discover it sooner. But it was so long since Old Lorimer had been a victim to the tender passion himself, that he had almost ceased to remember that such a thing existed, and had no more idea of the "child Kate's" falling in love with any thing but a pet-dog, or a favourite pony, than he had of flying.

Charles was of a different way of thinking; his pride was galled by the contemptuous manner in which his proposals had been received. He that had slain Bears aud Tigers to be called a child! a "precocious young rascal!" nay, to be treated as such. To be told that he had no business to make love! And, worst of all, to hear his darling Kate laughed at for a silly school-girl! Heavens and earth! the thing was intolerable. He felt his blood boil within him; and had the offender been any one but his own Uncle, there is no saying to what lengths his rage might have carried him. But fortunately his prudence got the better of his temper, he remembered that his Uncle—savage though he thought him at the time—was also Kate's Father, and he therefore replied with wonderful coolness, yet with firmness. He reminded his Uncle, that although young, he was not quite so much of a child as he had represented him; that he was of good family, and heir apparent to a good property; and although he had taken the liberty of ascertaining the state of his Cousin's affections towards him, that neither he nor Kate had any idea of marrying immediately. He had already made arrangements for starting that night to join his regiment, and only wished his Uncle, before parting, to give his consent to their union at any future period which he might think most advisable.

This Old Lorimer would not hear of. And we think he was right; for we hold it, that long engagements between young persons, are very unwise things, and by all means to be avoided. But he admired the boy's candour and spirit—perhaps his conscience smote him for having treated the matter with such levity—and although he still persisted in assuring Charles that it was all "calf's love," he shook hands with him kindly, and told him that evening, at parting, that if, when he became a General Officer, he still remained constant, and Kate unmarried, he might then, perhaps, allow him to talk of love. But in the mean time, that he was to banish all such foolish fancies from his mind, devote himself to his profession, and strive to become as good a Soldier as he was a Sportsman. Moreover he strictly forbade all correspondence between the young lovers. And so he gave Charles his blessing—for he really loved the boy—and sent him on his way, in a palanquin, by torchlight, with as heavy a heart as ever poor Subaltern carried under a buff belt.

We purposely avoid making any mention of the parting scene between the young lovers—not that we are ignorant of the particulars—but because we feel that it would be a breach of confidence on our part, to lay them before the public. We have a conscience, Lady!

The Doctor, however, remarked next morning at breakfast, that poor Kate's eyes were very red, and her spirits at a very low ebb, and his heart, as he said himself, "was wae for the poor young thing."

From this time forth, our friend Mc.Phee became a more frequent visiter than ever at the Lorimers', and was always a welcome one. His dry humour, and eccentricity of character, had long ago made him a great favourite with the Old Gentleman, and, in a very short time, he had completely won Kate's heart also.

The worthy Doctor, in spite of his broad Scotch dialect and rough exterior, had not only a heart overflowing with the milk of human kindness; but, when he laid aside his half-affected rusticity, and chose to make himself agreeable, he displayed a refinement of mind, and a depth of knowledge, which appeared quite marvellous in a person of such uncouth manners. His love for "Maister Charles" was unbounded, and his name ever in his mouth, which of itself, independently of his having been instrumental in saving his life, would have been sufficient to render him agreeable in Kate's eyes. But he also took a fatherly interest in herself; and strove with so much assiduity, yet genuine delicacy, to cheer her drooping spirits, that she must have been insensible indeed to kindness, had her heart not warmed towards the good affectionate creature.

It was some time after Charles had left Ootacamund, that the worthy Doctor was seen one fine fresh morning, striding with even longer steps than usual in the direction of Old Lorimer's cottage. He was dressed in his best sabbath-day suit. There was an elasticity in his step, and a joyous air of happiness pervading the whole man, which attracted the notice of all the gossips of the neighbourhood, and set them forthwith speculating as to the cause of these remarkable symptoms in the usually sedate Doctor.

Some Maiden Ladies of a certain age, who had lately remarked with much anxiety the frequency of the Doctor's visits to Old Lorimer's cottage, felt satisfied that the mystery was now about to be cleared up. It was self-evident that the Doctor, availing himself of the illness of Old Lorimer, who was confined to his room by an attack of gout, was now on his way to make his proposals to Miss Lorimer, and probably to arrange plans for an elopement. They had long ago seen through the old wretch's designs, and wondered how dear good-natured Mr. Lorimer could be so blind as not to perceive the very great, they might indeed say improper, intimacy which had for some time existed between Miss Lorimer and Doctor Mc.Phee. Others whose thoughts were less fully occupied by love affairs, were satisfied with the supposition that the Doctor had, through the interest of Old Lorimer, been appointed to the situation of garrison-surgeon on the Governor's staff, and was now on his way to announce the glad tidings to his Patron. Whilst some of a more gloomy temperament had it from undoubted authority, that the Doctor was hastening to attend the death-bed of Mr. Lorimer, who had been attacked during the night by a fit of apoplexy, from which there were no hopes of his recovery, and that the prospect of a good legacy was sufficient to account for the joyous air of the hypocritical old rogue. They had all along said that Mc.Phee was not devoting so much of his time to the Lorimers for nothing. His affectation of simplicity was all very well. But their hearers might take their word for it, he was more rogue than fool.

Our worthy Doctor, unconscious of the many good-natured remarks which his Sunday coat and happy face elicited—and which indeed would have given him very little annoyance had he heard them—went on his way rejoicing, his smile becoming brighter, and the execution of his favourite air "Johnny Cope" more energetic, the nearer he approached to the place of his destination. Arrived at the house, he walked in without ceremony, and availing himself of the privilege of an intimate and welcome friend, proceeded at once to the door of Kate's little boudoir, in which she usually sat during the morning.

By mine honour, Friend Mc.Phee, there is something rather suspicious in all this. We hope the surmises of our sagacious female friends may not prove correct after all!

The Doctor gave a modest rap at the door, and was desired by a sweet low voice to enter.

It was only now that poor Mc.Phee remembered it might perhaps be thought presumptuous on his part to intrude on the privacy of a Young Lady without being previously announced; and the idea of his having been guilty of a breach of good manners brought on a fit of nervous agitation, which rendered the poor man's manner, on entering the room, even more awkward than usual; he remained scraping and bowing with the handle of the door in his hand, and could not summon courage sufficient to venture beyond the threshold, till reassured by one of Kate's sweetest smiles.

"I hope I 'm no intrudin' on you, Miss Kate," stammered the poor Doctor, closing the door softly, and advancing towards the sofa on which Kate was seated, at the same time smoothing the nap of his hat with great care, and stepping as cautiously as if he feared to hear the sound of his own footsteps.

"Not at all, my dear Doctor," replied Kate, smiling, and extending her hand kindly towards him. "Pray be seated. You know you are always welcome here."

The Doctor drew in a chair, seated himself upon the extreme edge, and continued to smooth his hat with greater industry than ever, evidently at a loss how to open the conversation.

We shall avail ourselves of the awkward pause to introduce the Reader to Kate's boudoir.

On one side of the room stood her pianoforte, with a collection of the best and newest music, carefully arranged in a handsome music-stand within reach. In the bow-window was a stand filled with flower-pots, containing some of the rarest and most fragrant plants, their healthy appearance bearing ample testimony to the care bestowed upon them by their young mistress. Behind this was a table on which stood a half-finished clay bust, surrounded by modelling tools; and by it lay a portfolio, which being open, displayed to view some fine specimens of original drawings by the old masters. In various corners of the room might be seen writing materials, books, embroidering frames, and sundry little indescribable nick-nacks appertaining to a Lady's work-box, and in front of the sofa on which Kate sat, stood a table covered with drawing-materials, and a half-finished sketch of the Orange Valley in water colours. The floor was covered with the finest rattan-matting. In front of the fireplace a carefully-dressed Tiger-skin—one of Cousin Charles's trophies—was spread in place of a rug. And at the feet of his young mistress lay a beautiful tame Gazelle, wearing round his slender neck a richly-embroidered velvet collar. This too, we rather suspect was a present from "dear Cousin Charles."

The walls of the rooms were hung round with fine, boldly-touched drawings of some of the most picturesque views on the Neilgherry Hills. These were the produce of Kate's own pencil; but there were intermixed with them several spirited sketches of animals in a different style, but equally well executed, which the Doctor had no difficulty in recognizing as the handywork of "Maister Charles," who, he often used to remark, "was just extraordinar' for takin' off the likeness o' a wild craiter as natural as life."

Kate was seated on a sofa, dressed in the most simple white, and looking even more lovely than usual. The roses had forsaken her cheeks, and there was an expression of sadness in her soft blue eye; but this only served to heighten the naturally expressive character of her features, and render them more interesting. She had thrown aside her pencil like one whose thoughts are too much distracted to permit of their fixing their attention for any length of time to one subject, and was hanging in a pensive attitude over her guitar, as if overwhelmed by the host of tender recollections which the sound of its notes had called up around her. She laid the instrument aside as the Doctor entered, and with natural good-breeding, strove to relieve his evident embarrassment, by starting a subject of conversation.

"How did you find my Father this morning, Doctor?" she said, thinking that the Doctor had come as usual in his official capacity. "I thought him looking much better when I saw him."

"I didna gang to see him yet," replied the Doctor, with rather a sheepish air. "It was yoursel', Miss Kate, that I wanted to speak a word wi'."

"With me, Doctor?" replied Kate, smiling.

"Aye, just wi' you, Miss Kate. I hae somethin' in my pouch here, that I was thinkin' ye would maybe like to see, and yet maybe ye 'll no' be pleased wi' me for takin' the liberty o' showin' it to you. But it has made my heart light enough this blessed morning, and I 'm thinkin' it will no' do yours ony harm either." So saying, the Doctor drew a crumpled letter from his pocket, and handed it to Kate, with a broad grin of exultation.

Kate's hand trembled, and the blood rushed into her pale cheeks as her eye fell upon the well-known handwriting of her Cousin Charles. She hastily opened the letter, and strove hard to compose herself sufficiently to read the contents; but her agitation was so painfully apparent that the kind-hearted Doctor could not bear to witness it.

"You 'll maybe no' be able to make it out very

easily, Miss Kate," said he, gently withdrawing the letter from poor Kate's trembling hand. "He has been writin' in a terrible hurry, the wild birkie; and wi' an awfu' ill pen; and it 's that sore blotted, I could hardly make anythin' o't mysel' at first. But I hae manned it at last, so with your leave I 'll just tak' the liberty o' readin' it to you."

Kate faintly smiled her thanks, and the Doctor, after having carefully adjusted his spectacles, read as follows:—

"Fort of Koolgiedroog, 15th of May.

"My dear Doctor,

"We have taken the Fort of Koolgiedroog, said to be the strongest in the Southern Maharattah country. It was a sharp business while it lasted, but short and decisive. I was fortunate enough to have the honour of leading the forlorn hope, and thank God, escaped unhurt, or rather with a mere scratch, not worth mentioning. The Brigadier commanding has been pleased to compliment me in orders, and has promised to exert his influence in procuring my promotion. So you see I am in a fair way of procuring one step at least towards the *desirable rank of General Officer*. I address this to you because I am sure you will take the earliest opportunity of communicating its contents to my Cousin Kate. It will save the dear girl much unnecessary anxiety on my account, when she comes to see the rather heavy list of casualties, which I regret to say will appear in the next Gazette, and in which the stupid Surgeon may perhaps think it necessary to include my name. I shall write to my Uncle by next *tapall*, and enter more fully into particulars. Tell Kate, with my kindest love,—"

"Ahem! ha! and so on." The Doctor stopped short, coughed, wiped his spectacles, folded up the letter, and returned it to Kate.

"That 's a' the news worth mentionin', Miss Kate," said he; "the rest is just bits o' messages and civeelities, and the like o' that, to you and your Faither, honest man, that are no' worth my while to be readin' to you. You can just keep the letter and look it o'er at your leisure." So saying, the Doctor resumed the smoothing of his hat previous to taking his departure.

Kate, whose quivering lip and moistened eyelid betrayed the depth of her emotion, strove to master her feelings sufficiently to thank the Doctor for his kind visit, but the effort was too much for her: she allowed the letter to drop to the ground, and covering her face with her hands, burst into a violent fit of hysterical weeping.

"O Miss Kate! Miss Kate!" exclaimed the kind-hearted Doctor, his own eyes beginning to fill with moisture. "Ye maunna allow yoursel' to tak' on this way—else I 'll be fear'd e'er to tell you a piece o' good news again—and I 'm sure it 's a' good news ye hae heard the day, barrin' the bit scart Maister Charles got in the bruilzie—but that 's a mere trifle, and as he says himsel', no' worth the mentionin'."

"Pardon me, my dear Doctor," sobbed poor Kate, extending one hand to the Doctor, whilst she still covered her face with the other. "Pardon this weakness—it is childish, I know; but my nerves have been so shaken of late, that I feel quite weak and foolish. Leave me now, I pray you. I shall be better soon, and able, I hope, to thank you as I ought for your kindness."

The Doctor rose to depart; but ere he reached the door, the big tears of sympathy were rolling fast down his long thin nose.

"It 's maybe no good manners," murmured the worthy Doctor, turning back and dashing a tear from his eye, "but De'el tak' me if I can thale to leave this poor young thing, greetin' her very heart out, and no' sae ae word to comfort her. It gangs against my conscience.

"I crave your pardon,. my dear Young Lady," said he, trying to soften the naturally rough tones of his voice, and speaking with more confidence than he had hitherto done,—for his generous heart was swelling within him, and fast overcoming the painful feeling of bashfulness which had hitherto restrained him,—"I crave your pardon, my dear Young Lady. I 'm a rough auld carle, and maybe no' a very fit comforter for the like o' you; but I hae a heart, Miss Kate, I hae a heart, and it 's just at the breakin' to see you takin' on this way, and no' a leevin' soul to say a kind word to you. I canna thale to see it, that 's just the truth, so I maun e'en speak my mind, whether ye be angered wi' me for doin' it or no."

The Doctor paused for a reply, but Kate madé no answer, so he proceeded.

"You will see, Miss Kate, when you read the rest o' your Cousin's letter, that he has made me his confidant, and that I ken a' aboot the bit love affair that 's atween you two. If ye had ony friend to comfort and advise you, I wouldna hae ta'en the liberty o' mentionin' this; but as it is, I thought it better to break the ice at ance, and beg, if you think I can be of ony service to you, to command Jock Mc.Phee. I am auld enough to be your faither, Miss Kate—I feel a faither's love both for you and Maister Charles, and I hae a heart that would carry me through fire and water to serve you, so ye needna hae nae scruples about opening your heart to me. Poor Maister Charles! he was terrible down-hearted the day he left this; but I managed to cheer him awee afore we parted, and I dinna dispair o' bringin' the smiles back to your ain bonny face too afore lang, so keep your heart up, my dear Miss Kate, keep your heart up. I ken your Faither's nature weel; he 's no' sae dooms hard-hearted as he appears, and you 'll see that things will a' come right enough afore lang. And now, my dear Young Lady, I 'll awa', and I hope you 'll pardon me for the liberty I hae ta'en in speakin' sae free; for it 's just as true as Gospel that I couldna help it. You 'll maybe think it a daft-like thing for an auld carle like me to be takin' an interest in the like o' thae things; but I hae had experience, Miss Kate, I hae had sad experience, and though I 'm no' very young, I hae a soft corner in my heart yet."

Here the worthy Doctor laid his hand upon his heart, and screwed up his grotesque features into such an absurd expression of sentimental misery, that Kate could not help smiling through her tears.

"And so ye are laughin' at the auld Doctor," he said,

smiling in his turn. "Weel, weel, it does my heart good to see the smile upon that winsome young face again, for a' it 's mysel' ye'r laughin' at."

"Pardon me, my dear Doctor," she said, extending her hand kindly, whilst the smile brightened on her beautiful face like sunshine breaking through an April shower; "Heaven forbid that I should laugh at you. Pray sit down again. I am better now, and feel that your society cheers me, and does me good. And now that we have touched upon the subject, I should like you, if I am not taking too great a liberty in making the request, to tell me something of the passages in your past life to which you have alluded. You will find in me a deeply interested and truly sympathizing listener."

"A-weel, Miss Kate," replied the Doctor, twirling his watch-key and casting his eyes upon the ground, half bashful, yet half pleased at the evident interest which Kate took in his affairs. "Ye are askin' me to speak o' that which I hae na' mentioned to mortal man for the last thirty years, and which it wrings my very heart to think o', e'en at this distance o' time. But it will, maybe, do me good to speak o' thae things to you, Miss Kate, for I ken ye hae a heart that can feel for the sorrows o' others; and, at ony rate, I couldna refuse you anything, so I 'll just tell you a' about it."

The Doctor drew his chair a little nearer the sofa, took a nervous pinch of snuff, and thus began :—

"When I was young, Miss Kate, although ye 'll hardly believe it noo, I was no' that ill to look upon. My Mither, honest woman—she was a Heeland wife, and had a gae dash o' the Heeland pride in her—was for ever deevin' in my Faither's lugs that I had the air o' a Gentleman born, and that she could never dee contented till she had seen me wagging my head in a pulpit; till, for peace sake the poor man was at last obleeged to give up the idea o' makin' me an honest farmer like himsel', and sent me to the College o' Glasgow to study my Humanities. Findin', howe'er, that he had nae great interest to look to for gettin' me a Kirk, and as I was a gae throughother cheel in thae days, at ony rate, he determined to breed me up to the medical profession, in place o' makin' a Minister o' me.

"It was during my visit at hame, in my first vacation, that I became acquainted wi' Jeany Morrison, the daughter o' a new neighbour of ours that had ta'en the next farm durin' my absence. O Miss Kate! if ye had kent my Jeany ye wouldna wonder that I still cherish her image in my heart. In looks she wasna unlike yoursel', and that 's bonny enough. And O Miss Kate! she was as good as she was bonny. She was just a perfect Angel upon earth, and o'er good for this wicked world. I needna tell you I loved her—I did that in my very heart of hearts, and I believe she, poor thing, loved me as truly as ever woman did. But ye ken the old saying, 'The course of true love never did run smooth,' and in our case this was verified. Her Faither had nae great tocher to gie her; and I, a poor medical student, wi' very slender hopes o' obtainin' practice, after I had spent a' the little I was worth in education, what had I to look to? In short, our parents, although they had nae other objection to the match, wouldna allow us to think o' marriage till I had earned enough by my profession to keep a Wife respectably.

"I needna trouble you, my dear Miss Kate, wi' an account o' the mony difficulties I had to struggle through as a country Surgeon, and the mony thrifty expedients I had recourse to to scrape tegither a wee pickle siller. Suffice it to say that I, at last, obtained an appointment as Medical Officer, on board of one of the Company's ships, came out to this country, got into good practice, and have ever since been able, not only to scrape tegither some little savin's for mysel' but to keep my auld Parents in easy circumstances to the end o' their days—rest their souls!

"It was some five years after my arrival in this country that I found mysel' weel enough off to return to bonny Scotland, and claim the hand o' my Jeany. It was a joyfu' day to me, Miss Kate, when I landed once more on the shores o' Fife, and clasped my faithful Jeany to my heart. The day was fixed for our weddin'—the friends were bidden—and the very next mornin' Jeany was to have been mine for ever. We had strolled out, arm-in-arm among the bonny birk-woods, talkin' o' love and happiness, and forming plans for the future—short-sighted mortals that we were!—and sae interesting was our conversation that it was far in the glomin afore we thought o' returning. Fearing that our friends might be uneasy about us if we didna return afore dark, we determined to tak' a short cut which obleeged us to cross the burn at the back o' the hoose, by a ford. It had rained durin' the day, and the water was comin' down red and angry frae the hills. Poor dear Jeany!

she maun hae had some misgivin's, for I mind o'er weel her remarkin', at the time, that she thought the swirls o' the drumly water looked awfu' earie in the cauld light o' the full harvest moon, and that she was sure she heard the voice o' the *Kelpie* moanin' up the glen. However I kent the ford weel, and was laith to gang a mile roond by the brig; so, like a presumptuous sinner as I was, I laughed at what I called her supersteetious fears, and liftin' her in my arms, waded into the water.

"We had mostly reached the opposite side—the fire was glancing bright and cheerfu' through the cottage windows, the auld gudeman was standin' in the door, wi' his white hair glancin' like silver in the moonlight, waitin' to welcome his ain dear bairn to his arms, and I was just beginnin' to banter poor Jeany on her needless alarm, when my foot slipped on a smooth stane—my legs gaed frae under me—and next moment we were swept away down the ragin' water, clasped in ane another's arms. I was a strong swimmer then, but my poor Jeany clung to me wi' the grasp o' dispair, and my limbs were powerless. I mind nae mare till I came to my senses, mony hours afterwards, and found mysel' in bed, in the house of poor Jeany's Faither. My first thought was for Jeany. I asked if she was saved. They didna answer me, but the tears that blinded their een told the sad tale o'er weel. I sprung frae the bed wi' a yell o' dispair that gart them flee afore me, for they thought I was fae. I rushed into the next room, and there, on the very bed which was, that night, to ha'e been our bridal bed, lay the cold, blue corpse of my own loved

Jeany, streckit for the burial. O Miss Kate! Miss Kate! it 's thirty lang, weary, years sin' syne, but I canna thale to think o' that awfu' night, even to this day."

Here the poor Doctor's feelings completely overpowered him; he covered his face with his hands, and wept like a child.

Kate, whose tender feelings had been worked up to a pitch of painful excitement by the Doctor's tragical tale, was almost as much overcome as the poor man himself, and it was some time before either could utter a word.

The Doctor was the first to recover his composure.

"Ye maun think me a poor silly body, my dear Miss Kate, to gie way to my feelings in this way, but I see by that sweet smile that ye dinna think the waur o' poor Jock Mc.Phee for haein' a soft heart. God bless you, my dear bairn! God bless you!"

The Doctor had nearly reached the door, when he suddenly stopped short, and turning towards Kate, said, in rather a hesitating manner—

"I hae somethin' here, my dear Miss Kate, that ye would, maybe, like to see. Nae mortal eye except my own has ever looked upon it for the last thirty years, but after the kind sympathy ye hae shown in the sad fate o' my poor dear Jeany, I would like to think that ye had seen, even a faint resemblance o' her bonny face. There, dear, ye can look at it at your leisure, and return it to me in the evening, but dinna say a word aboot it to nae leevin' soul."

So saying, the Doctor drew from his breast something carefully enveloped in a small bag of chamois-leather, much soiled with use, and thrusting it into Kate's hand, rushed out of the room.

On removing the somewhat unseemly covering of chamois-leather, Kate discovered a miniature painting of a pretty interesting country Girl, dressed in the simple garb of a peasant, and having her fair locks braided with the silken snood of a Scottish Maiden. The painting, although somewhat faded, still bore traces of a master's hand, and there was a look of sweet simplicity in the face of the poor Girl, whose tragical fate she had just heard narrated, that she could not resist weeping afresh over her melancholy history.

But, Lady, we are forgetting ourselves!—for which we humbly crave thy pardon. We promised long ago to dispose of our characters forthwith, and retire; yet here we are running on as if thy patience were inexhaustible. We shall despatch, Lady, we shall despatch.

Know then that our young friend Charles, after a short but brilliant military career, succeeded, by the death of an old Uncle, to a handsome property at home. He lost no time in again suing for the hand of his Fair Cousin, and was this time successful. He soon afterwards returned to England, retired from the army, and is now living with his Kate, who, by the way, has become the mother of half-a-dozen fine children, in the full enjoyment of the most perfect domestic happiness.

Mansfield is still a bachelor, and a General Officer, well known among his sporting friends by the soubriquet of "Tiger Mansfield." He is no longer young, but is still universally acknowledged to possess the truest eye, and the steadiest hand of any man in India.

Old Lorimer still enjoys a vigorous old age, and annually accompanies his Son-in-law to the North of Scotland, where he rents an extensive Deer Forest, plentifully stocked with game. The Old Gentleman is no longer able to use his ponderous rifle with effect, but he cannot bear to have the favourite weapon out of his sight. It is therefore permitted to occupy a conspicuous place in the dining-room of the Shooting Lodge, where it affords to the Venerable Sportsman an ever ready excuse for holding forth on his favourite topic, the unrivalled exploits of his beloved "Kill-devil."

The worthy Doctor, to use his own words, "is still to the fore, and able to hirple about." He has purchased a pretty little Cottage in the immediate neighbourhood of Young Lorimer's Shooting Lodge, and spends the greater part of his time with him and his Wife, whom he still persists in calling "his dear Miss Kate." He is an immense favourite with all the children, but particularly with "young Maister Charles," who sits, for hours together, on the Old Man's knee, listening with childish delight to his long-winded stories about Bears and Tigers, *Mons Meg*, Wild Soos, and his Old Friend the Forest Ranger.

Gentle Reader, adieu! We have told our last tale, and now it only remains for us to offer thee our sincere thanks for having so long listened, like "young Maister Charles," to an Old Man's *clavers*.

GLOSSARY OF HINDOSTANEE WORDS.

Abba!—An exclamation of surprise, or complaint.
Ameldar.—The Native Collector of a district.
Ayah.—A Native female Servant.
Burrah Shikar.—The hunting of large animals.
Bagh-hie.—There is a Tiger here.
Buckshish.—A present.
Bangles.—Ornaments, generally of silver, worn round the wrists and ankles.
Bungalow.—A house such as Europeans inhabit.
Burrah Hakim Sahib.—The Great Doctor Gentleman.
Burrah Khamah.—A great dinner.—A feast.
Burrah Sahib.—Great Sir.—A Great Man.—A term of respect applied to European Gentlemen.
Bhot Atch Sahib.—Very good, Sir.
Bagh!—A Tiger.
Bagh-mar.—Tiger-slayer.
Chor do.—Let loose.
Cumberbund.—A shawl or sash worn round the waist.
Cumbley.—A coarse sort of blanket worn by the poorer class of Natives in India.
Cutch.—An Indian Province celebrated for a particular breed of Horses.
Coolies.—Men who carry burdens.
Chuprasee bolow.—Call the Tent-pitchers.
Cotwall.—A Village Dignitary.—The head man of the Police, whose business it is to supply Travellers with provisions.
Cowrie baskets.—Covered baskets for carrying provisions on a march.
Chunam.—A very fine sort of plaster, made from shells, which, when dry, has exactly the appearance of white marble.
Chowrie.—A bunch of horse-hair, or sometimes the tail of a Musk Ox, fixed into a handle, which Horsekeepers carry to brush away the flies.
Dekho Sahib.—Look, Sir.
Galee.—Abusive language.
Ghats, or *Ghauts.*—Mountain Passes.
Gram.—A kind of pulse on which Horses are fed in India.
Gorah lao.—Bring forth the Horse.
Gorah-wallah.—A Horse-keeper.
Ho Sahib.—Yes, Sir.

Huttee.—An Elephant.
Howdah.—The seat fastened on an Elephant's back.
Idder aon.—Come hither.
Inshallah.—Please God, or, Praise be to God. An exclamation ever in the mouth of a Mussulman when excited.
Jo hookum Sahib.—It is an order, Sir.
Jemmadar.—A Native Officer.—This title is often assumed by the head men of particular tribes.
Jagheerdar.—A landed Proprietor.—A petty Prince.
Jaggary.—A coarse sort of sugar.
Jungle Wallah.—Jungle Man.—A savage.
Kallion.—A small portable Hookah, or Hubble-bubble.
Koolgha.—A Buffalo.—The Natives of the Canara district call the Bison, *Jungle Koolgha*, or Jungle Buffalo.
Mussaulchee.—A Low Caste Native Servant, commonly called a Maty Boy, in the Madras Presidency.
Mahout.—The Driver of an Elephant.
Maugree.—A large species of Jessamine.
Nullah.—A small ravine.—A watercourse.
Ne Sahib.—No, Sir.
Natch Girls.—Dancing Girls.
Peon.—A Personal Attendant distinguished by wearing a shoulder-belt.—An armed Follower.
Pillaw.—A highly spiced Indian dish composed of meat and rice.
Puggarie.—The cloth of which a turban is formed.
Reench.—A Bear.
Ryot.—A Cultivator of the Soil.—A Peasant.
Shikar.—The hunting of wild animals.
Shikaree.—A Hunter.
Sunho Sahib.—Listen, Sir.
Swamy.—The Hindoo Deity.—A term of the highest respect, sometimes applied to a Superior.
Tapall.—The Mail, in India, is carried by men on foot, who are called *Tapalls*.
Todah Mund.—A cluster of huts inhabited by Todahs.
Tulwar.—A sword.
Topee Wallahs.—Men who wear hats.—Europeans.
Wallah! Wallah!—An exclamation of astonishment.
Wah! Wah!—Ditto.

NOTES.

"*Athol Brose.*"—Page 5, line 5.

A very delightful compound, for which Meg Dods gives the following receipt:—

"Mix with a cupful of heather-honey, two of mountain-dew, *alias* whisky."

We have little doubt that this was the tipple in which Father Jove indulged, under the classical name of nectar.

"*Climate of the Neilgherry Hills.*"—Page 7, line 2.

I have no hesitation in saying that the climate of the Neilgherry Hills is about the finest in the known world. Lying between the parallels of 11° and 12° North Latitude, they enjoy all the brilliancy and splendid moonlight of a tropical climate, whilst their great elevation (8,700 feet above the level of the sea) not only tempers the heat, but gives to the air a pureness and elasticity, unknown in less elevated situations. A meteorological table kept on the Hills, from March 1825 to March 1826, makes the maximum of the thermometer, at noon, 69°, and the minimum 55°; the maximum at 6 A. M. 60°, and the minimum 31°.—Is it possible to conceive a climate more perfect than this?

The first Europeans who ever visited the Neilgherry Hills, were a party of gentlemen from Coimbatoor, who made an excursion to them in 1819. They spoke in raptures of the appearance of the Country, and of the climate, and, soon afterwards, published an account of their tour, in the Madras journals. But, strange to say, this account failed to attract much public attention. In 1820, another party, accompanied by a Lady, ascended the Hills. In 1821, a pass was opened to the mountains, by Government, and some Families took up their temporary abode there. Since that time, the beautiful Cantonment of Ootacamund has been rapidly increasing. A handsome Church, a Military Hospital, a splendid mansion for the Governor, and many good houses have been erected. A Bazaar, and several excellent shops have been established, and, for some years back it has been a favourite place of resort, during the hot months, for the Inhabitants of Bombay as well as those of Madras.

I am so enthusiastic an admirer of the Neilgherry Hills, that I shall not trust myself to describe the scenery, lest I be accused of exaggeration, but shall take the liberty of making a few extracts from Mr. Hough's book, which gives a very correct account of this delightful Region.

" Neilgherry is a Canarese term, compounded of *Neil*, blue; and *gherry*, a mountain. The lofty Hills, so named, form the nucleus of the Ghats, described above, and are situated between the parallels of 11° and 12° North Latitude, and 76° and 77° of East Longitude. * *

" The acclivities of the mountains present a wild and rugged aspect, covered with impenetrable jungle, amongst which are seen numerous gigantic forest trees—teak, mango, ebony, black-wood, tamarind, &c. &c. But their character too much resembles that of other mountain regions in India to require, here, a more particular description."

* * * * * * * * * *

" The scenery of this interesting Country it is difficult to describe in adequate language. It presents very little of that bleak, rugged, and barren appearance, which is common to most other mountainous regions. Peringa and Maika Naads (districts) are composed of mountains which vary greatly in their elevation. Some of these eminences are almost perpendicular, towering to the clouds, and descending in deep and terrific precipices. Their sides are occasionally bare, but more frequently covered with fine grass, a rich profusion of plants, and a short brushwood, with almost every variety of fern." * * * * * * * * *

"The vast sides of some of the Hills are literally clothed with trees, occasionally forming extensive woods—the picturesque copses that fill or border their ravines, sometimes assuming a circular form, at others that of a crescent, which are so accurately defined that they appear to have been planted by the hand of man.

"They are adorned with the large crimson flower of the Rhododendron, and the white blossom of a species of Camellia, both of which trees grow here to the height of from thirty to forty feet. A species of Dog-rose, and the Jessamine, in their respective seasons, literally bespangle the woods, and perfume the air with their fragrance. These, with the pepper vine, intersect the branches, hanging in festoons, and climbing to the tops of the loftiest forest trees."

So much for Mr. Hough's description of the scenery—which is rendered doubly interesting to the Sportsman, by the fact of all these beautiful woods being plentifully stocked with game.

Here is a list of the animals and birds, with which I became acquainted during a sojourn of six months on the Neilgherries, —and of which I shall give a more particular description as they occur in the text.

The Samber, or Black Rusa Deer (*Cervus Aristotelis*), vulgarly called the Elk.

The Muntjack, or Rib-faced Deer (*Cervus Muntjack*), a variety of the Musk Deer—sometimes, very absurdly, named the Jungle Sheep.

A variety of the Ibex, which, for reasons hereafter given, I believe to have hitherto escaped the notice of Naturalists, and which I have therefore named the Ibex of the Neilgherry Hills.—He frequents the lofty precipices overhanging the Low

Country, and, from this circumstance, has been erroneously described as a species of Chamois.

Wild Hog (*Sus Aper*).

Tiger (*Felis Tigris*), not so numerous as in the plains.

Panther, or Leopard (*Felis Leopardus*).

Black Bear of India (*Ursus Labiatus*).

Jackall (*Canis Aureus*).

Wild, or Jungle Dog (*Canis Familiaris*).

The Crested Porcupine (*Hystrix Cristata*), the flesh of which is considered a great delicacy.

A species of black Ape, which I believe to be the Ouanderon, or Lion-tailed Baboon (*Simia Macacus Silenus*).

And the Common Hare.

The Game birds are, the

Woodcock (*Scolopax Rusticula*), the existence of which, in India, was, till of late years, unknown. They arrive about the end of October, and take their departure in March. They are not found in the Low Country.

The Common Snipe, the Jack Snipe, and the Painted Snipe (*Rhyncœa Capensis*).

Pea-fowl, Jungle-fowl, and Spur-fowl (*Perdix Spadiceus*), found in all the woods, but particularly numerous in the Orange Valley, about fifteen miles from Ootacamund.

And two varieties of Quail; the small brown Jungle Quail, and a larger variety with red legs, the name of which I do not know.

The Cobra Capella, and other venomous snakes of India, are unknown on the Hills. I only met with two small varieties of the snake tribe, one black and the other green, both of which are said to be harmless.

"*The enraged Boar no sooner got a glimpse of his white dress,*" *&c.*—Page 22, line 9.

The idea of poor Heels' adventure with the Boar was suggested by the following passage in my Indian Journal:—

" We had surrounded a sounder of Wild-hog in a ravine, and were, as usual, posted at the different passes.

" The Doctor, who was next to me, had taken his stand amongst some high grass, so that the Hog—which happened to take his pass—were within ten yards of him before he observed them;—he fired at the foremost one, an immense Sow, but missed her, and next moment the Old Lady was on board of him.

" The report of the rifle, followed by a savage grunt from the Hog, and a yell of despair from the unfortunate Doctor, attracted my attention to the spot. The high grass prevented me from seeing distinctly what had occurred; but some ten yards down the side of the hill, I observed a dark object, kicking and blaspheming in the midst of a thorn bush;—And —God forgive me—I could not help laughing, although, from the nature of the accident, it was more than probable that poor Mac was severely injured. The enraged Sow, having disposed of the Doctor, charged his Servant,—who was a little way behind with a spare gun—got her snout between his legs—tossed him over her head—and sent him flying down the hill, right on the top of his Master. This made the Doctor roar louder than ever, and the energetic manner in which he *blessed* poor Blacky's eyes, for falling on him, relieved me much, by assuring me that his wounds were not mortal. I tried to avenge his fall; but was so convulsed with laughter, that I missed right and left, and away went the Sow in triumph. On picking up the Doctor we discovered that he had escaped wonderfully well—thanks to his antagonist for being a Sow instead of a Boar. He had only received a severe contusion, and a pretty extensive abrasion of the skin from one of her blunt tusks, which had also ripped up his nether garment, from the knee to the waist-band;—but had the same blow been inflicted by the tusk of a Boar, the chances are it would have proved fatal. As it was, the poor Doctor felt the effects of the accident for more than a fortnight. His Maty Boy escaped with a few slight bruises.

"*Mansfield's Peon springs forward," &c.*—Page 31, line 3.

Your good Mussulman will not eat the flesh of any animal, that has not been blooded, and prayed over, either by himself or one of his own Caste. He is ever ready, therefore, to rush in, and draw blood from an animal, before he expires, for unless blood follows the knife, he is debarred from using any part of the flesh.

"*Thud.*"—Page 33, line 1.

Any one who has ever shot a Deer, must know full well, the very satisfactory sound which I have attempted to express by the Scotch word—*thud.*

"*The remains of the poor fellow presented a ghastly spectacle.*"—Page 41, line 3.

The first Tiger I ever assisted in slaying, killed one of the Beaters before our eyes, and his mangled body presented very much the appearance I have attempted to describe in the text.

"*Here 's at him at all events.*"—Page 43, line 15.

Bears are often speared on horseback—What is there indeed that an Indian Hog-hunter will not venture to attack with his spear?—but the chase is apt to terminate as I have described. A friend of mine had his horse pulled down, and narrowly escaped being killed in attempting to spear a Bear with a blunt weapon.

"*Have plenty of fireworks been sent to the ground?*"—Page 49, line 12.

In beating for a Tiger in thick cover, fireworks are often required to make him bolt.

"*Todahs.*"—Page 50, line 29.

The Todahs are certainly the finest and most interesting race of People I have met with in India. Here is a very good description of them, taken from Captain Harkness' work on the Neilgherry Hills.

"The appearance of the Todahs, who may be considered the original inhabitants of the Hills, is certainly very prepossessing. Generally above the common height, athletic, and well made, their bold bearing, and open expressive countenances, lead immediately to the conclusion, that they must be of a different race to their neighbours of the same hue, and the question naturally arises, *who can they be?*

"They never wear any covering to the head, whatever the weather may be, but allow the hair to grow to an equal length, of about six or seven inches; parted from the centre or crown, it forms into natural bushy circlets, all round, and at a short distance more resembles some artificial decoration, than the simple adornment of nature. The hair of the face also is allowed a similar freedom of growth, and in every instance, except from the effect of age, it is of a jet black, and of the same degree of softness, as that of the natives of the Low Country.

"A large, full, and speaking eye, Roman nose, fine teeth, and pleasing contour, having occasionally the appearance of great gravity, but seemingly ever ready to fall into the expression of cheerfulness and good humour, are natural marks prominently distinguishing them from all other natives of India.

"They usually wear small gold earrings, some of them a studded chain of silver round the neck, and rings of the same description on the hand.

"Their dress consists of a short under garment, folded round the waist, and fastened to a girdle; and of an upper one, or mantle, which covers every part except the head, legs, and occasionally the right arm. These are left bare, the folds of the mantle terminating with the left shoulder, over which the bordered end is allowed to hang loosely.

* * * * * * * * * *

"The women are of a stature proportionate to that of the

men, but of complexion generally some shades lighter, the consequence, perhaps, of less exposure to the weather. With a strongly feminine cast of the same expressive features as the men, most of them, and particularly the younger, have beautiful long black tresses, which flow in unrestrained luxuriance over the neck and shoulders.

" With a modest and retiring demeanour, they are perfectly free from the ungracious, and menial-like timidity of the generality of the sex of the Low Country; and enter into conversation with a stranger, with a confidence and self-possession becoming in the eyes of Europeans, and strongly characteristic of a system of manners and customs, widely different from those of their neighbours.

* * * * * * * * * *

Their life being in every respect a pastoral one, they do not congregate in towns or villages, but every family or the principal branches of each family live separately."

For further particulars of this interesting people, I must refer the Reader to Captain Harkness' work, which is well worthy of remark.

In my Journal I find the following description of their huts :—

" Their villages, which are called *munds*, generally consist of four or five huts, and are almost invariably situated in the most picturesque spots, the selection of which argues great good taste on the part of the Todahs. I cannot say as much for their taste in architecture.

" A Todah hut is, I think, the most uncomfortable habitation for a human being that ever was invented. In form it is an oblong square, about nine feet by seven, covered by a roof like the tilt of a waggon, formed of a pliant species of bamboo, covered with turf and neatly thatched, and is not more than six or seven feet high :—the ends of the hut are closed up by rough boards, and the only aperture in the whole building is a hole at one end about two feet square, which serves for door, window, chimney, and all. Four or five persons inhabit one of these bee-hives; but how they manage to exist in them is more than I can conceive. I once tried the experiment of entering one—an operation which is performed on all-fours, of course—and found the atmosphere so suffocating that I was glad to make my escape in less than five minutes."

"*The law of the Todahs allows but one Wife to the inhabitants of each village.*"—Page 52, line 21.

I find this statement recorded in my Journal, but have discovered since writing it, that it is not strictly correct. My ignorance of the Todah language, and the circumstance of my having visited some *munds* inhabited by several men, and only one woman, occasioned the mistake. The law of the Todahs, although it allows a plurality of Husbands to the Women, does not *oblige* them to become the Wife of a whole village, the selection of a certain number of Husbands, from those who aspire to her hand, being left either to the Lady or to her Father.

The following extracts from Captain Harkness' work will throw some light upon this curious subject:—

"Some of the Inhabitants from each of the monts we had visited, came to see us the following day. The accounts they had received from their Families, on their return home in the evening, having suggested to them one advantage to which our knowledge of their language might be applied, and which was to translate into that of their present masters the subjects of some disputes then existing among them. The opportunity was one of much promise, with regard to our desire of becoming better acquainted with their character; and the remainder of the day was passed in listening to their various statements, and in drawing up the following petitions.

"The petition of *Kerswan*, Kutan of Murzon.

"I gave my Daughter Pilluvāni to Wife, to Phori Pinpurz, Kutan of Koron, about fifteen years ago. She was then seven years of age; and I gave with her a portion of four buffalo kine, two of which were of a superior kind, and their milk drawn only for sacred purposes. Some seven or eight years subsequent to the above period, Pinpurz, and Swalt Khakhood, Kutan of Pirkon, came to me and asked my sanction for Pilluvāni to be Wife to the latter as well as to the former.

"To this I agreed, and, as is customary, Khakhood presented me with a buffalo. About a year subsequent to the latter period, Pinpurz, Khakhood, and Phori Tūmbŭt, Kutan of Koron, came to me and begged I would sanction Pilluvāni's being Wife to Tūmbŭt also. This I agreed to, and Tūmbŭt presented me with a buffalo. After my Daughter Pilluvāni had also become the Wife of Tūmbŭt, Pinpurz borrowed from him, at different periods, the sum of one hundred and twenty rupees. It is now about a year ago that Pinpurz refused to allow Pilluvāni to be Wife either to Khakhood or to Tūmbŭt, and at the same time refused to give them the customary equivalent. These two therefore complained to Mr. ——, who directed that the business should be investigated by a Panchayet, composed of individuals from the several Norrs. This Panchayet awarded that Pilluvāni was to be Wife to Pinpurz Kutan only, but that he was to pay to Tūmbŭt ninety rupees, in adjustment of all demands; and to present to Khakhood eight buffalo kine. To this award Pinpurz has hitherto refused compliance, although he will not allow Pilluvāni to be Wife to any one but himself; and he has now complained to the ———. The conduct of this Pinpurz is so infamous that I will not allow my Daughter Pilluvāni to be Wife to him any longer. I stated this my determination to the Panchayet, but was overruled by them. I now reclaim my Daughter, and petition that she may be returned to me."

In a subsequent part of the work the Author gives another version of the same case, as stated by Pinpurz, the following extract from which may prove interesting, as being farther illustrative of our subject :—

"Now, according to our customs, Pilluvāni was to pass the

first month with me, the second with Khakhood, and the third with Tūmbŭt; and the two latter, waiting in succession on the Father-in-law, were to ask his blessing, and claim their privilege in right. I was to give her raiment, the first year, Khakhood the second, and Tūmbŭt the third. I had the option of claiming the three first children, Khakhood the second three, and Tūmbŭt the third three, &c. &c.

* * * * * * * * * *

"We all three should have been equally bound to protect the whole of the Children, to marry and to give them in marriage; but the superior authority would always have rested with me. The case of Pilluvāni, and myself, however, was at variance with this custom. We were fond of one another, and determined not to separate. I offered to pay the usual fines, but the other party would not accept of them," &c. &c.

At the conclusion of the narrative the Author says—

"The above detail led to some questions from us, and we learnt that a Woman, besides this plurality of Husbands, may have as many cicisbeos, but with this proviso, that it must be with the consent of those to whom she is already contracted, —a consent which is not generally refused; but that a Man can only be contracted to one Woman. He may, however, be the cicisbeo of many."

"*Our hero found himself sprawling on his back in the bottom of the ravine.*"—Page 58, line 11.

My Brother, George Campbell, of the Bombay Civil Service, was the person who made this extraordinary escape from a Tiger. The adventure is related exactly as it occurred—even to the last long shot at the Tiger—with this one exception, that the Tiger was not in the act of charging any one at the time the fatal bullet reached him. The wonderful escape of Old Lorimer is also a fact, although it occurred on a different occasion.

Here are two similar instances of youthful rashness, selected from amongst many recorded in my Brother's Journal:—

"Dummul, 26th September.—A Tigress killed and completely devoured a Buffalo which was tied last night in the same nullah where we killed the Man-eater a few days ago. The unhappy brute, fastened as a bait, must have sold his life dearly, for the traces of a deadly struggle were manifest, and the neck appeared to have been dislocated, not, as usual, by the fatal wrench, but by repeated gripes. The long tusks of the Tigress's jaw had left many a deep impression in her victim's throat, and the ground, torn by claws, and ploughed up by hoofs, showed that the fight must have been a long one. The Tigress, although completely gorged, passed the Elephant, at the top of her speed, before the first rocket had ceased to smoulder in the covert where she had been lying. A succession of roars, and that indescribable shrinking, as the ball hits, made us feel satisfied that she was wounded, although she continued her long lobbing gallop, without showing any signs of weakness. A signal being made, from a tree, that she had lain up, we were soon at the spot, a very thick place on the side of the nullah. We could hear her growling inside of the bush, but from the howdah it was impossible to see her; and, when we found it in vain to attempt stirring her up, I dismounted, and, under cover of the Elephant, peeped in. There she was, looking very sick, and disgorging large masses of undigested flesh, mingled with her own blood. Her position preventing me from hitting either head or shoulder, I gave her both barrels in the back, and got under the Elephant's trunk, just in time, for she charged at me instantly. A rifle was now handed down from the howdah, and as the Tigress lay watching me, with her head between her fore-paws, I took her betwixt the eyes, which shone like emeralds, and 'put out the light.' She died, without a struggle, in the same position."

"Hungul, 24th December.—We have just returned from a very pretty day's sport, having killed a fine male Tiger, that held out for many hours before the *coup-de-grace* was administered. A labourer, in walking through a bed of chillies, came suddenly upon a Tiger, crouching among them, and ran to our tents with the intelligence." Here follows a long description of the hunt, during which the Tiger was several times wounded, and at last laid up in a thick clump of reeds, on the edge of a small stream. "I now went up to finish him, having a double rifle in my hand, pistols in my belt, and a double gun carried by a Peon, who engaged to stand firm. The Tiger commenced growling as we approached, and charged out, with a loud roar, when we were within about five yards. But the stream was between us, and he fell into the water sorely wounded, receiving both balls from my heavy rifle the instant he burst from the covert. He tried to swim towards me, dyeing the water with his blood, and I was obliged to finish him with the pistols, my valiant follower having bolted with the spare gun. After a few desperate struggles to keep above water, he sank and disappeared. We got him out, and found that he had been hit by the first volley, through the shoulder, in two places, and close to the heart by another ball; a fourth had hit him near the spine; and there were two other wounds in his hind quarters, besides the fatal shots which finished him—two in the chest, and one behind the ear."

"*And have no fancy to be haunted by your ghost now that you are dead.*"—Page 61, line 16.

The Natives of India have a superstitious belief, that unless the whiskers of a Tiger are singed off immediately after he is killed, his ghost will haunt those who have been accessary to his death.

"DEER STALKING AND IBEX SHOOTING ON THE NEILGHERRY HILLS."—Heading of Chapter, page 62.

The Deer found on the Neilgherry Hills is the Samber, or Black Rusa Deer (*Cervus Aristotelis*). He is a noble animal, nearly as large as the Elk, and indeed is generally so called by European Sportsmen in the Madras Presidency. I unfortunately neglected to make any memorandums of the size and weight of this animal, and can therefore only say, in a general way, that a full grown Stag stands about fourteen hands and a half—or five feet—at the shoulder, and weighs as much as a moderate sized ox.

A head now in my possession measures as follows :—

	Ft.	In.
Length of skull	1	5½
Breadth between eyes	0	6
Circumference of the burr	0	11
Circumference of horn above the brow antler .	0	7½
Length from tip to burr along the curve .	2	9
Distance from tip to tip . . .	2	7

He is found all over India, and in the Jungles of the Low Country is said to grow to the height of sixteen hands. This I can believe to be the case, from the immense size of some heads I have seen, although I have never met with a specimen myself, either on the Hills or in the Low Country, that exceeded fourteen hands and a half in height. The horns are as large, in proportion to the size of the animal, as those of the common Red-deer, and are nearly of the same form, differing only in this respect, that although they annually increase in size, they never acquire more than two antlers—the brow antler, and another near the top of the beam. The neck and shoulders of the male are covered with long shaggy hair, susceptible of being raised like the mane of the Lion, which gives the animal a very grand appearance when excited. The suborbital sinus is very large, and both Males and Females have canine teeth in the upper jaw, like those of the Horse. The Stag is very strong and vicious, and stands resolutely at bay when wounded and unable to escape. The Natives declare that he frequently attacks the Bison, and that they have witnessed desperate encounters between them. At the time I visited the Neilgherry Hills in 1833, Deer were so numerous that they used to come into the gardens at night; and in beating for Deer with a party of ten guns, I have killed as many as three, besides a Wild Boar, to my own share, within a few miles of the Cantonment.

Regarding the Ibex, I find the following remarks in my Journal:—

"The animal to which I have given the name of the Ibex of the Neilgherries is, without doubt, either a variety of Ibex, or Wild Goat, although the very inapplicable title of Chamois has been bestowed upon it by Madras Sportsmen; and I am inclined to believe that it is a variety which has hitherto escaped the notice of Naturalists. But this point I must leave to be decided by a better Naturalist than myself. He is a large animal, with a short stout body, and stands very high in proportion to his length. The male animal, from which my description is taken, measured as follows, immediately after death:—

	Ft.	In.
Height at the shoulder . . .	4	0
Length from point of nose to end of tail .	6	5

In figure he very much resembles the common Goat of India; but is much larger, and stouter, in proportion to his height. His horns are evidently those of an Ibex;—the section of them forms a triangle, flat and smooth on the inside, the anterior angle acute, and the other sides rounded off, and marked with transverse wrinkles, deep in front, and shaded off gradually towards the rear. The horns are nearly in contact at the base, and from hence they curve backwards, gradually diverging, till at the points they are about five inches apart. The length of the horn is ten inches. The nose is considerably arched, like that of a Highland Ram. The general colour of the animal is a dark ashy gray above, and white below, with a dark line along the back. The eye is surrounded by a spot of fawn colour, and the cheeks, fore part of the face, and muzzle are deep brown. The fore part of the legs is dark brown, and the hinder part white. There is a large callous spot on the knees, surrounded by a fringe of hair. The hoofs are large, coarse, and blunted—the hair short and thick, and of coarse texture, like that of the Indian Goat; and the male is furnished with a stiff upright mane on the neck and shoulders. The smell of the animal is particularly strong and disagreeable, like that of an old Buck Goat. They generally go in herds of eight or ten, and are only to be found amongst the wildest precipices, on the rocky summits of the Koondah range, or the precipitous Ghats which overlook the Low Country. The strength and agility with which they bound from rock to rock is perfectly amazing in so large an animal. They are so exceedingly shy, that it requires the greatest skill and perseverance to get within shot of them, and their favourite haunts being almost inaccessible to the foot of man, the pursuit of them is attended with great difficulty and fatigue, and even with danger, particularly if the Hunter is so unfortunate as to be overtaken by a fog. The female differs from the male in having more slender horns, no mane, a finer head, and being without the brown marks on the face.

"Now I can only find two animals to which this description will in any way apply, *viz.* 'The Caucasian Ibex,' and 'The Beardless Goat.' But in several particulars, the Ibex of the Neilgherries differs from either of them.

"Let us first take the Caucasian Ibex, as described in the enlarged English edition of Cuvier's Animal Kingdom. He agrees with our animal in colour, in his general figure, in the *form* of his horns, and in his habits. But he differs greatly in size, being only about five feet long, and two feet eight inches high at the shoulder, whereas the Ibex of the Neilgherries is six feet five inches in length, and stands four feet at the shoulder. The horns, also, although formed alike, in both animals, do not exceed *ten* inches in the Ibex of the Neilgherries, whereas in the Caucasian Ibex,—a much smaller animal,—they are described as being *twenty-eight* inches in length.

"The Beardless Goat is described as bearing a strong resemblance to the Caucasian Ibex, and, in so far, agrees with the general description of our animal; he has also got the ram-like head, and the mane on the neck. But he differs in having a dewlap, which is wanting in the Ibex of the Neilgherries, and in his colour, which is said to be variegated black and white *irregularly scattered.*

"Whether these distinguishing marks entitle this animal to be classed as a new variety of Ibex, is a question which I must leave for Naturalists to decide. In the mean time I consider myself justified in changing its name from the '*Chamois*,' to the *Ibex* of the Neilgherries."

"*And this with seven balls through his body!*"—
Page 75, line 6th.

This is no exaggeration. The incidents narrated in the text are taken, *verbatim*, from a Journal, kept by my Brother on the Neilgherry Hills. In my own Journal I find an instance recorded of a Stag receiving *ten* 1 oz. balls before he fell. Two, which he received at first, without even slacking his speed, passed clean through his body, about the centre of the ribs. After this he ran about a mile, and laid up in a wooded ravine to which I tracked him, and again beat him up; one ball broke a hind-leg, and another, entering above the rump, passed along the backbone and came out near the shoulder. I lost him for about an hour, but again found him, and when he broke cover I planted two balls close behind the shoulder, but still he went away strong. In the chase which followed I hit him twice in the body, and at last brought him down by a ball through the neck, when in the act of leaping a rivulet. He, however, got upon his legs again, and stood at bay in the water, when I was obliged to fire another ball into his head to finish him. I could quote a dozen similar instances of the extraordinary tenacity of life possessed by this animal.

"*Burgher Village.*"—Page 75, last line of page.

In a former note I have given a description of the Todahs, the aborigines of the Hills. We must now take some notice of the Burghers, who, although a more numerous, and more wealthy tribe than the Todahs, still look up to them with respect, as the acknowledged Lords of the soil, and pay to them a small annual tribute for the land which they cultivate. The Todahs, on the other hand, look upon the Burghers as an inferior race, calling them *Marvs*, or labourers. They call themselves (*par excellence*) men; and the question—"Is that a Burgher or a Todah?" would, with them, be literally —Is that a Labourer or a Man?

I extract the following description of the Burghers from my Journal:—

"The next class of People who inhabit the Hills are the Burghers. They are an Agricultural People, and although considerably more civilized than the Todahs—who are a purely pastoral Tribe—they acknowledge them as superiors, and pay to them a small annual tribute of grain for the lands which they cultivate. They are a people who have migrated to the Hills from the Low Country, from whence they say that their ancestors were driven, by the oppression of their Chiefs, about four hundred years ago. In size they do not exceed the natives of the Low Country, and their personal appearance is very inferior to that of the Todahs. Their dress is formed of the same materials as that of the Todahs, but is less gracefully arranged, and the head is covered by a turban. The ground in the neighbourhood of their villages is always well cultivated, and, I believe, they raise a considerable quantity of grain. Their mode of salutation is for the inferior to apply the top of his head to the breast of his superior, who immediately raises it up with both hands;—this has a very ridiculous effect, and looks as if they were butting at each other. The men are allowed to have as many Wives as they can afford to keep. The women have the power of divorcing their Husbands at will, after which they can marry again, and are allowed to repeat this as often as they choose. Their language is a corrupt dialect of Canarese. They burn their dead, but I am not aware what particular ceremonies are made use of on the occasion."

"*It is a melancholy story.*"—Page 86, line 12.

The tragical fate of the poor Dog-boy, here narrated by Mansfield, is a fact.

"*In the midst of our sport a large Panther sprang from the bushes.*"—Page 86, line 29.

I extract the following remarks upon the Panther, or Leopard, of India from a book of MS. notes by my Brother.

"The Panther, of which certainly two, and, in the opinion of some Sportsmen, three varieties are found in India, is scarcely less formidable than the Tiger. Its inferior strength is compensated by greater agility, and the extreme rapidity of its attack renders it, in my opinion, a still more dangerous animal to encounter on foot. Of the many fatal accidents which have come under my notice, as great a number was occasioned by Panthers as by Tigers. It is generally found in rocky ravines, or thickly wooded hills, and from the nature of its haunts, as well as its skulking habits, till once brought to bay, is difficult to mark down, and to surround when tracked to its lair. The description already given of the system pursued in Tiger shooting, applies equally to the hunting of this animal. Both are followed on Elephants, or beat up and shot from trees. Panthers have, on several occasions, been speared from horseback, but the serious accidents which have occurred, and which are always likely to occur in so very dangerous a sport, have prevented its becoming a general practice even amongst the most daring.

"I cannot pretend to offer, what has puzzled the greatest Naturalist to determine, *viz.* a definition of the distinction between those varieties of spotted Cats, which have been indiscriminately designated Panther and Leopard. I shall merely remark, that I have compared different individuals, amongst which I observed variations of colour and size, which lead me to suppose that they must belong to separate species.

"Some nearly equalled a Tigress in size. Of these, the ground colour was a pale fulvous; the spots, rose-shaped, were distinctly apart from each other over the sides, gradually amalgamating towards the back, down which they appeared to form a thickly studded line. Towards the shoulders the spots decreased in size, and imperceptibly changed their form, into small round dots, on the cheeks and fore-legs. This species is exceedingly fierce, and powerful enough to kill the largest cattle. It must have been one of these to which a correspondent of the 'Oriental Sporting Magazine' alludes, in the following words:—

"'I killed a Panther at Kirmar, in the Deccan, which measured upwards of nine feet, and a more savage and fearless animal I never saw: he charged, and struck down a Villager who was close to me, and held him down, till I killed the brute upon him. The unfortunate man, although dreadfully torn and shaken as a dog would a rat, is still alive, but with the loss of an arm.'

"The other variety which I noticed is much more common. In size it is at least a third smaller than the preceding, less strongly made, and less ferocious. Its prevailing colour is much darker, the ground being of a rufous tint. The rose-shaped spots, so close as to be almost united, are thickly studded over the whole body, except on the head and fore-legs, where, as in the preceding animal, they form small dots. Both are generally called Panthers by European Sportsmen, and *Cheetah*, by Natives; the Hunting Leopard (*Felis Jubata*) being the only animal in India known by the appellation Leopard.

"So much has already been said of the Tiger, that I shall conclude this article with the relation of an incident which occurred near the station where I resided. A Panther having killed a Bullock was traced by a party of *Shikarees* into a garden. The men advanced cautiously, with their matchlocks loaded, and one of them was in the act of taking aim when the Panther charged; he fired, and slightly wounded the animal, who instantly struck him down by a blow on the head, that killed him on the spot,—and springing from the shoulders of one to another, without once touching the ground, lacerated three dreadfully, before they had time to raise their guns. He then crouched in a small bush, where he lay growling at the people, who were hesitating how to act. It was at last proposed, by a daring young fellow, to fire a volley into the bush, and then run in upon him with their swords. To this proposal all assented, and advanced to within ten yards, blowing their matches. Out of six of their miserable weapons, two only exploded, and they probably were harmless in their effect. The Panther dashed out, as if thrown among them by the impetus of some projectile engine, and the nearest man was pulled down like a child in a giant's grasp. The swordsmen, assisted by some *Peons*, armed with spears, rushed to the rescue, and literally hewed the Panther to pieces with their heavy sabres. But seven men were carried from the ground at the conclusion of the conflict; of these, two never spoke again."

" *Charles and the Doctor returned to the road, dragging along their snake in triumph.*"—Page 97, line 23.

This adventure with a snake was achieved by my Brother and myself in our early *griffinage*, in the Canara forest: and in those unsophisticated days was looked upon by us as an exploit no ways inferior to Sir Guy's famous victory over the Dragon of Wantley. The incidents are narrated in the text exactly as they occurred, my Brother having performed the part of Charles, and I that of the Doctor.

" BISON SHOOTING."—Heading of Chapter, page 100.

The Great Forest, which extends along the western coast of the Peninsula of India, being the only part of the world in which that rare animal, the Indian Bison, has hitherto been found, and the extreme wildness of the animal, together with the unhealthy nature of the jungle which he inhabits, rendering the pursuit of him a work of considerable difficulty, and even of danger, his name has not, till of late years, found its way into the pages of Natural History; and even now the animal is only known, by name, to the Naturalists of Europe; no perfect specimen having ever been brought to this country.

The only account I can find of the animal is in the notes, by Edward Griffiths and others, to the English edition of Cuvier's Animal Kingdom, and here only two authorities are quoted; the *Mém. du Mus. d'Hist. Nat.*, vol. ix., in which this animal, under the name of Gaour, is absurdly described (upon the authority of some English Sportsman, whose name is not given) as having the *vertebræ* of the withers *projecting externally;* and Mr. D. Johnson's Sketches, &c., in which the following description of the animal is given. I quote the passage as it appears in Cuvier's Animal Kingdom:—

"In Mr. D. Johnson's Sketches, &c. the Gaur is described as a sort of wild bullock of a prodigious size, residing in the Ramghur district, not well known to Europeans. That Gentleman continues:—'I have never obtained a sight of them, but have often seen the print of their feet, the impression of one of them covering as large a space as a common China plate.—According to the account I received from a number of persons, they are much larger than the largest of our oxen; are of a light brown colour, with short thick horns, and inhabit the thickest covers. They keep together in herds, and a herd of them is always near the Luggo-hill; they are also in the heavy jungles between Ramghur and Nagpoor. I saw the skin of one that had been killed by Rajah Futty Narrain; its exact size I do not recollect, but I well remember that it astonished me, never having seen the skin of any animal so large. Some Gentlemen of Chittrah have tried all in their power to procure a calf without success. The *Shikarees* and Villagers are so much afraid of these animals, that they cannot be prevailed on to go near them, or to endeavour to catch any of their young. It is a prevailing opinion in the country, that if they are in the least molested, they will attack the persons disturbing them, and never quit them until they are destroyed, and should they get into a tree, they will remain near it for many days.'"

This account is tolerably correct as far as it goes, but it is not sufficiently explicit.

During five years which I spent in India, I have more than once had the good fortune to fall in with, and shoot the Bison in his native haunts.—And although my knowledge of Zoology is very limited, I trust that even the following undigested memoranda, noted down in my jungle encampment, may prove interesting to such of my Readers as are more deeply versed, than I am, in that interesting study.

"The Indian Bison,* *Gaour*, or *Jungle Koolgha*, (*Bos Gaurus*,) is the largest known animal of the Genus *Bos*. The following are the accurate dimensions of two specimens, male and female, which I have just killed. The measurements were taken immediately after death, and without following the curve of the body. The length was taken with a tape, between two upright sticks, one placed at the nose, and the other at the insertion of the tail; the height was measured, in like manner, from the spurious hoof of the fore-leg, to the top of the shoulder, the length of the foot being omitted, to allow for the diminution of the length of the limb, which would be occasioned by the weight of the animal when standing:—

		Ft.	In.		Ft.	In.
Height at the shoulder . .	Bull,	6	1	Cow,	5	5
Height to top of dorsal ridge .		6	5		5	10
Length from nose to insertion of tail .		9	0		8	5
Girth of body behind shoulder .		8	0		——	
Girth of fore-leg, above the knee .		2	6		2	0
Girth of neck . . .		4	3		——	
Breadth of forehead . . .		1	3½		——	

* The following remark upon the name *Gaour* appears in Griffiths' notes to Cuvier's Animal Kingdom:—"This name of Gaour, or Ghau-ur, originating in Central India, shows how far the root *ur*, urus, is extended. *Gaur*, a giant; *Ghaur-ur*, the gigantic, ancient, mysterious, terrible ox."

"I had no means of weighing the animals, but judging from the weight of the Bull's head, which was as much as two men could carry, slung between them on a bamboo, it must be enormous.

"The head is more square, and shorter in proportion than that of the common Ox, and the nose, particularly in the male animal, is considerably arched, like that of a ram. The forehead is broad, the frontal bone slightly concave, and surmounted by a thick arched ridge of solid bone, which is sufficient, of itself, to distinguish the skull of the Indian Bison from that of any other animal of the same genus. The horns turn slightly backwards, and upwards, with a sweep, in continuation of the arched bony ridge. They are of a light gray colour, tipped with black, rather short, and exceedingly thick at the base. The forehead, above the eyes, is covered with a thick coat of short close hair of a light dun colour, which, below the eyes, runs into a dark brown, approaching to black. The muzzle is large and full. Eye rather small, with a large pupil of a light blue colour, which gives the animal a very remarkable appearance. The tongue is extremely rough, and covered with sharp *papillæ*, which turn backwards. The pallet, which is white, is also armed with *papillæ*. The neck is short, thick, and heavy, and, in the male, is covered with large folds of skin. The skin on the neck, shoulders, and thighs, is nearly two inches thick, and is much prized by the natives, for the purpose of making shields. The dewlap is small in the male, and hardly perceptible in the female. The shoulder very deep, and muscular. Chest broad. Fore-legs short, and the joints particularly strong. Fore-arm extremely large and muscular, but the leg, below the knee, fine like that of a deer. Hoofs small, black, and finely formed. Behind the neck, and immediately above the shoulder, rises a thick fleshy hump like that of the Zebu, and from this commences the dorsal ridge, which forms the most striking feature in the appearance of this animal, and is a peculiarity which I have not remarked in any other. The ridge, which is about two inches thick, and of a firm gristly texture, is about six inches in height at its junction with the hump, and gradually diminishes to the height of three inches, at the point where it terminates abruptly, a little beyond the centre of the back. The hind quarters, as in the common Bison, droop considerably, and the tail is short, the tuft of hair at the end not reaching below the hocks. The young animals are covered with a short thick coat of woolly hair, which becomes more scanty with age, and, in very old animals, the back and sides are nearly bare, showing a dark shining skin, like that of the Buffalo. The colour of the animal is a dark coffee brown, which becomes gradually lighter, till it terminates in an ochrey yellow, on the belly and inside of the thigh. The legs below the knee, and the forehead above the eyes, are dirty white, or rather a light dun colour. The female differs from the male, in having the hump on the shoulder hardly perceptible, horns less robust, finer and more graceful head, slender neck, hardly any dewlap, and in the dorsal ridge extending less far back, not beyond the middle of the back.

"The Bison inhabits the heavy forest jungle, along the whole line of the western coast of India. They generally go in herds of from ten to fifteen, and are found in the morning and evening, in the small open glades of the forest, where they feed, during the night, on the rich grass and tender shoots of the bamboo, which spring up in these spots, after the monsoon. They retire for shelter, during the heat of the day to the thickest recesses of the forest, where it is very difficult to find them. The native Hunters say that the Cow goes nine months with young, and drops her calf in November, for which purpose she retires to the more open jungles, on the outskirts of the forest, to the eastward. In the month of May the old Bulls are generally found solitary.

"The Bison is naturally a fierce animal, and particularly so when wounded. If not brought down or disabled by the first shot, he almost invariably charges, and I have known instances of his being the first to commence hostilities. They are much dreaded by Native Hunters, more so even than the Tiger—indeed there are few, except the *Seedees*, who will venture to attack them on foot, and I have met with many who refused even to act as guides in those parts of the forest which they frequent.

The description of Bison Shooting, in the body of the work, gives a correct idea of that sport. The incidents are narrated exactly as they occurred to myself, with this exception, that, having no companion but the *Jemmadar*, I was obliged to finish the Bull without assistance.

"*He is a Seedee*"—Page 101, line 9.

A wild race who inhabit the jungles on the western coast of India are called *Seedees*. They are evidently of African origin, and are said to be descendants of African slaves, who fled from the early Portuguese settlers at Goa, and took refuge in the jungles. They are fine bold fellows, and the only *Shikarees* I have met with, who care to attack the Bison.

"*Allow me to introduce my friend Kamah, the Jemmadar.*" —Page 103, line 10.

The following extract from my Brother's Journal, gives a good description of the old Savage as he appeared in his holiday garments, on my first introduction to him at Dharwar:—

"*Dharwar, May* 1831.

"Old *Kamah* showed his grinning visage in camp yesterday, looking as much out of his element in the open country, as one of his Bison would be, were he removed from the forest, and turned loose in the black plain. His long woolly hair fluttering behind his ears, from beneath the greasy skull-cap that covered the frizzled mass; the sharp eye, keen as a falcon's—one redeeming point in his African features; the independent manner; the springy step, lean wiry figure, and national costume of a spare *langoutee*, and ample blanket thrown across his shoulders; the long black matchlock, and well worn *crease*, marked old *Kamah*, the *Jemmadar* and bloodhound of the forest. He was actually, from instinct, following up the trail of R——'s tame Deer, as he entered the compound; and could not resist giving his wild 'whooh!' like the cry of a horned owl, as it cantered past him. The old Savage had come in as usual, with accounts of game swarming in the forest, and a lament that brandy was not to be had at Dandilly. His eloquence always overpowers me, for the very sight of his sporting visage recals scenes of Bison glancing through the green bamboos; Samber, with their noble antlers, clearing their path through the interwoven jungle; the graceful Axis wandering in painted herds, along the banks of the Black River; and recollections of the many happy hours spent in their pursuit, amidst the eternal forests of Canara. Well did he know his powers of seduction; and the production of a pair of gigantic horns, the trophies of his last successful shot, settled the matter at once. I gave him a bottle of brandy to comfort him by the way, on his return, and promised to meet him at Dandilly."

"*The ball had flattened against the massive skull of the animal.*"—Page 112, line 7.

The skull of the Bison is fully two inches thick, and I have known several instances of the bullet flattening upon it, although, as a general rule, one may calculate upon a well-directed shot in the forehead proving mortal. I once lost a Bison after having planted an ounce ball directly between his eyes, when in the act of charging. He dropped, apparently dead, with a stream of blood pouring down his nose, but before I could reload he had recovered himself and made off. I tracked him for some miles by the blood, but never saw him again.

"Bear Shooting."—Page 115, Heading of Chapter.

The Black Bear of India (*Ursus Labiatus*) is frequently described as a harmless animal, but this is quite a mistake. For although he feeds principally upon roots and insects, yet from mere wantonness he frequently becomes a most savage and dangerous animal, seizing his victim generally by the head, and inflicting wounds which seldom require the Surgeon's aid. My Brother shot one which had inhabited the same cave for many years, and was the terror of a tribe of shepherds who fed their flocks on the hills near his haunts. During the month previous to his death he had killed three men, besides attacking and wounding several others.

On the march from Belgaum to Dharwar, my Brother and I sent on our spare horses a stage during the night. They were attacked by Bears, the Horsekeepers wounded, and one of the horses so severely injured that his life was despaired of for many days.

During my residence on the Neilgherry Hills, a Beater, in driving the woods for Deer, was attacked by a Bear, and killed on the spot, his chest being torn open so as to expose the lungs.

I could adduce many other instances of ferocity to prove the accusation I have made against the Bear of India, but I think the above will be sufficient to justify me in bringing in a verdict of guilty against him.

"A Wet Night under Canvass."—Page 142, Heading of Chapter.

This chapter is a presumptuous attempt, on my part, to give an idea of one of the grandest sights in nature, the breaking out of the North-west Monsoon among the Western Ghats of India. I have often witnessed it, and it has each time impressed me with renewed feelings of wonder and admiration. A good explanation of the causes of this phenomenon will be found in the "Encyclopædia Britannica," under the head "Meteorology."

"*Bushing the tent-pegs.*"—Page 143, line 22.

This operation is performed, on the approach of heavy rain, by digging a hole near the tent peg, and burying in it a bunch of brushwood, which is fastened to the peg. This not only helps to secure the peg by its own resistance, but acts as a sort of drain, and prevents the water from saturating the ground, so as to make the pegs draw.

" *Riding down a Wolf and an Antelope.*"—Page 152, line 3.

These two extraordinary feats were performed, exactly as described, by my Brother, George Campbell, of the Bombay Civil Service. I never knew another instance of an Antelope having been fairly ridden down; and, previous to his having done so, the thing was considered impossible. I have heard of one or two other instances of a Wolf having been speared from horseback, but only after he had gorged himself with food.

" *Charles, who was the last of the party, happened to spy the head and antlers of a noble spotted Buck.*"—Page 167, line 10.

The Spotted Deer of India (*Cervus Axis*) nearly resembles the Fallow Deer, but is distinguished from it by having round horns, without the terminal palm. One antler arises at the base which points forwards, and another half way up the beam, on the internal side which turns to the rear. The suborbital sinus is small, and the canines wanting. They go in herds of fifteen or twenty, three or four of which are generally Bucks. They pass the greater part of the day in sleep, when it is difficult to find them, but in the morning and evening they may be found in great numbers in the open glades of the forest, and among the long grass on the banks of rivers. They are extremely shy, and when once disturbed it is hardly possible to get a second shot at them. A four year old Buck weighs about 178 lbs.

" *The Doctor's body was perfectly uninjured.*"—Page 185, line 14.

This extraordinary adventure with a Wild Elephant occurred in the forests of the Coimbatoor district, at the time I was upon the Neilgherry Hills. The person who made so narrow an escape, was a gentleman of high rank in the Company's Civil Service. I have narrated the facts exactly as they were told to me, by an eye-witness, a few days after they occurred.

" *The Banshee.*"—Page 196, line 23.

A female Spirit peculiar to the Highlands of Scotland, and to Ireland. She attaches herself to particular families, and is heard wailing and lamenting round the house, previous to the death of any of its members.

" *Cowrie baskets.*"—Page 210, line 25.

Circular baskets, covered with oilcloth, in which provisions, &c. are carried on a march. One is suspended from each end of an elastic slip of bamboo, which the bearer balances across his shoulder.

" BOAR-HUNTING."—Page 222, Heading of Chapter.

The following remarks upon this noble sport are taken from a book of MS. Notes by my Brother, who was one of the best riders in the Deccan, and has seen as much of Hog-hunting as any man in India.

" If excitement be the test by which to estimate the comparative merits of any sport, Hog-hunting must rank before every other. Try it by another standard, its universal popularity, the enthusiasm of its followers, and the preference given to it in a country where the Tiger even is less noticed than the Boar, and it must be granted that there is some peculiar fascination in this noble sport. Men who have followed hounds at home, and shared in all the field sports of Europe and Asia, talk of it with rapture; and such a scene of animation, of generous rivalry, and true sporting feeling as is exhibited at the great hunting meetings surpasses any thing I have ever met with elsewhere. One word in explanation of rivalry, lest I should mislead. Killing a Boar is quite a secondary consideration to taking the first spear. This is the powerful incentive which causes the keen excitement of Hog-hunting, while men are struggling, as if for life or death, to draw first blood. There must be an antagonist to conquer as well as a Boar to overcome, and a true Sportsman would scarcely value the fastest run, ending in a brilliant death, without an opponent to ride against him for the spear of honour. The slightest touch that stains his blade with one crimson drop is enough. He is said to have killed the Hog, and the others who assist in despatching him, even he who gives the death-blow to a furious Boar at bay, claim no share in the honour which belongs exclusively to him who first drew blood. The influence of this feeling makes men ride with desperation beyond what the best contested steeple-chase, or the hardest struggle for the lead with hounds generally exhibits.

"Those who have never seen a Wild Boar could hardly credit his speed. Upon a dead plain, like a race-course, a fast Arab cannot overtake a lanky, outlying Boar, with a start of fifty yards, in less than half a mile. Conceive, then, what such an animal can do across a country cut up by deep ravines, many not practicable except by an in and out jump. These the Boar can cross much quicker than the cleverest horse can follow, and his bottom is so great that unless you can press him hard enough to blow him, he will run for ever. Hog are generally found in the worst part of a difficult country, and they invariably select a line abounding in obstructions. Nullahs with blind banks, steep rocky descents, thorny jungles which nearly tear the rider from his horse, and frequently nail his boots to his legs, are the usual variations of ground, which, even in its best parts, frequently resembles a plate covered with walnut shells. Over this country the game little Arab is pressed at his utmost speed, spurs clashing to get one more stride out of him—no holding—no craning—you may throw him down, but you must go your best, be the ground what it may. When the Boar is overtaken, after a long run, then comes the thrilling moment, if a man worth beating is at your haunches. The spear is perhaps quivering within an inch of the mark, and every nerve is strained to gain that inch, although, perhaps, your good honest horse has done his best, and answers only by a groan to every stroke of the spur. Your rival is coming up—his horse's head reaches your knee—he creeps nearer, nearer—every thought is absorbed in one whirling maddening feeling, the thirst of conquest. The two foaming Arabs are neck and neck, panting with fatigue, yet still struggling with the same spirit of rivalry as their Riders.—First one head is in front—then another—Oh, for one yard more and the deed were done!—Spears are lengthened to their utmost stretch—a blade disappears, is withdrawn, dimmed with blood—and the spear is won!—If a Boar is reached before he gets blown, he turns with great rapidity as soon as the leading horse is within a few paces of him, throwing him out, and making him lose much ground, even when well in hand, and turning readily. The second man then prepared to make his rush frequently takes the spear; but it sometimes happens that half a dozen riders are thus baulked, in succession, by a speedy Hog, before the contest ends. By this time being usually too much blown to run farther, the Boar stands at bay, and charges every one who approaches.—It is at this period of the chase that horses are apt to get ripped, without good management. Going slowly at the Boar is very dangerous, for not only may a miss occasion an accident, but even if you spear him through the body, he can run up the shaft, and tear the horse's entrails out. But with a steady, bold horse, you have no right to expose him to any great danger. Go at the Boar, at a smart gallop, and, as he meets you, strike straight down, while he is under your right stirrup, and whether you kill him dead or not, your speed will generally save you by wheeling off at the moment of delivering the spear.

"Fox-hunting and Hog-hunting have often been compared. I never could trace the resemblance. Can you compare a sport where you hunt and kill your game without the assistance of dogs to one in which they do both?

Can you compare the wild mad struggle for a mile or two, at the utmost pace of a fiery Arab, to the steady gallop of an hour or more, with Foxhounds?—Can you compare the chase of a Boar, an animal that has frequently been known to kill a Tiger, that stands at bay as soon as he gets blown, that fights to the last gasp, and displays more ferocity in his charge, and more determined courage in his last moments, than any other animal I have ever encountered, with that of the Fox, which runs perhaps for twenty miles, and then dies a poor broken-hearted devil, torn to pieces by a hundred jaws? —No, no! the sports are totally different, and require very different qualities both in man and horse. The Hog-hunter of the Deccan would be as much out of his element at Melton, as Dick Christian would find himself on the Poonah Hills, with a gray Boar in front, rattling down one of the steep ravines, and a dozen men of the right sort laying into him at a killing pace, over ground where an English hunter would knock himself to pieces.

"The favourite covers for Hog are fields of sugar-cane, bauble jungles, date groves, and ravines upon the sides of hills. Those which feed on sugar-cane become too fat to run far; but the Boars are extremely savage, always charging as soon as they are blown, whilst some refuse to run at all, standing at bay as soon as they are driven into the plain. The best Hog, for speed and bottom, are those found on the hills; they are always in good wind from the distance they have to go daily, in quest of food, and although hardly so pugnacious as their fat brethren of the plain, they afford better sport than any others. Hog are found nearly in the same way as Tigers, by marking them down as they return from feeding, or by following up their trail to the cover where they repose during the day. They are very numerous in some parts of the country, and do extensive mischief to the grain, from which the Natives are unable to drive them without the assistance of large parties. A hundred and fifty Hog have been killed at one meeting, which lasted for twelve days."

" *Now for the spear of honour.*"—Page 230, line 24.

I have already, in the preceding note, sufficiently explained what is meant by the spear of honour. The following extract from my Brother's Sporting Journal, affords a curious instance of taking a spear cleverly. After describing the first part of the run, he thus continues:—

" By the time we had forded the nullah, the Boar was a full mile ahead, making strong running for a distant cover, across a country admirably adapted for showing the difference between a real Hunter, and a thing to canter on a parade ground. The nullahs were so numerous, that an in and out jump occurred at every hundred yards, and it required most determined cramming to keep the Boar in sight at all. The pace was beginning to tell. S—— pulled up lame. R——'s long-legged dragoon, from not being quick enough in getting over the nullahs, was a long way behind. And the Boar was champing his foaming tusks with very little running left in him, when I came up, after a gallop of four miles. He tried to throw me out by practising some of his cunning tricks in a ravine, and I feared now that chance might lose me the spear, for R—— was coming up, hand over hand, whilst we were playing at hide and seek. However, I caught him at last, by cutting off his retreat to the bank, and he stood at bay. Challenger, now pretty well blown, poked out his little sturdy fore-legs, refusing to move an inch, whilst the Boar, with his back to a bush, planted himself directly in front, gnashing his tusks, and twinkling his fiery gray eye, just out of reach. R—— was spurring up his sinking horse close behind. I shall lose the spear, after all, from the brute's obstinacy. There was just a chance remaining. Reaching over my horse's neck I made a long stretch and succeeded in pricking the Boar's snout. On he came like lightning. I threw myself back, reversed my spear, and just as he was under my right stirrup, a straight *job*, between the shoulder-blades, sent him down with a stream of blood and foam gushing from his mouth.

"'Just in time!' cried R—— as he galloped up,—'I thought I might have had it yet.'"

"THE MAN-EATER."—Page 248, Heading of Chapter.

The term Man-eater is applied to those Tigers, which, deserting their usual haunts in the jungle, frequent the neighbourhood of Villages, and prey chiefly on men. They are almost invariably found to be old animals, and generally females. They are usually very cunning and cowardly.

The following remarks upon the Tiger, written by my Brother, may prove interesting:—

"It was my lot to be stationed, for several years, in a remote part of our Indian possessions, adjoining the Mysore frontier, and in the immediate vicinity of the great chain of Western Ghauts. In the pathless thickets of their eternal forests, untrodden by the foot of Man, the Tigress reared her young, and wandered, with her savage partner, into the smaller jungles of the plain, proving a scourge that drove every feeling of security from the humble dwellings of the wretched inhabitants.

"In such a country, inhabited by the poorest classes, living in small villages surrounded by jungle, and forced to seek their subsistence amongst the Tiger's haunts, numerous casualties, of course, occurred, and I had frequent opportunities of studying the habits, and witnessing the ravages of this formidable animal. Some idea may be formed of the havoc committed by Tigers, when I mention, from returns made to Government, that, *in one district, three hundred men, and five thousand head of cattle were destroyed during three years.*

"Whilst confined to the forest, the Tiger is comparatively harmless. There, feeding principally on deer, he rarely encounters Man, and when the solitary Hunter does meet the grim tyrant of the woods, instinctive fear of the human race makes the striped monster avoid him. But in the open country he becomes dangerous. Pressed by hunger, he seeks his prey in the neighbourhood of villages, and carries off cattle before the Herdsman's eyes. Still he rarely ventures to attack Man, unless provoked, or urged to desperation. But under whatever circumstances, human blood is once tasted, the spell of fear is for ever broken; the Tiger's nature is changed; he deserts the jungle, and haunts the very doors of his victims. Cattle pass unheeded, but their driver is carried off; and from that time the Tiger becomes a *Man-eater*.

" A notorious old Tigress, which I assisted in killing some years ago, used to lie in wait near the ford of a rivulet, daily crossed by travellers, and after carrying off several mail-bearers, she became so dreaded, that the road which passed her haunt was deserted. For years she had frequented the same covert; repeated attempts had been made to destroy her; she had been caught in nets, and pit-falls, but always escaped; and, at last, she became so cunning as to baffle the most experienced Hunters of the district. In the course of a tour through the province, accompanied by a friend, we encamped close to the scene of her depredations. Our *Shikarees*, always on the look-out for information of Tigers, heard of her, and most fortunately hit upon her trail next morning. It was followed up, into a small, but impenetrable clump of brushwood on the banks of the rivulet, which was surrounded so effectually as to render escape impossible, till our Elephant arrived. He was a very good one, and beat the thicket, inch by inch, wherever it was practicable; wading through masses of interwoven creepers, and tearing down trees which opposed his progress, without once hearing a growl, or observing a symptom of our game. Finding that we could not thus dislodge her, the Elephant was withdrawn, and showers of rockets, and other combustibles, were thrown into the covert, whilst we posted ourselves on a tree, which commanded a view of the whole clump. It was soon in a blaze, and when the whole had become one vast sheet of flame, the heat grew so intolerable, that we were obliged to abandon our post. My friend had already reached the ground, and I was in the act of dropping from a branch, when the Tigress burst from the midst of the flames, lashing her sides with her tail, and roaring furiously. We fired, and broke her leg by a rifle ball. Fortunately she did not charge, for we were both completely in her power. She appeared stupified by the smoke, and crept into a date bush, where she lay concealed till we remounted the Elephant. We found her lying like a hare in its form, in which position she received several shots, without making the slightest show of resistance. Nothing would induce her to charge, and, after skulking from one extremity of the thicket to the other, the fatal shot was at last administered. This Tigress evinced, both in appearance and disposition, all the marks of a true Man-eater. Her skull bore the traces of great age, the sutures being unusually closed, and the teeth worn nearly to stumps. She was not much larger than a Panther; her fur was mangy; and her lean gaunt figure seemed diseased by the human flesh on which she fed.

"I recollect another instance of a Man-eater obstinately remaining in a small patch of jungle, till it was burnt down around him. We could see him, completely exposed, sitting on his haunches, surrounded by fire; his hoarse roar rising above the fierce crackling of the flames; his glaring eyeballs rolling from side to side, watching the rockets which fell thick around him; his natural size magnified in the intense glare of light; and his brilliant colours glowing with unnatural brightness. At last the heat became intolerable—The flames scorched him—Uttering a roar that startled even the old *Shikaree* who stood beside me, he sprang, with one tremendous bound, over the blazing barrier, and dropped dead the instant he alighted. In both these cases rockets were used unsparingly, without forcing the Tiger to quit his strong-hold. But, in general, fireworks prove most effectual in beating up Tigers, and the strongest covers may thus be driven, without exposing the Beaters to any danger.

"To give an idea of the muscular strength possessed by a

Tiger, I shall mention two remarkable instances, from among many that have come under my observation. A Bullock was killed by a Tiger near our encampment, on the banks of the Tumboodra, in a field enclosed by a hedge of prickly pear, about six feet high. The carcass, still warm, was observed by some persons, who brought intelligence to the tents. On going to the spot we found the carcass of the Bullock, partly devoured, on the outside of the hedge; not a branch was ruffled, and the only clue to account for its removal were the deeply impressed foot-prints of a large Tiger, where he must have sprung over the barrier with his prey in his jaws. The impossibility of the Bullock having been carried there in any other way, alone convinced us, otherwise we could not have believed that an animal weighing under 600 lb. could have exerted such prodigious strength. I have weighed many Tigers, and found that full-grown males attained the weight of 500 lb.; larger specimens might probably be found, but I should think that none exceeded 600 lb. Any one who has studied the anatomical structure of the Tiger, would, however, more readily believe the power he can exert. The fore-leg is the most beautiful piece of mechanism conceivable, measuring upwards of two feet in circumference, and displaying a mass of sinew and muscle to be found only in that most formidable weapon of the most agile and destructive of all animals. His jaws, neck, and shoulders evince corresponding strength; and if it be considered that the Cattle of India are, in general, less heavy than a Tiger, this extraordinary feat appears less impossible.

"The other instance to which I alluded was the following: —Four very fine large Oxen, harnessed in the same team, were destroyed by a Tiger, while their owner was driving them in the plough. He described their death as the work of a few seconds. When in the act of turning his cattle, at the end of a furrow, a Tiger sprang from some bushes on the leading Bullock, broke his neck by a single wrench, and before the other terrified animals could disengage themselves, all were overcome in the same manner. Their owner fled to a tree, from whence he saw the monster finish his work of death, and then trot back to the jungle, without touching the bodies, as if he had done it from mere love of slaughter, and not to satisfy the cravings of hunger. I saw the Bullocks immediately after they had been killed; one of them had been thrown backwards with such force, that his horns were driven a considerable depth into the ground.

"It is a common opinion, and as a general rule correct, that Tigers, in their wild state, devour only what they have killed. But there are exceptions. A *Peon*, in my employment, who was watching a jungle, at day-break, observed a Tigress, with four Cubs, feeding upon a Buffalo which had died of disease on the preceding day. We killed the Tigress some hours afterwards, and saw from the Buffalo's torn remains that the man's account was correct. Still more unusual was a circumstance which occurred in Kandeesh. An Officer stationed there having shot a Tigress from his Elephant, sent out people, on his return to camp, to bring home the spoils. To his astonishment they came back, declaring that the Tigress was still alive, and that she had charged them as soon as they came in sight. So incredible a story was laughed at; but to satisfy the people the Gentleman returned, with an Elephant, to the spot, and was amazed to find a second Tiger greedily devouring the body of the first. This one also was shot, after a desperate resistance.

"All the Cat tribe are remarkable for their tenacity of life, and this alone is sufficient to render Tiger shooting on foot a most hazardous attempt. Allowing that a man has sufficient confidence in his own nerve to permit a Tiger to approach quite close, in the certainty of hitting him between the eyes, he is still far from safe. Any old Sportsman can assure him that a ball through the head is not certain to stop a Tiger. I have, myself, seen two, run a considerable distance, and even charge an Elephant, after receiving a ball in the forehead.

"Fatal accidents too often occur from men heedlessly approaching a fallen Tiger. A Madras Sepoy was killed some years ago, whilst measuring a Tiger which had just dropped, apparently dead. The expiring brute struck at him, and fractured his skull by one blow of his tremendous paw. And it is only a few months back that an Officer of a Native Regiment was struck dead by a dying Tiger under precisely similar circumstances. I recollect another instance of a poor fellow who was rendered a cripple for life, in the same way.

"It is a curious fact that Tigers never attempt to climb, although their form appears peculiarly adapted for doing so. Their great weight may perhaps prevent them; but, more probably, the nature of the animals on which they prey precluding the necessity of resorting to this means for seizing them, they do not employ the power which they possess. One *Shikaree*, whom I knew, was pulled down from a tree by a Tigress, and killed; but he was not at a sufficient height from the ground to require any great exertion to reach him; and I believe, that had he been two feet higher, he would have been quite safe.

"I have frequently shot very savage Tigers from trees, at an elevation of not more than nine feet from the ground, but never saw any attempt to climb, although they saw plainly from whence the shot was fired.

"A circumstance occurred, in the Southern Mahrattah Country, while I was there, which shows how a wounded Tiger singles out the man who fires at him. A Tiger was found in a small patch of jungle, near camp, by a party of *Shikarees* who had been out looking for Hog. They surrounded the place, and blazed away with their matchlocks till sunset without doing much harm. The Tiger, slightly wounded, was lying in the middle of the thicket; and there he remained, answering every shot by a roar that deterred any one from approaching near enough to take a pot shot. Well, when they could no longer see the muzzles of their long barrels, these sagacious fellows resolved to squat round the cover all night, determined, if the Tiger did not die before morning, to make him 'eat some more bullets' as soon as it was light. It was getting very dark, and somewhat cold. One of the *Shikarees* proposed to smoke, and while the poor fellow was indulging in a long whiff, that made the *chillum* glow brightly, a rush was heard from the bushes, a roar rang in their ears, and the Tiger was among them. The ill-fated smoker, with the pipe to his lips, was smashed by a blow, like the stroke of a sledge hammer, and away went the Tiger, roaring through the stillness of the night. It is evident that the Tiger, observing the light, fancied it to be the flash of a matchlock, and rushed to revenge himself on his adversary.

"In countries well stocked with Cattle, Tigers prey almost entirely upon them. Even the huge Buffalo falls beneath his strength, when taken by surprise; but, when prepared, he resists, and, not unfrequently, beats off the aggressor. In herds, Buffaloes, far from fearing the Tiger, are the first to attack. I have been assured, by Herdsmen, that they never felt the least alarm, even in the most dangerous jungles, whilst their Buffaloes were feeding by them, for no Tiger dared to molest them. I remember a poor little Boy, who had charge of a number of fine Buffaloes, that used to graze in a valley frequented by a very savage Tigress, and four cubs. She had repeatedly tried to carry him off, but, in every instance, the faithful brutes which he tended rushed to the rescue, and drove her off. One day, whilst playing with another Boy, at some distance from his cattle, the Tigress, with her cubs, was seen approaching. They ran towards the Buffaloes, who charged in a body as soon as they perceived their enemy;—but it was too late. One of the Boys was overtaken, and his terrified companion saw him carried off to the jungle, and devoured on its edge. He came to our tents with the melancholy intelligence, begging of us to destroy the Tigress, which we did next day; and, to our surprise, on reaching the ground, we found this fearless Boy following his Buffaloes with perfect unconcern, through the thickest part of the jungle. He said he was not afraid; he had only to keep close to this Bull—pointing to the leader of the herd—and no Tiger in India would venture to attack him."

The natural history of the Tiger is so well known that it is unnecessary for me to make any further remarks upon it here. But although I have already extended this note to rather an unreasonable length, I must add a few words regarding the size of Tigers. We constantly hear of Tigers measuring twelve and fifteen feet in length, and I lately saw an account of one, which was said to have measured *twenty-four* feet!

But, during a residence of five years in India, I never met with a Tiger that exceeded ten feet in length, from the point of the nose to the end of the tail; and although I have been at some pains to collect information on this subject, I never could obtain any authentic account of a Tiger exceeding eleven feet in length. I subjoin the dimensions of an average sized male Tiger, which I measured myself, with great accuracy, a few hours after his death:—

	Ft.	In.
Length from point of nose to point of tail .	9	5
Length of tail	2	10
Height, from heel to shoulder . . .	3	2
Extreme length, from shoulder to point of toe .	3	11
From elbow to point of toe . . .	2	0
Girth of body, immediately behind the shoulder	5	3
Girth of fore-arm	2	7
Girth of neck	3	0
Circumference of head	3	3

I conclude that the measurements of the fifteen feet Tigers we hear of have been taken from raw hides, stretched out to their utmost extent; and that the enormous size of my friend of twenty-four feet, must be attributed to some mistake of the Printer.

"The Sacred Village."—Page 274, Heading of Chapter.

The description of the Island of Sevasamoodrum, Rhamaswamy's house, and the Falls of the Cauvary, as well as the

Hindoo legend relating to them, are given as I find them in the pages of my Journal, written on the spot.

" *Behold that far winding procession.*"—Page 284, line 16.

Since writing the above I have been fortunate enough to become possessed of a rare and curious old book, entitled " The Voyages and Adventures of Ferdinand Mendez Pinto, a Portugal, done into English by H. C. Gent, A. D. 1663." Pinto being a great traveller avails himself of a traveller's license to a large extent, and tells marvellous tales of " Anthropophagi and men whose heads do grow beneath their shoulders"—so much so indeed, that he has obtained for himself the honourable distinction of " The Prince of Liars." But the greatest romancer will occasionally stumble on a bit of truth in spite of himself, and accordingly our travelled friend gives an account of an Indian religious feast, which is described in such delightfully quaint language, and,—barring a few exaggerations, which it was not in his nature to avoid—so nearly what we see at the great festival of Juggernaut to this day, that I cannot resist the temptation of transcribing it.

Our Author sailed from Portugal, A. D. 1537, and, after a most disastrous voyage, arrived in India. In the course of his travels, in that Country, he visits " The great Temple or Pagode of Tinagoogoo," and in the LVI Chapter, page 218, thus describes the feast :—

" Whilst the Feast of these *Gentiles*, as also the Fair, which was kept all the time thereof, endured for the space of fifteen days, with an infinite concourse of Merchants and Pilgrims, that came flocking thither from all parts, as I have declared before, there were many sacrifices made there with different ceremonies, not a day passing without some new thing or other. For amongst many of great charge, and very worthy of observation, one of the chiefest was a *Jubile*, after their manner, which was published the fifth day of the moon, together with a Procession, that was above three leagues in length, as we could guess ; it was the common opinion of all, that in this Procession there were forty thousand Priests, of the four and twenty sects, which are in the Empire: most of them were of different dignities, and called *Grepos*, *Talagrepos*, *Roolims*, *Neepois*, *Bicos*, *Sacarens*, and *Chanfaranhos;* now by the ornaments they wear, as also by the devices and ensigns which they carry in their hands, they may be distinguished; and so every of them is distinguished, according to his dignity; Howbeit, these went not on foot as the other ordinary Priests, for that they were as this day forbidden upon pain of great sin to tread upon the ground, so that they caused themselves to be borne in *Palaquins*, or Arm-chairs, upon the shoulders of other Priests their inferiors, apparelled in Green Sattin, with their Stoles of Carnation Damask. In the midst of the ranks of this Procession were all the inventions of their Sacrifices to be seen, as also the rich Custodes of their Idols, for the which each of them had a particular devotion. They that carried them were clothed in yellow, having each of them a big wax candle in his hand; and between each every fifteen of these Custodes went a triumphant Charet, all which Charets put together were in number an hundred and twenty six. All these Charets were four and some five stories high, with as many wheels on either side; In each of them there were at the least two hundred persons, what with the Priests and the Guards, and on the top of all, an Idol of Silver, with a Mitre of Gold on his head, and all of them had rich chains of Pearl and precious stones about their necks; round about every Charet went little Boys, carrying silver maces on their shoulders, and between them were a many of caskets full of exquisite perfumes, as also divers persons with Censors in their hands, who ever and anon censed the Idol to the tune of certain instruments of musick, saying three times with a lamentable voyce, *Lord asswage the pains of the dead, to the end they may praise thee peaceably;* whereunto all the people answered, with a strange noise; *Such may thy pleasure be and so may it come to pass, every day wherein thou showest us the sun.* Each of the Charets was drawn by above three thousand persons, who for that purpose made use of very long cords, covered with silk, and thereby gained for themselves plenary remission of their sins, without restitution to be made of anything at all: Now that they might participate in this absolution, by drawing the cords, they set their hands to it, one after and close to another, continuing doing so to the very end, in such sort that the whole cord was covered with their hands, and nothing else to be seen; but that they always which were without might gain this indulgence, they helped those that had their hands on the cord, by putting theirs about their shoulders; then they that were behind them did the like, and so, consequently, all the rest. In this manner throughout the whole length of the cord there were six or seven Banks or Files, and in each of them about five hundred persons. This Procession was environed with a great number of Horsemen, that carried staves with pikes at both ends, who, riding all about, went crying to the people, which were infinite in number, that they should make way, and not interrupt the Priests in their prayers: Many times, also, they struck those so rudely whom they first met withal, as they beat down three or four together, or hurt them grievously, no man daring to find fault with, or so much as say a word against it. In this order this marvellous Procession passed through above one hundred streets, which to that end were all adorned with boughs of Palms and Myrtle, amongst the which were many Standards and Banners of silk planted; There were also many Tables set up in divers places, where all that desired it for God's sake were admitted to eat of free-cost; yea, and in other parts they had clothes and money given them; There likewise Enemies reconciled themselves one to another, and the rich men forgave them their debts which were not able to pay. In a word so many good works were done there, more proper for Christians than for Gentiles, as I must needs conclude, that if they had been done with Faith and Baptism, for the love of our Lord Jesus Christ, and without any mixture of the things of this World, assuredly they would have been acceptable unto him. But alas! the best was wanting in them, and that both for theirs and our sins. Whilst the Procession, together with the Charets in which the Idols were, passed along in this manner, and that with a dreadful noise of Drums and other such Instruments, behold where out of a certain wooden shed, made expressly for the purpose, six, seven, eight, or ten men, all besmeared with odours and wrapped up in silk, wearing Gold Bracelets about their Wrists, start forth all at once, and room being instantly made for them by the People, after having saluted the Idol which was on the top of the Charet, they went and laid themselves down athwart on the ground, so that the wheels coming to go over them crushed them all to pieces, which the Assistants beholding, cried out aloud together—*My soul be with thine.*—Presently whereupon nine or ten of the Priests descending from the Charet took up these blessed, or rather accursed, creatures, that sacrificed themselves in this sort, and putting the head, bowels, and all the other members so crushed in pieces, into great Bowls made for the purpose, they showed them to the people from the highest part of the Charet where the Idol stood, saying with a pitifull voyce—*Miserable sinners, fall ye to praying that God may make you worthy to be a Saint as this here is, who hath now offered himself up as a sweet smelling sacrifice.*—Whereunto all the People, prostrated on the ground, answered with a fearful noise, *We hope that the God of a thousand Gods will permit it to be so.* In this manner many other of these poor Wretches sacrificed themselves, to the number, as we were told by certain Merchants worthy of credit, of six hundred and more. After these followed other Martyrs of the Devil, whom they called *Xixaporans*, which sacrificed themselves before the said Charets, by most mercilessly slashing themselves with sharp razors, that to behold them how they did it, one could not think but what they were altogether insensible; for they cut off great gobbets of their flesh, and holding them on high at the end of Arrows as if they would shoot them up to Heaven, they said, *That they made a present thereof to God for the souls of their Fathers, of their Wives, of their Children, or of such an one for whose sake they did this wicked work.* Now wheresoever this gobbet of flesh chanced to fall, there ran so much people to catch it up, that oftentimes many were stifled in the press, for they held it as a very great Relick. In this sort these miserable Wretches stood upon their feet, all bathed in their own blood, without Noses, without Ears, and without the resemblance at all of a man, untill at length they fell down stark dead on the Earth; then came the *Grepos* in all haste down from the top of the Charet, and cutting off their heads, showed them to all the people, who kneeling on the ground, and lifting up their hands to Heaven, cried out with a loud voyce—*Let us, O Lord, live to that time wherein for thy service we may do as this same here hath done.* There were others also whom the Devil drew thither after another manner. These same, craving an Alms, said, *Give me an alms for God's sake, or if thou dost it not I will kill my self.*—So that if they were not presently contented, they would instantly cut their own throats with razors which they held in their hands, or stab themselves into the belly, and so drop down stark dead; whereupon the *Grepos* ran suddenly to them, and having cut off their heads, showed them, as before, to the people, who reverenced them prostrate on the ground. We likewise saw some named *Nucaramons*, men of a very ill look, clothed with Tyger's skins, and carrying in their hands certain Pots of Copper full of Excrements, and filthy corrupt Urine, the stench whereof was so horrible and insupportable, that it was not possible for any nostril to endure it; These craving an Alms of the people, said, *Give me an Alms, and that quickly, otherwise I will eat this Ordure which the Devil eats, and bespatter thee with it, that so thou mayst be accursed as he is.* They no sooner uttered these words but that all ran hastily to give them Alms; for if they stayed never so little, they straightway set the Pot to their mouths, and taking a great sup of the stinking stuff, they therewith all to bedashed such as they pleased; in the mean time all others that beheld them so dressed, holding them accursed, fell upon them, and entreated them in such a strange fashion, as the poor Wretches knew not which way to turn themselves; for there was not a man of the company that drove them not away with blows, and that railed not at them, saying; *That they were accursed for having been the cause that this holy man had eaten of this beastly filth which the Devil feeds upon, and therefore was become stinking before God, so that he could neither go into Paradise nor live amongst men.*—Behold how strange the blindness of the people is, who otherwise have judgment and wit enough" * * * * * * *

"As for the Image of *Tinagoogoo* it was placed in the midst of the Temple, upon a stately Tribunal, in the form of an Altar, environed with a number of Silver Candlesticks, and a many of Children attired in Purple which did nothing but cense it to the sound of Instruments of Musick whereupon the Priests played reasonably well. Before this Idol danced, to the tune of the said Instruments, certain Ladies which were wonderfull fair and richly clad."

In another place, talking of the Dancing Girls, our Author thus quaintly expresses himself.

"Then began the Women to play on Instruments of Musick, and six of them danced with little Children for the space of three or four *Credo's*. After that other six little Girls danced with six of the oldest Men that were in the room, which seemed to us a very pretty fantasticalness."

There is, I think, something delightfully primitive in worthy Pinto's method of computing time, and his concluding remark is surely the very perfection of simplicity.

After this long stretch of *almost* unadulterated truth, I feel it would only be doing justice to my travelled friend, to bring forward a few specimens of *the marvellous*, in support of his well-earned character for stupendous mendacity. But as my limits will not permit me to indulge myself so far, I must leave such of my Readers as have a taste for the *wonderful* in nature, to seek out the immortal Romancer himself, with this assurance, that, if they are fortunate enough to meet with him, they may indulge their fancy to the fullest extent.

"*A chance shot at an Antelope or a Bustard.*"—
Page 274, line 10.

The common Antelope is found in great numbers on the open plains, in almost every part of India. They afford good sport to a man who is gifted with patience, and can stand fatigue, but their extreme shyness, and the open nature of the ground which they inhabit, renders it so difficult to approach within shot of them, that there are few who take the trouble of acquiring that intimate knowledge of the animal's habits which is absolutely necessary to ensure success. The various devices employed in approaching Antelope are too numerous to be described here. But the following extract from the Journal of my Brother—who was the most successful and indefatigable Antelope stalker I ever knew,—will serve to give some idea of the extreme difficulty of approaching this animal.

" Sudegee, 1st November.—Antelopes were seen all along this morning's march, twelve miles from Hookerry, chiefly upon a barren, stony soil, very different from their usual haunts to the eastward. I found them shy, and apt to run long distances when disturbed, before they settled again to feed. Some of the herds were unusually large, containing not less than sixty individuals. After following one of these herds for a considerable distance, without getting within shot, it joined another equally numerous. Both went on together till they met a third, when there must have been, at least, one hundred and twenty Does, and twenty black Bucks, besides Fawns, collected in one spot, forming the most beautiful group of Antelope I have ever seen. As their numbers increased, they became more shy, led on by an old suspicious Doe, which kept bounding along in front, and never allowed the main body to halt. Occasionally a pair of Bucks would leave the ranks to settle a private feud by a passage at arms, but they never engaged in earnest, so as to allow me to creep up, and pick off one of the combatants. They led me in this way from the plain where I had first found them, within sight of Sudegee, nearly back to Hookerry, a distance of twelve miles, gaining fresh recruits at every feeding ground they passed. The fights among the males became more frequent as they pressed up against each other, and several pairs would stop at once, to engage, some on their knees, with horns interlaced, others racing up to each other, and tilting with lowered heads, till all the Bucks, becoming infected with a fighting mania, selected antagonists, and the plain was covered with contending pairs, whilst the Does and Fawns watched against surprise. This internal discord proved their ruin, as it has often done among Men as well as Antelopes. I kept gradually edging nearer, keeping carefully out of sight of the old skittish Doe, who was jealous of every moving object, and, with the assistance of some broken ground, stole up within a hundred yards of two pugnacious fellows who were too busily engaged to mind me. One dropped to the shot, hit through the shoulder, so fatally, that he was dead before I reached him. His companion dashed off towards the herd; and all, throwing up their heads together, broke away into their long striding gallop, never stopping till they appeared like white specks on the horizon, leaping up from the cloud of dust raised by their bounding hoofs."

The Indian Antelope stands considerably higher than the Roebuck, and is altogether a larger animal. The horns, eighteen inches to two feet in length, are twisted spirally and annulated to within a few inches of the point. The old males are nearly black above, and white on the belly and inside of the legs. The females, which are without horns, are a light fawn colour above, with a whitish line running horizontally along the side, and white beneath. The young males are, at first, of the same colour as the females, but become gradually darker with age, till they attain their full growth, when they are, as I said before, nearly black.—An average sized black Buck weighs about ninety pounds, a Doe about seventy-five pounds. The male of the Gazelle, a smaller species of Antelope, also found in India, averages about sixty-two pounds, and the female about forty-seven pounds.

Bustard frequent the same sort of ground as Antelope, and are approached much in the same manner. The Cock weighs about twenty-two pounds; the Hen from eighteen to twenty pounds.

"Tiger Hunting at the Falls of the Cauvary."—
Page 289, Heading of Chapter.

During my visit to the Falls of the Cauvary, I encountered a Tiger in the manner described in the text, and tried to surround him with nets, which is the method of hunting practised in that part of the country. But the nets not being sufficiently numerous to surround his lair, and the Beaters having failed to drive him in the proper direction, he escaped without getting into them. The latter part of the adventure is therefore pure invention; but it *might* have happened.

My Brother, in his Journal, gives the following description of this method of driving the Tiger into nets:—

"A curious method of killing Tigers, practised by the Natives of the Wynad Country, deserves notice. When one of these animals is discovered, the cover in which he lies is enclosed by a net, supported upon bamboos of a sufficient height to prevent his leaping over them. All being prepared, the Villagers, headed by their Priests, surround the outside of the net, armed with long spears, and, provoking the Tiger to attack them, meet him as he charges, and pierce him through the meshes of this apparently feeble, but impassable barrier, till he falls. A Gentleman, who was present at one of these scenes, describes it as most interesting, and exciting in the highest degree; for there existed the appearance of imminent danger, although, in reality, it was almost impossible for the Tiger to reach his assailants."

"*Wi' that wee towsie tyke sitting on her back, as conceity as you please.*"—Page 357, line 20.

The female Bear is in the habit of carrying her young on her back, and when attacked, frequently charges with a fierce little brute of a Cub standing upright on her shoulders, and showing his teeth as savagely as the mother. This, as the Doctor remarks, has a very absurd effect.

"*Kelpie.*"—Page 386, line 5.

A Water Spirit, said to haunt fords and ferries at night.

THE END.